DREAMING TO SOME PURPOSE

Other works by Colin Wilson:

The 'Outsider Series':

The Outsider Religion and the Rebel
The Age of Defeat
The Strength to Dream
Origins of the Sexual Impulse
Beyond the Outsider
The New Existentialism

Works on the Paranormal:

The Occult
Mysteries
Beyond the Occult
Poltergeist: A Study in Destructive Haunting
The Psychic Detectives: The History of
Psychometry
Afterlife
Strange Powers
The Geller Phenomenon
Enigmas and Mysteries
Men of Strange Powers
The Supernatural

Biographies:

Rasputin and the Fall of the Romanovs
Bernard Shaw: A Reassessment
The Quest for Wilhelm Reich
Gurdjieff: The War Against Sleep
Rudolf Steiner – The Man and His Work
Jung: The Lord of the Underworld
Aleister Crowley: The Nature of the Beast

Criminology:

An Encyclopedia of Murder (with Pat Pitman)
An Encyclopedia of Modem Murder
(with Donald Seaman)
A Casebook of Murder
Order of Assassins
A Criminal History of Mankind
Written in Blood: The History of Forensic
Detection (with Damon Wilson)
Jack the Ripper: Summing Up and Verdict
(with Robin Odell)
The Serial Killers (with Donald Seaman)
A Plague of Murder – The History of Serial
Murder

Other Non-Fiction:

From Atlantis to the Sphinx
The Atlantis Blueprint (with Rand Flem-ath)
Atlantis and the Old Ones
Alien Dawn: An Investigation into the Contact
Experience
The Misfits: A Study of Sexual Outsiders
Poetry and Mysticism
New Pathways in Psychology: Maslow and
Post-Freudian Revolution

A Book of Booze
Brandy of the Damned (Essays on music)
Eagle and Earwig (Essays on books and writers)
Sex and the Intelligent Teenager
Starseekers: A History of Science and
Astronomy
The Craft of the Novel
The Strange Genius of David Lindsay
(with E. H. Visiak and J. B. Pick)
An Encyclopedia of Scandal (with Damon
Wilson)
An Encyclopedia of Unsolved Mysteries
(with Damon Wilson)
Frankenstein's Castle
Access to Inner Worlds
Marx Refuted (with Ronald Duncan)
The Necronomicon (with George Hay)
Voyage to a Beginning (A Preliminary
Autobiography)
Tree by Tolkien
The Essential Colin Wilson
A Directory of Possibilities (with John Grant)
The Book in My Life

Novels:

The Sorme Trilogy
Ritual in the Dark
The Man Without a Shadow (The Sex Diary of
Gerard Sorme)
The God of the Labyrinth
Adrift in Soho

The World of Violence:
Necessary Doubt
The Glass Cage
The Black Room
The Killer (Lingard)
The Magician from Siberia
The Personality Surgeon

Detective Fiction:
The Schoolgirl Murder Case
The Janus Murder Case

Science Fiction and Fantasy:
The Mind Parasites
The Philosophers' Stone
The Space Vampires (Lifeforce)
Spider World: The Tower
Spider World: The Delta
Spider World: The Magician
Spider World: Shadowland

Play:
Strindberg

DREAMING TO
SOME PURPOSE

Colin Wilson

arrow books

Published by Arrow in 2005

1 3 5 7 9 10 8 6 4 2

First published in the United Kingdom in 2004 by Century

Arrow Books Limited
The Random House Group Limited
20 Vauxhall Bridge Road, London, SW1V 2SA

Random House Australia (Pty) Limited
20 Alfred Street, Milsons Point, Sydney,
New South Wales 2061, Australia

Random House New Zealand Limited
18 Poland Road, Glenfield
Auckland 10, New Zealand

Random House (Pty) Limited
Endulini, 5a Jubilee Road, Parktown 2193, South Africa

The Random House Group Limited Reg. No. 954009

www.randomhouse.co.uk

A CIP catalogue record for this book
is available from the British Library

Papers used by Random House are natural, recyclable products made from wood grown
in sustainable forests. The manufacturing processes conform to the environmental
regulations of the country of origin

ISBN 0 099 47147 7

Printed and bound in Great Britain by
Bookmarque Ltd, Croydon, Surrey

To Paul Copperwaite – who suggested it.

I would like to acknowledge the help of my daughter Sally, who read and sorted out hundreds of letters I wrote to my family over the years. My wife Joy, as usual, spent weeks correcting the proofs and index. Friends like Robert Lomas, Howard Dossor and Ted Brown read the book as I wrote it and made many invaluable comments. Most of all, I want to thank my publisher (and editor) Mark Booth, whose extensive suggestions not only improved the book, but made it more than fifty pages longer – the only publisher, in my experience, who wanted me to lengthen an already long book.

Cornwall, December 2003

Contents

List of Illustrations

In order of appearance

Analytical Table of Contents

5: *Anarchism and Soho.*

The anarchists on Speakers' Corners. The Western Hospital. *Tristan* and a peak experience. Bix Beiderbecke. Irmgard and the Hitler Youth. The Coffee House and Laura. Bill Hopkins. 'He's says he's a genius too'. The *Saturday Critic*. Bill and Celtic Romanticism. A night with Kay. Sexual failure. *The Twentieth Century Revue. The Metal Flower Blossom*. Laura and I get drunk. Boredom and blackouts. Return to France.

6: *Joy.*

Back to Paris. Working for *The Paris Review*. Bill arrives in Paris. The *Merlin* crowd. Christopher Logue. Alfred Reynolds and Die Brücke. Back to Leicester. The carpet department in Lewis's. Joy teaches me the cash register. Flax Halliday. Getting with drunk with Flax. The 'will to power' game. Strip tease. The mechanics of seduction. A weekend foursome. The Christmas play. The dominance syndrome. 'Are you a virgin, Joy?' Back in a factory. The run to Great Glen. The New Year party. Persuading Joy to come to London. Flax in trouble. Maurice Willows. Back to London.

7: *London and The Outsider.*

Joy's father pays me a visit. The room in North Finchley. The Victoria Wine Company. The Scottish clerk. The St. Neot margin insight. Joy and I get engaged. Sleeping outdoors. Hampstead Heath. The Reading Room and Angus Wilson. Discovering existentialism. The dairy at Chiswick. Camus's *Outsider*. A holiday at Windermere. First trip to Cornwall. The insight at Teignmouth. 'Truth is objectivity'. The room in New Cross. Reading the mystics. Christmas alone. The job in the laundry. Notes for *The Outsider*. Barbusse's *L'Enfer*. The three types of Outsider.

8: *Breakthrough.*

The Coffee House in the Haymarket. Writing *The Outsider*. The move to Baker Street. Sexual experiments: playing with fire. Carole Ann. Dorothy. Found out. The trip to Canterbury. Religion or humanism? Alfred again. Stuart Holroyd becomes an ally. The reading. Stuart begins *Emergence From Chaos*. My mother's illness. Acceptance of *The Outsider*. Holiday in Cornwall. My first restaurant meal – smoked salmon. Gollancz and Fred Warburg. *Daddy Long Legs*. Gwenda David. Viking reject *The Outsider*. Christmas in the post office. The move to Notting Hill. Living in a bathroom. Angus Wilson lends me his cottage. Publicity photograph. My first literary party – Iris Murdoch and Elias Canetti. A day with Burns Singer. John Wain. First interview. Publication day. 'A major writer and he's 24'. Kenneth Tynan and Osborne's *Look Back in Anger*. The 'Angry Young Men'.

9: *Backlash*

Success – and disillusionment. Outsiders and 'world rejection'. Mary Ure and John Osborne: 'The greatest playwright since Sheridan'. Samuel Beckett. Ionesco: 'The rain is falling – what is the meaning of that?' Meeting Marilyn Monroe. Publicity and its backlash. Stuart Holroyd's *The Tenth Chance*. '– get out of my life Wilson'. Dan Farson and Francis Bacon. A holiday in the West Country – Negley Farson. 'Are you a genius?' Meeting T.S.Eliot. Advice from C.P.Snow. Tom Maschler and *Declaration*. Attacks on Stuart Holroyd. 'Colin Wilson Admits He Is a Fraud'. 'Bubble of the year – *The Outsider*'. Joy has her tonsils removed. Her family and the 'horse-whipping incident'. We flee to Devon. Dublin – with the *Daily Express*. Tralee. 'Why don't you sue *Time Magazine*'. 'The Genius Returns'. 'Get out of London or you will never write another book'. The move to Cornwall.

10: Getting Away

Temptation removed. Living in Cornwall. I teach myself to drive. Drinking in the back room of the *General Wolfe*. *Religion and the Rebel* is slaughtered. Trip to Norway. Oslo lecture. On to Hamburg. *The Divine and the Decay* panned. A night in the Reeperbahn. The rats in the walls. Lecture tour in Germany. An afternoon with Camus.

11: John Braine in Leningrad.

The search for a house. My parents come to live with us, but return to Leicester. Joy announces she is pregnant. Publication of *Ritual in the Dark*. Braine's *Room at the Top*. Our trip to Bingley. How *Room at the Top* came to be written. 'You are all figments of my imagination'. The room in Notting Hill. Tom Greenwell. Female groupies. Pat Pitman and *An Encyclopaedia of Murder*. Dan Farson becomes a television celebrity. Negley's death: 'This is the perfect place for a journey's end'. The trip to Leningrad. John Braine falls off the wagon. Soup with melted butter. Across the Baltic. Bright red tights and orange slacks. Caviar for the price of icecream. The reception at the Astoria. 'Murder is virtually unknown under Communism'. John Braine flies on to Moscow. John Wain travels back with us. Amis tries to kill me. Braine distraught. Bill Hopkins launches *Penthouse*. My quarrel with Braine. Braine's later novels. The frog prince. Death of John Braine.

12: America.

Our daughter and the *Daily Mail*. A visit from John Brinnin. My lecture trip to America. The Algonquin. An evening with Graham Greene. Was Greene a paedophile? Meeting with Robert Shaw. Night train to Washington. Dan Danziger. 'A literary Elvis Presley'. The sex life of Paul Tillich. In Old Virginia. The lecture circuit. Providence and H.P. Lovecraft. Los Angeles and Christopher Isherwood. The party at Stephen Spender's. Sandy Wilson's boyfriend. Angus Wilson and Sonia Orwell. Long Beach College and Hugh Smith. A meeting with Henry Miller. Aldous Huxley and Charles Laughton. Elsa Lanchester and H.G. Wells. 'The British press is the dirtiest in the world'. Marilyn Monroe and the Royal Court debate. Back to Cornwall.

13: The Peak Experience.

A letter from Abraham Maslow. The monkeys in the Bronx zoo. Do monkeys have an 'appetite for knowledge'? Peak Experiences – the American marine. 'Aren't I lucky?' Underfloor lighting. Robert Ardrey and *African Genesis*. The Dominant 5%. High dominance women. Dominance and its problems. John Calhoun and overcrowded rats. Einstein and charladies. Why are Outsiders so pessimistic? Losing Sally in Cheltenham. The problem of the robot. 'Normal consciousness is half asleep'. The pen trick. The Miles Gifford murder case. Dinner at the murder house. 'Reluctance'. The hot baths at Esalen. 'Intentionality in action'. Syd Banks has a revelation: 'You're not unhappy, Syd, you just think you are'.

18: The Occult.

Ghost stories and Spiritualism. 'How many unbelievable things you can believe before breakfast'. The invitation to Majorca. Life in Deya. The fruit rats who played football. Robert Graves. The 'Traverse'. 'Poetry is written in the fifth dimension'. Graves's romanticism. George Cockcroft and *The Diceman*. George attacks me. Anthony Burgess and language. 'A pompous know-all'. Burgess and 'free floating guilt'. Burgess's accident-proneness. Joyce and resentment. The quiz. Burgess attacks me in his autobiography. Burgess as a novelist. Completing *The Black Room*. Beginning *The Occult*. Osbert Sitwell and the palmist. Synchronicity. The book that fell off the shelf. My digital clock. Foreseeing the future. Mark Bredin and the taxi. Osborn's music master has a vision. Yeats and astral projection. 'The abominable Mr Gunn'. Smilley, the calculating prodigy. Prime numbers. Graves on the school roller. Publication of *The Occult*. 'Poor devils, they'll lose their money'. Philip Toynbee and Cyril Connolly recant. Back from the wilderness?

19: Breakdown.

Becoming a television presenter. Attacks of nerves. The '*Occult* sequel'. Joy discovers T.C. Lethbridge. Dowsing at the Merry Maidens. How does dowsing work? The 'other self'. The part-work on crime. Kathie comes to visit. How to avoid being seduced. My back problem. Launching *Crimes and Punishment*. Overwork. Ten articles a week. The panic attacks. Holiday in Normandy. The panic attack on the train. Three months in Philadephia. Visit to Beyrout. Red carpet treatment. Damascus and General Tlas. More television: *A Leap in the Dark*. Christine Beauchamp and multiple personality. Julian Jaynes and the 'bicameral mind'. The double brain. *The Space Vampires*. Meeting Uri Geller. Geller reads my mind. What is a poltergeist? The Rosenheim case. The trip to Pontefract. Meeting Guy Playfair. 'Poltergeists are footballs'. The Pritchards and the 'Black Monk'. I change my mind about poltergeists. Max Freedom Long and the 'three selves'. The Kahuna death prayer. Is spirit-possession real?

20: Criminal History.

Another panic attack. Three books in three months. *The Space Vampires* is optioned. Self-discipline and overwork. 'When life fails'. 'The mind itself'. The car that decided to stop. A trip to Viitakivi. Brad Absetz and the Right Brain. The two tennis players. *Access To Inner Worlds*. 'Now un-depress yourselves'. Reichian breathing. Combining Reichian breathing and the pen trick. The split-brain and the Hillside Stranglers. Buono is caught faking. Billy Milligan and his twenty-three sub-personalities. *World History Of Crime* commissioned. The Right Man. Ian Brady and the Moors Murders. *The Gate of Janus*. Writing *A Criminal History Of Mankind*. 'No Mean City'. History increases its pace. The birth of the modern novel – *Pamela*. The 'magic carpet'. The rise of sex crime. Interview with my bank manager. Buchanan invents psychometry. Tasting brass in the dark. Telescope into the past. Why psychometry was ignored: the rise of Spiritualism. Denton and the dinosaur fossil. Cicero and the emperor Sulla. *Life Force* – the worst film ever made.

21: Dreaming to Some Purpose.

Invitation to Japan. Donald Seaman and *Spider World*. *The Encyclopaedia Of Unsolved Mysteries*. I begin collaboration with Damon. The trip to Tokyo. The foundations of Buddhism. The Esoteric Buddhism of Kukai. 'Enlightenment in this very life'. Jet lag. Drinking whisky with the monks of Koyasan. Bullet train to Tokyo. The guest of honour.

22: The Ancient Ones

Epilogue

CHAPTER 1

Giving God Back His
Entrance Ticket

When I was sixteen, I decided to commit suicide.

This was not a sudden emotional decision. When I made it, it seemed entirely logical.

I had left school in July 1947, a month after my sixteenth birthday. If it had been a possibility, I would have applied for a university scholarship. But my father wanted me to go to work and contribute to the family budget. He was in the boot and shoe trade, and had worked throughout the 1930s for about £3 a week; even now, he had to work as a barman in the evenings to make ends meet. My younger brother Barry had left school at fourteen to become a butcher's boy, and my father was resentful that he had had to support me for two years longer.

It was my ambition to be a scientist. Ever since reading Sir James Jeans's *Mysterious Universe* at the age of twelve, my daydream had been to become Einstein's successor. But to become a scientist I needed a Bachelor of Science degree, and the first step was to be an apprentice at some large chemical firm like ICI, and study for a degree in my spare time. In my final exams at school. But I failed to get a credit in maths, which meant taking the exam again after leaving school. Meanwhile, I took the only job the Labour Exchange could offer me, working in a wool-processing factory.

Going to work came as a shock. I started at eight in the morning and left at six at night, with an hour for lunch. The upper part of the factory was occupied by women standing in front of winding machines. It was my job to keep them supplied with hanks of wool and, when this had been wound on to bobbins, to take it downstairs and pack it in crates. The work was hard, but dreary and repetitive, and by the time I cycled home I was exhausted and depressed. I would spend the evening reading poetry as an emotional relief. I loved Keats and the Romantics, but in this state of dejection found that my mood was reflected best by Eliot's *The Waste Land* and 'Hollow Men'.

One day, when I had returned to my old school to borrow some maths books, the headmaster told me that if I got the extra credit in maths, I could return to school and work as a laboratory assistant. And I would be given free time to work for my inter-B.Sc. The idea sounded wonderful, and if this had happened a few months earlier, it would have filled me with delight. But there was now a problem. Since I had been spending all my spare time soaking up poetry, I had lost all interest in science.

I felt it would be unwise to admit this. So I took my maths exam, gained my extra credit, and before Christmas 1947 was back at school and wearing a white lab coat.

I had taken the exams in Birmingham, thirty miles from my home town, Leicester, travelling there daily on the train. I loved the train journey, for I had so far done little travelling, and even the flat Midland landscape seemed exciting. And one day I walked into Birmingham public library, which was far bigger than Leicester's, and was overwhelmed by the high shelves that stretched to the ceiling and had to be reached on ladders. There were books I had always wanted to read; like most teenagers I loved horror stories, and the sight of Maturin's *Melmoth the Wanderer* and Lewis's *The Monk* made me wish I lived in Birmingham. Standing in the library I suddenly knew what I wanted: to spend my days reading from morning till night. I had realised that books are a world in themselves, as immense and varied as the real world.

I found the laboratory job an enormous relief after the factory; it was like being let out of prison. But the question of my future still worried me. The three months in the factory had been a glimpse into an abyss of boredom and repetitiveness. And now my loss of interest in science meant I no longer had a future. It seemed that society had no place for people like me, people who had no desire to 'get on in life'.

Sooner or later, the headmaster would find out that I had no interest in applied mathematics or analytical chemistry, and I would be without a job. And then I would go to the Labour Exchange and be offered a choice of a dozen or so jobs that I found equally repellent. As far as I could see, I was going to have to spend my whole life doing jobs I hated.

I continued to find an escape in literature, spending my weekends devouring poetry. But this only made it harder to go back to work on Monday morning. And the physics master who was my immediate boss soon realised that I was there under false pretences, and took every opportunity to inflict petty humiliations.

But I discovered one marvellous way of restoring a sense of purpose: writing. I had listened to a radio programme about Samuel Pepys, and decided to start keeping a journal – not just a diary of my daily activities, but a record of what I thought and felt. I had borrowed from the library a book called *I Believe*, full of statements of faith by people like Einstein,

Julian Huxley and H. G. Wells. One Saturday, after spending the morning in the laboratory, I bought a fat notebook, and settled down to writing my own statement of what I believed about my place in the world.

I wrote for page after page, with a sense of freedom and release. I was objectifying doubts and miseries, pushing them to arm's length. When I put down my pen, after several hours, I had a feeling that I was no longer the same person who had sat down at the writing table. It was as if I had been studying my face in a mirror, and learned something new about myself.

From then on, I used my journal as a receptacle for self-doubt, irritation and gloom, and by doing so I wrote myself back into a state of optimism.

After spending the weekend writing myself back into a state of optimism, however, I had to go back to school, to the niggling of the physics master and the bafflement of crystallisation curves and the hydrodynamics of incompressible, inviscid fluids. The optimism had evaporated by Monday afternoon, and by Wednesday my mind felt dead.

After one particularly irritating day, I returned home at teatime to find the house empty, and started pouring my frustrations into my journal before going off to my analytical chemistry class. It had been a very hot day, and I felt exhausted. After an hour of writing, I began to feel the burden lifting, and experienced a trickling of relief that was like cool water. But I knew I would be feeling the same boredom and frustration at the same time tomorrow and the next day and the next. And suddenly it struck me that it was simply not logical to go on living like this. I felt angry with God – or fate, or whoever had cast me down into this irritating world – for subjecting me to these endless petty humiliations. I did not even believe human life was real; it had often struck me that time is some sort of illusion. But surely, I could turn my back on the illusions by killing myself?

As soon as that thought occurred to me, I felt oddly calm and relieved. Suddenly I felt in charge of myself and my destiny. If God was responsible for putting me here, then I could spite him by declining to go on playing this silly game.

As I cycled through the heat to my chemistry class, I felt strong and almost exalted. I arrived late, as usual, and endured the sarcasm of the professor with total indifference. And at the first opportunity, I went into the other room, to the reagent shelves, and took down the bottle of hydrocyanic acid, with its waxed glass stopper. I removed this, and smelled that distinctive almond smell. I knew that hydrocyanic acid would kill me in less than half a minute. Mentally, I had already raised the bottle and taken a swig of the bitter liquid.

Then an odd thing happened. I became two people. I was suddenly conscious of this teenage idiot called Colin Wilson, with his misery and frustration, and he seemed such a limited fool that I could not have cared less whether he killed himself or not. But if he killed himself, he would kill me too. For a moment I felt that I was standing beside him, and telling him that if he didn't get rid of this habit of self-pity he would never amount to anything.

It was also as if this 'real me' had said to the teenager: 'Listen, you idiot, *think how much you'd be losing,*' and in that moment I glimpsed the marvellous, immense richness of reality, extending to distant horizons.

So I re-stoppered the bottle and went back to my analytical chemistry. I felt relaxed and light-hearted and totally in control.

This mood of strength lasted for two or three days, then gradually went away. But I no longer felt trapped and vulnerable.

Forty years later, Marilyn Ferguson told me, as we walked by a lake in California, that she believed that everyone who achieves anything original in literature or philosophy has been at some point on the brink of suicide. I suspect that this is because anyone who has looked into this abyss achieves the separation of the real self from the inessential self, which is like being reborn.

When, in 1955, I began to write my first book, *The Outsider*, I knew that its central question was whether we would all be more sensible to commit suicide. By that time I was aware that Albert Camus had written a book, *The Myth of Sisyphus*, declaring that suicide is the only serious philosophical question. I was also aware of the many 'misfits' who had committed suicide: Kleist, Beddoes, Stifter, Van Gogh, Hart Crane.

Van Gogh especially fascinated me because of that feeling of life-affirmation in canvases like *The Starry Night* and *Road With Cypresses*, in which trees like green flames surge towards stars that are whirlpools of light. Yet when Van Gogh committed suicide by shooting himself in the stomach, he left a note that read: 'Misery will never end.' He seemed to epitomise the question that Carlyle called 'Everlasting Yes versus Everlasting No'. The question raised by *The Outsider* is: which has the last word?

I was inclined to come down on the side of everlasting yes because the noes seemed to me often to be weak and to lack self-discipline, or to be indulging in pessimism because it tends to be more artistically effective.

One day in the late 80s, I attended a day-long seminar in the Plymouth Arts Centre in which I shared the platform with the poet David Gascoygne and the psychologist R. D. Laing. I had known Gascoygne at the time of *The Outsider*, and been impressed by the force of his religious poetry. Laing I had never met before, although we had often come close to it on the 'New Age' lecture circuit in America. He told me he had decided to write his first book, *The Divided Self*, because he had read *The Outsider* and felt he ought to be able to write something equally successful.

That day, Gascoygne lectured on surrealism, and seemed to take the view that life itself is bizarre and surrealistic. Laing argued his theory that the mentally ill are not really ill, but are simply reflecting the sickness of our society. I explained why I had come to reject the pessimistic existentialism of Sartre and Camus, to create a form of existentialism whose implications are fundamentally optimistic.

To my surprise, Laing and Gascoyne seemed to take this personally. When the three of us finally got together on the platform for a symposium, they turned on me, taking the view that if I could be optimistic, it must be because I was shallow and superficial. They made no attempt to argue their case, but behaved like two schoolboys ganging up on a third. I suddenly realised that they were actually affronted by my optimism, not simply on a level of ideas, but on a personal level.

Thinking about this later, I began to understand the reason. Gascoyne had had several nervous breakdowns, and his haunted eyes showed it. Laing was an alcoholic whose drunkenness led to his deregistration as a medical practitioner – although I did not know about this until I read a biography of him written after his death in 1989.

'Outsiders' – and both Laing and Gascoyne were undoubtedly of the Outsider type – are abnormally sensitive to this problem of 'Everlasting Yes' versus 'Everlasting No'. A friend of mine, the poet Charles Wrey Gardiner, wrote an autobiography entitled *The Answer to Life is No*. Gascoyne and Laing had reached the same conclusion. That was why they saw my optimism as some kind of criticism of themselves.

What they were failing to grasp was that this optimism was not a matter of temperament, but of logic. My starting point in *The Outsider* had been those nineteenth-century Romantics who had experienced moments of overwhelming delight, of visions that filled them with optimism and affirmation – and then awakened the next morning to wonder what the hell they meant by it. So many of them had died insane or committed suicide – in effect, having decided that 'the answer to life is No'.

They felt that life is ultimately tragic because the 'moments of vision' seem to evaporate and leave nothing behind. Pushkin compared the poet's heart to a coal that glows red when the wind of inspiration blows on it, but turns into a black cinder when the wind dies away. Most of my 'Outsiders' seemed to feel that everyday life is a bore – what de Lisle Adam's Axel meant when he said: 'As for living, our servants can do that for us.'

The problem, clearly, was that there was no simple method of summoning the 'moment of vision'. What human beings seemed to need, as far as I could see, was a kind of pump on the front of their heads, like the pump of a primus stove, so they could increase the inner pressure with a few strokes. It was true that drugs or alcohol could sometimes do it, but they obviously carried heavy penalties. There had to be some other way.

In 1962, I made the acquaintance of the American psychologist Abraham Maslow, who had identified what he called 'peak experiences', feelings of sudden bubbling happiness. Typical was the experience of one of his students who was working his way through college as a jazz drummer. One morning, in the early hours, he suddenly had a burst of new energy, and found himself drumming perfectly, unable to do a thing wrong.

But Maslow believed that such experiences occurred by chance, and that there was no way of inducing them. I could not wholly accept this view for I had noticed that peak experiences often occur after a sustained effort, or with sudden release of stress, with its surge of relief.

One such occasion happened in the mid-60s, when I was driving back from Scotland with my family. We had set out from Biggar, in Lanarkshire, and I had assumed we had a journey of a hundred miles or so to reach the border. After driving for about an hour, I saw a signpost and realised I had greatly overestimated the distance; England was only about ten miles ahead. This meant we could easily reach Leeds, where an old friend lived, and stay the night there.

The realisation that I was closer than I thought brought a surge of cheerfulness, and since it was a sunny morning, I was soon in a mood of supercharged optimism. This feeling increased as the great hills of the Lake District came in sight. This had always been one of my favourite places, and I was familiar with its geography. But soon I began to experience the odd sensation that I could somehow see through the mountains, to what lay on the far side. I do not mean, of course, that the hills seemed literally transparent; but I felt as if I was a bird who could look down on them from a great height. This state of intensified awareness lasted an hour or more.

Maslow discovered that when his students began to discuss their peak experiences, they began having peak experiences all the time, and this makes sense. During the course of an ordinary day, we are constrained by a kind of natural caution, an anticipation of possible difficulties and problems, which tints our consciousness a shade of grey. Talking and thinking about peak experiences makes us realise how lucky we are, and that we can dispense with the caution and constraint. It is like realising that you have more money in the bank than you thought – or, in the case of the drive from Scotland, realising that the border was closer than I thought, and that I therefore had energy to spare.

Still, Maslow would point out that my Lake District experience was a matter of chance, and I would have to agree. But there was another occasion, in January 1979, when I achieved an intensity of experience through deliberate effort.

On Saturday 30 December 1978, I had to travel to a village called Sheepwash, in Devon, where I was due to lecture. It was raining when I set out, but as I drove through Launceston the rain began to turn to snow. I arrived at the farm called Totleigh Barton in the late afternoon, and gave my talk to a group of poetry students after dinner. That night, as I went to my chalet, the snow was thick on the ground and still falling. The next morning, it was obvious that I was not going to be able to drive back home. I phoned my wife and told her I might be stuck there for several days. That night – New Year's Eve – the cold froze the water supply.

The next day I tried to get my car up the slope and out to the main road. As the wheels began to spin, the others pushed me. Then we all took shovels and began the slow business of clearing the snow to the gate.

The narrow country lanes had ditches on either side. If I landed in one of those I would be stuck until the rescue services arrived. But with everything deep in snow, it was hard to see where the road ended and the ditch began. I sat forward in my seat, driving in second gear and staring through the windscreen with total concentration.

It took about two hours to reach the main Exeter road, where the snow had been churned to dirty mud, and there I could relax. I now discovered that the two hours of frantic concentration had induced a state of heightened consciousness. Everything I looked at seemed deeply interesting, as if twice as real as normal, and the cottages I passed seemed to be so fascinating that I almost wanted to stop and look more closely.

This state of intensity lasted all the way home, where I found that the electricity was off, and that my wife had delivered nine puppies in the night by the light of a torch.

The experience proved to me beyond all doubt that Maslow was mistaken. States of heightened awareness could be induced by sheer concentration.

I soon discovered the basic technique. When we are slightly bored, we allow our inner pressure to leak away. And suddenly it seems obvious that the world is a rather dreary place, for when our inner pressure is low, everything looks boring. On the other hand, when we have something to look forward to – even our favourite meal at dinnertime – there is something inside us that resists such leakage. The trick seems to be to induce this state of pleasant anticipation by the use of imagination, the exercise of inner freedom, even if you have nothing in particular to anticipate.

This could be compared to a concert audience awaiting the arrival of the conductor. There is a murmur of conversation; everyone's attention is focused on something different. Then the conductor comes in; the buzz dies away. Everyone's anticipation is suddenly focused in the same direction.

What happens in boredom is that we feel there is nothing 'out there' that is worth our full attention. But there is a fallacy involved here – a fallacy I began to grasp on that drive back from Sheepwash. Concentrating my attention because I might otherwise land in the ditch generated a certain 'energy of attention'. And when I was able to relax on the main road, all this accumulated energy made me see that *everything* is interesting. And this state was sustained during the rest of the drive home because I was now aware that the world around me *was* interesting, so that I was looking at it with an eager attention that generated yet more energy. I labelled this state 'positive feedback', as opposed to the negative feedback in which boredom generates yet more boredom.

It has been the aim of my life to learn to generate 'positive feedback' by an act of will.

CHAPTER 2

Romantic Nihilist

When I was about fourteen, my mother, who was always singularly frank about sex, told me that she knew the moment I was conceived. She and my father, who was then nineteen, had been saying goodnight outside the garden gate when the urgency of physical contact had led them to make love in the upright position. My mother felt her knees buckle and almost slid to the ground.

This was in late September 1930. Two months later, after missing her second period, she went to the doctor, who verified she was pregnant. They were married on Christmas Day.

My grandfather had taken aside Frank Tarratt, the boyfriend of my mother's elder sister Dora, and said: 'I hope you aren't getting up to that kind of thing?' Frank looked shocked and assured him that Dora was still a virgin. But one year later, Dora and Frank had to marry, and my cousin John soon made his appearance.

It seems that my mother's eldest sister Connie was responsible for her downfall. She had become engaged to an optician named Frank Carlyle, who was a widower. Together with my mother, they had been invited to stay with Aunt Ethel, who lived near Doncaster. Frank and my father were assigned to one double bed, Connie and my mother to the one in the next room. Halfway through the night, Connie went and climbed into Frank's bed, and my father had no alternative than to replace him in the other.

My mother, whose name was Anetta (but whom everybody called Hattie), told me all this when I was about ten years old. She also confided to me that Aunt Ethel was not really my aunt, but a friend of my grandmother's who had got herself pregnant, and been taken in by a kindly relative. Although Ethel had married and moved to Doncaster, she remained a close friend of the family.

All this talk of unmarried pregnancies shocked me, not because I was a prude (at ten I was indifferent to the moral issue), but because it seemed such a disastrous thing to happen. I swore that it would never happen to me, and when it actually did – some nine years later – I felt there was a kind of inevitability about it.

My mother did not particularly enjoy being married, any more than my father did. Like most working-class people, they simply made the best of it. My dad (I always called him Dad, and it sounds more natural than 'my father') liked his beer, and spent most of his evenings in the pub. My mother stayed home and looked after the children – I was soon joined by my brother Barry – and read True Romance magazines and library books. Dad was bad-tempered and irritable – no doubt resentful at being forced into marriage and having to spend his life at a factory bench – and we all breathed a sigh of relief when he went off to the pub. He was a hard worker and a good breadwinner, but working a forty-eight hour week must have struck him as a poor substitute for living.

I was a bright and – as my photographs show – rather a pretty child, and was always regarded as the clever one of the family. Cousin John was also clever and, being an only child for many years, rather spoilt. His father Frank turned out to be rather odd; he used to slap Dora around, suspecting her of infidelity, and slept with a knife under his pillow.

My father never hit my mother, although they often quarrelled, for my mother was also a strong character. She confided in me, I think, because she was bored by the drudgery of working-class life. So while she was doing the ironing, or putting wet clothes through a mangle that screwed on to the sitting-room table, Barry and I would lie on the rug in front of the fire and say: 'Tell us about when you were a little girl.'

She had been a member of a family of seven, so they were relatively poor compared to us (with dad's £3 a week), and her stories of poverty seemed romantic, and made us feel a pleasant sense of having come up in the world.

Looking back on a working-class childhood, what strikes me most is that everyone we knew seemed to accept the situation fate had thrown them into. No one dreamed of escape, because no one thought there was any escape. Instead they contented themselves with the pub, and the football match on Saturday afternoon, and dreamed of winning the football pools. And my mother and Aunt Dora, who were both readers, devoured library books, and enjoyed writers like D. H. Lawrence and A. J. Cronin because they often described poverty and the frustration of intelligent women trapped in working-class life.

I naturally followed my mother's example and read a great deal, often the books she had just finished (her plot summaries of *Wuthering Heights* and *Sons and Lovers* made them easier to absorb). I had taught myself to read from comics like the *Dandy* and *Beano*, then progressed to boys' papers like *Wizard* and *Hotspur*. But I found 'grown-up' books more satisfying because I disliked being a child; I seemed to be devoured by a permanent dissatisfaction.

Things began to improve when I was about ten. Uncle Frank Carlyle gave me a book called *The Marvels and Mysteries of Science* and I became fascinated by astronomy, learning to recognise a dozen or so nebulae at a glance, and memorising the order of the planets from Mercury to Pluto. Percival Lowell's speculation that the canals of Mars might be irrigation channels across its deserts led me inevitably to Wells's *War of the Worlds*, then on to *The Time Machine* and *The Invisible Man*. There and then I had the first dim inkling of the desire to be a scientist.

My mother gave me a chemistry set for my eleventh birthday in 1942; it was a cheap one with a dozen chemicals in drums and a few test tubes. But there was an instruction book, and I was soon showing Barry how to add two colourless liquids together to make bright blue or cloudy orange. It was at this time that I left junior school and won a scholarship to a secondary school, where I discovered a coverless copy of Holmyard's *Elementary Chemistry* on top of some lockers, and felt no guilt about stealing it. And after I had read Holmyard, I began borrowing large leather-bound volumes on chemistry from the public library.

During that year when I discovered science, I suddenly felt that an immense psychological gap had opened between myself and the people around me; I dreamed of a day when, as Wells suggested, men would be like gods.

What began to worry me slightly was my own awakening sexual impulse. In spite of my mother's stories, sex had never interested me as a child; I was a rather puritanical little boy who felt vaguely disgusted when schoolfriends told dirty jokes. One day when I was about ten, I walked with two friends to the fields a mile away at Humberstone, and we lay on the grass and drank water from lemonade bottles. Then the others began to talk about girls, and how delightful it must be to undress them. Soon they became so excited that they took off their trousers, obviously enjoying the feeling of the air on naked flesh. One of them lay on his stomach while the other placed his erect penis in the crack of his bottom, and began to move it up and down. There was, of course, no thought of sodomy – their excitement would never have carried them that far. It was simply an obscure urge, the knowledge that penises could be placed inside girls, and the desire to play at sex. Their talk of girls caused me to feel sexually aroused, but I had no desire to join in the game.

I am not, of course, claiming that I was devoid of interest in sex before that time. At a very early age, before I had ever heard of sex, I used to put on my mother's knickers when I was alone in the house, and experience a curious thrill at the silky feeling of the rayon against my body. And from then on, the sight of knickers always caused a certain sexual arousal. Many years later, I asked a girlfriend why she thought knickers were sexually stimulating to males and she replied: 'Because they're associated with that part of the body.' But I am not sure this simple explanation explains anything, since I knew nothing about female anatomy at the age of three.

My own suspicion is that this is not learned behaviour but some kind of instinct that has somehow been 'imprinted' in males in the past century and a half. Knickers (or 'drawers') were invented in the mid-nineteenth century, and began to figure in the pornography of the time. Because they were 'forbidden', men would soon be as excited by a glimpse of a woman's drawers, which came down to her ankles, as by a glimpse of bare flesh under her skirt.

The biologist Rupert Sheldrake believes that new forms of behaviour can be transmitted by what he calls 'morphic resonance', which could be regarded as a kind of telepathic induction. In an experiment to test whether morphic resonance was real, children were asked to learn a nursery rhyme in a foreign language, and a piece of 'verse' that had been made up. If morphic resonance really existed, they should find it easier to memorise the genuine nursery rhyme because millions of children already knew it. And that is just what happened. I am inclined to believe that the male response to knickers has been transmitted down to us by morphic resonance.

By the time I reached adolescence, the tingling in the loins became so powerful that it never seemed to go away. I found myself thinking about sex all the time, and glancing into the windows of ladies' underwear shops and at knickers on clothes-lines.

When I was about fourteen, I was lying in bed, thinking about the French mistress, who used to sit with her feet on a desk in the front row – the boy who sat there claimed (probably untruthfully) that he had caught glimpses of her underwear. As I pressed my hips against the mattress I experienced a sensation of intoxicating sweetness, more intense than anything I had ever felt. I was amazed to discover that my body possessed this power to generate ecstasy.

After this discovery, I came to accept that my body needed relief from sexual tension, and was glad when masturbation had relieved me of the desire so I could give my full attention to science. But the tingling in the loins returned so often that I sometimes masturbated seven times a day.

Shaw claims in one of his prefaces that his only teenage sexual experience was 'the involuntary emissions of dreams', which seems to confirm the speculation of some of his critics that he was sexually cold. As to me, I suspect that I inherited my lively sexuality from my father – my mother once hinted that his sexual demands were fairly continuous – so the six-year period from thirteen to nineteen, when my sexual experience was purely imaginary, seemed to last for ever, and I longed for the experience of penetrating a girl. In these imaginative seductions, I never began by conjuring up a naked girl, but by picturing myself lying on top of a girl wearing rayon knickers, and rubbing my penis against her until I reached orgasm.

I read somewhere the statistic that adolescent boys think of sex every quarter of an hour; in my case this was a gross underestimate. On my way to school, the bus passed an enormous advertisement for Bile Beans, a remedy for constipation, that was illustrated by a picture of a girl in green bra and panties standing on a bathroom scale; I never passed it without staring furtively and licking my lips. Just beyond the advertisement, the bus made a turn past small back yards with clothes-lines, and I always gazed down intently for any glimpse of knickers.

By the time I was thirteen I was writing my first book. I had bought at a church bazaar two volumes of a work called *Practical Knowledge for All*, a kind of home educator which included 'courses' on every subject from aeronautics and astronomy to philosophy and zoology. And one day during the long August holiday of 1944, I decided to begin a book that would try to summarise all the world's scientific knowledge in a single small volume. I gave it the title *A Manual of General Science*, and began with the subjects I knew best, physics and chemistry. I soon filled that volume, and had to buy a second notebook.

Carried away by the sheer pleasure of writing, as exhilarating as free-wheeling downhill on a bicycle, I decided to venture into subjects I knew nothing about, like geology and biology, and found this experience so enjoyable that I simply carried on scribbling, even when the holidays were over. I had never been so happy in my life. I had discovered the sheer immensity of the world of ideas, which seemed to stretch, like some marvellous unknown country, to limitless horizons. Every day, when I started writing, I felt like an explorer preparing to discover new lakes and forests and mountain ranges. I felt sorry for the other boys at school, who were ignorant of this magical kingdom where I spent my evenings and weekends.

I even wrote a section on philosophy, from Plato to Berkeley and Hume. I loved explaining to school-friends Berkeley's argument that the external world is unreal, and might vanish if there were no human beings to see it.

Having finished the book – or rather, given it up, as I realised I could go on for ever – I set myself a new project, and spent the next school holiday trying to read all the plays of Shakespeare and his contemporaries, Marlowe, Jonson, Middleton, Webster and the rest. During another holiday I read works by all the major Russian writers – Dostoevsky, Tolstoy, Gogol, Aksakov, Chekhov. Later I turned to the history of art, and discovered Van Gogh, Gauguin and Cézanne.

In 1946, when I was fifteen, I switched on the radio one night to the BBC's new Third Programme, and found myself listening to the third act of Shaw's *Man and Superman*. In the previous year I had seen the film of *Caesar and Cleopatra*, and thought it an impressive historical extravaganza, but felt no desire to explore Shaw's other work. But this third act of *Man and Superman* – Don Juan in Hell – left me stunned, and convinced that Shaw was the greatest playwright since Shakespeare.

The scene is a discussion between Don Juan, Mozart's Commendatore, his daughter Doña Ana, and the Devil. Doña Ana has just died and, finding herself in Hell, is indignant. Was she not a faithful daughter of the Church? Don Juan explains that Hell is not a place of torment, but of endless pleasure, and that he finds it thoroughly boring. Her father joins them, and explains to her that heaven is the most beatifically boring place in the universe, and that all the best people prefer Hell, including the fathers of the Church. Then the Devil arrives, and explains that he stands for love, beauty and warmth of heart, and organised this place to epitomise them. Don Juan then describes his own view of the purpose of evolution: the creation of the Superman.

What impressed me so much was that Shaw is asking: what is the purpose of life? It was the first time that I had heard anyone ask the question that had haunted me since the age of thirteen. Wells had written a little book called *What Are We To Do With Our Lives?*, but it was basically about politics and sociology. Shaw obviously understood the basic problem: meaninglessness.

Yet Shaw's answer: that the purpose of life is to understand itself, failed to satisfy me. How could that supply an answer to the question of good and evil, right and wrong?

So at the age of sixteen, when it was time for me to leave school, I had no strong sense of purpose. Worse still, I was suffering from that typical problem of teenagers: boredom and futility. I spent a great deal of my time experiencing a complete lack of motivation. On a hot Saturday afternoon I would go for a walk in the park, and feel like an alien from Mars, looking at a world that meant nothing to me.

One July day, when I had been reading too much in the hot sun (it was a gloomy book on Russian literature) I went into the kitchen to switch on the stove, and had a blackout. I stood holding on to the stove, and felt my mind swept away completely, and with it all I knew as my identity. When my sight cleared, I was overwhelmed with horror. Through all the hatred and distrust of the world I had at least been certain of one thing – my own existence. But in the blackout I had felt my existence taken away from me as simply as you might take a sweet away from a baby. Suddenly, I wanted badly to know who I was, if I could still exist when my identity slipped away. I understood what Eliot meant when he spoke about the mind under ether being 'conscious, but conscious of nothing'. What I seemed to have been conscious of in the blackout was a kind of electrical flow of pain in the nothingness. Later, I wrote in my journal that life is not a movement towards something, but an escape from something – from some ultimate pain on the other side of existence. For days, after this experience, the world became an absurdity; watching it was like listening to a foreign language. What made it worse was that I could not feel: 'This is frightful', or 'This is a tragedy.' It simply negated every possible human value and therefore every human description. I felt as if I should not be alive.

This is why I read so much. I knew that, with luck, a book would draw me into it and excite a feeling of being alive. So I ploughed my way through gloomy Russians like Goncharov – I felt Oblomov was my first cousin – and Saltykov-Schedrin and Zamyatin, and read *Ulysses* for the fifth time. (When, years later, I met my first publisher, Victor Gollancz, he asked me: 'How on earth have you managed to read so much?' and I answered 'Boredom'.)

In fact, I glimpsed the solution in that preface that Constance Garnett used in all her translations of Dostoevsky: his description (in a letter to his brother Mikhail) of how he and other condemned 'revolutionaries' were taken out on to Semyonovsky Square in St Petersburg to be executed by firing squad. 'They barked orders over our heads, and made us put on the white shirts worn by persons condemned to execution. Being the third in the row, I concluded I had only a few minutes of life before me. I thought of you and your dear ones, and I contrived to kiss Plescheiv and Dourov, who were next to me, to bid them farewell. Suddenly the troops beat a tattoo, and we were unbound, brought back to the scaffold, and informed that his Majesty . . . had spared our lives.' One of his fellow-prisoners went insane. It struck me that if Dostoevsky had been offered his freedom *on condition that he promised never to be bored for the rest of his life*, he would have accepted gladly, and been quite certain that he could carry out his promise.

I again saw the answer in Boswell's life of Johnson – which I bought myself for Christmas – when Johnson remarks: 'When a man knows he is to be hanged in a fortnight, it concentrates his mind wonderfully.' That was obviously what was wrong with my mind – lack of a sense of urgency. But how could you generate a feeling of urgency when your whole life lacked direction?

My only salvation obviously lay in becoming a writer. In the year as a lab assistant I had written a sequel to *Man and Superman* called *Father and Son*, in which Shaw's hero Tanner finds himself father of a son who shares none of his belief in socialism, and who feels that the evolutionism of *Man and Superman* still fails to address the question of whether life is an absurd joke.

It was shortly before this that I came upon a discovery that put an end to the nihilism and the suspicion that life was a malicious joke. In the *Selected Essays* of T. S. Eliot I had come upon a reference to the Hindu religious classic, the *Bhagavad Gita*. Since Eliot was my main literary guide – I read every book he mentioned – I immediately bought a copy of the book when I saw a new translation – by Isherwood and Prabhavananda – in our local bookshop.

It is a small extract from the vast Hindu epic *The Mahabharata*. Its hero, Arjuna, is told that he must fight against an army that includes kinsmen, and he is horrified at the thought that he might kill some of his own family. His teacher, Krishna, the incarnation of God, tells him that his misery is unnecessary. 'There never was a time when you did not exist, nor I, nor any of these princes, nor is there any time when we shall cease to be. Worn-out clothes are shed by the body; worn-out bodies are shed by the soul, like garments.'

Krishna then goes on to teach Arjuna the essence of the religious life. Although we are obliged to live in the world, it is important to refuse to become the slave of desire. We must learn to practise non-attachment. Human beings spend their lives tangled in a web of illusions, of Maya, and this is the cause of all their unhappiness. We must recognise them as illusions, and refuse to allow them to gain power over us.

This can be done by teaching yourself to meditate and to recognise that 'you' are not your body, or your emotions, or even your mind. The essence of your being is identical with Brahman, the power behind the universe, the reality that creates this web of unreality . . .

I was a frustrated teenager, continually tormented by desires and emotions. The *Gita* taught me to grasp the knowledge that my soul, the Atman, is of the same nature as Brahman. It brought a tremendous sense of relief. When I was tormented by embarrassment – as teenagers are most of the time – or a feeling of humiliation, I simply had to create that sense of looking down on human life from above:

> Though a man be the greatest of sinners,
> This knowledge will carry him, like a raft
> above his sin.

So I no longer needed to feel guilty about masturbation, or mortified by social blunders and errors. I was not an adolescent; my essence was immortal and timeless.

It was an incredible relief. And I soon discovered that 'meditation' was not the important part of the discipline. Merely sitting, cross-legged, for half an hour, and focusing my mind, brought a sudden feeling of inner control. I would still my mind, then I would concentrate hard, often screwing up my face until I must have looked like a demon. When, years later, I acquired one of those steel syphons for making soda water, it reminded me of that mental trick. Concentrating hard was just like screwing the little metal cylinder on to the hollow spike, and hearing the hiss as the carbon dioxide rushed into the water and made it effervescent. Suddenly my mind was sparkling.

So the kind of misery that had brought me to the verge of killing myself now seemed an absurdity. I would get up in the morning at half past five, and sit on the floor of my bedroom repeating:

> Brahman is the ritual
> Brahman is the offering
> Brahman is he who offers
> To the fire that is Brahman.
> When a man sees Brahman in every action
> He shall find Brahman.

Then I would put on running kit, and go for a jog around the park before setting off to my job as a lab assistant, walking across Spinney Hill Park and through the back streets of the slums where I had often visited members of my father's family in childhood. Sometimes I would stop, and simply stare at some cracked windowsill, aware that *anything* on which we focus our full attention becomes interesting. And at the laboratory I became indifferent to the petty nagging of the physics master; his stupidity and spite could no longer touch me.

It was during this period that I realised I had discovered one of the secrets of human existence: if I maintained a high level of inner pressure, and declined to allow my mind to collapse into tiredness or boredom, everything went well. When I didn't, they went badly. The major problem of human beings is a tendency to allow our energies to *leak*. And as soon as they leak, consciousness is dimmed, and we become subject to accident. I seemed to have spent years of my teens going through life with a continual sense of anxiety, as if anticipating a blow. Now I realised that I caused the blows myself by allowing my inner pressure to escape. All I had to do was to concentrate hard, to set my mouth in a firm line and clench my jaw, and perhaps stretch my muscles like an animal waking from a nap. And as soon as I had induced this feeling of control, problems evaporated.

Again it was necessary to look for a job. Ideally, I would have liked to work as a junior reporter for the *Leicester Mercury*, but they had no openings. The Labour Exchange sent me instead to the office of the Collector of Taxes, which was opposite the *Mercury* building. I was interviewed by an amiable Londoner called J. W. Sidford, who quickly divined that I did not have the slightest interest in becoming a tax collector, but offered me a job that might serve as a stopgap until I could make a living by writing.

Predictably, the tax job bored me. I had to begin the day by filing Schedule A forms, after which there was very little to do. Fortunately, Mr Sidford seemed to find me amusing, and often invited me into his office, where we would discuss literature – his favourite author was Howard Spring, who wrote novels about Manchester working-class life. I escaped to Leicester Central Library around the corner far more often than I should have done. And I was allowed to read at work when there was no filing to be done – it was there I first read *War and Peace*. That boring first chapter had so far deterred me, but within half a dozen chapters I was living in Tolstoy's world, carried away – as E. M. Forster says – by the 'effect like music'.

At least my father was pleased; if his friends in the pub asked him what his son was doing, he could tell them I was a Civil Servant. So I worked throughout my seventeenth year in the office in Albion Street, and even allowed myself to be persuaded to take the Civil Service examination, which I passed in the spring of 1949. When I was told that I would be posted elsewhere, probably out of Leicester, I was delighted.

This did not last. I arrived at the Collector of Taxes in Rugby at the beginning of an intensely hot summer. This was the home of Rugby School, made famous in *Tom Brown's Schooldays*, celebrated in the nineteenth century for the regime of Dr Arnold, the father of the poet Matthew. It was also the place where Rupert Brooke had grown up – I had come to greatly admire his poetry.

But Rugby was a small town, and there was little to do in my spare time but read. My landlady took a dislike to me, finding me too bookish and abstracted, unlike my fellow lodger, who was red-cheeked and outgoing. Finally, she gave me notice. But this turned out to be a piece of excellent luck. I found that there was a hostel for young men in Rugby, where no one cared when I came and went, or what I read. So I thoroughly enjoyed the rest of that summer. But I continued to dislike office work, and was overjoyed when a summons arrived to enter the RAF for my National Service.

By the time I took the train to Padgate, in Lancashire, to become an airman I had already turned eighteen. I had the worst expectations of military life, since my father had often told me grimly that National Service should knock some sense into me. But it proved pleasanter than I had expected. The flight lieutenant who interviewed me decided I was officer material – by that time I had taken some care to get rid of my Midlands accent – but this notion was dropped when I revealed that my family background was working-class, and there was not enough money to pay my mess bills. After a week in Padgate, being issued with a uniform, I was sent to Bridgnorth, in Shropshire, a picturesque place with a railway that runs up a cliff. There I did my 'square-bashing', starting at half past six in the winter dawn, and I wrote a poem that began:

> The sun is a white diamond in the morning
> Tearing a pale scar across the sky.

The day was long and exhausting, and when I collapsed into bed, I was too tired to be kept awake by the noise that went on until lights out.

After eight weeks of this, there was a passing-out parade, and I was surprised to experience a surge of sheer delight as several hundred of us snapped to attention, then went through our drill and marched to the sounds of the brass band. It made me realise that we all contain this immense, irrational energy of joy, and that our problem is to gain access to it. The insight reinforced what I had learned from my 'suicide attempt' – that the thin walls of personality separate us from an immense world of sheer happiness and affirmation.

After that parade, the rest of my career in the RAF was an anticlimax. I had hoped that I might learn to fly aeroplanes, but was told that I could only do that if I signed on for five years. My next choice was to become a medical orderly – I had met one during a brief spell in hospital, and decided that the job seemed interesting. But I suspect that fate had no intention of allowing me to relax and enjoy life yet. I was assigned to general duties as a clerk, and posted to a run-down camp called Wythall, not far from Birmingham, for training.

It was a slovenly, cheerless place, but since I had already taught myself to type, I was allowed to write letters during the typing lessons. It was there that I read Aldous Huxley's *Antic Hay*, which I found exhilarating – I envied Huxley his early success, and his association with figures like T. S. Eliot and D. H. Lawrence. It made me daydream of weekends in country houses and intellectual discussion that went on until dawn. In Wythall I seemed to be a thousand miles away from the kind of life I wanted to lead.

I also recall going to see the Graham Greene film *The Third Man*. As I was standing in the queue, a tramp came and asked me for money, and I gave him a shilling. At that moment he noticed a policeman watching us, and hastily handed me a cigarette, so that he could not be arrested for begging. I had never smoked – although both my parents were addicted – and decided to try it. The man next to me gave me a light, and I puffed away, trying to breathe in the acrid smoke without coughing. It made the time pass more quickly, but also filled my mouth with such a bitter taste that I was never subsequently tempted to try another.

I had one odd experience at Wythall, which later played a part in getting me discharged from the RAF. When I was billet orderly, I had been placed on a charge for failing to polish the dilapidated, discoloured linoleum to the level required. This involved extra duties in the evening, and one day I was sent to polish the floor of a warrant officer. He seemed a pleasant, friendly person and engaged me in conversation. Then he began to talk about the joys of flogging, and asked if I would tie him up and beat him. The idea did not appeal to me, and I declined as politely as I could, saying I had to report back to the guard room. The next day I went home for Christmas, and after I came back, was relieved to learn that the warrant officer was still on leave.

Soon after that, my training over, I was posted again, this time to Hucknall Torkard in Nottinghamshire. It was close to the birthplace of D. H. Lawrence, and to Byron's Newstead Abbey, to which I cycled one rainy January afternoon. But the camp itself was as run-down as Wythall, sunk in a permanent lethargy like a Russian novel. There were soldiers there, as well as airmen and airwomen, and I was transferred to the RAF regiment and assigned to work as the clerk in an auxiliary unit whose members came in for training only at weekends.

During the week, it was not unlike being in the tax office, with not enough to do. I remember it mainly through the books I read – William Gaunt's *The Aesthetic Adventure*, and the poems of Swinburne and Dowson. I was also studying *Finnegans Wake*, using the *Skeleton Key* of Campbell and Robinson. At that time, *Ulysses* was reissued, for the first time since the war, and I hastened to buy a copy. I had been reading it since I was sixteen, and knew much of it by heart. Although my first reaction had been disgust and irritation, I soon realised that this is a writers' manual that could teach me the precise science of describing actuality.

One week, everything went wrong. Believing the adjutant was on leave, I walked into the office late one morning, and my weekend leave was cancelled. On the weekly parade I had been singled out for growing my hair too long, and placed on a charge. And at that time, feeling thoroughly sick of the RAF and its stupidities, I was reproved by the adjutant for typing a letter badly. He waved it in front of my nose and shouted: 'Aren't you ashamed of yourself.' My patience finally snapped, and I shouted back, 'No.'

He stared at me in astonishment, and so did the corporal and sergeant. The adjutant told me to go and wait for him in his office.

The next step, I could see, would be the guard room and 'jankers' (prison). But I felt reckless and disgusted. I even contemplated throwing the inkwell through the glass door when I saw the adjutant's shadow on it.

When he came in, however, the adjutant looked concerned, and asked me in a fatherly way what was wrong. I decided to play up to his idea of me as a dangerous neurotic, and strode up and down the office denouncing the RAF as a stupid Boy Scouts organisation. He asked me what I would prefer to do, and I said I would like to be transferred to the Medical Corps. Cheered at the prospect of getting rid of me, he told me to go and see the Medical Officer, and see if he could be persuaded to sign a certificate stating that I was emotionally unfitted to be an efficient clerk.

The M.O. was a young man, and had obviously received a phone call from the adjutant asking him to try and get me assigned elsewhere. It was plain that he did not feel that dislike of the RAF was enough to prove my emotional instability. But he said he would do what he could. As I started to leave his office, I was thinking hard for some other reason why I should be transferred. Then I had an inspiration. I turned back and said: 'There *is* one more thing, sir . . .' 'Yes.' 'I'm a homosexual.'

The effect was impressive. When I wrote home about the episode, I said: 'He seized two pencils in both hands and began writing with both at once.' With an expression of deep concern, he told me to sit down and asked how long I had known I was homosexual. I said ever since I was fourteen. Then I invented a history for myself, based on a homosexual friend called Alan. I said that my mother had wanted a girl, and had intended to call me June. (This happened to be true.) She had kept me dressed as a girl until I was nine years old. But my days of active homosexuality had started when I had been seduced by a schoolteacher named Eric, and discovered I enjoyed it.

What was causing me stress at the moment was being surrounded by beautiful male bodies in the billet.

The M.O. explained that active homosexuality was a serious offence that could land me in jail. Which meant that AC2 Wilson might not be allowed to remain in the RAF.

I looked horrified, trying to conceal my delight, and said I hoped not.

Back in the office, the adjutant asked me what had happened, and I told him. He was obviously fascinated, and made me repeat the most scandalous details several times. Then he told me I could take the rest of the morning off to recover. I cycled out to Newstead Abbey, overwhelmed by an intoxicating sense of freedom. When I got back, the adjutant had another long talk with me, enjoying every moment of this break from the dull routine, and repeating: 'But Wilson, I don't understand. There's nothing *like* a woman . . .'

The next day there was an unpleasant complication. The adjutant had gone on leave, and I was told that the S.I.B., the Special Investigations Branch of the RAF police, wanted to see me. They wanted to know if I knew other homosexuals in the camp, and if I had had sexual relations with any of them. Of course, everyone knew the queers – a certain cook, a certain sergeant, even a WAAF officer – but I wasn't going to involve any of them. The interrogation went on for two hours, then I was allowed to go. The next day they sent for me again, and this time tried increasing the pressure. Unless I was willing to name names, they could not guarantee that I wouldn't spend the rest of my eighteen months in jail . . . Then the officer asked if I had known a Warrant Officer called Rutherford at Wythall. I admitted I had – this was the man who wanted me to beat him. Rutherford, he said, was now under arrest for sadistic cruelty to a cat, putting out its eye. If I would give evidence against him at his trial, they would drop the threats. Apologetically, I once more said I couldn't do that. I was finally allowed to go, but told to think it over.

The next day the adjutant returned, and I told him what had happened. He immediately wrote me out a leave pass, and told me to go and stay there until contacted.

I went home chuckling with delight. I could hardly believe my luck. For the next four weeks I returned to Hucknall only to collect my pay. Eventually, I was told to go to Wendover to see a psychiatrist. He was a large and sympathetic Wing Commander, who told me I would probably be discharged from the RAF. A few weeks later a medical board proved to be tougher, obviously suspecting that I was shamming. I put on a show of mild hysterics, and accused them of treating homosexuals like criminals, and they had no alternative but to discharge me.

CHAPTER 3

Mary

So six months after entering the RAF I was a civilian once more. The day after my discharge I hitch-hiked down to London. A signpost pointing to Wendover reminded me of Rupert Brooke's lines:

> Thank God that done! and I'll take the road
> Quit of my youth and you,
> The Roman road to Wendover
> By Tring and Lilly Hoo.

Getting out of the RAF was one of the most decisive events of my life. I suddenly felt, like Wells's Mr Polly: 'If you don't like your life you can change it'. Until that point I had felt like a football kicked around by destiny, forced to work at jobs I disliked and swallow boredom and irritation as my inevitable lot in life. Now one single impulse – the decision to say no – had changed everything.

In the state of optimism that followed, I turned my back on the Romantic literature that had formed my staple fare so far. The major influence on my thinking during this period – as strange as it sounds – was Rabelais's *Gargantua and Pantagruel*, which I had stumbled on through reading J. M. Synge's free translation of Ronsard's lines on Rabelais:

> If fruits are fed on any beast
> Let vine-roots suck this parish priest,
> For while he lived, no summer sun
> Went up but he'd a bottle done,
> And in the starlight beer and stout
> Kept his waistcoat bulging out.
>
> Then Death that changes happy things
> Damned his soul to water springs.

Gargantua became for me an affirmation of delight in living. This was not the Motteux and Urquhart translation, but that of Jacques LeClerc. I particularly liked Gargantua's poem on emptying his bowels:

> Whilst I was shitting yesterday, I sniffed
> The daily tribute that I owe my tail.
> Alas, the odours from my penetrail
> Proved quite the worst a human ever whiffed.
> O had some power but granted me the gift
> Of bringing her I waited for (sweet frail!)
>   Whilst I was shitting
> I would have rammed and dammed her water-rift,
> Engrossed and settled her estate entail,
> Whilst she with skilful fingers would avail,
> To guard my nozzle from the turdous drift
>   Whilst I was shitting.

Rabelais was more than a bawdy priest; he was a symbol of ultimate acceptance of life.

My admiration for Synge led me to dream of going to the Aran Isles – the Islands of the Saints – and trying to find myself some ancient stone hut where I could spend my days in meditation.

One result of this new optimistic state of mind was the determination to resign from the Civil Service. I had had enough of offices. But my father was horrified. He felt I was ruining my life. First I had changed my mind about becoming a scientist, and now I was throwing away the chance of becoming a Collector of Taxes. What *did* I want to do? When I said I wanted to become a writer, he asked me how I thought I was going to go about it, and I had to admit I didn't know. So he ordered me to leave home.

Looking back on it, I have to admit that I never liked my father much. He was a man of strong character and fixed opinions, and my obsession with reading struck him as unhealthy. One day when I had been using a screwdriver from his tool box, and had forgotten to put it back, he slapped my face, and in that moment I hated him. And when I was a teenager, and would listen to plays or symphony concerts on the radio, he would come back from the Coleman Road Social Club and mutter, 'Bloody rubbish,' and change the programme to comedy or a variety show. I so detested him that, until I had children of my own, it never struck me that any son could love his father.

Meanwhile, I had to decide what to do next. I had a little money from the RAF, but not enough to support me for long. But I was in a bubbling, happy state, and was sure that whatever happened would be interesting.

Synge had wandered around Ireland as a tramp. Why should I not do the same in England. I set out from home wearing my old RAF uniform – I found it made hitch-hiking easier – with a haversack on my back. I was carrying one or two favourite books, including the *Bhagavad Gita*, Plato's *Symposium* and *Phaedo* and the collected work of William Blake. My immediate purpose was to see whether I could find a job as an assistant stage manager in the theatre. Someone had recommended that I try the Playhouse in York. But they told me that although they had a vacancy, I would need to pay a premium of a hundred pounds, which was as far beyond my resources as a hundred thousand. I tried the theatre in Harrogate, but they had nothing to offer. In retrospect, I can see that this was a piece of good fortune, for if I had become an actor or stage manager, I would certainly have given up the idea of writing books.

I went on to visit the Lake District, which I had explored on a bicycle before I went into the RAF, but as my money ran low, I decided to return to Leicester to see if my discharge papers had arrived. My father was not pleased to see me, particularly when I told him I intended to take a labouring job on a building site, but reluctantly he allowed me to stay. Building jobs were easy to obtain, and the employers didn't care if you only stayed a short time.

My workmates were amiable enough, and did not seem surprised that I had decided to be a labourer – students often worked on sites during the holidays. The only thing I found a strain was the dreary talk about sex. The first question in the morning was who had been 'on the nest' the night before. One habitual drunk, who had been in jail for wife-beating, described how he had made love to his wife, then to his daughter. Another had ten or so children, but still insisted on ignoring his wife's protests and having sex without a condom. I began to feel that these men had settled for living in the present because they had been hypnotised by sex.

I stayed two weeks, wheeling barrowloads of concrete, and made ten pounds or so. Then I set off to hitch-hike to Southampton, where I hoped to find a boat to India – the *Gita* and various Buddhist scriptures had filled me with the idea of becoming a 'tathagata', or wanderer there.

I also had the romantic idea of spending the night on Stonehenge, which I had seen pictured in Blake's *Jerusalem*. I found that it was surrounded by a barbed-wire fence, which I had to climb over. It had been a warm summer day, but by two o'clock in the morning the temperature had fallen, and my teeth began to chatter. So I made my way to a haystack in the next field and crawled into it. I had intended to get up before dawn and watch the sunrise, but I overslept, and when I emerged from the stack, found I looked like a teddy bear, with thousands of little needles of hay stuck into my overcoat.

When I saw a signpost to an RAF station, I decided to try and get a free breakfast, and went to the guard room and explained that I was waiting for my discharge papers from the RAF, and wanted to find out what had happened to them. In fact, they gave me breakfast and lunch but kept me waiting while the RAF police contacted the civil police in Leicester. My mother was upset when a policeman came to the front door, and told him to send me home immediately. Twenty-four hours later I found myself back at home, where the atmosphere was still cool. But at least there was no more talk of throwing me out.

It was a hot summer. I worked for a few weeks at another building job and, when I got tired of that, went back to the Labour Exchange to be directed to something else. I no longer felt any conscience about changing my job as often as I felt inclined. Why should I be tied to the same dull job until I felt bored and exhausted? I was sent to a fairground that had opened on the edge of Leicester, where I had to sell tickets on a gambling machine called a 'spinner'. A lighted beam would spin around to music, and bulbs would flash on and off over a bank of numbers. When the machine stopped, the illuminated number won a prize. My job was to walk around the circular booth shouting invitations to the passers-by.

I was so good at this that my boss offered me a permanent job, and I was tempted – a life that involved continual change sounded perfect. But it was not to be. I was literally seduced away from this life as a wandering showman.

One evening, a girl who looked about twelve stood staring at me, and when I asked her if she wanted to buy a ticket, said: 'Do you want to sell yourself?' She had a pretty oval face and a cold sore on her lip. She waited for me until I finished work, then I walked her home – a few streets away – and kissed her goodnight. Her name was Mary, and I realised from the way she gazed at me that she offered me the prospect of finally losing my virginity. We arranged to meet the following afternoon – she was an assistant at Woolworths, and Thursday was her afternoon off – and take a bus out to Swithland Woods. It would have to be a short afternoon, since I was due at work at six.

It turned out that Mary was nearly sixteen, and lived on a slum estate near Gypsy Lane. She spoke with a broad Leicester accent, in which 'bum' is pronounced 'boom' and 'get out' 'gerrout'. She was easy to talk to, being a born chatterbox, and in the depths of the woods we found a grassy space and lay down and kissed. I was startled and pleasantly surprised when she inserted her tongue between my lips, a mode of kissing I had never experienced. I moved away from her in case she noticed my sexual excitement, but she could undoubtedly deduce it from the pounding of my heart.

Finally, we went to a cottage that advertised afternoon teas, and had a pot of tea and buttered scones. By the time we reached the bus stop, we found that we had missed the six o'clock bus, and had an hour and a half to wait. I was obviously going to miss the fairground job, but it seemed worth it. As we had walked back to the bus, with my arm round her waist, she had taken my hand and placed it on her small flat breast beneath her thin blouse.

It was becoming dark as we kissed goodnight on the corner of her street. She kissed me with her tongue, grinding her pelvis against my erection. And as I walked home, I knew that my curiosity about sex was soon going to be satisfied.

The next morning I went to the fairground, and was told I was sacked. I took a bus to the centre of town and went to see Mary in Woolworths. She looked harassed and miserable, and told me that her parents had thrown her out for being home after dark. She had tried to catch me up, but failed, and had ended by knocking on a door in Coleman Road – not far from my home – to ask if they knew where I lived. A kindly bus conductress had given her a bed for the night. And now, as we sat in a cheap cafe, she asked me if I would be willing to marry her.

The thought made my heart sink – the last thing I wanted was a teenage wife. But since I had been to blame for her present predicament, I said I would. First I would go to her home and talk to her mother.

She proved to be a short lady with large breasts and few teeth, and the sitting room she asked me into was furnished with wooden boxes instead of chairs. I found something very sensible and likeable about her, and could see why Mary was so fond of her. She told me indignantly that her husband had had no right to throw Mary out, and said I was to order her to return home immediately.

That was a huge relief – I had already envisaged myself working in an office and living with Mary in lodgings. Now I hurried back to Woolworths and told Mary, who was overjoyed. And I was overjoyed to feel that my world of poetry and music and philosophy had been restored to me.

It was necessary to find another job immediately, and again I took one on a building site, starting the next day. And that evening, Mary and I took a bus out to Evington Village, where there was a common. As we sat kissing, and I became feverishly excited, she reached down, squeezed my erection through my trousers, then, to my delight and incredulity, unbuttoned me and took my penis in her hand. I found it amazing that a fifteen-year-old girl was not afraid to make the first advances, but deeply relieved – it would have taken me a month to overcome my inhibitions. Since she was sitting down and wearing slacks (cherry-coloured), it would have been imposs-ible for me to attempt any response. We took the bus home, and she kept my hand tightly pressed into her lap.

The next day was a Saturday, and we went for a walk in Humberstone Park. Unfortunately, this was flat and offered no kind of shelter. We sat among some spaced trees and kissed, and when she squeezed me through my trousers, I managed to slip my hand under her dress. Then some people went past, and I had to hastily remove it.

The following day we had agreed to meet early and go into the country. I already knew what was bound to happen. We caught a bus to Scraptoft village, then walked on into the green countryside, where the temperature was already in the sixties, with my hand on her breast.

We went into a field, and unpacked our sandwiches and orange cordial. But the farmer ordered us to move on. We walked a quarter of a mile, found another field with a stream that flowed through a grassy dell, and this time made sure we were no longer within sight of the road. We put the bottles in the stream to cool, then lost no time in lying down.

As soon as we began to kiss, she unbuttoned my khaki shorts and examined my penis. For some reason, its underside was covered in tiny spots, and she christened it 'spotted Oscar'. I did what I had dreamed of so often, and reached up her skirt and inside her knickers, but she had to take my hand and push it further back – so great was my ignorance of female anatomy that I supposed the vagina to be the fold of flesh that as a child I had glimpsed in small girls at bathtime. It came as a surprise, and a slight disappointment, since all the sexual fantasies of my teens had involved entering at the front of the body, over the pelvis, and my imagination had to be readjusted. When I inserted a finger she sighed and pushed her tongue into my mouth.

The time had obviously come for us to curtail these frustrating explorations, and she gasped, 'Shall I take them off?' And she knelt on the ground, pushing down her cotton schoolgirl knickers, repeating gleefully: 'Aren't we wicked?'

I was not sure what came next, and clumsily tried to mount her. But she told me to lie on my back, took my penis firmly in her hand, and sat astride me, holding it with one hand behind her, and the other pulling down her vest, since she had a fruit rash of which she was ashamed. Then she sat carefully down on me, giving a cry of pain as the head penetrated her, and with more gasps of discomfort, went on pressing down until she was sitting on my thighs.

I found it hard to believe that this is what I had imagined so often. Where was the ecstasy, the surge of intoxication? This felt as clinical as having a cut finger bandaged.

When I tried to move she groaned, 'Hold still.' Then she began to move up and down very slowly and cautiously until I said, 'Move off, quick,' and she raised herself and looked down curiously at the semen bubbling out and rolling towards my stomach.

After that we ate our sandwiches and drank lemonade. I found it hard to believe that it had all been so down-to-earth. Was this the reality behind all those feverish daydreams?

We made love again, this time in the normal position, and I had to put my hands under her buttocks to raise her. Her reactions to lovemaking were gratifying; she gasped, her eyes rolled, and she wriggled and moaned, apparently unconscious of anything but the pleasure in her loins. Again, I had to withdraw quickly. As she stood up and pulled on her knickers, bracing her legs apart, I observed that my sexual response – if not the capability to satisfy it – returned immediately. And half an hour later we were making love again.

Now, suddenly, I realised that I was beginning to understand one of the basic features of sex: that it depended to a large extent on visual stimulus. Two years before, I had been cycling along this road, and passed two women, one of them lying with her hands behind her head and her legs apart, showing her knickers. I felt as if a mine had exploded under my bicycle. But the actuality of lovemaking meant that the only sense involved was the sense of touch, so all the frenzied excitement was absent. Real lovemaking, the lovemaking I had dreamed about for years, would require *a sense of reality* that made the visual stimulus unnecessary. I would one day label this sense 'Faculty X'.

And as we went on to make love five times more, I noted that as the desire became increasingly diluted I was maintaining my excitement by *telling* myself that I was inside her. It seemed that actual sex was more like masturbation than I had expected.

An interesting thought occurred. Now I knew that sex was this practical activity, no more intrinsically exciting than eating a sandwich, would I be able to turn my back on it, like a monk? After all, if we have been to some place that we always wanted to visit, the curiosity is satisfied, and more often than not, it hardly matters if we never go there again.

But as we walked back to the bus stop in the late afternoon, with the faint smell of cow dung on the breeze, and her head on my shoulder, I had other things to think about. Mary had returned to the subject of marriage, and I had to explain that if I intended to become a writer, a wife and family would have to wait.

Another problem nagged at my mind: was it possible she was pregnant? I had withdrawn each time, but had read somewhere that sperm cells are incredibly hardy, and can travel the equivalent of dozens of miles to reach their objective. This was a depressing thought. Meanwhile Mary was daydreaming aloud about how nice it would be to live in London as the wife of a famous writer, and her mother somewhere nearby.

To tell the truth, I was tired of all this loving and kissing. I wanted to get back home and write in my journal, and then sit cross-legged on the floor and concentrate.

It seemed that Mary was not a virgin; she told me she had been raped on the 'recky' (recreation ground) by two boys when she was thirteen. This experience had not, as might have been expected, put her off sex; in fact, the contrary seemed true, and her sexual urge was clearly as strong as my own. If it had been socially permissible I think she would have unbuttoned the trousers of every attractive male to inspect his endowment.

The affair soon settled into a kind of routine. On Saturday evenings I would go to babysit at the house of Uncle George and Aunt Muriel, near Humberstone Park. As soon as we were alone, we would take off our clothes and make love on the rug. Now her strawberry rash had gone she was no longer embarrassed to let me see her naked. She had a beautiful little body with tiny breasts, too small for a bra, and she soon got rid of her school-girl knickers and began wearing grown-up nylon panties.

Something else became clear: that nature has baited the sexual hook with a curious kind of honey that is a mild and addictive poison; its taste fills us with a bubbling sense of exultant indecency, so the mind begins to look around for something that will satisfy this appetite for the forbidden. It was amusing to reflect that even vicars would feel no desire for their wives without this touch of wickedness.

I soon had my answer to the question of whether I could rid myself of sexual desire now I knew the reality of sex. One day when we had finished lovemaking, Mary pulled on her pink knickers, and looked so desirable that I instantly removed them to start all over again. This was clearly absurd. The visual stimulus was obviously about ten times as powerful as the physical sex urge itself.

After lovemaking I had a pleasant sense of relaxation and freedom from desire. But I only had to catch a glimpse of a girl whose panties made a V-shape through a tight dress to feel the desire once more.

It seemed to be a kind of swindle. I knew that if I could persuade the girl into bed, I would feel the same dissatisfaction once it was over. In other words, fate had taught me that sex was an illusion, but my loins disagreed. Like a child that wants to put a coloured toy into its mouth, my body simply refused to learn from experience.

When I grew bored with working on the building site, I asked the Labour Exchange what they could offer me. They suggested that I might become an agricultural student and work on farms, for which I would be paid a grant under a government training scheme. It sounded worth trying, so I went to the village of Newbold Verdon, where the squire wanted a farming assistant. I learned to milk the cows at six in the morning and shovel the dung into a wheelbarrow and dump it on a heap. After breakfast there would be haymaking. This was the kind of life I loved reading about in poetry but, as with lovemaking, the reality was too real, too solid. After a short time, the squire realised I was not a committed farming student – 'You're doing this for a lark, aren't you?' – and sent me back to the Labour Exchange.

I had two more farming jobs, the second at Houghton-on-the-Hill, which was close enough for me to be able to commute to work by bus. I was replacing a farm labourer who had been caught practising animal husbandry with a cow. But the old problem was still there. I simply didn't want to do this kind of thing. I felt I was marking time.

The affair with Mary went on pleasantly, the only problem being that she would be carried away by moods of violent emotion like summer storms. Perhaps she felt insecure, or perhaps her temperament required sudden outbursts of emotion to clear the air. Whatever the reason, she would suddenly take offence at something I had said quite innocently, and quarrel or burst into tears.

She was also prone to explosions of amusement when she would laugh helplessly, and make everybody around her laugh. One day, an old Gypsy woman stopped us in the street and asked me to buy some trinket or other. She wanted far more than it was worth, but I gave her what she asked. I commented to Mary, 'She cheated us, of course,' then added, 'God bless her – we've all got to live.' The words struck Mary as uproariously funny, and she screamed with laughter for five minutes.

We made love at every opportunity, but with nowhere to go these were few. On one occasion when I took her to my home, we found the house empty and retired upstairs – the first time we had actually made love in a bed. My brother Barry came back and we had to get up and dress hastily. Before the end of that summer we had two pregnancy scares, and each time I realised I was tempting fate. I had no intention of marrying her, but if we kept on like this, we would end up getting married by force of habit.

So I went and had my photograph taken, and sent off for a passport. Then I gave my notice at the Houghton farm. I was surprised that I felt so sad about it as I made my way to the bus stop on my last day. I had finally begun to enjoy farming, and working in the open air. But if I wanted to write for a living, I had to find some way of life that would carry me in the right direction.

Mary cried a great deal when I told her what I intended to do, so I decided to take her on a farewell holiday to the Lake District. It was not a wise decision because it meant spending the little money I had saved. As it was we had to hitch-hike, and stay in youth hostels. But I felt grateful to Mary. She had changed my life, and I felt a different person. The world-weary romantic had vanished and been replaced by a realist.

I remember a windy hillside in Derbyshire where we made love sitting against a tree, since the hill was too steep for any other position. Then we went to the top of a tower, and the wind blew away my beret. It began to rain heavily, and we took shelter in a wood, and lay under a ground-sheet cape, listening to the rain drumming against it. Finally, walking down the hill, with leaves flying past us, carried along like ships in full canvas, and looking across at the great circle of hills on the edge of Lancashire, I was overwhelmed with a consciousness of power and freedom, with a sense that made the boredom of my teens seem negligible. I knew at that moment that I had discovered a secret: never quietly to accept boredom and unfulfilment. 'If you don't like your life, you can change it . . .' With a knowledge of this secret, I felt the future could hold nothing but triumph, and that whatever happened, I would somehow survive it.

Mary was overwhelmed by the beauty of the lakes, and kept saying: 'Oh, I wish me mam was here.' I could see that she somehow felt it was all unreal unless she had her mother to share it with. I felt very protective about her, and sorry for her. But I knew that marrying her would be a disaster, and that if I stayed any longer, these silken threads would end by wrapping me up into a cocoon.

Back in Leicester there were tearful goodbyes and last-minute sex, and Mary swore she would wait for me for ever. Then, with half a crown borrowed from my mother in my pocket, I set out for Dover.

My first stop was the home of a homosexual friend in Northampton. His name was Jackie Shepherd, and I had met him through Alan – the friend whose story I had adapted to escape the RAF. He was as infatuated with me as Mary was, but since I have no homosexual tendencies, there was nothing I could do about that. To make things worse, his parents, who had no suspicion of his tastes, put us in a double bed together. I liked him, and wished I had been bisexual, just to oblige him. But it was no use.

The next day he took me to a birthday party in the home of friends – a twin brother and sister, both incredibly good-looking and sophisticated. There I met a plump, soft-skinned, very pretty girl called Marion, and the attraction between us was immediate and strong. We met again the next day in the home of another acquaintance. I had not forgotten Mary, but the realisation that Marion was also ensnared tempted me to stay on in Northampton and find a job. The Sirens were singing again, and even more sweetly than in Leicester. But I knew it would be foolish to tempt fate. So I set out again the next day, feeling rather like the hero of some musical comedy who has just said goodbye to his lifelong love.

Fortunately, Jackie decided to come with me as far as Dover, for I had no money left. He was able to support us for a few days, until we found work near Canterbury as hop pickers. The farmer provided a tin hut with straw beds. Since we had only two blankets, we had to sleep together, and Jackie became a nuisance because he would wake up before dawn in an amorous mood, and I had to curse indignantly to be allowed to go back to sleep.

Bored with unaccustomed physical labour, Jackie returned to Northampton. At that point, my friend Alan – the homosexual from

Leicester – joined me, and we found work apple-picking at Marden, in Kent. But he and I could never get along for very long. He was an aesthete who read Proust over and over again, while I had *Gargantua and Pantagruel* in my haversack. Possibly I produced in him the same frustration I produced in Jackie. At all events, we quarrelled, and he crossed the Channel and – I discovered later – met a rich male friend who took him on to Rome.

I found myself a job picking potatoes, and the farmer let me sleep on the first floor of a ruined cottage – the downstairs was full of potatoes – but since half the floor was missing, I had to take care not to roll over in the night. This job paid me enough money for my fare across the Channel, with about a pound to spare.

I must admit that I did not enjoy being in this homeless state. I love my home comforts. Wandering around like this was like a chilly wind that brought a continual sense of unease. I came to the conclusion that I didn't much like physical reality.

France seemed very strange – I can still remember its raw impact, the flat, dull area around the Calais docks, the tramlines, the bomb-damaged houses, the cobbled streets. The map showed me that it was a long way to Strasbourg, where I hoped to stay with a penfriend, Willi Schwiscka, in return for a holiday he had spent with us two years before.

I went into a shop and bought a long loaf of French bread, a bottle of red wine (it cost a hundred francs – there were a thousand to the pound) and some onions, and ate my first meal in France sitting by the side of one of those long tree-lined roads, with flat countryside stretching all around. I had never tasted wine before – except port – and wondered why it tasted so sour. Then, with a series of lifts, I managed to get to Lille, where there was a youth hostel. I had left my Nonesuch edition of Blake in the back of a van that gave me a lift; it seemed a bad beginning.

I had a curious adventure in Lille. There were two English girls in the hostel, typists from a bank in Redditch; their names were Wendy and Jean. As I was cooking my breakfast the next morning, they approached me and asked me what I was doing that day. I said I was going on to Strasbourg. They explained that a Frenchman had offered to show them the town, but he struck them as a suspicious character; would I go with them? It was hard to refuse; I decided to spend an extra day in Lille. The Frenchman called himself Michel de Ryoveur, and explained that he came of an old and aristocratic family – this should have alerted me, for he looked distinctly unaristocratic.

He was interested in Jean, so I was left to accompany Wendy. Before the end of the day, Michel was walking with his arm around Jean's waist and kissing her in the bushes; Wendy obviously expected me to do the same; so, although I was not particularly interested in her, I obediently put my arm round her and kissed her in the bushes. Later, at the hostel, as we sat on the steps in the dark, she said: 'Why don't you come to Paris? I shall miss you.' 'Will you?' I was astonished. The idea that she could be emotionally involved with me after a few hours seemed absurd; but she assured me she was. Then I thought of the few francs I had left in my wallet, and explained that I had to get on to Strasbourg.

We had breakfast together the next morning. 'Come and see us off, anyway?' said Wendy. Michel knew a truck drivers' café, where they could find a lift all the way to Paris. We went there – it was on the outskirts of Lille – and after ten minutes, Michel came out with a truck driver. 'He will take you.' I kissed Wendy, and Michel kissed Jean. The girls climbed in. Then Michel slapped me on the shoulder. 'We go too, huh?' 'But I have no kit – it's all at the hostel.' 'Never mind – we come back tomorrow.' 'I have no money.' 'I will lend you some – I have a sister in Paris.'

We climbed in, to the truck driver's astonishment. It was an exhausting trip. The truck broke down after dark; finally, we managed to get another lift. We arrived in the Place de l'Opéra at about two in the morning, all very tired and in low spirits. Michel decided we would sleep at the police station, so we went in and explained our situation. I was a little puzzled about the way Michel behaved with the police. He told them he was an American, and spoke French with what he evidently considered an American accent. None the less, they let us sleep in a cell. It had no bed – only a big, hard table. All four of us slept on this, covered with our coats. And at six o'clock, the police woke us up, and we went out into the cold Paris dawn, and looked at the globes burning down the Avenue de l'Opéra, and wondered where we could find coffee.

I suggested we find Michel's sister, but he now became very evasive. Instead, he insisted on dragging us around the Louvre and Jeu de Paume. We were all exhausted and getting bad-tempered. Finally, when Michel disappeared into a pissoir, Jean said to me: 'For God's sake take him away – he's driving us mad!' He had apparently decided he was in love with Jean and wanted to marry her, and was plaguing her with all sorts of insane schemes. When Michel came back, I said: 'I'm going back to Lille this afternoon. The girls want you to come too.' He shed some tears, but finally agreed to come.

The trip back to Lille was much worse than the trip to Paris. We spent a great deal of time walking through the dark in the rain. Michel came back with me to the hostel – and then vanished. The *mère de l'auberge* was furious; he had gone off without paying his bill. But he had good reason. The next morning, the police came searching for him. He had been working for a hire-purchase company, and had absconded with a large amount of money. His name, of course, was not de Ryoveur – in fact, it was Maréchal.

By this time, I was in no condition to care much. I had caught the worst cold of my life; my head rang, my throat burned and my eyes streamed.

Unfortunately, I had no money – not only for food, but to pay my hostel bill. Luckily, other guests left their provisions in cupboards in the kitchen, and I managed by helping myself cautiously to small amounts from everything. To make it worse, a postcard came from Wendy, begging me to rejoin them in Paris, and signed: 'Your lonely Wendy'. She was staying at the youth hostel at Porte de Châtillon. Suddenly, Strasbourg no longer seemed important. I explained to the *mère aub* that I had no money, but that I would send it as soon as I got to Strasbourg, and I left some shoes as security. Then I set out for Paris again.

It was hopeless. My head was spinning, and my legs felt strange. There were no lifts, and an hour after dark it began to rain again. I crossed the road and hitch-hiked back to Lille. A kindly Frenchman saw I was in a fever, took me into a café, and insisted that I drink two brandies with hot coffee. Then he took me back to the hostel. That night, I perspired as I had never perspired in my life. But when I woke up in the morning, the fever had gone; I just felt very weak. It was sunny, and my 'lonely Wendy' was waiting for me.

Once again, I packed my bag. I had made the acquaintance of a travelling salesman in the hostel, a short, handsome man with a crew cut and a Clark Gable moustache. I asked him if he could lend me any money. He said he hadn't much – a hundred francs was all he could spare. But he gave me his address in Paris. At one point on the road, I found trees loaded with small but sweet apples. I filled my knapsack and a spare bag with them, and the pockets of my RAF overcoat. For the next few days, these were the main item of my diet.

I was in Paris by evening, and took the métro to Porte de Châtillon. I tried to imagine Wendy's face when she saw me – delight, astonishment (I hadn't told her I was coming) – or would she be shy and undemonstrative?

She was neither: only irritated. During the past few days she had met a tall Norwegian, and when I saw her, she had her arm round his waist. Clearly, there was no point in reproaches; they were on holiday, and they intended to enjoy themselves. I shrugged my shoulders and tried not to brood on it. I had other problems: no money, and no bed – the hostel was full, and people were sleeping on the floor in sleeping bags. (Wendy was sharing the Norwegian's.)

But at this point, there was a slight improvement in my luck. An American received a telegram and had to leave suddenly; I asked him not to notify the warden, and so was able to sleep in his bed. Since I was not signed in, I managed to slip out of the hostel the next day without paying. I did not say goodbye to Wendy.

It was a dull day, and the wind was blowing the leaves from the trees in the Avenue de Châtillon. I have never been prone to self-pity, and I was determined not to give way to it at this point; but I had a feeling that the memory of Wendy was going to sneak up and take me unawares when I was thinking of other things, and give me a few days of twinges like toothache.

At that moment, an interesting thing happened. The sun came out and shone on the trees opposite. I was suddenly struck by the beauty of their foliage. The thought arose: they are here whether I am here or not; and I saw myself detachedly, as if looking at myself from an aeroplane, a limited human being, wrestling with transitory emotions as if they were all that mattered. I felt a rush of delight, and a desire to laugh, and I knew that this sudden happiness had tossed Wendy out of my mind. It was true. She never gave me another twinge.

The address of Claude Guillaume, the kindly Frenchman who had lent me a hundred francs in Lille, was in the rue Bayen, near the Étoile. When I knocked on the door, it was opened by one of the most beautiful girls I had ever seen, with translucent skin and lovely eyes. This was Claude's wife, Marie, and when I explained who I was, she invited me in. I was in luck again; she was studying for a teacher's examination and was wrestling with *The Canterbury Tales*, finding it impossible to understand the language. I had read much of Chaucer in my mid-teens, and spent the next hour helping her with 'The Knight's Tale'. She immediately offered to let me stay there – although they had only a single room. Claude soon came home, and seemed equally pleased that his wife had found herself an English instructor. That evening, I ate steak with vegetables, and slept on an air mattress. When I look back on all this I wince: it was hard work being young.

But fate seemed to be on my side. The next day, I picked up a curiously printed book from Claude's piano; it was called *Étincelles de mon Enclume*, and seemed to be in an extremely weird French ('*seconde edition*' said the title page). It was full of vaguely humanistic sentiments: '*L'homme a plus de valeur que l'or*,' '*Plus important que le théâtre et la musique est la parole humaine.*' The name of the author was on the title page: Raymond Duncan. Claude saw me reading it. 'Ah yes, he is an American millionaire who runs a school for writers in the rue de Seine.' I pricked up my ears. Claude showed me another volume by Duncan, this time in English. It seemed to be full of a kind of Whitmanesque poetry:

> Look above to the sky and under
> Your feet the earth
> Here is our theatre.

The sentiments struck me as sloppy and vague, but if this man was a patron of young writers, I was not going to be choosy. Claude gave me a couple of métro tickets, and I made my way to the rue de Seine. Number

31 was halfway down the street, close to the hotel where Wilde had died. There was a large open courtyard with sculptured objects lying around. I found the office, and spoke to a large woman in a white sackcloth garb like a nun's. This was Mme Aia Bertrand, Duncan's second-in-command. When I told her I admired Raymond's writing – a flat lie – she became quite friendly. I asked her what order she belonged to. She looked indignant. 'No order. I am an atheist.'

Raymond Duncan came in. I was disappointed. His photographs – there were many of them around – showed a keen, hawklike man with long white hair held around his forehead with a band like an Indian headdress, wearing a white toga. He looked like the prophet of some Californian cult. This man was small, and he was so old that his face had lost the stern, piercing look; he was nearsighted and wore thick glasses, and his toga was a kind of dirty white nightdress made of towelling. His manner was kindly, but one got the impression that he was thinking of other things, or perhaps was just deaf.

He explained to me that his philosophy was that men should return to the old standards of medieval craftsmen; everybody would be happier if they worked with their hands. As far as I could make out, his philosophy was a kind of humanistic anarchism rather like William Morris's. He felt that modern society had fragmented man and removed him from the old ideal of the 'all-rounder', the Leonardo ideal. He himself painted, sculpted, wrote poetry and produced his own plays – all very badly, I later discovered – and he told me that he could also mend a clock, build a wall, or make his own clothes.

He and his two sisters – one was the famous Isadora Duncan – had left San Francisco as children and come to Europe. Isadora became a dancer who had a habit of propositioning any man who attracted her – she caused a scandal with her creed of sexual freedom – and Raymond went to Greece and started to build a temple. In Paris, he spent one night inventing a pair of comfortable sandals from a piece of leather and some thongs. He set up a shop to sell them and made a fortune. He devoted this to publishing his own poetry and producing his own plays; he became a figure in the Paris of Tristan Tzara and the Dadaists. He endorsed the sentiment of the American humorist Will Rogers: 'I never met a man I didn't like.' Raymond felt a Whitmanesque affection for everybody, particularly the 'ordinary people'. He told me how he had stayed at one of New York's most expensive hotels, and when he left, the staff were all lined up waiting for their tips; but instead of tipping them, Raymond went down the line shaking hands with everybody. 'They preferred that,' he said earnestly. 'They didn't really want money.' I tried not to smile.

After rambling on for a quarter of an hour – and explaining, incidentally, that he was not a millionaire, although he had made and lost several fortunes – he made the offer I had been hoping for. 'Come and stay here, and learn how to work with your hands. I'll teach you how to print your own books, present your own plays . . .' When Mme Bertrand came in a few minutes later and was told the news, she looked dubious but resigned,

I went back to the rue Bayen bubbling with excitement. I would learn to print, I would finish my novel in the evenings, and then set it up myself. I would write plays . . . Claude and Marie were as happy as I was, perhaps because they were finding the room cramped with three in it. The next day, I moved into 31 rue de Seine. I hoped that this time I had landed on my feet, found something that would last. It certainly looked hopeful. It was what I had always dreamed about in Leicester – a place for artists, where I could use my energy for creation instead of for jobs I hated . . . But it was hard to believe that my luck had changed so abruptly. Surely, such things just didn't happen. Yeats says of his hermits:

> They are plagued by crowds until
> They've the passion to escape.

When I felt low, I re-inflated my optimism by reflecting that perhaps this was why fate never allowed me to relax, why life was always difficult and uncomfortable, why every job became unbearable after a week or so. But I couldn't help wishing that fate would give me a breathing space. And it looked as if the Akademia Duncan might be the answer to my prayer.

It was not. I found work in the printshop unexpectedly boring. I was given blocks of type to break up and put into various small trays. I was a kind of odd-job man. On my first evening there, Raymond gave a lecture in the large hall. He spoke in French so bad that even I could understand it, waving his hand up and down rhythmically while he reclined on a couch. Everything he said sounded incredibly platitudinous. 'La beauté est la seule morale des hommes, et la vertu compte seulement parce que la vertu a de la beauté.' He declaimed it all slowly, as if reading poetry. 'Mais l'univers est tout la beauté, tout la sublimité, mes amis . . .' I thought of that line from *The Man Who Came to Dinner*: 'I may vomit' – and had to stop myself from laughing. During the last year I had begun writing an early version of a novel I called *Ritual in the Dark*, a gloomy book about a murderer. I was obsessed by the concept of original sin and the notion that modern society is a wasteland. And there was Raymond declaiming: 'L'une des plus grandes vertus de l'homme est d'être original. Cherchez nos poètes dans la vie, mes amis.' And I was supposed to be his disciple . . .

However, I had no money and no prospects, and the rue de Seine seemed as good a place as any until something better turned up. I didn't like the deception, but I could see no alternative. It was, however, a depressing place. There was only one other guest, a Swedish girl called Sybil, a plain little thing with spots and glasses, who disliked it as much as I did. Mme Bertrand bullied her, and I hated to see this. The rooms were gloomy, and I slept on a couch in the wings of the stage without a light.

There was a cult of Isadora about the place. I read parts of her autobiography, and found her amusing but silly. She was described as beautiful, although Shaw said her face looked as if it was made of sugar and someone had licked it. The death of her two children, who had been drowned when her car rolled backwards into the Seine, seemed typical of the misfortunes she seemed to attract. So was her death, when a long scarf she was wearing caught in the rear wheel of a car, and she was strangled. But Raymond was a good, decent man, honest and well-meaning. It wasn't his fault if I was just about the most unsuitable person in the world to be anyone's disciple.

I wrote to my penfriend in Strasbourg and almost immediately a letter containing five thousand francs came back, with an urgent request to go and see him.

I needed no second bidding. After a mere two weeks I had a sense that Mme Bertrand was growing tired of me – I spent every evening at the Bibliothèque Ste Geneviève writing my novel. Sybil had decided to leave unannounced, and I had to help smuggle out her clothes. After playing a Chopin recital, a homosexual pianist named Victor Gille had invited me to go and live with him, and for a moment I had even toyed with the idea as a way of giving myself the freedom to write, but the idea of being sodomised did not appeal to me.

Finally, a rich American woman had invited me to her hotel for tea. She allowed me to read her some of my poetry, and told me enthusiastically that she thought that one day I might be as great as Mr Somerset Maugham. Raymond and Mme Bertrand seemed to think this was a shameless piece of opportunism, and Raymond even told me so that evening over dinner – it was unusual to see him so stern – and went on to say that I had come there on false pretences. I could say nothing, since it was true.

So, when the money came and I told Raymond and Mme Bertrand I wanted to visit Strasbourg, and added that I might be back some day, Mme Aia said very firmly: 'No, no one who leaves here is allowed to come back.' I could sympathise with them – no one wants cuckoos in the nest. (I have put up with many of them since then.)

The journey took me three days. Willi lived in a flat with his middle-class family – his father, who was a scrap merchant, his plump mother, a typically hard-headed Frenchwoman, and a plump and pretty sister. When he had stayed with us in Leicester, he and I had laughed and joked and made atrocious French puns. But we had both changed a lot. He had become a Communist, who thought that the workers should murder the rich. I still thought seriously that I might eventually end up as a monk.

So now we could not get into a discussion without getting exasperated with one another. After three weeks, the family had clearly had enough of me, and one morning his mother explained regretfully that they needed my room for someone else.

I called at the British Consulate and explained that I wanted to be repatriated. There was no difficulty; they gave me my rail tickets within an hour, took away my passport as a pledge and gave me a temporary one, good only for the return trip. I caught a train to Calais late that afternoon. There was a certain excitement in being in motion again, even though I had nothing much to look forward to in England.

Suddenly, life seemed interesting and adventurous, and the last two months to have been worthwhile. I now remembered sitting alone in the square in Lille, and feeling that if I now vanished into thin air, no one would know I had gone – a sense of total contingency and unimportance. Now this seemed self-evidently false; as the train clattered on through the night, there was a feeling like getting the exam results at the end of term, and seeing you have passed.

CHAPTER 4

Marriage and London

It was pleasant to be back in Leicester, but the problems that had driven me away – how to earn a living while teaching myself to write – were still unresolved. The only difference was that I no longer felt stifled and depressed by my home town.

And there was still the problem of Mary. She had written to me in Paris and Strasbourg, and her letters were full of talk about missing me, and how we should get engaged as soon as I got home. Now that the actual habit of seeing her daily was broken, I knew that it would be pure stupidity to renew our relationship. On the other hand, she would have to know I was back sooner or later.

I shirked the problem for a week, then went along to Woolworths to meet her as she went off for lunch. She looked startled to see me; and yet, I thought, not particularly happy. 'How long have you been back?' 'A few days,' I said evasively. 'Why didn't you contact me?' 'Oh, I wanted to find a job first . . .'

We were walking along Charles Street, and the wind was freezing. She said suddenly: 'I suppose I'd better tell you . . . I've been going out with a bloke I met at a dance.' I should have been pleased, but I felt an irrational jealousy.

Yet the situation had not really changed. I met her that evening and we went to see my grandmother. When we were alone for a moment, I kissed her, and her mouth opened after a moment, as it always had. I raised her dress and pulled aside the leg of her knickers. She gasped: 'God, it's so long since I've had it.' 'What about your new boyfriend.' 'He'd be shocked if I even mentioned sex.'

I gathered that he was a quiet, shy man, an engineer, who wanted to marry her right away.

The next day was Mary's afternoon off and she came back to our house. My mother was out shopping. Mary told me she would visit only on condition that I 'behaved myself', and I agreed. I knew her by this time. When she kissed, she seemed to lose control of herself; her lips parted, her hips began to move, and when I put my hand up her dress, she opened her legs to make it easier. Afterwards, she lay on the rug gasping, her eyes closed. I said, 'You'll have to be careful you don't do that with your boyfriend. You'd frighten the life out of him.' She said, 'I know. But he's so shy.' She opened her eyes. 'I'd much rather marry you.' And so we were back in the old stalemate.

My feelings about her were divided. I felt strongly protective, and had to acknowledge that, as she was growing up, she was becoming beautiful. Her oval face, regular features and pink cheeks made men stare, and her smile made people smile back. She was naturally generous and good-natured. Her slim figure and long legs were beautiful. But she had the strongest Leicester accent I have ever heard, with its gutteral u's and dropped aitches. There were times when I felt she was exaggerating it out of a kind of defiance, and I doubt whether Professor Higgins could have persuaded her to abandon it. And quarrelling and bursting into tears were part of her nature, which I found wearing.

It was midwinter – uncomfortable weather for building jobs. Moreover, my father wanted me to go back into the Civil Service. We finally compromised, and I took a job in the office of an engineering works, Richards (Leicester) Ltd. The pay was absurdly small – £3 a week – but the work was not hard and, to begin with, not too boring. I had to file receipts and orders. I also had to wander around the works – which were spread over a large area – delivering sheaves of paper to the foremen of various departments. It was fascinating to watch the molten metal pouring out of the furnaces, or showers of sparks leaping into the air. Under different circumstances, I might have been happy enough there – certainly, my trip to France had reduced the inner tension and made me more comfortable with myself. But I had to write books, and all this had nothing to do with it. I didn't want to marry Mary and settle down to an office job. I didn't want to do any of the things that society and my parents seemed to want me to do. But while I was working forty hours a week for three pounds, my freedom of movement was limited.

I continued to see Mary; but both of us had the sense that something was ending. She knew I wasn't in love with her and that her new boyfriend was; she wanted security. One day I came back from work to find all the books I had given her piled up in a pram on the front lawn, including a lavishly illustrated edition of Shakespeare in four volumes. I made no attempt to see her after that. She had done the sensible thing, and I knew it. Still, it was difficult not to experience a neurotic sense of having been rejected. I tore out the inscriptions from the books and put them in a cupboard.

One day at work, I went to see the resident nurse about a sore throat.

Betty was a fair-haired girl; not pretty, but with an attractive mouth. The first time I saw her, I thought her cool and forbidding; she had a cut-glass, upper-class accent, and her look could be frigid. She was nine years my senior (I was still nineteen), and her coolness and self-control were an attraction, after Mary and her violent emotions. At first, the relation was casually flirtatious – before going into her office, I would pull my tie askew, knowing that her innate tidiness would make her straighten it, and that I could try to put my arms round her. On closer acquaintance, the icy manner proved to be superficial; she was a friendly, shy, level-headed sort of person. I found myself liking her increasingly. Her background was in many ways the same as mine – working-class; and her childhood had been thoroughly unhappy. She had left home at the beginning of the war and become a nurse in London, working there throughout the Blitz. The man she was engaged to was killed in the RAF. Since then, she had concentrated on her career. Unlike me, she had no basic trust in life. I once said to her that she was like a rabbit hiding in its hole, and she replied: 'I suppose so, but every time I stick my head out, someone hits me on it.'

I made excuses to call in at her office. After a while it was no longer necessary to make excuses; she was obviously glad to see me. One day, she invited me back to her flat for coffee. The very word 'flat' had a romantic ring for me. Cycling there that evening, I wondered if she had had many lovers, and whether I was a likely candidate for the next.

The answer – that evening at any rate – was no. She made it clear that the invitation to her flat was for coffee and nothing else. Cautiously flirtatious in her office, she became defensive on home territory. When I left, she allowed me to kiss her, but she kissed stiffly, with her lips tightly closed. I pushed my bicycle out into the road thinking: Oh, well, that settles that . . . I still winced when I thought of Mary; I had no intention of being rejected again.

But when I saw her over the next few days, she was friendly and, when I kissed her in her office, made no strenuous objection. At this time I was reading Hemingway's *A Farewell to Arms*, and couldn't help feeling that my attitude towards Betty was much the same as that of Frederic Henry towards Catherine Barkley. I liked her, and the cool, rather distant attitude aroused the usual masculine desire to break down resistance – perhaps the nurse's uniform had something to do with it.

When I'd got over my irritation at her aloofness, I found I liked her air of self-possession and her sense of responsibility. Her temperament was much closer to mine than Mary's had been. I enjoyed going to her flat to eat supper, and then perhaps listen to an opera on the Third Programme, or read her the latest chapter of *Ritual in the Dark*, or a play in the manner of Granville-Barker that I was struggling with.

Slowly, her sexual reserve melted. She was completely unlike Mary in that she seemed to have no sexual drive that was independent of her personal feelings. She didn't even enjoy flirting to any great extent. She started by liking me, then grew fond of me and became accustomed to seeing me around; it would never have occurred to her to conceal that she was fond of me or indulge in a Lawrencian sex war. I realise in retrospect that I became her lover because she was already thinking of me as a husband, and recognised that the platonic relationship was bound to end eventually. I was too restless to put up with it for long, and was already making plans to return to London.

I had a number of friends in Leicester. I still saw Alan, although I got tired of his petulance and desire to dominate. Jackie, my other homosexual friend, was still at Leicester University. There was also a painter, Stanley Rosenthal, whom I called 'Rab' because of his Rabelaisian sense of humour, and I saw a great deal of a poet called Maurice Willows, whose wife Freda typed the early version of *Ritual in the Dark*.

The original story had been about a man who murders a prostitute in the act of possessing her; the murder is a sudden welling up of total frustration at a civilisation that starves our souls. The story was about a frustration and exhaustion that have gone so deep that the man lives in a daze: he never feels anything; he lives automatically; and when he has killed the girl he feels no guilt because it all seems unreal. He confesses the murder to a girl he sleeps with, but she doesn't believe him. Then he attempts suicide by drinking rat poison, but it only makes him vomit. Obviously, he has to go on living somehow, find some sense of motive. But when I finished the story, I had no idea of the answer.

In later versions, I decided that it would be more interesting if the reader is never sure whether the hero is a murderer or not. The hero suffers from a constant sense of unreality and from hallucinations. The question he wants answered is: if I did kill her, and I feel no guilt, am I still guilty? And if the answer is yes, then perhaps I am guilty even if I didn't kill her, for I am obviously capable of it; if I weren't capable of it, I'd know I didn't kill her. At a certain point, the novel was entitled *Things Do Not Happen*.

It turned into a story about a man under extreme mental strain, who reads that a prostitute has been found strangled in her bed, and thinks he may be the killer. What I wanted to do was to write the definitive novel of mental strain – it was at about this time that I read Charles Jackson's *Lost Weekend*, and felt that he had missed the opportunity to write a masterpiece.

I immediately encountered one of the major problems of the modern novel. If you ask what *Ulysses* or *Manhattan Transfer* or *Alexanderplatz, Berlin* is about, the answer is: the essence of Dublin, or of New York, or of Berlin. And because these books are about the essence of a place, they cannot have a straightforward plot, or a single hero; they have to move around, to present a panorama. A 'story' would run away with the book and falsify the author's intention; the reader would concentrate on the story instead of on what the author is trying to tell him.

This was my problem. What I wanted to tell the reader about was the sense of unreality that comes from frustration, long periods when there is nothing you want to do, and consequently you never use the will. And the real question this points to is: what ought we to be doing with our lives? Are they supposed to be a useless movement to keep ourselves alive: 'birth, copulation, and death'?

I wanted to write a novel in which the central character goes around with this question on his mind all the time, so that ordinary situations arouse a perpetual sense of irony. The values of ordinary people strike him as illusions. History is fuelled by illusions. Armies fight, patriots rant, lovers swear everlasting vows, the religious talk about eternal fire – but it is all sound and fury. Nothing really happens. *Time is, in some sense, an illusion.* Perfectly ordinary situations would do; it is the way he sees them that counts.

And this raised the problem of the structure of the novel. A novel should have a purposive forward movement. How could I give it some kind of form? It was at about this time that I discovered *The Egyptian Book of the Dead* in the local library, and saw the possibility of using it as the basis of a novel, as Joyce had used the *Odyssey*. It is a series of prayers for the use of the soul on the night after death, to protect it against the various perils that it encounters – such as blood-sucking worms – before it emerges the next morning into Amentet, the Egyptian underworld.

I structured the later versions of the novel on *The Egyptian Book of the Dead*. I was even struck by the coincidence that the book was also known as *Ritual of the Dead*, one of the early titles I had chosen for my novel. The notion of the underworld suited me perfectly. If working in a bank had made Eliot see the crowds crossing London Bridge as souls in Limbo, my own years in dreary jobs had made me feel that our situation is Hell itself. I wanted my 'outsider' to walk through its trivialities and complex- ities possessed by some foreboding of judgment, seeing his world as the culmination of the agony of centuries.

I started a kind of literary group that met once a week in the upstairs room of a café near the Clock Tower. We ate cheese rolls and drank tea, and read aloud our poems and short stories.

It was impossible for me not to be aware that I was a long way ahead of most of them as a writer. The years of endless scribbling in my diary were paying off. I had read more than any of them, and could produce a pastiche of almost anybody at a moment's notice. On one occasion, when Maurice Willows sent me a message that he could not come and read his poetry, I wrote a five-page poem in jazz rhythms in an hour before going to the meeting, interspersed with limerick-style stanzas that shamelessly imitated Auden:

> Come to our jungle paradise
> Where the laws are ineffectual,
> Where tigers play
> Shooting crap all day
> And the elephants are homosexual.

It was a huge success and they encored it.

I was becoming something of a character in Leicester, at least among the young. It was time I had something published. But in spite of our literary group, I lacked any real desire to socialise. Old problems were still acute. To begin with, there was work. After a month or so, the engineering works began to suffocate me every time I walked into the building and smelled its individual odour of dust and machine oil. Betty could not understand my moods; one evening, when I was tense and irritable, and left early, she thought I had gone off to meet another girl. In fact, I was thinking about my obsessive creative drive and hating this comfortable life of meeting friends in coffee bars or eating meals in Betty's flat. The spur was digging in again.

As soon as the weather became a little warmer, I gave up the job at Richards, and went to work for the Leicester Electricity Board as a navvy. On my first day, it started to snow, and went on for two weeks. Having lost the habit of physical labour, I would get home exhausted. But at least the exhaustion dulled the sense of wasting my life. Betty was also going through a difficult period: she was a senior member of the firm, and was having differences of opinion with its managing director, who both admired her and quarrelled with her. Sometimes she burst into tears, the rigid self-discipline suddenly cracking; and embraces that were intended to comfort her lost in restraint what they gained in excitement.

But I wanted more time to write and think. Digging trenches to lay electric cables was less boring than office work, but very nearly as repetitive. I didn't want to do other people's work; I wanted to get on with my own. One day, returning from work in a state of irritable fatigue, it struck me that this manual labour was so much better paid than the office that I could afford to work only half the time. This was obviously the solution! Two or three days at work, and the rest of the week in the Central Library, working on my novel. At that rate, the book could be finished in six months.

In a state of optimism and excitement, I went to the offices of the Electricity Board and explained my problem – that I was a student, and would like to work part time. They said they had no objections if my foreman was agreeable. They contacted him, and he said he didn't mind either. I went back to work in a state of elation, already planning a rigid writing schedule. But when I got there, the foreman explained that he had had to change his mind: the other men thought it was favouritism to allow me to work half-time, and threatened to walk off the job. It was the typical spirit of the British workman: since they couldn't afford to work half-time, they saw no reason why I should be allowed to. I told the foreman that I would prefer not to work with such a mean-spirited crew, and went to the office for my cards.

The next job was the pleasantest so far: I was engaged as an odd-job man in the Dalmas chemical factory. The work was varied and interesting, and I liked the people I worked with. I had various tasks to complete at different hours of the day: boiling up the resin and lanoline that was the basis of the adhesive on sticking plasters, disposing of empty crates, supplying half a dozen machines and coordinating their activities. It was a responsible kind of job, with a certain amount of free time. I was reading *The Magic Mountain*, *The Brothers Karamazov* and William James's *The Varieties of Religious Experience*.

I had made a list of books that struck me as saying something interesting or worthwhile: D. H. Lawrence's *Man Who Died*, Nijinsky's *Diary*, Hemingway's *Across the River and Into the Trees*, Wells's *Mind at the End of its Tether*. I decided to write a series of essays, raising the same concepts in each, applying them to each of the books to show their relations, the way in which each is concerned with the basic problem of values. These essays later became the foundation of *The Outsider*.

And then, one evening, Betty told me she thought she was pregnant. I could only hope she was mistaken. At last I was working at a job I enjoyed, writing well, and optimistic about the prospects of publication. Nothing could have been more irrelevant than a baby. I was fond of Betty, but I didn't want to marry anybody.

A few days later she told me it had all been a false alarm, and I heaved an immense sigh of relief. I had just bought myself a record of the final dance in Stravinsky's *Firebird* (I could not afford the whole ballet), and as I was listening to it in the shop, experienced a great upsurge of sheer delight. We decided to take a weekend's break in Wales, and for two days I was walking on air. Then she told me that she had been mistaken and was pregnant after all, and once again I felt like a condemned man.

I asked friends about it: one suggested hot baths and gin, another oil of fennel; another said that the best thing would be to have the baby and have it adopted. Betty rejected all these suggestions, and said that there were really only two alternatives: I should marry her, or go away and leave her to have the baby alone.

It was as disastrous for her as for me; she had just received promotion, and won her long argument on some important point of policy with the boss.

I felt that this was a repetition of the basic Mary situation: a conflict between my common sense and my desire not to hurt. Finally, my parents cast the deciding vote by advising marriage. On 6 June 1951, Betty and I were married at the Leicester registry office in the lunch hour, then she hurried back to work. Our best man was a brawny Welshman called Alan Nottingham. Betty paid for the ring. I spent the evening with her, in a rather subdued mood, then set out to hitch-hike to London. We had to live together somewhere, and I was determined that it shouldn't be Leicester.

I spent the next night in the youth hostel in Great Ormond Street. John Clements and Kay Hammond were doing *Man and Superman* at the Princes Theatre, and I went to see it (the first of six times). It had always been my favourite Shaw play, but now some of the dialogue had a ring of irony. 'The true artist will let his wife starve, his children go barefoot, his mother drudge for a living at seventy, sooner than work at anything but his art.' Clearly, I was not a true artist. And when Ann tells Tanner that he doesn't have to get married if he doesn't want to, he asks: 'Does any man want to be hanged? Yet men let themselves be hanged without a struggle for life, though they could at least give the chaplain a black eye.' The cap certainly fitted.

I found myself a room in Camden Town and moved in. It was at the end of Rochester Road, and cost thirty shillings a week. The landlady was one of the most tolerable I ever met; Shaw's description of Mrs Warren as a 'genial and fairly presentable old blackguard of a woman' fitted her exactly. On my first day there, she told me in confidence that the honeymoon couple in the basement were decorating it, and that as soon as they were finished she meant to give them notice and charge a higher rent for the place.

I went to the Labour Exchange, and was directed to a building job at the Catholic church of St Etheldreda's. It is one of the oldest churches in London, and all the beams in the ceiling were being replaced. It was a dangerous job, for the new ones had to be manoeuvred past the scaffolding, and the ropes often slipped as the heavy beams were hauled aloft. One of them slid free and made a six-inch dent in the floor; luckily there was no one underneath.

I looked through the evening paper every day and made a list of the flats and double rooms to let, then spent an hour in the telephone box ringing the landladies. It was a discouraging business. Unfurnished flats always wanted a large down payment for 'furniture and fittings', since they were rent-controlled, and this was the only way the owners could evade the law.

Furnished flats were all well beyond our means. Double rooms were easy enough to find, but as soon as I mentioned that my wife was pregnant, the landlady always said: 'Sorry, no children,' and hung up. My present landlady hinted that she might have a place for us in a month or so, but I knew her too well by this time to rely on it.

I had come to London with three pounds borrowed from my grandmother, but my money ran out before I was due for my first week's wages – which, as is usual in England, were paid at the end of the second week of work. Then, one day, I came from work to find that Betty had sent me money and an enormous parcel of food. This was not simply a relief and a pleasant surprise; it also made me recognise that marriage has other aspects besides mere responsibility; there were benefits as well as drawbacks.

A few days later, Betty joined me in London for the weekend of my twentieth birthday. During the course of that weekend, our relationship changed; I ceased to feel that this marriage was a nuisance and a misfortune, and realised with a shock that I was probably going to enjoy being married. In my relationship with Mary it had come as a surprise to me that I have a strong protective streak. With Betty, this had never had a chance to appear, because of her tendency to emotional reserve. Now we were married, she had no more reason for reserve; she trusted me and accepted me, and my response was to become protective. And I knew suddenly that her need for affection and understanding was as strong as Mary's. I am naturally affectionate and demonstrative; I find that the noisy expression of affection is good for my soul. Betty could take all I had to give. Blake rightly points out that 'what men in women do require', and vice versa, is 'the lineaments of satisfied desire'; that is, that each should need what the other has to give. Also, Betty, unlike Mary, had a great deal to give besides affection and trust; she had self-discipline and practical ability, and was used to cooking and running a home.

The result of all this was that when Betty returned to Leicester on Sunday evening, we were both perfectly happy about the marriage, and parted on the tenderest of terms. She intended to give up her job in about a month – by which time her pregnancy would start showing – and move to London. I had to step up my search for a home. But at least, I was now doing it because I wanted to; we were both impatient to live together.

In spite of all this, it was an ill-fated marriage from the beginning. Two days after Betty returned to Leicester, I received a furious letter from her. The telephonist at work had asked her if it was true she was married. The culprit was a friend of mine called Millicent, whom I had known since we were together in the tax office, who was in the same amateur dramatic group as the telephonist. Obviously the point was that she had also mentioned why we had got married, and this was what really hurt. Betty's attitude toward sex was rigid and prudish. (She could not even bring herself to tell her mother the reason we married, even after the baby had been born; I had to make a special trip to Leicester to tell her that she now had a grandson, some six months after his birth.)

I was equally furious about her prudishness, and the way she had turned on me, and pointed out in my reply that she had promised to love, honour and obey, and that this burst of fury was hardly an example of wifely tolerance and understanding. Her reply was even angrier; and since I am an impatient person, the marriage might well have come to an end there. I was so angry, I took a day off from work and hitch-hiked to Leicester. But as soon as we actually saw each other, the old sexual magic began to work; we made it up within minutes. Still, the episode is an example of the kind of clash that would finally break up the marriage. The chief emotional component on my side was protectiveness; as soon as this was rejected, I felt the links dissolve. They could be resoldered, but each time they became slightly weaker.

I found a small double room in East Finchley, and also changed my job: I moved to Frazer and Glass, a plastics factory in North Finchley. The work was repetitive but not difficult, and I liked the place; I could usually earn about ten pounds a week. Betty left her job and joined me at the beginning of August, and suddenly I was quite contented with life.

It was also at this time that I discovered *Seven Pillars of Wisdom*, through reading the anthology *The Essential T. E. Lawrence*. Betty had the complete book in two volumes, but I had found it too long to read. I now saw that Lawrence was one of the few modern writers who was aware of the same problems that obsessed me. Why was he so little known? Why had Eliot never written about him? I seemed to have stumbled upon a large number of important books that no one else seemed to know about: Nijinsky's *Diary*, Wells's *Mind at the End of Its Tether*, Granville-Barker's *Secret Life*, Hesse's *Steppenwolf*. It was also in the Finchley library that I found *The Gospel of Sri Ramakrishna*. I decided that I must one day write a book relating them all.

I found this new routine of marriage very satisfying: I would return from work to find my supper waiting for me. Then we might go to see a film, or I would walk to the library. At half past nine or so, we would open up the bed-settee, and both get into bed and read. On weekends, we took bus trips to other parts of London, or went for walks around the Finchley area; or I might take a bus to the British Museum and spend Saturday afternoon writing my novel in the Reading Room. This was not because the place was any more convenient for writing than at home, but because it was enjoyable to think that I was writing in the same place as Samuel Butler, Karl Marx, Bernard Shaw and H. G. Wells. (When *The Outsider* came out, I was gratified when some press cutting about the Reading Room added my name to this list.)

I think I know why I enjoyed being married so much: it was another version of the old craving for order. Children like stories because they are less chaotic than the real world; they do not have choices to make, they do not have to 'interpret'. The story channels their emotions cleanly and simply, like a canal; in real life, there are too many distractions, and it is only in rare moments of happiness that the emotional response to real life can be so uncomplicated. Very young children are protected by parental love, but this becomes less protective at about the age of seven, as the child becomes more independent. Thereafter, the child has to learn to deal with the chaos as best he can.

I had got through most of my teens without much love or attention; I had learned to deal with the chaos on my own. And now, suddenly, I was back in something very like the secure world of childhood; one other person in the world thoroughly approved of me and believed in me, and cooked my meals and allowed me to remove her clothes. It was like relaxing in a warm bath after a hard day's work.

And then, a month before the baby was due, our landlady gave us notice. She had already warned us that we would have to find new lodgings when the baby arrived, but she suddenly became panic-stricken at the idea that it might be premature, and her family kept awake by its wailing. I had now reached the stage of expecting this kind of thing from landladies, and subsequent experience with them convinced me that becoming a landlady is the surest way to forfeit your immortal soul. I used to daydream of a dictatorship that would pack all England's landladies on to ships and send them to a remote part of Patagonia, where they could torment one another with their malice and stupidity.

The foreman at work offered me a room in his house, and we were living there when the baby arrived – a boy whom we called Roderick Gerard – the second name being that of the hero of *Ritual in the Dark*. But a few weeks later, our new landlady gave us notice – the baby's crying had been more than she had bargained for. I spent the next week searching for another room, but when it became clear that I wouldn't find one in time, Betty decided to return to Leicester for a while. She stayed with my parents, because she had still not told her mother about the baby. I quickly found myself a single room in Golders Green, on a convenient bus route to the factory. My new landlady was a hard-faced woman with genteel pretensions, and I knew as soon as I saw her that I would have trouble.

On the day I moved in – with half a dozen cases, a trunk and two tea chests full of books – she stood by the front door, wailing that she would never have rented me the room if she had known I had so much luggage. From then on, I usually found a note from her in my room when I returned home from work: 'Please take care not to spill sugar on the carpet', 'Please do not leave teacups on windowsill'. She nagged about the empty tea chests, although they were stored away in a corner, and finally paid the dustman to take them away; then she demanded the money back from me. I gave it to her for the sake of peace. I should have been spending my weekends looking for a new home for us, but I was getting tired of moving around; instead, I worked on *Ritual*.

Luckily, Betty decided to advertise in a nursing journal for a job that would include accommodation, and received a reply from a Mr Penman, who lived alone and wanted a resident nurse–housekeeper. And so, with immense relief, I gave my landlady notice – she was furious that I had been there such a short time, although she had done everything to drive me out. In the spring of 1952, Betty and I moved into a comfortable, semi-detached house in Queens Road, Wimbledon. Mr Penman suffered from asthma; he was a retired businessman, and at first struck us as extremely generous. He was so anxious to retain Betty's services that he told her at an early stage that he intended to leave her the house in his will; he also gave me permission to use his typewriter whenever I liked. We were understandably sceptical about the house offer, but I made full use of the typewriter. I spent Saturday afternoons writing in the British Museum, and then typed it up on Sunday morning. It was on one of these Saturday afternoons in the Reading Room that it suddenly struck me that I should set my novel in the East End of London, and perhaps bring in the locales of the Jack the Ripper murders of 1888.

I cycled to Whitechapel after the museum closed; and there I realised that I needed two main characters in my novel: the hero, and the murderer with whom he becomes involved. And the Whitechapel murders would provide a storyline that need not interfere with the major theme of the book. As far as *Ritual* was concerned, this was the breakthrough that turned it from a rather muddled and impressionistic account of boredom into a narrative that had a sense of flow.

It was in the Wimbledon Public Library that I came across a book called *In Search of the Miraculous* by P. D. Ouspensky, and knew at once that this was one of the most important books I had ever read. It describes, of course, how the young Moscow journalist Ouspensky is introduced to an exotic-looking stranger whom he calls G, a man with the 'face of an Indian rajah'. G explains that he and his pupils are engaged in a task which they call 'the work', but offers no further explanation. It is only after several meetings, when Ouspensky complains that people are turning into machines, that G tells Ouspensky that the simple truth is that we are all machines, possessing virtually no free will, and that moreover we are all asleep. It is only gradually that Ouspensky begins to understand what G means when he says that our lives are lived on an entirely mechanical level, and that only with a tremendous effort can we cease to be machines. This effort is what G calls 'the work'.

The book influenced me so deeply because I had long recognised that a large part of me was 'mechanical'. T. S. Eliot has a line in *The Family Reunion*: 'partial observation of one's own automatism'. Of course, what really interested me was the question Ouspensky asked G: how is it possible to become free?

I was even more delighted when I discovered in the library a book called *Venture With Ideas*, which explained it all in far simpler language, and which made clear that G was George Ivanovitch Gurdjieff. I immediately recognised the name, for I had glanced at a great fat volume called *All and Everything* in a bookshop in Kensington Church Street, and had been deeply curious to know what its author had to say that took him over a thousand pages. Now I was about to find out.

The author of *Venture With Ideas* was a doctor named Kenneth Walker, and nothing would have amazed me more than to learn that one day he would become a friend. Meanwhile, I tried to learn all I could about this amazing man Gurdjieff, who was quite obviously one of the greatest minds I had ever encountered.

It was also in the Wimbledon Public Library that I discovered the *I Ching*, the Chinese book of 'oracles', newly published in a two-volume translation by Richard Wilhelm, and introduced by Jung.

Being an aspiring writer, the first thing I wanted to know was about my own future. I followed the procedure described by Jung: shook three pennies in my cupped hands and threw them down six times. A preponderance of heads signifies an unbroken line, meaning yang, the positive principle. A preponderance of tails signifies a broken line, the negative or yielding principle. These lines are placed on top of one another like a sandwich, forming a 'hexagram' which is one of sixty-four. The 'Judgement' of the *I Ching* then interprets their meaning.

The answer to my question about my future was six unbroken lines, the first hexagram in the book, 'The Creative':

> The creative works supreme success
> Furthering through perseverance.

This, of course, told me what I had hoped to hear. And in the hundreds of times I have consulted the *I Ching* since then, I have never thrown six unbroken lines.

I consulted the oracle about our present situation with the old man, and received the hexagram Sung, Conflict, which stated: 'You are sincere but are being obstructed'. It advised caution, and added: 'It does not further to cross the great water'. This answered my question about the old man, who was becoming so difficult that we were tempted to move immediately; the *I Ching* made us decide not to be rash. As to crossing the great water, we had thought of moving back north of the Thames, and when we finally did so, the move was – as I shall describe – something of a disaster.

One of the 'lines' struck me as oddly appropriate. The old man had an infuriating habit of giving my wife presents when in a good mood, and taking them back later. The *I Ching* told us: 'Even if you are given a leather belt, it will have been snatched away three times by the end of the morning'.

I had decided not to leave my job in the plastics factory, even though it meant a long journey from Wimbledon to Finchley. I was satisfied with my job, which consisted of spraying models of Piccadilly's Eros and the Houses of Parliament, or stamping the label on plastic deodorant bottles. So I travelled back and forth on the Northern line for two hours every day.

But the persistent fate that refused to allow me a sense of security began to interfere. The old man became increasingly capricious. He obviously resented my presence in the house and would have preferred Betty to himself. He made a habit of having asthmatic attacks a few minutes after we had got into bed, as if his aim was to interrupt lovemaking. He would get Betty out of bed half a dozen times in the night, when there was clearly nothing wrong with him, and would often stay locked in the bathroom for hours, although there was only one lavatory in the house and it caused us some inconvenience. He told his part-time secretary to take away the type-writer; supposedly to do work at home, but actually to prevent me from using it. Our patience began to wear thin.

I still enjoyed being married, but it was not quite as quarrel-free as I had anticipated. The trouble was partly the difference in age, partly the fact that Betty had established an independent way of life before she met me. The episode of the telephonist who asked her if she was married demonstrated her capacity for working up a resentment. Married people are bound to do things occasionally that strike the other as tactless or thoughtless, or just selfish, and when this happened, she was likely to end by telling me that I was immature, and that I would see things differently when I was ten years older. This kind of thing would, of course, throw me into a fury.

One or two quarrels were due to her strange prudishness. One day when I was adjusting the blind on our bedroom window, I realised that I could almost lean across to the bathroom window, a few feet away, where I could see Betty washing before coming to bed. I was tempted to say Boo, but didn't want to startle her. When she came into the bedroom a few minutes later, I told her I could see her from the bedroom window. She flew into a rage that I found incomprehensible and called me a Peeping Tom. I pointed out that Peeping Toms spy on strangers, and that she was my wife, but it made no difference.

The prudishness made me laugh when she got undressed. She would remove her skirt and stockings with her back to me, put a nightdress over her head, then give a sudden wriggle so that her underskirt and knickers fell round her feet as the nightdress descended. But on the two or three occasions when her prudishness caused a quarrel, I felt less amused by it. One day I dismounted from my bicycle with a bottle of orange cordial in my pocket, and it shot out and exploded on the pavement. We had very little money, and I went into the house cursing loudly; she bridled and told me to wash my mouth out. This struck me as completely unreasonable; I was swearing to relieve my exasperation and, in fact, I had been feeling almost cheerful when she spoiled everything. My feeling towards her was based on protectiveness; it turned to fury when she treated me as a foul-mouthed stranger.

The old man finally became such a nuisance that we decided to leave. Betty warned his sister that she intended to give notice. The sister begged her to stay, and offered twenty-five pounds as an inducement, telling her that there would be a similar present every six months. This certainly made a difference. What is more, it enabled us to take our first holiday since we were married. We went to Hayling Island, leaving the old man in the charge of a no-nonsense hired nurse. It was a delightful week, which seemed a presentiment of a better future. We went to see Blake's cottage at Felpham, spent a day looking at Chichester Cathedral (where I discovered Eliot's excellent pamphlet on cathedrals, emphasising the need for leisure), and went to look at the *Victory* at Portsmouth. On Felpham Beach, I felt as if I could see Blake's angelic forms hovering over the sea. I was also sick from eating too many tomatoes.

At the end of the week, we returned to Wimbledon, en route for Leicester, and discovered that Mr Penman was dead. Perhaps the no-nonsense nurse had induced a heart attack, or perhaps he induced one himself in a transport of self-pity. But I also recalled a curious experience that had happened a few days before we left. The old man had done something more than usually infuriating, and as I thought about this, I felt a rising tide of sheer rage and hatred. And then, quite suddenly, it seemed to reach a sort of climax, like an orgasm, and went away. I found myself wondering if I had somehow directed a curse at him. The novelist John Cowper Powys once said that people he had reason to detest often met with sudden misfortune, until he felt forced to discipline himself into a state of 'neurotic benevolence'.

The old man's sister told us we could stay in the house for a while, and I was also able to recover the typewriter, which she told me I could keep. Now at last I began to type up *Ritual in the Dark*.

The next few months were the happiest time of our marriage, with no landlady to nag us, no quavering voice to call 'nurse' in the middle of the night. If we could have continued like this, the marriage would have lasted for ever. However, there was again the problem of where to live. Finally tired of two hours' travel a day, I changed my job to a local plastics factory, where I worked nights; but everyone was expected to work at a tremendous speed and earn time-and-a-half. I preferred to work at my own speed and earn single-time. After a few weeks, they sacked me, and I signed on the dole, which was then about £4 a week.

Then we had the idea of making a bid for independence by starting a rug-making business; Betty bought a loom, and hanks of strong wool, and I spent days walking around London's biggest stores, trying to establish a market for the rugs; but they cost too much to make to sell at a profit.

Betty advertised for another nurse–housekeeper post, and eventually found one in Courtfield Gardens, Kensington. Her new employer was the retired matron of a private nursing home for alcoholics; she had married one of her wealthy patients. Most of the house was let out in rooms, but Mrs Deacon retained a large flat, where she liked to entertain writers and people from the arts world – provided, of course, that they were successful.

We moved in the autumn of 1952, and the next six months proved to be the worst ordeal of our married lives. I was still on the dole – jobs were very scarce. We lived in a basement with a minimum of light: the lamps had to be kept on all day. And if our previous employer had been a doddering Tiberius, this one was a female Caligula. She was insanely neurotic; so much so that she had never been able to keep a housekeeper for more than a few weeks. She began by accusing Betty of steaming open her letters; Betty, who was rigidly honest, was outraged: there was a quarrel that ended with Mrs Deacon ordering her to leave the room.

After this, the woman became steadily more paranoid, and used to shriek at Betty, inventing insane accusations. When I first realised about this bullying, I went upstairs to talk to her; she began very sweetly reasonable, and ended in one of her strange furies, telling me that if we weren't satisfied, we could leave the following day. We had spent every penny we possessed moving Betty's furniture down from Leicester, so that was out of the question. I was ignominiously forced to climb down and apologise. I went downstairs cursing her with every drop of hatred in my being; all my natural conceit as a writer and my conviction of my own genius was outraged by her insults. Once more, as in the case of Mr Penman, the anger seemed to reach a climax, then suddenly drain away, leaving an odd sense of relief. A few weeks later, Mrs Deacon went into hospital for an X-ray and they discovered she had a cancer of the womb that would kill her in a matter of months. This had no doubt been the cause of her insane rages.

For a few days after she had been told the news, our landlady was subdued and good-tempered; then the rages returned more violently than ever. One day, Betty heard that she was about to be sacked; she forestalled it by giving notice; our furniture was put into storage, and she returned to Leicester with our year-old son to wait until I could find another home for us.

But it was actually the last time we would live together, and I had a premonition of this on Christmas Day, when we had another of our absurd quarrels.

I had decided to spend Christmas trying to meditate. Accordingly, while Betty got the breakfast, I opened a volume of Blake, and tried hard to put myself into a state of inner calm. I had often done this kind of thing in my teens; sometimes it took all day, but sooner or later, the immense relaxation would descend on me, and then, slowly, the old optimism and sense of affirmation would awaken. I had not experienced it for a very long time, and Christmas seemed a good opportunity.

Unfortunately, I had only been focusing my attention for a few minutes when Betty came in, asking me if I would look after Roderick for a while. I burst out angrily, and she went away; but meditation was now impossible. I got up feeling guilty, but Betty had retreated into one of her icy, unapproachable moods, and we hardly spoke all morning. After lunch, when Roderick was asleep, I made an attempt at reconciliation. I often used to read to her; now I suggested that I should read her Lawrence's 'The Man Who Loved Islands' – an interesting study of a paranoiac whose need to be alone becomes so obsessive that he finally buys a tiny island and even has the sheep removed. Lawrence intended it as a sermon on the theme that no man is an island, but I sympathised with his hero, and found the ending of the story – with the snow drifting in great banks against his hut – strangely moving. I began to read it to Betty; but after a few pages, she interrupted with: 'This is the most boring story I've ever heard. I can't stand another word of it.'

This enraged me; I put on my coat and left the house. It was a grey, cold afternoon, but without snow. I cycled aimlessly down the Earl's Court Road and King's Road to Wandsworth Bridge, and then stood looking at the cold water. I was not thinking of suicide; but trying to look inside myself to discover what I really wanted, what I ought to do. This deadening frustration had gone on for long enough. I was thinking about Nijinsky, whose wife had also been an honest, straightforward woman who had failed to understand why he was under such strain. It seemed to me that Betty was always trying to reduce me to some sort of lowest common multiple, to work out my motivations in the crudest terms. On that evening when I had left her flat early, my mind full of Van Gogh, she had believed that I had left to see another girl, and had continued to believe this after our marriage, although I told her often enough it was untrue.

What was worse, she tried to impose this crude, oversimplified version of my motives on me, implying that she knew me better than I did myself.

Now I thought again about Van Gogh, of that obsessive quest after the purely affirmative vision that ended with the cry 'Misery will never end', and I saw that this marriage was an irrelevant interlude, a long diversion from my purpose; it would have to end. It was not an emotional decision; I suddenly saw it with clarity as a fact that could not be evaded, I felt an immense sense of relief, and began to feel sorry for Betty. When we were newly married I used to have nightmares in which I left her, and I woke up choked with emotion. The nightmares sprang out of self-division; now I had ceased to be self-divided.

When we parted, in January 1953, a part of me knew we would never live together again, although we were then on the most affectionate of terms, and I promised her to find us another home as soon as possible. Betty was in tears when I saw her off.

CHAPTER 5

Anarchism and Soho

One result of our separation was that I suddenly became more involved with the London Anarchist Group.

I had been a member for the past few months, having first come across them one Sunday afternoon, when Betty and I were taking a walk in Hyde Park. On Speakers' Corner, we heard a red-bearded man preaching anarchism. He seemed to be intelligent and widely read, and when I heckled him, his answers were witty, if not convincing. When someone asked him if he thought clergymen really believed what they preach, he said: 'Of course. Their salary depends on believing it.'

A week later I returned to speak to him, and asked if I might join the group; he said there was no formal membership, but that if I was a convinced anarchist, I was welcome as a comrade. His name was Philip Sanson, and he offered to let me try speaking on his platform. So the following Sunday, tense and excited, I went to Hyde Park. I travelled by tube from Wimbledon, and tried to get out of paying the full fare by claiming that I had boarded the train much nearer my destination than I had. The inspector asked me whether the station I had started from had had an escalator or a lift, and I was not able to answer; so I admitted that I had intended to swindle London Transport. (He took my name, and in due course, I received a summons and was fined ten shillings.)

This experience stimulated all my anarchistic inclinations, and I began my speech by telling my audience – a very large one, since other speakers had attracted it for me – exactly how I had been caught, and advising them on how to avoid paying their fares. This was a huge success; I found it easy to talk in the open air since I had to shout, and this prevented me from being nervous. I talked for half an hour and doubled the size of the audience. When I climbed down, several members of the group thumped me on the back, and hauled me off to Lyons's to celebrate on tea and sandwiches. One of them, Tony Gibson, seemed particularly enthusiastic, and we became friends. But when we rejoined the others I was told that my speech had not pleased the rest of the group: it might have been stimulating, but it was not anarchism. So I was instructed that I would have to spend a few months studying Malatesta and Kropotkin before I could be allowed to speak again.

The truth was that I thought the political theory of anarchism nonsense. Anarchists are, of course, anti-authoritarian; they believe that human nature is basically good, and that if men were left to themselves, laws would be unnecessary because men would quickly learn to regulate themselves, and crime and war would vanish.

I could see, of course, that one might hope for an increasingly democratic and intelligent society that would finally dispense altogether with authority, but it seemed obvious that in our present stage of political evolution we were not ready for it. On the other hand, I felt that the real aim of anarchism was to create a society of 'free spirits' who would help one another openly and generously. This was very close to my heart. It seemed clear to me that the disease of our civilisation was the self-interest and power mania of businessmen and politicians. I had worked for a while in a large toy factory in Wimbledon, and a few days there had been enough to make me want to destroy the place with dynamite: the workers were expected to work at top speed for every single second between clocking-in and clocking-out; there was no freedom of any kind, and to be a minute late was a serious offence. A week there had been enough for me. It seemed to me disgusting that this land of England, that had produced Sir Thomas Browne and Newton and Shelley, should have come to this: demoniacal, ruthless money-grubbing.

Of course, it was because this money-grubbing was a threat to me as a writer that I hated it so much. The aim of anarchism, as I saw it, was to create an England fit for men of talent, and a society whose aim would be the encouragement of individualism.

However, the anarchists seemed to feel that my aims were somewhat too idealistic, and not nearly political enough. So I was banned from their platform. I then joined the North London Syndicalist group, who were glad enough to get speakers and allowed me to say what I liked on their platform.

My rather guardedly friendly relations with the London Anarchist Group came to an end when I offered to deliver one of the Tuesday lectures. In a basement near Fitzroy Square, I talked about the late Roman emperors, from Tiberius to Nero, and read them extracts from Suetonius; then I moved on to Jack the Ripper and the problem of the steady rise in the crime rate. They all thought I intended to draw the moral that power corrupts, but I was far more interested in trying to make them understand that there is an irrational element in human nature that will make the establishment of the anarchist millennium impossible. I drew my text from

Dostoevsky's *Notes from Underground*. Half my audience walked out, and the remainder attacked me violently: one of them said that I had used the lecture to get some sadistic compulsion out of my system, treating the lecture platform as an analyst's couch. After that, I saw very little of the group.

The breakup of my marriage to Betty was not entirely due to me. I have said that various resentments and strains had built up in the eighteen months we had lived together. We were on close terms for a great deal of the time, but a clash of temperaments had developed. I was sufficiently certain of what I wanted to do to want to be taken at my own valuation. I had spent long enough in my teens fighting self-doubt, imposing self-discipline. If a relationship could not be established on my own terms, I was prepared to forgo the relationship. I classified myself with Nietzsche, Van Gogh, T. E. Lawrence, Nijinsky, as a mystic and an outsider, as someone driven by an evolutionary urge that transcends normal personal motivations. I do not mean that most of my motivations are not personal; but there are certain important moments when they are not.

It is also true that the evolutionary obsession can be interpreted as a manic egoism or will to self-assertion. Many would-be artists and rebels can be regarded almost entirely in terms of a will to self-assertion. It is an accusation that can be made to stick to almost anyone whose motives sometimes transcend the personal. In our quarrels, Betty hurled it at me fairly frequently, for example, that when I got carried away by ideas, I talked *at* her instead of *to* her – implying that I had forgotten her presence and was indulging in a kind of intellectual masturbation, when in fact my chief desire was to get her as interested in the ideas as I was myself, so we might share the excitement.

These were the resentments on my side, and when we had been apart for a couple of days, I wrote her a letter in which I expressed them. It crossed in the post with a letter from Betty in which she expressed her own resentments: that I was basically selfish and self-indulgent. All that was really happening was that the strain of eighteen months of continual crisis and worry had vanished too suddenly, and we were being hurled into violent reaction. Neither of us saw this at the time. The recriminations went on, and we decided by post that we did not intend to live together again – at least for a long time.

I now found a job in the Western Fever Hospital in Fulham, as a -hospital porter. I was one of about a dozen porters whose job was to receive patients and wheel them to the wards on a stretcher, as well as emptying dustbins, taking meals to the wards, cleaning windows and generally looking after the maintenance of the hospital. I was to live in: my room was a cubicle big enough to contain a bed and chest of drawers; and by standing on the bed I could see into the next cubicle, or down the full length of the building. There was not much privacy, but for someone who had been in the RAF this was no hardship.

I started in January 1953. The work was easy. We spent most of the day lounging around the porter's room waiting for the phone to ring. When this happened, two of us had to collect a stretcher and move a patient from the ambulance to the reception room, or from the reception room to the ward. No one was overworked – and this was the trouble. The long periods of inactivity were demoralising. The porters played cards, listened to football matches on the radio, made tea every half hour, and quarrelled among themselves.

The place reeked of sex; it was the perfect atmosphere for incubating some future Jack the Ripper. The job involved lifting half-naked women on and off stretchers, and walking into wards where the female patients might be wandering around with very few clothes. The porters talked of nothing but sex, and at least one of them pursued nurses and ward maids with some success. A pimply male nurse spent most of his wages on grubby hand-printed booklets of pornography obtained from a shop behind Leicester Square, and they were passed from hand to hand – I recall one about a man who has sex with his dog, then seduces his niece.

In *The Magic Mountain* Thomas Mann observes that tuberculosis heightens the sexual urge. My own experience of the T.B. wards confirmed this, but it seemed to be true of most departments of the hospital with which we came into contact. It may be due to the continually felt presence of death. This came home to me when I walked into the mortuary one day and saw a particularly attractive young girl lying naked on the slab. I had seen her alive a few days before; a few hours later I saw the body after the postmortem, the brains and intestines piled on the end of the mortuary slab, all suggestion of a fellow human being having now disappeared. She was the mother of children, and happily married, and I found myself asking for the first time, with a real desire to understand: why did she die? Could I die like that? Are we so unimportant to Nature? Or did she die because she had no passionate desire to live, no real purpose? Was Shaw right when he said we die because we are too lazy to make life worth living?

I had one near-mystical experience in the hospital. I was lying on my bed listening to a concert on the radio; they played the 'Liebestod' from *Tristan and Isolde*, one of my favourite pieces of music. At that time, my admiration for Nijinsky often made me improvise a dance to music, as Nijinsky and Isadora Duncan used to. (It is unnecessary to say that I was always alone when I did this) So I now stood up and, in the fairly small space between my bed and the opposite wall, began to perform slow, sinuous movements with outstretched arms. As I did this I tensed the muscles of my arms, legs and torso. As the music reached a climax, it seemed to penetrate the depths of my being, and for a brief moment consciousness reached a clarity that made me feel I was above time, as if I could look down on it like a bird on the earth.

I remain convinced that what I did that day was to achieve a glimpse of man's evolutionary possibilities, of freedom from the slow, inevitable movement of time. Shaw had talked of the necessity for man to live to be three hundred, but could not suggest a method by which this could be achieved. I feel that the 'timeless moment' I induced that day by sheer concentration was a flash of insight into the answer. The body's flow in the direction of death could be slowed, or even halted, by using the will as a brake.

The anarchists had begun to produce a composite revue of the twentieth century just before the group was split by the poet Herbert Read's acceptance of a knighthood. I had written parts of it myself. After the schism the idea was dropped; but I was unwilling to scrap my work, and decided to finish writing it and to find my own cast to perform it. The cafés and coffee houses were full of restless art students with no idea of how to kill time. A number of these I recruited for my revue. A young commercial artist called Jonathan Abraham let us use his room in Fellowes Road, Hampstead, for rehearsal, and played us jazz and records of French cabaret. (He introduced me to the records of Bix Beiderbecke, who is still my favourite jazz trumpeter.) I continued writing the revue as we rehearsed it – 'rehearsing' meant reading it aloud, for we had no idea of how it could be staged.

Sexually speaking, that summer was almost completely continent. I was chiefly interested in an eighteen-year-old girl named Laura del Rivo. I also took out a few girls from the hospital. There was a pretty Finnish student called Laura Kokalla who was working for the summer as a ward maid. I took her along to rehearsals, and sometimes we went out for the day on Sunday, wandering around London or Surrey. Since Laura spoke very little English, I started to learn Finnish. She was a shy, gentle girl with beautiful skin, and intensely frightened of sex. Whenever she started to enjoy being kissed and allowed herself to relax, she would say: 'We must stop. I am excited.' And I had to jam on the brakes.

An equally pretty German girl called Irmgard Huckmann was more interesting, but just as frustrating. She was also a student working as a ward maid, and on her first evening at the hospital she went out with the porter who was interested in nothing but sex. After that, she refused to speak to him, and went out with me instead. The porter would leer at me and offer to lend me a condom; years later, in Germany, I discovered why. Irmgard had let him get her drunk, after which he took her to a piece of waste ground behind the hospital and took off her clothes. The experience had disgusted her so much that she determined to stay virtuous for the rest of her stay in London. This was my bad luck.

Irmgard has always stayed in my mind as a symbol of a certain kind of revolt. She had been born in a small German town, Besigheim, in the early 30s, and in due course joined the Hitler Youth. She was so intensely vital that she soon became the youth leader, and used to arrange their parades and games. She worshipped Hitler; for her, the war was a crusade to make the world a more beautiful and heroic place. Since Besigheim is a small town, everyone knew her and liked her. And then, quite suddenly, her hero was dead and the war was over, and the town was drab, and everyone was half-starved. Now there was nothing to satisfy the craving for purpose. She openly mourned Hitler. She agreed that Dachau and Belsen had been horrific, but they had only been the dark side of a magnificent enterprise.

She was an exceptionally beautiful girl, with a strong, Slavic face and thick dark hair. She emitted vitality like sparks. But she was a manic-depressive. On some days, everything was funny to her: she laughed, joked, wanted to do absurd things; on other days, she talked of the meaningless-ness of life. In this mood, she was also likely to do absurd things. We were standing on Westminster Bridge one evening, and she gestured at the people: 'Look at them – dummies, puppets. They are not even half-alive. What would they do if I suddenly took off all my clothes? Or lay down in the middle of the road?' 'Why don't you?' I said, hoping to see her strip. 'I'm not afraid.' She strode out into the traffic, to the middle of the road, crouched on all fours, and began touching her forehead on the ground. Nobody seemed to pay much attention, and the traffic was crawling past her as if she was invisible. I was relieved when she stood up before the policeman on traffic duty spotted her. But she was cheerful for the rest of the evening. I could understand her frustration: she had learned to develop huge reserves of energy, and channel them into things she felt important. Then the channels had suddenly been closed. She was like a mother without a baby, her breasts swollen with milk. Five years later, when I was doing a lecture tour in Germany, I saw Irmgard again. The good looks had vanished. The strength of the face was still there, but the vitality had gone; she seemed burned out, listless; she had accepted that civilisation has no room for her kind of vitality.

The girl who occupied most of my thoughts that summer was, as I say, Laura del Rivo, whom I met in the Coffee House in Northumberland Avenue. She was not pretty; her face had the flat planes and healthy colour-ing of Gauguin's paintings of Breton women. Her voice was sweet and childish, with an accent that indicated she had been to a good school, and she talked and dressed like a twelve-year-old, in cotton frocks with green and white stripes. The fact that she had full breasts and an excellent figure made the schoolgirlishness very piquant, and made me long to find out if she wore white cotton knickers.

I felt she was bored and unhappy, curiously at a loose end. She told me she wanted to be a writer, and I asked her to let me see some of her work. The next day, we met in a café opposite Charing Cross underground, and she produced her manuscript. She smoked all the time I read it, and I noticed that the hand holding the cigarette was trembling; there was something very tense about her, like a frightened animal. The story was called 'Emil' and was obviously autobiographical; it was about a Russian youth she had met when she was working in Foyle's bookshop. She had become completely infatuated with him, but he was indifferent to her. The story had a discipline and lack of self-pity that were startling, coming from an eighteen-year-old.

Suddenly, it seemed to me that Laura was the girl I had been looking for: intelligent, completely feminine, devoid of resentments or self-assertion. The only thing that bothered me was the fact that I was married, for she was a Catholic and attended mass every Sunday. But when I finally told her I was married, she said casually: 'Oh, yes.' That was all. It was typical of Laura; she didn't even express curiosity.

Her unusual personality fascinated me. Emotionally, she was completely innocent, Blake's 'soul of sweet delight' that can never be defiled. I was invited to her home in Cheam to meet her parents: it was a quiet, secure household, with a long back garden full of apple trees; her father was a bank manager; her younger sister, Lucy, was a pretty, very lively child, and used to sit on my knee while I told her stories. There was a statue of Saint Joseph on the stairs, and a crucifix on the wall of the sitting room.

I began to understand the nature of Laura's inner conflict. It seemed that her twelve-year-old mannerisms and teenage frocks were an attempt to stave off the responsibilities of adulthood. She had enjoyed her peaceful, secure childhood, but physically she was now in an adult world, a world in which you experienced a compulsive urge to leave your innocence behind and give your virginity to immature young Russians who worked in Foyle's. Soho fascinated her, intellectually and emotionally. She spent her evenings there, at parties where couples would neck until they were obviously in a fever of excitement, and then hurry to the bedroom; where sixteen-year-olds talked casually about abortions, and drank strong tea, and smoked endlessly – pot when they could get it. Her closest friend, Olivia, who was seventeen, was having an affair with a plump Cypriot who was much older than she was and already married. Olivia got pregnant but took something for it, and one night rushed to the lavatory and had a miscarriage. She flushed it down the toilet, spent the weekend in bed, alone, then went to work as usual on Monday.

Laura could turn away from this world, which she found so exciting and disturbing, to the middle-class home at Cheam where nothing had changed since her childhood. She told me that as a child she used to roll up into a tight ball in bed and say: 'Isn't it nice to be me?' She still wanted to do this. She wanted to keep a foot in both camps.

Laura was my type, but I, unfortunately, was not hers. She submitted to being kissed, but she was a bad kisser, and never seemed to know what to do with her nose. She was all tense self-consciousness. On the other hand, she was physically fully developed, and when she walked into the Coffee House, the tight green sweater she sometimes wore made all the men look up. I had been sexually deprived since January, and it was now June; being alone with Laura was a continual exercise in self-control.

One Sunday, in a field near Box Hill, I asked her if she understood why she was so sexually unresponsive. She said calmly: 'Oh, yes. It's because I'm keen on someone else.' The bottom fell out of my stomach. 'Someone else? Who?' 'I can't tell you that.' I said: 'But good God, do you mean to tell me that with England's foremost man of genius kissing you, you can think about anyone else?' She said: 'But he says he's a genius too.' 'Pooh, the world's full of imposters.' 'And he's published, too.' This was an unkind cut. I asked her the man's name, but she wouldn't tell me; she suddenly became tense and reticent again.

Eventually she volunteered the information that he was a journalist and had published poetry. She also mentioned his first name. It was Bill.

A week later, we were sitting in a jazz club, and I was talking to a strange, pale-faced girl named Jackie Noble. She was telling us about her boyfriend, Philip Veen, and Philip's closest friend, Bill Hopkins. She said that Hopkins was the most brilliant man she had ever come across; that his flow of words was incredible, and that she had never seen anyone beat him in an argument. I was struck by a suspicion. I looked at Laura. 'Is that the Bill?' She blushed and looked away. 'No.' But she had said it too quickly. I determined to seek out Bill Hopkins and find out if he was all that brilliant.

He was not difficult to find, for he was attempting to launch a magazine called the *Saturday Critic*, and half my cast was working for him, selling subscriptions. I first saw him in the A and A Club, a taxi drivers' rendezvous; a crowd of people were sitting and standing round a table, listening to someone talking. I asked who it was. 'That's Bill Hopkins.' So I hurried over and stood on the outskirts of the group. He had a pale face, very good-looking in a Scott Fitzgerald sort of way, with clean-cut features and a strong jaw. He was arguing with someone about literature. He certainly had a dominating presence, yet I found him disappointing. I had expected a man of calm and discipline, who had read as much as I had, and who had carefully calculated his assault on the literary bastions. Instead, I found this intense, good-looking man with a romantic idealism as innocent as Shelley's, who declared he never read other people's books because he preferred to be original, and whose taste for rhetoric made it obvious he was a compatriot of Dylan Thomas.

But there could be no denying the immense power of his personality. He seemed born to be a leader. His humour was so constant and individual that I found it exhausting after the first half-hour or so. By comparison, I seemed sullen and brooding.

I introduced myself to him, but he seemed brusque and absent-minded as he shook my hand. I said I was a friend of Laura's, and he looked blank, then said, 'Oh, yes?'

At our second or third meeting I lent him the uncompleted manuscript of *Ritual in the Dark*. A few days later, I met him in Charing Cross Road. He was wearing a yellow T-shirt stained with red wine, and was in an exuberant mood: but when I asked about the manuscript, he was evasive. I suspected – rightly – that he had not read it. Laura was with me when I met him, and he hardly seemed to notice her.

It was after this that she told me what had happened between them. She had seen Bill talking in cafés, and had developed a romantic crush on him. She used to wait until it was time for him to go home, for they lived in the same direction – he was in Streatham – and often caught the same bus. They seemed to get on well enough, but he was apparently not interested in her sexually. And then one evening as they were walking to the bus, he said seriously: 'Look here, Laura, I find you rather sexually attractive. I'm not in love with you or anything like that. I'd just like to sleep with you. I promise I wouldn't talk about it afterwards.'

Laura was tongue-tied. She finally said: 'I'm sorry, I can't.' 'Why not?' She seized the first excuse that came into her head. 'Because I'm a Catholic.' He held out his hand decisively. 'Well, goodbye, Laura.' 'And he hasn't paid me any attention from that day to this,' she told me. 'Are you still attracted to him?' She hesitated. 'I suppose so. I wouldn't have minded sleeping with him, but he put it so clinically.'

This was a knife turning in my bowels. But obviously Laura would be of no use to me while she nursed this passion for Bill. I said: 'Why don't you offer to help him launch the magazine? He told me the other day he needed a typist.' 'He wouldn't have me, and I wouldn't ask him.' 'Shall I ask him?' 'No.'

I did, nevertheless. And Bill said testily: 'No, no, I don't want that female. I once asked her to go to bed with me and she said she was a Catholic. What's that got to do with it? The girl's a fool.'

'Perhaps you put it a little too bluntly. She's only eighteen. You probably scared her.' He looked thoughtful. 'Well, if she can type . . . Tell her to come to the office one evening.'

This was not noble disinterestedness on my part; neither did I want to play pandar. But I was fond of Laura, and it was obvious that Bill had become an obsession. So I gave her Bill's message, and left them to it.

What then happened was what I had expected. Bill re-presented his proposal to her; this time she accepted. They became lovers briefly. But he found her frightened and shy, and lost interest. I did not see the result of my experiment; by then I was in France. It had been a frustrating summer.

But before all this happened, I walked into the A and A one day and found the manuscript of *Ritual in the Dark* waiting for me, together with a note that said: 'Welcome to our ranks! You are a man of genius.'

Bill had finally got around to opening it, and been struck by the discipline of the writing.

On the other hand, I found his own writing disappointing when I first saw it. A short story was full of vague romanticism: it was about a soldier who is badly wounded in battle, and who has time to fall in love with a beautiful peasant girl before he dies.

The truth was that our standards of writing were completely different: I had 'trained' under Eliot and T. E. Hulme, and had been equally influenced by Shaw, Yeats and Hemingway. Bill was a self-taught Romantic, writing in a tradition akin to Musset and Hugo. The shade of Hugo seemed to haunt him, and he was once told at a spiritualist meeting – which he was reporting for a newspaper – that the French poet was standing behind him and wished to present his regards. This brought to my mind Gide's comment when asked who was the greatest French poet: 'Victor Hugo, alas!'

There were times when I suspected that Bill subscribed to Poe's dictum that the most appropriate subject for poetry is the death of a beautiful woman. A story he told me later was somehow typical. In Paris he was asked to help in the search for a girl who had disappeared from her parents' home in Belgium, and was reported to be making for the Left Bank. He was given a photograph of an exceptionally beautiful girl, and told to comb the cafés. Understandably, he fell in love with the photograph, and spent weeks in feverish search for its original. Then he was told the search had been called off: the girl's body had been found buried near her home; a disappointed suitor had murdered her, and then claimed that she had left for Paris.

Bill told me this story in connection with an episode in one of his novels (still unpublished at the time I write). A young and romantic German officer goes into a Polish castle that has been wrecked by shellfire. He enters a bedroom that obviously belongs to a girl; her photograph on the dressing table shows her to be remarkably beautiful. But one wall of the bedroom is missing, and the bed is soaked in blood.

I am telling these stories – out of sequence – to illustrate the way in which Bill Hopkins's imagination works, and also to explain why it was that I found his short story disconcerting. His aim has always been to create a certain kind of intensity that has more in common with the German nineteenth-century Romanticism than with Hemingway.

But the reason that I was immediately fascinated by Bill was that he was the first man I had met who was as conceited and as assured of his future greatness as I was. Soho had disappointed me; I had expected to find a kind of *La Bohème* spirit; instead, I found the easily recognisable lack of self-confidence that I had thought to be the characteristic of provincial towns; after six months I had met no self-professed artist or writer who seemed to rise much above mediocrity. All seemed to be oppressed by some suspicion of future failure – what I later came to call 'the fallacy of insignificance'. Moreover, I had not met anyone who seemed to be seriously determined to produce major work. (Laura was, at this time, extremely modest about the value of anything she might produce.) Although we live in an age of specialisation, where years of study are required to become a technician or mathematician, few would-be writers seem to recognise that their trade requires an equally long self-discipline.

It was true that Bill also seemed to rely largely on native inspiration in his writing; but he gave the impression that he had never, in all his life, entertained a moment's doubt about his future eminence, and about the dignity that attaches to the destiny of being a writer.

It soon occurred to me that his main problem was simple: his immediate personal effect on people was so great that he might easily have spent his whole life dazzling a small circle of admirers (who would never cease to assure him of his genius) and never writing a line. The temptation was doubled because he comes from a family of actors, and he would therefore only be following the family tradition to rely on the spoken rather than the written word. This came to me even more strongly when I heard him talk for the first time about the plot of his novel *Time of Totality*. As he told it, it was irresistibly dramatic. The romanticism was welded neatly into a plot that had the movement and economy of a Graham Greene thriller; listening to him, it was impossible to doubt that he had the material for a best-selling novel. And yet I had only to cast my mind back to the occasion when he had first outlined to me the plot of his novel *The Divine and the Decay*, and then to recall his years of effort in writing and rewriting it, to realise that there can be an immense gap between conception and execution. (I was, in any case, already aware of this from my own years of rewriting *Ritual*.) In telling a story some difficult point is glossed over, some relationship made to sound more plausible than it will on paper. In writing, a conception that seemed watertight may appear more like a beggar's coat – more holes than cloth. There is no alternative but to work and rework, until the original vision is no more than a distant memory.

However, in this digression I have left the story of the *Saturday Critic* suspended; and yet, when I first met him, it seemed to me – and to many people in Soho – that Bill Hopkins was about to become the new Frank Harris, whose *Saturday Review* was the most successful periodical of the 1890s. If the *Saturday Critic* had ever appeared, the legend of the Angry Young Men would have started three years earlier; for the magazine was to be devoted to violent demands for higher standards in all the arts, and ruthless condemnation of all that failed to meet these standards. (I have no idea how he proposed to keep the goodwill of his advertisers.) His army of contributors were all pledged to make the fullest use of satire, irony and downright abuse in their reviews.

Aware that confidence is most easily inspired by an appearance of success, he took an office in Southwark, close to the tavern from which Chaucer's pilgrims had set out, and had two telephones installed. Various publishers sent him books for review. Jonathan Abraham drafted a dummy copy of the first number, and this was printed with blank pages and a combative editorial explaining the magazine's policy.

I learned that Bill had worked in Fleet Street since his teens, become a protégé of Beaverbrook, and had at one time edited several local north London newspapers simultaneously, each one requiring a minimum of effort. The *Saturday Critic* seemed to have every chance of success. However, the problem was always money, and the free help and the few subscriptions were not enough. Eventually, the whole scheme collapsed under its own weight.

During all my time in Soho I was still speaking on the anarchist platform: in fact, since I was the only speaker for the Syndicalist Workers, I kept their platform at the hospital, and cycled in with it strapped to my back on Sunday afternoons. Shaw had gained his experience as a public speaker in Hyde Park; it seemed to me the best way to learn to speak to audiences. I had been a good debater in my schooldays, but I had lost some of the fluency since I had grown up. I had once tried to make a few comments after a meeting of the Theosophical Society – I had been a member for a brief period in my Wimbledon days, but found their thinking too woolly – and my voice shook, and I had to grip the chair in front of me to conceal the trembling of my hands. In the open air, I had to shout, and the nervousness vanished.

It was after one of these afternoons in Hyde Park that I had my only sexual experience of the summer, and it was a disquieting one. In the A and A, I fell into conversation with an attractive girl who told me she was a Communist. Her name was Kay, and we talked about Russian literature and argued for a while, and then I walked with her as far as Marble Arch. Here she suggested that I go back to her room for coffee. I knew what she had in mind, and I was willing enough.

She lived in a mews flat in Maida Vale. I parked my bicycle outside with the platform tied to it, and went up. We drank coffee, talked for half an hour, then I said I'd better be going. 'Why don't you stay the night?' I said I'd like to. So she went off to the bathroom, and I undressed and got into the double bed. I was already beginning to feel tense. Kay was not really my type. She was sophisticated, with a drawling upper-class voice, and talked openly about her sexual experiences. She had been married to an actor who had left her for another woman; since then, she had satisfied her sexual needs by sleeping with various men.

Her room was sordid. There was an enormous stain on the ceiling shaped like an eye; the wallpaper was peeling; the bedsheets were crumpled, and there was an old menstrual stain on the lower one.

Kay strolled in wearing a gauzy nightgown; she had a good figure. She got into bed, and we kissed. Then she touched my erect penis, and said: 'Wait a moment,' and sat up to take off the nightgown.

As she lay down and opened her legs, my excitement collapsed; so did my erection. I said: 'I'm sorry – it's overexcitement.' She didn't seem to mind; she turned towards me again, and we talked and occasionally kissed; but as far as sexual excitement was concerned, I felt as if I had blown a fuse. Finally, we dozed off for a while. I woke up and felt her pressed against me. The excitement revived like a tiny spark; I was aware that if I was not careful, it would go out again. I stayed relaxed, tried to direct my thoughts to the girl beside me, and felt the spark turn gradually into a flame. I moved on top of her; luckily, she was easy to enter, and once that much had been accomplished, there was no further difficulty. I tried to make up for the earlier failure, and at the end of half an hour we were both exhausted. I made love to her twice more before morning.

Later in the week, I went to see her in a new flat – she had been thrown out of the old one for not paying the rent. We had a meal and went to bed. This time it was no use. I simply didn't want her. My body refused to respond in any way at all. And it suddenly came to me what was behind all this. My life with Betty had produced a subconscious conflict. Ever since we were first married, the act of getting into bed together had aroused an intense physical excitement in me; perhaps her demureness produced a sense of male conquest, of violation. After quarrels, it had often been physical contact that had started the reconciliation. But the more we quarrelled, the more a part of me didn't want to be reconciled, so that I began to apply an automatic brake to the excitement she aroused in me. The brake had become a habit, and it was working with other women.

It was frustrating to be unable to control my physical responses, yet I felt less defeated about it than I might have. My inability to respond to

Kay made me more aware of the things I *did* hold valuable. Human beings were not intended for this insipid lovemaking:

> Those who sit in the stye of contentment, meaning
> > Death
> Those who suffer the ecstasy of animals meaning
> > Death.

Mathematics, music, the mystery of the universe and of human existence: these were what really mattered, not this sensual girl whose hips worked like a machine.

A few evenings later, I was talking in the A and A with a friend of Bill Hopkins named John. I was due to see Kay, but since we were having an interesting discussion, I invited him to come along with me. We went to Kay's flat in Percy Street. John was telling me about the problems he was encountering with a novel; I was explaining my difficulties with *Ritual*. Kay made tea for us and we carried on talking. Then Kay turned the conversation to sex, and at some point my friend admitted he was a virgin. Kay was delighted. Towards midnight, I said I had to go. Kay said: 'Well, I've got to sleep with somebody . . .' We both looked at John, who blushed. But he stayed. I saw Kay a few days later and asked what he had been like. 'Fantastic. He nearly killed me.'

I made no further attempt to sleep with her. But I found myself wondering if I would fail as ignominiously if it was Laura who was in bed beside me.

My *Twentieth Century Revue* was finally presented some time in July 1953. We hired a hall near Holborn, a large upstairs room of a café called The Garibaldi that the anarchists used sometimes. We had put up advertisements in all the coffee houses, and we had a large audience. We read it aloud, seated around a table; it went on for two hours, and was more successful than we had expected. We charged no admittance, but the money donated for coffee and cakes also paid for the hire of the room.

Afterwards, the cast was gloomy. They had been rehearsing for months, and now felt the anticlimax. Soho was not really the vital, bohemian place that our elders assumed it was. Most of the younger generation were bored and only vaguely rebellious. Bill Hopkins and I had produced a certain discipline for a month or so, offered a centre of gravity to draw them together and give them something to do. Now the revue was over, and the *Saturday Critic* was already encountering production difficulties, the old aimlessness was back. The cast urged me to write them a play, and I began *The Metal Flower Blossom*, about a Soho artist and his involvements with his models. (Parts of it were later incorporated into my second novel, *Adrift in Soho*.)

The trouble was that this required far more rehearsal and coordination than a revue, and they were not willing to give it that much attention. Half of them were always absent from rehearsals. One day, Laura and I decided that we would skip a rehearsal and get drunk. Neither of us had ever been drunk before – I had never been able to afford it. We went into Henekey's wine bar in the Strand, and drank several glasses of cheap burgundy, then took another bottle with us to the gardens of the newly built Festival Hall, and drank it on a seat overlooking the river. At first the effect was disappointing, but by the time the bottle was empty, we were undoubtedly drunk.

We walked to the Coffee House in Northumberland Avenue and drank black coffee; and then, crossing Trafalgar Square, Laura was sick in one of the fountains. After a few minutes, a disapproving policewoman came over and told us we were causing a scene. I looked up and saw that a crowd had gathered and was watching us. I travelled to Cheam with Laura, delivered her home, then caught the last train back to Fulham. Waiting for a connection at Putney Bridge, I too was suddenly violently sick in the bushes. The next day, I felt exhausted, and had a headache. It happened that I had been chosen for a particularly strenuous job that day – the window-cleaning detail. I got through the day somehow, and swore I would never repeat the folly.

I didn't enjoy life in Soho; there was too much meaningless activity. When Laura started working for Bill – dropping out of *The Metal Flower Blossom* – I decided it was time to return to France. I was tired of the hospital, and bored – so bored that no amount of spare-time activity could stop me feeling as if I was rotting, spiritually and mentally. Somehow, a mere five minutes in the porters' room could reduce my thoughts to a repetitive babble. I made tremendous efforts against it, but it was no use; I stewed in my own apathy. I frequently sneaked off to a room above the laundry, sat cross-legged on the dusty floor (breathing in a smell of dead mice) and tried to concentrate on the *Gita* and on freedom. I was haunted by an image from Lancelot Cranmer-Byng's *Vision of Asia*, a picture of 'Corea, the Land of Morning Calm' – an idea not without ironic implications in 1953 – and of three old men standing in a green basin in the hills, each tasting a jar of vinegar. Buddha finds it sour, Confucius is calm and indifferent; Lao-Tzu looks delighted. The brew, of course, is life.

This image filled me with sick longing as I breathed in the dust, and then went downstairs again to hear the same conversations about football and sex, and watch the endless card games. It was history that had died for me. I had an unusual degree of freedom; the work was easy; I had many friends; but my mind was like a mouse in a bucket that cannot climb over the sides, and can only leap up and then fall back to the bottom.

At about this time the Christie murders were discovered, and the newspapers were full of photographs of detectives digging up the back garden of 10 Rillington Place. Reg Christie was a middle-aged sex maniac, impotent except with unconscious women; so he persuaded a succession of women that he could cure catarrh by getting them to breathe in a potion of Friar's Balsam in hot water. Once their heads were under the blanket he introduced a rubber hose attached to the gas tap and waited for them to collapse; then he raped and strangled them. The bodies were found by his landlord in a large kitchen cupboard after Christie had left the house, and for days the newspapers were filled with the hunt for the sex murderer.

These murders seemed to symbolise for me the sordidness and futility of my life in the hospital. I drove myself on by willpower, but I could not recover the delight and confidence of that summer of working on farms. I now often remembered that day of my last holiday with Mary, on the windy hillside in Derbyshire, and the sheer exultation I had felt as we were blown downhill. Was it, I wanted to know, possible to re-create this exultation at will?

And here I was in a job that brought me constantly into contact with sickness, aware of the moral consequences of our stagnation in the porters' room, and making no real effort to escape. My mind was like a wet tinderbox that no spark can ignite.

One day I met in Northumberland Avenue an old acquaintance, John Drury, from the Vaughan College in Leicester, who congratulated me on looking so healthy and full of energy. I was interested in this observation, for I had been deliberately driving myself for many months, refusing to acknowledge exhaustion; yet I was aware of an immense listlessness inside me.

Two events led to my deciding to leave the hospital and return to France. The first was renewed turbulence in the relationship with Betty. One weekend I went to Leicester and found that my parents had invited Betty – she was living again with her mother – in an attempt to reconcile us. They had put us into the same bed but I was determined not to make love. Then, halfway through the night, I woke up with my penis erect and tingling with excitement. Betty was lying on her back, and I realised that her finger was touching my penis. From this there was an electrical flow of energy. It was obvious that she was fast asleep. Then after perhaps ten minutes, she raised her knees, and I reached out and let my hand rest on the stretched cotton at the bottom of her nightdress. Another five minutes, and she had stretched out her legs again, so my hand took the nightdress with it. I touched her between the thighs, and found she was completely moist. Afraid of waking her, I climbed on top of her, and my penis slid inside her. She woke up and said: 'What are you doing?' and I felt like laughing and saying: 'What the hell do you think?' Then she became excited too, and I reached orgasm before I could withdraw. She said: 'I wasn't prepared.'

At that moment Roderick woke up, and Betty asked me to go downstairs and warm the bottle. While I waited for the water to boil, I sat on the back doorstep, and reflected that I seemed to be caught in the spider's web again.

The next day, I took Roderick out for a walk in his pram. I walked over Spinney Hill Park, then decided to go and show the baby to Millicent, who lived nearby. I knew, of course, that Betty disliked her – for revealing the secret of why we got married – but felt sure she could hardly object to me taking my eighteen-month-old son to see her.

I was wrong. When I got back she was furious, and snatched up Roderick and marched off home, leaving me baffled at the sheer illogicality of the reaction – after all, Roderick could not even talk. However, I followed her, and we had a reconciliation, and agreed to make a joint effort to find a home for ourselves in London.

I was not entirely happy about this, for while I loved my wife and son I had no particular wish to repeat the experience of the previous year. However, Betty borrowed money from her mother; I registered with an agency that offered to find us a flat for five pounds, and we started the search for a home again. The agency offered us a flat in Forest Gate, East London. I went to see it and liked it; they wanted one hundred and twenty pounds for 'furniture and fittings', but the rent was low – two pounds ten shillings a week. I gave the agent a cheque for fifty pounds as a deposit, and sent for Betty to come and see it.

She was reluctant – she thought the premium high, and was suspicious of the terms of the agreement: the lessor refused to allow her to take the agreement to a solicitor. However, she finally agreed to the price, and returned to Leicester.

Later the same day, back in my hospital room, I received a telegram from her telling me that she had changed her mind, and wanted to call the whole thing off. I was furious. I had taken a great liking to the woman who offered us the flat – a plump Irish Catholic who was completely charming – and had told her that we would quite definitely be taking it. I sent her Betty's telegram, with a letter of apologies – she returned our fifty pounds by the next post – and I wrote to Betty saying that if she wanted a flat now, she could look for it herself. But I suspect I was also relieved that things had turned out as they had.

I had another reason for wanting to leave London. Exhaustion was bringing on curious attacks of dizziness, probably due to low blood pressure, like the one I had experienced as a teenager in Leicester. One day in my bedroom in the hospital, I stood up and yawned. Everything dissolved; in a half-conscious state I groped about the floor, aware of a curious trickling noise in my head and ears, and of separation from my body and all I called 'myself'. My identity dissolved; there was nothing left to hang on to; I was 'conscious, but conscious of nothing'. Then my head cleared, but as I went downstairs to work, the ordinary world seemed a mockery, a pointless ritual of machines.

A few days later it happened again, on the deserted upper deck of a bus, as I was returning from seeing Laura in Cheam. I stretched and yawned, and became unconscious. I knew that this was because I was causing the blood to rush from my brain, but this was no answer to the sense of horror, the feeling that all human life was futile.

It occurred once more when I returned home late one night, a little drunk, and lay in bed in the warm darkness. Abruptly, I felt a sense of the absurdity of being there. It was suddenly very clear. I wanted to ask: who am I? What am I doing here? What lies beyond life? We take this world in which we live for granted, as if it were the most ordinary and reasonable thing to be alive. What guarantee have we that we are not sitting in an execution chamber? For us, 'life' is all there is, but we are not afraid because there is always some alternative, some 'beyond' around the corner. But since we are living beings, what alternative is there to life? I suddenly felt like a rat in a trap, and it seemed that our stupidity and incomprehension were all that lay between us and some ultimate horror.

The irony was that all these questions were irrelevant to my life. If the foreman said: 'Why are you looking ill this morning?' could I reply: 'Because I suspect that all life is false' or 'Because I suspect you are a delusion of my brain'?

As I saw it: we cannot live except as human beings, pursuing the human ritual; all we do must be 'human'; we must travel along our tramline of time, and make time pass by various purposes that all relate to other people. We seem to be individuals; in fact, we cannot even breathe for ourselves; every act of self-expression of which we are capable is a human, a social, act.

It seemed to me that I was like a slot machine, standing on some corner and believing itself free, believing that it stands there of its own free will and disgorges each packet of cigarettes by an act of volition. Suddenly I had realised that 'I' was wholly mechanical, depending entirely on coins inserted by other people, that therefore no act of mine was meaningful, that I could claim to be nothing more than an observer, a witness of life, consciousness trapped in matter but completely helpless – helpless even to observe except by the body's grace, which might cut off consciousness at any moment.

Plainly, there was nothing to be done about such a vision, but it saps the delusions that keep us moving. It seemed to me that the only sensible alternatives were suicide or leaving the hospital. Neither would be as sensible as simply not being, but since I 'was', I had no choice in the matter.

I sold all my books at Foyle's, collected together all the money I could muster, and wrote to Betty to tell her that I was on my way to France. (This meant that, technically speaking, I had 'left' her, although we had in fact been separated for nine months.) I spent a night sleeping on the floor of Bill's office in Southwark, and hitch-hiked toward Dover at a leisurely pace the next day. The following night I slept in a wood near Canterbury – in a sleeping bag, of course – and was up early the next morning, prepared to see what life had to offer next.

CHAPTER 6

Joy

By midday I was back in France. This time, I had a little more money than I had had before – a few pounds. I went into a restaurant in a great barnlike place near the docks, and ordered a meal and some wine. I had not yet had breakfast. The wine soon made me drunk and happy; the place was decorated with paper streamers, and the radio was playing Spanish music very loud. I was given an immense and tender steak. For the first time for a year – it seemed to be many years – the joy welled up in me, the strength of the powerhouse, as it had on the windy Derbyshire hillside, and I was certain I had made the right decision in leaving England. I felt that the gods were back with me again, and had sent me this glimpse of power as a sign of approval. I was in Spain and Calais and all over Europe at the same time; I could catch history like a bus.

Two days later I arrived in Paris, and went straight to the room of Claude Guillaume in the rue Bayen. He no longer lived there, but his mother kept the room on for her occasional visits to Paris. The concierge had been told to give me the key; so I moved in.

The first problem was to find some way of making a living. It looked as if I might have found a solution on my first evening in Paris, when I saw an advertisement for a new American magazine called the *Paris Review*. I went to visit the editor in his office in the rue Garanciere; he proved to be a clean-cut young American called George Plimpton.

George suggested that I should sell subscriptions for the *Paris Review*, keeping a large share for myself. He supplied me with a list of Americans living in Paris, and a map of the city.

It seemed an excellent idea. The subscriptions cost a thousand francs each (about one pound in 1953), of which I would retain four hundred francs. This meant that I could live by selling only one or two subscriptions a day. I went back to the rue Bayen in a very cheerful frame of mind.

The next day I discovered that the work would be harder than I had anticipated. To begin with, the addresses on my list were often a long way apart: I would either have to pay heavily in bus fares, or walk. Secondly, very few Americans seemed to be interested in a new literary magazine. After a long day's work, and walking about twenty miles in oppressive heat, I had sold one subscription, but had spent about a thousand francs on cool drinks and bus fares. When the addresses were on the telephone, I tried ringing them up, but discovered that this method of approach was hardly ever successful; it was too easy for the potential client to make an excuse and hang up.

One American told me to call the next day at his office. But his home address happened to be very close to the rue Bayen, so I called there on the off chance of selling him a subscription on my way home. He came to the door and, when I told him my business, shouted: 'I thought I told you to come to my office! What the hell do you think I am! If you want to see me, you'll do it my way! Now get out!' He slammed the door in my face. I stood there, feeling the same hatred that I had once felt for the landlady at Courtfield Gardens, and invoking all the gods to bring on him the nastiest and messiest death possible. I went home wondering why it is that Americans can be the vilest and rudest people on earth, as well as the most charming.

After a few days I found various means of supplementing my income. The most useful was to sell individual copies of the magazine to possible subscribers who wanted more time to make up their minds. Many people were unwilling to part with a full year's subscription but were happy enough to buy a single copy. As far as my job went, this was strictly 'illegal', but I had to live; and I felt that George Plimpton had misled me about the profits to be made.

About two weeks after I arrived Laura wrote to me to say that Bill Hopkins might be on his way over to look for a French printer for the *Saturday Critic*. I spent the next day in my room, hoping he might turn up. I was glad enough of an opportunity to read poetry and Shaw's plays, for I detested knocking on doors. But there was no sign of him, so the next day I went out and left a note on the door, saying I would be back at six o'clock. Still no one came, so the next day, I stayed in, and read. Towards seven in the evening there was a faint knock on my door. It was Bill's friend Philip Veen, who told me that he and Bill had been waiting on the pavement downstairs all the afternoon. They had arrived at midday, seen my note (which I had forgotten to remove) and assumed I was not at home.

I was delighted to see them, for Paris had me in a defeated frame of mind. Bill, as usual, was a tonic. He also had no money. Philip had to return to London the following day – he had come for a weekend trip – and we discovered that we had just enough for his fare by clubbing together. Bill decided that he would stay in Paris and sell subscriptions with me until we had enough money to return to England. Things would be different now, he said; a little fast sales talk was all that was needed to make us rich.

In this he proved to be over-optimistic. We tried the address of every American in the Champs Élysées, sold half a dozen copies of the magazine, and took one or two subscriptions. But Bill was a non-stop smoker and I ate large quantities of chocolate, so the money soon vanished – including George Plimpton's share of the subscriptions. We saw George that evening and explained to him that we had been forced to 'borrow' the money, and handed him the addresses of the new subscribers. We were also introduced to the editors of the small English review called *Merlin* – and met a cadaverous young poet called Christopher Logue. We decided to add *Merlin* to our subscription drive, and equipped ourselves with a large armful of copies of the magazine. The *Merlin* subscriptions, like those for the the *Paris Review*, had to be impounded to feed us, but we did not starve.

We shared the room in the rue Bayen, taking turns sleeping on the bed. Bill is a night worker; he would often type (on *Time of Totality*, a novel that was never to be finished) until three in the morning, and then wake me up and insist on taking a walk round the empty boulevards.

In the long discussions on our temperaments and methods, each of us was frank about his low opinion of the other's approach. I felt, with instinctive resentment, that Bill was patronising me. Since I had worked for years on the assumption that I was the only important writer in Europe this astounded me. I was glad enough to acknowledge him as the only potentially great writer I had ever met, but to be aware that he did not regard me in the same light was irritating. Consequently, I was as candid as I could be about the defects of his own writing, about his lack of serious discipline, and about the time he wasted on trying to influence people directly – either by conversation or in the magazine – instead of concentrating on creating major works.

He in his turn declared that I was too subjective and introverted, and that this revealed my fear of having my conviction of superiority shattered by contact with other people.

We wrangled for days, and ended in a kind of agreement, both partially acknowledging the justice of the other's criticisms. We ended by achieving a degree of respect and liking for one another that has never changed. (After the success of *The Outsider*, a few mischief-making critics enjoyed suggesting that Bill was one of my 'followers', but this was as absurd as suggesting that I was one of his. We regarded one another in every sense as equals.)

We were also in agreement that a new phase of modern literature had begun when we decided to form an alliance. Certain misunderstandings were also aired and cleared up and all this left us feeling optimistic, and we often celebrated a long day of selling subscriptions with a few bottles of cheap wine at the expense of the *Paris Review*.

Still, this did nothing to advance the fortunes of the *Saturday Critic*. So after several weeks of working on our respective novels and drinking with the *Merlin* crowd in the Café Tournon, we decided that the British Consulate must once again be called upon for repatriation. It was a hard decision: I had come to Paris with every intention of living there. Chris Logue and the rest of the *Merlin* writers managed to make a thin living from teaching English, and they offered some helpful advice. (When Claude Guillaume arrived unexpectedly at the rue Bayen one day, Bill spent the following night sleeping – or trying to sleep – on Logue's floor, and listening to an interminable sonnet sequence until dawn. This, I think, hastened the decision to return to England.)

So in late November, after a mere two months in Paris, I returned. I had no heart for London, and in any case, had no money to find a room. I stayed for a few days with a Hungarian acquaintance, Alfred Reynolds, who had recently moved into a house in Dollis Hill; he ran a kind of humanistic political group which he called Bridge and preached a gospel of absolute tolerance to a group of young men once a week. I stayed long enough to attend one meeting, decided that this kind of vague and unspecific tolerance had nothing to teach me, and went on to Leicester.

The Labour Exchange directed me to Lewis's, the department store in the centre of town. They needed temporary salesmen for the Christmas rush and I was allotted to the carpet department.

I had come to Leicester hoping vaguely that fate might have changed its policy towards me. It seemed to me that I had been a dissatisfied wanderer for as long as I could remember, either enduring futile jobs, or drifting at a loose end. I felt myself a perpetual misfit. And yet it was not because I had the temperament of a drifter or a bohemian. All I wanted was a room lined with books and enough money to live on tinned tomatoes and fried eggs. But for years now, the pattern of my life had been repetitive: finding myself in situations that grew slowly unbearable, breaking away, and then landing in another situation that slowly went sour.

The trouble, I suppose, was my introversion. Life in modern society means mixing with other people, and I didn't want to. The few jobs I had really enjoyed had been jobs in which I was allowed to work alone – at Frazer and Glass, in North Finchley, I had worked in a spraying shed half a mile from the main factory, and often saw no one all day. The woven rug business I had tried to set up with Betty would have been ideal. As it was, I saw I was going to be forced to stick at jobs until they bored me, then go and look for another.

Still, working at Lewis's was not disagreeable. The manager questioned me for half an hour on the morning I applied for the job; he was obviously rather intrigued by someone who had moved around as much as I had. But he ended by taking me on, emphasising that it was on a temporary basis – for I was obviously not 'respectable', and didn't even possess a suit. The work was enjoyable enough. The Christmas rush kept us busy. The loudspeakers blared carols all day, and I liked the other salesmen in my department.

My first day was spent in a classroom at the top of the building, learning to use a cash register. There were two other trainees: one was a mild youth whom I have forgotten, the other, a young army officer named Martin Halliday, who had a square, clean-cut face, close-cropped blond hair, and a public school accent.

I found the girl who taught us about the cash register intriguing. Travelling up to the classroom in the lift, it had struck me that she was vaguely the same type as Betty, although the oval face reminded me of Mary. In profile, she was not especially pretty, her nose being perhaps too Roman, but as soon as she smiled, this impression vanished, for her smile was dazzling, and gave an impression of extraordinary sweetness and good temper.

I expected her to have the awful Leicester accent, which I hated, but when she spoke her accent was that of a well-educated middle-class girl, although completely free of the nasal drawl to which well-educated young women are prone.

I was more interested in watching her than listening to what she had to say about the cash register; she was slim, rather tall for a girl, and had a graceful way of moving. The ex-army type remarked afterwards that he liked the way she braced her legs slightly apart, and turned from the waist to gesture towards the board behind her. It made the black skirt stretch across the thighs in an interesting manner, so that one couldn't help speculating what she would look like without it. I thought I noticed a wedding ring on her finger, and remember thinking that she must give her husband a great deal of pleasure. Mrs Batty, the lady in charge of the teaching department, called her 'Miss Stewart', but that meant nothing, since all the girls were addressed as 'Miss'.

As I watched her, my heart sank. Two or three years earlier I would have become hopelessly infatuated, but now I realised there was probably no point, and suppressed the feeling immediately. Six months' frustrating pursuit of Laura had taught me that much self-discipline.

At lunchtime, I ate in the staff canteen with Halliday, and found him interesting. He also had the rolling-stone temperament. He had spent three years in the army – after the war, of course – having trained at Sandhurst. He liked the army; he liked the idea of discipline. Civilians struck him as unbearably sloppy. (He stared with disapproval at my chin – I had not bothered to shave that morning.) He suspected that life as a civilian was going to be tiresomely devoid of challenge.

We discussed our teacher. He told me her name was Joy, and that she was a friend of the girl he was at present hoping to get into bed – another trainee manager called Pat. Joy was apparently not married, but she was engaged to someone she had been at university with, and expected to marry him soon. (I must have mistaken the engagement ring for a wedding ring.) That was much as I expected; girls like that were not left lying around for long. Joy and her fiancé intended to move to Canada where they would be married.

That evening, when I left work, Halliday suggested we go and have a drink. I didn't have much money, but I could afford a couple of pints, so we went into the hotel opposite Lewis's. When we had both drunk a pint, he seemed to relax and become happier. He told me to call him Flax – the nickname was obviously due to the colour of his hair – and we ordered a second pint; he also insisted on buying two whiskies. Obviously, he missed the companionship of the officers' mess; I was a second-best, but better than nothing.

There began immediately a kind of 'will-to-power' struggle between us. I agreed that discipline was important, but I detested the armed forces and everything to do with them. The only kind of discipline that mattered was the self-discipline of dedicated men. T. E. Lawrence proved that the intellectual will-to-power could be geared to physical purposes, but the physical will-to-power cannot rise above its own level.

Flax disagreed with me; he said he had never met an intellectual who was not also a weakling. We went on arguing, and we moved to another pub, where we ate sandwiches, for which he paid – I had now run out of money. I found his mystique of power interesting. He had noted that certain army officers, sons of rich or titled men, seemed to give orders without effort, and were obeyed mainly because they took it for granted they would be. One day in the mess, the son of a duke had called across to him: 'Halliday, get some more drinks,' and he was on his way back with the tray before it struck him that the form of the request had been hardly polite, and that he ought to have been offended.

He was intelligent: there could be no doubt about that. I argued – we were in our third pub – that physical existence was futile and repetitive, and that only the power of the mind could leave a permanent mark on human existence. He then began to expound his own metaphysical theory: that acquired experience was not lost, that in some strange way every evolutionary advance made by every living creature was stored up in a kind of universal computer, and the computer might be what the mystics call God. It was a curious kind of monistic idealism.

He suggested we go back to his place, where he had some bottled beer.

It was a house in New Walk, within easy reach of Leicester's town centre; the upstairs was unoccupied and Flax lived in a single room with an attached kitchen downstairs. We stood in the upstairs room in the freezing darkness, and watched the woman in the next house undressing. He told me she always did it about the same hour, without drawing the curtains, and he strongly suspected that she knew he watched her. In fact, when she had finished, he openly turned on the light before we went downstairs to a sandwich and more beer.

There he went on outlining his basic power theory: his notion that the force that holds society together is the will of dominant human beings, and that this will is fundamentally mystical in nature. He cited Hitler as an example, and later gave me his copy of *Mein Kampf* inscribed 'Halliday to Wilson'. He felt that the foundation of modern society is rotten, since our civilisation fails to provide enough challenge for the men of power, and a man can develop only through surmounting a series of challenges. (I noted here the same basic frustration I had observed in Irmgard.)

He spoke with admiration of certain officers who played Russian roulette with a revolver, or who would offer to prove they were not drunk by spreading their fingers out on a tabletop and stabbing between them at an incredible speed with a sharp stiletto. He told me that one of them had missed, and pinned his hand to the table. He produced his own army revolver, and told me that he had once played Russian roulette with it. Then, as he sat fingering it, he asked me casually to pass him a pipe that lay on the floor beside my chair. As I bent over, there was a deafening explosion, and the wood of the cupboard near my nose splintered. I picked up the pipe and handed it to him as if nothing had happened. 'Hmmm, your nerves are good,' he said, peering into the smoking revolver.

The will-to-power argument led on to sex, a subject that fascinated him above all others. A healthy male is naturally a stallion, he explained (a view with which Bill Hopkins would have concurred). There is a magic about women that touches his deepest springs of will. ('What is life without conquest?' I had made Jesus ask, in a story I had written about the crucifixion.) But no one has ever written honestly about this aspect of sex – certainly not Lawrence or Joyce.

Artists were not qualified to write about it, Flax insisted, because they were basically weak, romantic. Who had ever really written honestly about the details of seduction, the physical minutiae; about the way that a girl may allow a man to slip his hand into the waist of her skirt at the back as he is kissing her; and, if she is not wearing an underskirt, into the elastic of her knickers? This strikes her as natural, while an attempt to fondle her breast or unzip her skirt might frighten her into frigidity. If the skirt waistband is elasticated, she might even allow him to caress her buttocks, still without feeling that he is going too far.

In the same way, girls feel it less of a liberty for a man to kiss their breasts than to caress them. A shy girl in a swimsuit would not be unduly alarmed if the man she had only allowed to kiss her goodnight placed his head on her breasts, then turned sideways and pressed his lips to them, then slipped off the shoulder strap so he could suck the nipple. It is his hands she worries about, then his penis, and it never strikes her that his mouth, used upon her breasts or genitals, can bring about her undoing more effectively than either of these.

(I later put a portrait of Flax into a book of mine called *The World of Violence*, and included some of his sexual theories; but my publisher cut them out.)

I left him after the last bus had gone, and walked unsteadily home. He reminded me of certain officers described in Russian fiction of the nineteenth century: Pushkin's Herman, Tolstoy's Dologhov, Lermontov's Pechorin. And the significant thing about these three is that they are basically tragic. Flax was basically a nineteenth-century romantic.

I was sorry when our brief training period in the classroom was over, since it meant that I would have no more opportunity to see Joy. But at coffee break that morning, I was sitting with Flax when she came in. Flax asked her to come and sit with us. I said very little; I was more interested in listening to the sound of her voice, and watching the smiles that transformed her face as completely as sunlight passing over a lake. Flax seemed to be on familiar terms with her; he addressed her as 'Joy' and asked after the health of her 'rock-tapper' – her fiancé was apparently a geologist.

I remember looking at her and thinking: a few years ago, I would have allowed myself to get completely moonstruck by her; now I have enough self-discipline to know there is no point in wanting something you can't have. I envied Flax his bachelor's flat; he was already working out the details of his plan of campaign to seduce Joy's friend Pat in several easy stages. The first was to get Joy to join the two of us for a drink, and then invite her back to the flat. Then Pat could be asked back too. And then perhaps the two girls might be persuaded to stay there over a weekend.

When Flax left me alone with Joy for a moment, I asked her when she had left university. She said a year before. 'How old are you?' I asked, half-expecting her to tell me to mind my own business, but she said, 'Twenty-one.' I was astonished. Perhaps because she reminded me in some respects of Betty, perhaps because of her poise and self-possession, I had assumed her to be in her mid-twenties. If she was younger than I, perhaps the poise was only skin-deep, and I could make some impression after all.

Later that day, I had an idea. Why not organise some kind of Christmas show – perhaps a production of the *Twentieth Century Revue* that I had written for the anarchists, or my *Metal Flower Blossom* – and try to get her to take a part in it? It would enable me to see her without having to rely on Flax. I already felt that he was capable of being capricious.

At the next opportunity, I suggested the idea to the manager. He agreed immediately – on condition that he be allowed to see the script. I then approached Joy. She seemed doubtful; she said she couldn't act, but would perhaps take a minor part. I chortled, and put on Bill's favourite expression of the villain alternately twisting his moustache and rubbing his hands.

I went along to see Betty at her home near Hinckley, and there was vague talk of living together again. But when a relationship has been broken and stuck together again as many times as ours had, it becomes as unserviceable as a patched saucepan.

Thinking back on our quarrels, I suddenly recognised their basic cause. It was an insight I owed to Flax: it was all a question of dominance. I suppose that I take after my father in being of fairly high dominance. Betty's nine-year seniority and her years of independence had also developed a dominance in her that was acquired, a shield against the world rather than something natural. It overlaid her naturally feminine and dependent personality. The Betty I loved was the feminine essence; the Betty with whom I quarrelled was the dominant alter ego.

Now I thought about it, this question of dominance seemed the key to a great deal of human nature. The inner conflicts of my teens had been due to my attempt to turn my dominance inwards, into ideas. The weight of my literary talent was due to this dominance turned into ideas. Like Flax, I had a natural tendency to feel that all artists or thinkers must be sissies. As a child I had been a good scrapper and a natural leader, although I hated sport. I had inherited from my father a natural ability to use my fists, and he had even tried to teach me the rudiments of boxing. Under different circumstances, perhaps in a different age, I would have developed naturally into a man of action. The dominance had turned inwards, and I was outwardly mild and unquarrelsome. So I fitted easily into ordinary jobs, and at first my employers were always impressed by my intelligence, which seemed to predict that I would go far. But the dominance unfitted me for ordinary work: it made me contemptuous of the people I worked with, who – aware only of the mild exterior – reacted by feeling a natural resentment.

Obviously, the dominance syndrome explained my complex relation with Bill Hopkins; it also explained why I found Flax interesting. We were amusing each other with a game of clash of wills, like a friendly sparring match; and every time I looked at him, I could see that, under different circumstances – perhaps if, like Flax, I had been born of middle-class parents – I might have been very much like him.

The dominance syndrome certainly explained why Shaw meant more to me than any other writer; all his plays are about the clash of wills; and one in particular – *Major Barbara* – is about the clash between a man whose dominance has been directed mainly at other people (Undershaft), and a man in whom it has been forced inwards into intellectuality (Cusins). And significantly, Shaw writes of the latter that the 'chronic strain . . . has visibly wrecked his constitution'. My health was, fortunately, still unimpaired, except for stomach upsets, but it would obviously not remain unimpaired if the chronic strain of unfulfilment lasted too long.

The dominance theory also explained why Joy attracted me so enormously. A few evenings after I started at Lewis's, she came out for a drink with the two of us, and we ended back in Flax's place. In close contact with her, it was easy to see that the soft voice and the sweet smile indicated her basic disposition: gentle, good-tempered and – oddly enough – rather vague. She seemed unoffendable. At one point in the evening, Flax asked her casually: 'Are you still a virgin, Joy?' and she looked embarrassed and said, 'That's the kind of thing I don't talk about,' but she said it without reproach, almost apologetically. Her background was middle-class: her father was an accountant; she had attended Trinity College, Dublin, taken a degree in French, and got engaged to an Irishman with the same kind of background as herself. The apparent grace and poise were natural, not acquired, and they concealed her shyness. Like myself, she had spent a great deal of her childhood curled up in corners with a book. She was lucky that she possessed this natural poise that concealed the fundamental romanticism, and made her seem relaxed and efficient.

On our first afternoon off – on early closing day – I asked Joy to come to the home of Stanley Rosenthal, the painter, and I read her the first two acts of *The Metal Flower Blossom*. She said she couldn't imagine the manager of Lewis's allowing it to be performed there, but the afternoon served the purpose of placing me in a direct relation with her, instead of having to use Flax as an intermediary. I couldn't invite her back to my home: with my sister Susan and my brothers Barry and Rodney there would be nowhere in the house where I might get her alone, although in recent years my mother had managed to furnish the front room, which had always been empty during my childhood. Besides, my parents wanted a reconciliation with Betty; Joy would hardly have been welcome.

It was on that afternoon, leaving Stanley Rosenthal's, that I remember looking at Joy and thinking: I wonder what it would be like to be married to her? and trying to envisage a future with her. It was only a casual daydream, and it seemed about as unlikely as anything I could think of.

Subsequently, I introduced her to other friends: to my homosexual friend Alan (who disliked her, but not as much as he had disliked Mary), to the poet Maurice Willows, and to John Crabbe, a new acquaintance – a man of my own age, who looked at least forty, with a small moustache and the mild eyes of Wells's Mr Polly. Crabbe was a music lover; he had a record player and access to complete operas on LP (which was fairly new at the time, and which struck me as miraculous). I spent long evenings with him, listening to the complete *Bohème*, *Flying Dutchman* and *Meistersinger*, and the symphonies of Brahms and Beethoven. I took Joy there one evening to listen to opera, and to read her – and John Crabbe – some of my favourite poems (I was much given to reading poetry aloud in those days – with Yeats, Eliot and Rupert Brooke at the top of the list, and Wilfred Owen's 'Exposure' a special favourite). Walking home with her, I reached down for her hand, but she was wearing a coat with turned-up cuffs, like a highwayman's, and my hand found its way into this, and I groped bemusedly. At this point, she decided to help me, and offered her hand. I had no idea whether she regarded this as a light flirtation, to be kept strictly within the bounds of decorum, or whether she was really interested in me. But I was beginning to hope.

On the next occasion I called for her, her landlady told me she was still in the bath, and asked me if I would wait. She did not invite me to wait inside, so I stood on the doorstep, my coat collar turned up. When Joy came down she said, 'I'm so sorry,' and gave me her hands completely naturally.

Otherwise, she was not particularly encouraging. But I had grown used to Betty's shyness and detachment, so this didn't bother me. My own intentions were still not definite; my emotions were uncommitted. She was due to go to Canada in a few months to get married, and in all probability she would do so; there was no point in building plans around her.

But there came an evening when I decided that, if it was possible, I would persuade her out of the marriage. We were crossing Victoria Park in the dark, and I asked her what books she had in Leicester with her – her home at the time was near Peterborough. She listed Yeats's poems and plays, Proust (in French), Virginia Woolf, and *Ulysses*. Most of the attractive girls I had known had been definitely unliterary; and the few literary ones had been unattractive. Even Betty, who was intelligent enough in a practical way, had never really shared my interest in literature and ideas. Plainly, if I intended to settle with a girl, Joy would be about as close to the ideal as I could find.

Flax and I continued to play the dominance game. The steeple of the nearby St Margaret's Church was being repaired, and there was some scaffolding. One icy night, Flax proposed that we should climb it. In childhood I had been terrified of heights, but I was not now willing to acknowledge this. We clambered up the ladder, and then up the scaffolding round the steeple. When I made the mistake of looking down, my stomach seemed to fall into the void below, and I had a terrifying sense that only the grip of my hands prevented me from landing on those hard paving stones. I decided it was better not to think about it, and completed the climb to the top.

After an exploit like this, Flax and I were on extremely close terms, the dominance question having sunk temporarily into abeyance.

I introduced him to Alan, Maurice Willows, John Crabbe and Stanley Rosenthal. I wanted to make the point that external dominance can turn into intellectuality. Obviously, he considered them all weaklings. He dismissed Alan as a bitchy queer. It would have been interesting to see what would have happened if Flax and Bill Hopkins had come together.

Joy was right when she told me that the manager would never pass *Metal Flower Blossom* for performance, and he was equally definite about the *Twentieth Century Revue* when he came to the poem about homosexual elephants.

It was true that I had now achieved my purpose in getting close to Joy, even to the extent of being allowed to kiss her goodnight, but I didn't like to admit defeat about the show, so I suggested that we do the first act of *Man and Superman*. The manager found this unexceptionable, so we put it into rehearsal, with Joy playing Ann. We used to rehearse at the Capital T, the temperance club in Granby Street. When Joy and I went into the dark backyard for our bicycles, I would seize the opportunity to kiss her. She always struggled and protested, but could not have really objected, or she would have stopped going into the yard with me.

I suppose the turning point in our relation was when Flax persuaded her and Pat to spend the weekend at his flat, with me as a fourth. The original idea had been to seduce Pat that weekend, but she had ceded her virtue several evenings earlier. Flax told me how, as he lay beside her in a state of sexual excitement, she had masturbated him to a climax, then smiled at him triumphantly. But his virility had been equal to the challenge and he had another erection within ten minutes.

We all worked Saturday, of course. On Saturday evening, we went to Flax's house, taking beer, wine and food. The two girls prepared a meal; I read them the latest chapter of *Ritual*. Afterwards we went to the pub and had more to drink, then came back and talked until the early hours of the morning.

Pat and Flax got into bed together; Joy and I lay on two mattresses in front of the fire, each with a blanket. We were both fully dressed. After the fire had burned low enough to make us invisible to the occupants of the bed, I moved under her blanket and spread mine over us. As we lay there in the firelight, I whispered that I thought she was the most marvellous girl I had ever met. I saw from her smile that she wanted to believe I meant it.

It was a night of virtue; I sensed that she did not want me to try to force her in any way. I didn't mind; it was a considerable advance to sleep under the same blanket, even if she pushed my hand away when I tried to put it up her skirt.

The four of us spent Sunday together, talking, cooking meals, taking walks and drinking in the local pubs, and late in the evening we separated. When Flax saw me alone on Monday, he asked me what kind of knickers Joy wore; I said I didn't know. He shook his head sadly, and confided that Pat had started wearing winter woollies, which were a sexual depressant.

Man and Superman was finally performed (the first act only) in the canteen a few days before Christmas. It was, on the whole, disappointing. I knew Tanner's part by heart, and even acted it quite well, since I had seen Clements play it at least a dozen times. But at the last minute the actor who was to play Octavius let us down. A poet called Barry Hipwell – a friend of Maurice Willows – agreed to take the part at short notice, but since he could not possibly learn the lines, he had to read them from the book, which spoiled the effect. Joy, being shy, was as bad an actress as she had said. The audience – mostly consisting of the girls who served behind the counters – stared at us in a baffled manner. Luckily, we had two excellent comics in the second part of the show – both from the carpet department; one looked and sounded like Arthur Askey, the other did Red Skelton's routine of Guzzler's Gin. The audience livened up and began applauding all the turns enthusiastically, so that the evening ended in an atmosphere of Christmas cheer.

Flax and I had something like a quarrel on Christmas Eve. There was a dance for Lewis's employees, held in the Bell Hotel opposite the shop; I naturally took Joy. Towards the end of the evening, after calling in at a few pubs, we walked home up New Walk, and I decided – against Joy's advice – to knock on Flax's door. Just as we were about to go away, a light came on and we heard a female voice. Then Flax appeared, looking bad-tempered. He said, 'Oh, it's you, Wilson. Would you mind going away,' and slammed the door. I was furious, and even angrier that something like this had happened in front of Joy. Flax and I were back on speaking terms after Christmas; but it was impossible to think of him as a friend any more. Bill Hopkins would have been incapable of this kind of rudeness – as I would myself.

Joy went away for Christmas, then to Southampton to see her fiancé off to Canada. When she came back, I thought she seemed subdued; I put this down to a feeling of guilt about me. She had probably rationalised her relationship with me by arguing that she could not be expected to spend six months in Leicester without friends, and that she had not encouraged me. What I did not know was that the relationship with her future husband had imperceptibly weakened during a year she had spent teaching in France, and that the relationship with me had made her aware of this. Being a vague sort of girl, she preferred to avoid conflict, but a point would obviously arrive when she had to make up her mind.

Now Christmas was over, the manager called me to his office, and pointed out that I had been taken on in a temporary capacity, and that I had promised to buy a suit. What did I intend to do – buy a suit and stay on, or leave? I was feeling restless again, and besides, I had been selling rugs to some of my relatives at cost price, and this was bound to appear in the stocktaking. So I said I would leave. I had already decided to return to London.

The episode on Christmas Eve might have ended my relation with Flax, but he had persuaded Joy and a trainee named June to take his upstairs rooms as a flat. They needed redecorating, and I offered to do it. And so, when I left my work at Lewis's, I delayed taking a job for another week, and spent the time painting the walls and ceilings. I knew June well, having worked with her and taken her to the Capital T on a couple of occasions. Although she was engaged to be married, our relationship was vaguely flirtatious.

Maurice Willows proposed giving a New Year party, and Joy and I were invited. By this time, I was pressing her to leave Leicester and come to London with me, but so far she had refused flatly. But John Crabbe, to whom I'd mentioned the idea, showed unexpected insight when he said: 'Don't worry. She will.'

Joy and I went to the New Year party at Maurice's on Saturday evening, after work. We had bicycles, but Maurice announced that anyone who wanted to could sleep on the floor. I tried to persuade Joy to stay, but she said no. We had an argument about it in the corridor. She told me later that at this point, I seized her face between my hands and banged her head several times on the wall. If this is so, I had drunk more than usual; I cannot recollect it. Apparently this gentle persuasion made her decide to stay.

Again, we slept on the floor, covered with a blanket – again, fully clothed. But she made no resistance when I reached up the back of the skirt and put my hand on her knickers. I felt it a major step forward. If she made a habit of sleeping with me, even fully clothed, she could hardly persist in the belief that she was not encouraging me.

I spent the following day decorating the flat. Joy had gone home for the day, and I met her off the train in the early evening. She came and joined me and cooked me a meal. Afterwards we lay on a bad settee, kissing, but she strenuously resisted my attempt to unzip her jeans. Finally, mildly exasperated, I said: 'Don't you care for me at all?' She said nothing for a long time and I repeated the question. Finally, she said, almost inaudibly: 'Yes.' I said: 'Good. Then you'd better come to London and break off your engagement.' And although I had to return home that night, I felt a sense of deep satisfaction.

The next day, a Monday, Joy went to work, and I again spent the day decorating the flat. In the evening she once again joined me and cooked a meal. It came to the time for her to go home, and I knew this would be crucial. I had made up a mattress for myself on the floor; I asked her to stay too. She said she couldn't – her landlady would begin to wonder what was happening. I pointed out that she was leaving shortly anyway. Finally she agreed, and then, to my delight, removed her skirt before getting into bed. (Since she had to go to work in it, she could hardly sleep in it.) As she climbed between the sheets in her underwear I couldn't believe my luck – I said later that I felt like a cat that has been given a whole chicken.

Sensing her nervousness I made no attempt to force her. In fact, I was delighted just to lie there kissing her. My marriage had left me with certain sexual inhibitions – for on one occasion when I had ejaculated prematurely Betty had burst into tears. So in bed with Joy, what Viktor Frankl calls 'the law of reverse effort' operated in my favour. (Frankl was the Viennese psychologist who realised that when a stutterer is *asked* to try and stutter, he is suddenly unable to stutter – obviously because the tension that causes the stutter has now disappeared.) Knowing that Joy was nervous removed my own inhibitions.

In any case, it was such an intoxicating sensation lying beside Joy that I wanted nothing more. It seemed incredible that, only six weeks earlier, I had felt my heart sink as I looked at her, feeling she was one of the most desirable girls I had ever seen, and now she was in bed with me without any clothes on. (I had soon removed the rest.) It was one of those moments when all life seems wonderful, and I was carried away by sheer delight.

This was not primarily sexual, although obviously there was a sexual element in it; it was one of those moments when you feel that the gods are on your side, and that life is wholly good. I felt as Van Gogh probably felt as he painted *The Starry Night* – total affirmation. It seemed appropriate that her name was Joy; no one had ever given me such joy.

She had gone when I woke up next morning – she had to return to her room to change before going to work. At mid-morning, I cycled down to Lewis's to join her for the coffee break, and I noted my feelings with interest. It was a revival of what I had felt during the early months of my marriage to Betty – the same comfortable sense of not being alone any more. Although I had only kissed Joy, I had a sense of being married to her; what had happened the previous night was like an exchange of rings. She also seemed quite different as we drank coffee together; she knew that something had changed permanently.

When I suggested that she ought to write to her fiancé to explain that she had changed her mind, she said, 'Yes, I suppose I ought.' It was also settled that she would come to London. I did not press her too hard; I could see she was worried and self-divided. But I was certain of one thing: we were in it together now.

I found a job in a boot-and-shoe factory. It paid well, which was the main thing I was interested in. The work was very hard. I was doing a job called 'bottom polishing': a man to my left pushed a trolley full of shoes at me; I had to polish the soles and hand them on to a man on my right; all three were geared together, and we were all on piecework, being paid by quantity. At the end of the day, I ached from head to foot. The machines pounded; considerable force had to be used in holding the shoes against the brushes revolving at a high speed; if my grip relaxed, the shoe flew out of my hand and across the room.

I went to see Joy that evening. She was not yet in, but Flax was; he invited me in for a beer. When Joy came, she made food for the two of us. Flax was talking about his increasing boredom in his job, the craving for action. The previous Saturday, two teddy boys had got into an argument with him in the shop. He told them he would see them on the car park next door at six o'clock, and they were waiting for him. It was the kind of situation he loved: he left them both half-unconscious, and the memory of it was obviously a source of satisfaction, although his knuckles were skinned. As we talked about the need for action, Flax said: 'I think I'll go for a run. Care to come?'

It was the old dominance game. I said 'All right,' and changed into running kit which he provided. 'To the Stoneygate Terminus and back?' That was about two miles along the London Road. He even persuaded Joy to come with us, and she ran alongside with an easy, graceful stride. When we reached the terminus, Flax said: 'Let's go on to Great Glen, Ok?' That was another five miles. I agreed. Joy went back home by bus, promising to make us coffee, and we ran on, up the hill past the racecourse and along the double concrete highway.

I remembered from my old running days at school that the important thing was to get the body into a machine-like rhythm, ignore the pain in your side, and wait for second wind. My second wind came some time before we reached Great Glen. As we ran into the village, I saw there was a bus waiting there. But Flax said, 'Round the island and straight back, all right?' I was too winded to do anything but nod.

Long before we reached Leicester, I was wondering what would happen if I slowed to a walk for a moment. I could not feel my legs; they had become numb, and so had my lungs, but my legs were obviously working. I had a floating, detached feeling; my body was carrying on without me. Then, at the top of the hill by the racecourse, I saw a bus at the Stoneygate terminal, the last bus of the evening. I pointed to it and shouted: 'Let's run and catch it?' He nodded, and we sprinted downhill as the engine of the bus revved up. It started, and we made a last spurt; I jumped on board ahead of Flax. He waved ironically to me, and went on running. It was typical of him; the need to go one better at any cost.

Years later, Joy and I were in Edinburgh, having dinner with the bookseller Anthony d'Offay, who was selling some of my manuscripts to American universities. He had known Flax well in recent years, and mentioned the story of our run. I told him what had happened. He said, 'Then you didn't collapse?' I said no, I hadn't. 'That's odd. Flax said that when you were halfway back to Leicester, you had a blackout and fell down. He said, "Poor old Colin, he was game, but his body let him down." Are you sure you didn't collapse?'

I said I was sure, and Joy verified that I had arrived back twenty minutes or so before Flax. I had run a hot bath and climbed into it. Flax came in and joined me in it. We were both feeling pleased with ourselves, and for the rest of the evening we were on almost the same terms as before Christmas.

Flax and Pat had decided to get married; they certainly seemed to suit one another as well as Joy and I did. But Flax's will to power was still getting him into trouble.

On the evening Joy had slept on the mattress upstairs with me for the first time, he had been out at the engagement party of an old army friend who was marrying a beautiful model named Sybil, who worked at Lewis's demonstrating perfumes; she had apparently moved her lodgings only that afternoon. The party went on late, and the future bridegroom was in no condition to escort his fiancée home. Her new lodgings were somewhere near New Walk, so Flax and she shared a taxi. But when they got out in the street where she lived, she said she was unable to recognise the place in the dark, and she had left the address in her room. They walked up and down for half an hour, then Flax said she had better come and sleep at his place. Arriving back at three in the morning, he chuckled to see Joy's bicycle and mine still outside the door. Inevitably, he and Sybil shared the same bed, and she left early the next morning.

However, she left some hair pins in the bed, and Pat found them. There were also a few platinum blonde hairs on the pillow. Flax pleaded with her, but Pat said this was the end. In fact, she showed unusual strength of character in refusing to see him again. Her previous boyfriend had treated her badly, and no doubt she was determined not to repeat the disaster. Flax reconciled himself to Pat's defection by persuading Sybil to break off her engagement, and they were still together when I saw him some six months later in London.

My meeting with Joy represented a turning point for me. With her, I had a feeling that a permanent element in my life had fallen into place. Since I left school, my life had been an awkward, out-of-joint thing. My destiny was imposed on me by circumstances; the only part of it that really seemed to belong to me was my writing. The rest was often an irrelevant bore. Nothing ever went right for long. I was a clumsy person, always fated to knock things over. Yet I was basically optimistic, for I believed Pound when he wrote:

> What thou lov'st well remains, the rest is dross
> What thou lov'st well shall not be reft from thee
> What thou lov'st well is thy true heritage . . .

I also knew Auden's lines:

> Beloved, we are always in the wrong,
> Handling so clumsily our stupid lives,
> Suffering too little or too long,
> Too careful even in our selfish loves.

I had pursued science, then become a writer because I wanted to escape this sense of always being in the wrong, of clumsiness and stupidity; to impose order on a small area of my existence. Our vision of what we would like to be, and the actuality of our lives, always seem to be in conflict, until most of us end by accepting the compromise. Those who insist on clinging to their self-image in spite of reality often end in madhouses insisting they are Julius Caesar.

In my moments of depression, I often found myself wondering what happens if reality keeps on repelling your assaults on it, your attempts to impose your own terms? When did it first strike Keats's friend Benjamin Robert Haydon that he was not the world-shattering genius he always believed, that he was simply a painter of inflated and grandiose pictures? Or did it ever strike him? Human beings have many means of escaping the truth; I had been observing my fellow men for years, and meant one day to write a book called *The Methods and Techniques of Human Self-Deception*.

But here, with Joy, was at least one human relationship that seemed to conform with my inner world, with what I 'loved well'. She was like a sexual daydream come true. She accepted me at precisely my own valuation, as a child accepts parents. After two years with Betty I was touchy and tense, on the lookout for any hints of patronising superiority. With Joy, they never came.

I must admit that her sexual shyness also came as a relief. The Kay episode in London had forced me to recognise that my marriage had implanted an element of sexual self-doubt. 'Le fiasco' (as Stendhal called it) is a nervous ailment, like a stutter, and the more one worries about stuttering, the worse it is likely to become.

The limit of Joy's sexual experience so far had been a little petting. She didn't want to be hurried, and neither did I. We slept together as often as possible, but I was free of that sense that I had experienced in bed with Kay – that I was expected to demonstrate my masculinity. What made abstinence easier was that she was the most kissable and cuddly girl I had ever known; although slim, she was as soft and warm as a baby. I sometimes felt guilty at monopolising her.

After a few weeks of the shoe factory, I had had enough of Leicester. I had no special motive in moving to London; no nostalgia for Soho or the cast of *The Metal Flower Blossom*. But while life remained fundamentally unsatisfying, I had to keep moving.

CHAPTER 7

London and *The Outsider*

The next year in London was the worst so far. In spite of having found Joy, some demon with an ironic sense of humour was still driving me from pillar to post. I suspect it was trying to make a writer of me.

I found myself a room in Archway, in a house run by a Scotsman. I had hoped that a landlord might be preferable to a landlady, but I was soon disillusioned; he was as fussy and trivial-minded as any old woman.

I went to the Labour Exchange in North Finchley, and was directed to a job in a laundry. It was heavy work that involved loading wet laundry into spin dryers, and unloading it fifteen minutes later. I handled tons of wet linen a day.

Joy wrote to me often, but I now began to realise that one of the disadvantages of her sunny and easy-going personality was an extraordinary vagueness: she would forget to write for a week and I became convinced that something was wrong or that she had changed her mind about living in London. She finally came a month later, took a room in Fellowes Road, Chalk Farm, and found a job at Peter Robinson, a big store at Oxford Circus.

I found something frustrating in my relationship with her, something I could not define. I knew that she was not sure of me – Flax had warned her that I would leave her within six months – but this didn't explain it. I know now that the problem was that I had been used to Betty and, before that, to Mary; both of them rather insecure, craving affection, driven by strong emotions. By comparisson Joy seemed oddly understanding and this was because her early life had been so secure and conventional.

Like any middle-class young lady, she had learned to ride a horse, joined the local tennis club, and worn an evening gown to attend dances with young men in dinner jackets. Whenever she talked about her relatives, they sounded to me like characters out of *The Forsyte Saga*. Her life had flowed on like a quiet stream: a private school for young ladies (where the novelist

Beryl Bainbridge was a fellow pupil), university in Dublin, and weekends fishing on the west coast of Ireland.

She had spent a year as a teacher in France and, when I met her, was filling in time as a trainee manager, with every intention of getting married and settling down to a routine middle-class existence in Canada. I had disrupted this existence, made her take an irrevocable decision – she had written to break off her engagement. And I was touchy, impatient, arrogant and demonstrative, and inclined to bully her when she arrived an hour late or had me sitting by the telephone waiting for a call that, in her sweet vagueness, she had forgotten to make.

One rainy day in March I had just got out of the bath when my landlord told me there was someone to see. An elderly gentleman announced that he was Joy's father ('My name is Stewart, sir') and that he would like to speak to me. I invited him in; he said he would prefer that I came out to the car.

It was an unfortunate interview. Joy's parents had been shocked when she told them she had broken off her engagement – her future had seemed comfortably settled. They had looked through a suitcase she had left at home, and found some of my letters, 'devilishly clever letters', said her father sternly. As far as they could see, Joy had been lured astray by a plausible young rogue, a bohemian waster who no doubt only wanted to seduce her, or perhaps send her to work and live off her earnings.

What her father had to suggest was that I should change my address and never see Joy again (his actual words were: 'Get out of town, Wilson'); otherwise, they would take her back to Peterborough. I pointed out that that depended entirely on Joy: if she asked me to go away and never see her again, I would, but since I had persuaded her to come to London, I could hardly walk out on her simply because her parents disapproved of me. Anyway, what right had he to disapprove of me since he didn't know me? He said that my letters told him all that he needed to know – that I would obviously 'end in the gutter'.

To me it seemed an unreal situation. I could not take it seriously. I had told her father that I was in love with Joy because it seemed to be expected of me, but it was not wholly true. I was somehow not the sort of romantic to 'fall in love'; that was the kind of thing that happened to teenagers. She attracted me immensely, yet she seemed detached and undemonstrative. Surely all that had happened was that two people who strongly attracted one another had embarked on an affair, which might or might not last?

I had been in the car about half an hour, getting colder and colder. I was certain that I was developing a cold (and proved correct). I ended by telling her father that we were obviously never going to see eye to eye, and went indoors again.

I rang Joy and told her what had happened. In due course, her father arrived at her lodgings and placed the alternatives before her: to stop seeing me, or be taken home. After a long discussion, she was allowed to remain in London on condition that she promised never to visit me at my lodgings. When I went over to see her later on, I was furious: she was over twenty-one; what right had her parents to offer her ultimatums? I found it hard to understand that she didn't feel hostile toward them. She could see, of course, that they were simply worried; for all they knew, I might be a white slaver. And Joy was such a gentle girl she could probably be bullied into anything.

To add to my problems, I was having trouble with my landlord. My gas fire was working badly, and I dismantled it, saw that it was blocked, and asked my landlord to get it repaired. When the workman came, he told the landlord that a dismantled gas fire could be dangerous. My landlord promptly gave me notice.

Again I had a feeling that it was some malign destiny that kept devising these stupid situations. It was midweek and I demanded a full week's notice – which he was obliged to give me by law. But I was so angry that I went out looking for rooms the next day, and found the whole upper floor of a house in Summers Lane, North Finchley, for thirty shillings a week. I moved my books there, and on Saturday morning told the landlord that I was moving out.

He was indignant. He said he had turned away an inquiry for a room only that morning, and that if I wanted to leave I would have to pay the week's rent, or he would refuse to let me take my baggage. I went to the local police station and asked their advice; they told me that the landlord would have to sue me if he thought he had a case. I returned to my room; the landlord was out, so I left him a note telling him where he could find me if he wanted to sue me, and left. I never heard from him.

I worked in the laundry for about a month, but I found it boring as well as exhausting; moreover, they were underpaying me for the work I was doing. I decided to change my job and, in spite of my resolution never again to work in an office, I applied at the local exchange for an office job. They directed me to a garage near Finchley Central station. I was taken on as a storeroom clerk, and my role was to keep a check on thousands of spare parts, and to issue them to garage repairmen. Since I have never looked under the bonnet of a car, the various names were Greek to me, and they bored me so much that I had no desire to learn them. After two weeks, the foreman sacked me.

I then found a job with the Victoria Wine Company that consisted in entering orders in a ledger. I knew almost as little about wine as about cars, so found this equally boring.

The Scottish clerk with whom I worked had a pink, girlish face, a slight stutter, and incredible belligerence. He was strongly anti-Semitic, refer-ring to Hampstead as Abrahampstead, and Golders Green as Goldstein's Green. And he seemed to regard it as a kind of insult that a 'bohemian' should occupy the seat next to him (the word 'beatnik' had not then been invented), and he played the dominance game for all he was worth. I didn't regard him as worth wrangling with anyway, and my indifference infuri-ated him. (In 1960, I was to meet him by chance in Stockholm, and his first words to me were: 'You know, I'm far more of a genius than you are' – he had been irritated by some Swedish journalist's fulsome description of me.) After a few weeks, the Victoria Wine Company sacked me too.

It was at about this time that I received a letter from Betty saying that she intended suing me for maintenance. This seemed to me one more attempt to tie me down to a respectable job and turn me into a 'husband and father'. My first impulse was to go back to France, or at least move far away to some obscure town. But she finally agreed to drop the idea when I offered to pay her a weekly allowance – which, under the circum-stances, I could obviously not afford.

There were also minor irritations about my lodgings. The old lady who rented the house lived off National Assistance; she had a daughter in her mid-thirties – a large, owl-like girl – and a fat grand-daughter. The daugh-ter soon made me her confidant, explaining that her husband had left her and that she supplemented the National Assistance with a little street-walking. I did not in the least object to the streetwalking, but I found it tiresome to discover in my bedroom unmistakable signs that it had been used to receive her male friends. The girl herself seemed to have a curious preference for eating fish-paste sandwiches in bed, and I often had to remake the bed to remove the stale crumbs.

I had had a quarrel with Joy about her refusal to visit my lodgings; I was so angry I determined never to see her again. But we had already started to get used to each other – the real basis of all marriages – and after two days, I went to see her in the Oxford Street shop.

I pointed out that I had now changed my lodgings, so her promise to her parents did not apply to this flat. And since she was also missing me, she allowed herself to be convinced by this piece of casuistry, and agreed to come that evening.

My room contained no settee on which we might sit together – only a chair and a bed. Joy had been too well brought up to accept an invitation to lie on a bed in the early evening, so we sat on the floor, to my immense frustration. Finally, I had an idea; I tossed a coin and said: 'Heads we lie on the bed, tails we stay where we are.' To my relief it came down heads, and Joy kept her part of the bargain.

We were still not lovers. This may sound strange, but her shyness made it seem natural. Besides, I found it so pleasant just being in the same bed that I was perfectly contented, realising that one of the main problems with sex is that it so easily becomes a habit, and wanting to make the anticipation last as long as possible. I recognised that the pleasure of love-making lies to a large extent in the imagination, and the sight of Joy in her underwear often struck me as so beautiful that I forgot to feel sexual desire.

Joy's parents were hoping we had split up, for she had told them so during that weekend when we were quarrelling about her refusal to return to my room. When they learned we were still together they summoned me to come and see them at their home at Orton Longueville. And since it was obvious that Joy would get no peace until I agreed, the two of us set out one hot Saturday afternoon to hitch-hike there.

The journey would result in one of the most important insights of my life. What happened was this.

We took the bus as far as Barnet. But beyond that there was little traffic on the road, and we tramped on in the heat. I didn't care much whether we got a lift or not, for I was not looking forward to being grilled by her parents. But then, I was also bored with London. So I had no strong motivation to go forward or back.

Finally, a lorry stopped for us. The cab was hot. And after about half an hour, there was a knocking noise from the gearbox. The driver explained that he would have to let us off at the next garage, so in due course we clambered out and resumed waving our thumbs at passing traffic.

After a walk of several miles, another lorry stopped. I was feeling so disgruntled by now that I felt no particular relief, merely a feeling of 'About time too . . .'

And then – the preposterous coincidence: there was a knocking noise from *his* gearbox, and for the second time in an hour, the driver told us he would have to drop us at the next garage. I found myself thinking indignantly: Oh no, not again! And realised that this was the first positive thing I had felt since leaving London.

The driver discovered that if he slowed down to about twenty-five miles an hour, the knocking stopped. So he kept his speed low, and we ground on through the hot, dull afternoon. But by this time, Joy and I were listening intently for a resumption of the noise, for we were now as anxious to get there as the driver was. And when he said: 'I think if we stay at this speed we're going to make it,' I felt a surge of relief.

Then I was struck by the absurdity of the situation. There we were, in the overheated cab of a lorry driving at twenty-five miles an hour, and actually feeling grateful to be there.

I thought: it is as if there is an area of the mind which is indifferent to positive stimulus (i.e. the lorry stopping for us) but which can be stirred into activity by a negative stimulus (the threat of the lorry breaking down).

We happened to be passing through a small town called St Neots, whose name I misread as St Neot. Knowing how easily such flashes of insight are lost, I scrawled in my pocket notebook 'St Neot Margin'. And, weeks later, I found it and wondered that the hell I meant. Then the name 'St Neot' brought it back. Later, I came to call it 'the indifference threshold'. In psychology, a threshold means a level at which some stimulus becomes noticeable. We have a noise threshold, a pain threshold, and so on. The 'indifference threshold' is the level at which we feel *that a certain effort is worth making*. Bored, spoiled people develop a high indifference threshold.

When Joy and I finally arrived in Orton Longueville, her mother and father made us sit down on the settee, and asked us the kind of questions that might well have been regarded as impertinent: for example, whether Joy was still a virgin. To that we could reply affirmatively, although we went on to admit that we slept together. And when Joy admitted that she had also slept with her ex-fiancé, Mrs Stewart's expression indicated that she wondered what the younger generation was coming to. Finally she said firmly: 'All right, you'll have to get engaged.' And when we both said we would, I fancy that Joy's mother looked relieved. The situation was once again normal, and life could go on as before.

In fact, I was sleeping with another girl at this time, although, oddly enough, it was completely innocent. Jackie Noble, the girlfriend of Philip Veen (who had come to Paris with Bill), had been turned out of her lodgings and had no money. I told her that there was a spare bed at my place, provided she crept in quietly, and left early. Then the old lady moved her grand-daughter into the spare bedroom. Jackie used to arrive at one in the morning, after an evening drinking tea in Soho cafes, and climb into bed with me; she usually left the next morning before I was awake.

Bill Hopkins asked her whether I never tried to make love to her. She said that one night I began to caress her, then rolled over on to her; then I woke up, recognised Jackie, and rolled off again . . . This is probably true. Jackie was an attractive girl, but she was a true bohemian, and simply not my type. My temperament was definitely non-bohemian.

One evening, as Joy and I were sitting in bed together drinking tea, the landlady's fat grand-daughter walked in without knocking. We usually locked the door, but Joy had forgotten. The next morning, as Joy was sneaking out of the house, my landlady emerged from the kitchen and told me I would have to leave – this kind of thing might corrupt the child . . . Since I had been carefully preserving the secret of her daughter's spare-time occupation, this struck me as an absurd piece of irony. If my mild half-deaf and half-blind landlady could give me notice, my ironic demon must have some powerful grudge against me.

By that time I had found another job at a plastics factory in Whetstone, and I found this less boring than the offices. But after a few weeks of it, I quarrelled with the foreman. I had gone into work one Saturday morning (Saturdays were overtime, and we could refuse to do it if we wanted to). After clocking in, I went to a shop next door to buy some chocolate (I was a voracious eater of chocolate and sweets in those days). When I got back, a few minutes later, the foreman caught me going in, and ordered me to clock in again. A few years before I would have done what he said, and cursed under my breath, but endless irritations and frustrations had ground my patience to a fine point. I told him to go to Hell, and went home. On Monday, he told me I could collect my cards at the end of the week. This was when my landlady gave me notice.

I was beginning to feel like Raskolnikov just before the murder in *Crime and Punishment*, when he suddenly has the feeling 'he would not go on living like that'. I was sick of putting up with fools, working at jobs I hated, never having the leisure to work continuously at *Ritual in the Dark*. I had been wrestling with it now for six years, since I was seventeen, and it really needed a month's hard and unbroken work to turn it into a novel instead of a series of fragments. There were whole chapters in it that seemed to me good, but it would not be a novel until I could start at the beginning and write on to the end.

I read Graham Greene's entertainments – with considerable impatience – and it seemed clear to me that I could do as well as that. Why not, since Balzac had launched his career by writing potboilers under assumed names? What was I doing in these pointless jobs? It was time I started being a writer.

And in this mood of total frustration, it suddenly struck me that part of my problem was that I had to pay rent. It was low enough by ordinary standards, but rent and fuel and National Insurance and income tax meant that I was earning about three times as much as I needed to feed myself. At this time, Johnny Abraham, the friend in whose room we had rehearsed the *Twentieth Century Revue*, was proposing to go off to the Middle East and wander around for a year, seeing the world; he had bought a tent and waterproof sleeping bag. It came to me that this might be the answer. Once you had paid for a tent, it was yours. And you could put up a tent anywhere in a field. I was living near the outskirts of London – half an hour's cycle ride from the open country north of Barnet.

I put the plan into operation at once. I bought a cheap tent and a sleeping bag. Barry Hipwell, the Leicester poet who had played in *Man and Superman* at Lewis's visited me that weekend. He told me he had decided to move to London, and asked my help in finding lodgings. I told him he could have my room. I took my books to Joy's lodgings in Chalk Farm. And before the end of my last week at the plastics factory, I was sleeping outdoors in my tent. For the first few nights, I stayed in a field on the edge of a golf course near the factory. But I soon decided that the tent was superfluous; it was too much trouble to put up and take down, and attracted too much attention. It was enough to have the waterproof sleeping bag. If it rained, I could pull the top over my head, then sleep securely while the rain pattered on the impenetrable rubber.

All this meant, of course, that I could not continue to send Betty money. But by this time, she had found another nurse–housekeeper post at Billesdon, near Leicester, so this was not too serious.

I had about twenty pounds to come when I left the plastics factory. This ought to last me a month if I spent it only on food (and resisted the temptation to buy books). I started sleeping on Hampstead Heath, which was conveniently close to Joy's lodgings, and within easy distance of the British Museum. I knew of a busman's café opposite the Chalk Farm underground station where I could get a cup of tea and two thick slices of bread and dripping for sevenpence. I went there every morning for breakfast. Then I would cycle to the museum, and leave my rucksack in the cloakroom. (The attendant obviously regarded this as an imposition, and threatened to complain to the museum authorities, but nothing came of it.) At once I began to work hard on rewriting *Ritual in the Dark*.

This new routine was infinitely preferable to working every day in an office or factory, but it was by no means ideal. I was mentally exhausted by the wear and tear of the past two years; leading the life of a tramp in London did nothing to ease the strain. When I told Bill Hopkins that I was sleeping on the heath and writing in the museum during the day, he said enthusiastically, 'That's the idea, Col, build up the Wilson legend!' But I could not live on legends.

Through the Reading Room I met one of the most interesting characters so far. I was reading Bretall's *Kierkegaard Anthology*, which has Kierkegaard's name splayed down the back in gold letters. As I was sitting outside the museum eating a sandwich, a young man approached me and said: 'I see you're reading Kierkegaard. I'm studying Heidegger,' and we fell into conversation. He was a Canadian named Alan Detweiler, and he was also studying music – particularly the Swedish composer Berwald. As we talked, I mentioned that I sometimes spoke on Hyde Park Corner. Alan immediately suggested that I should go to meet a friend of his. And a few days later, I took the tube to Warwick Avenue, and was introduced to a middle-aged man with a faint European accent and a kindly smile. His name was Alfred Reynolds, and he lived in a room lined with books and gramophone records. Alfred was a Hungarian Jew, and in the 1930s had been forced to flee from Europe by the Nazis. He had changed his name from Rheinhart to Reynolds, and become an intelligence officer in the British army.

At the end of the war, Alfred had been assigned the difficult task of de-Nazifying young Nazis. The first time he entered the classroom, he felt a wall of sheer hostility as they waited for him to start telling them that Hitler was a monster and Nazism was wicked. Instead, he sat down on a desk, and began asking them why they had joined the Hitler youth. He listened to their stories sympathetically, and interjected the occasional question, using the same method as Socrates to make them aware of their own contradictions. Soon he had won them all over; there was not a Nazi left among them. And they had transferred all their loyalty and affection to Alfred, and his faith of tolerance and understanding.

He became the leader of a movement called 'Die Brücke', The Bridge – or simply Bridge. It swept all over post-war Europe, with thousands of members. But with the German economic recovery, the young idealists turned their attention to money-making, and the movement shrank until it was now limited to a group who met in Alfred's rooms in London.

Alfred now asked me if I would demonstrate my speaking abilities. So we took a bus down to Hyde Park Corner, and I found myself a folding chair and proceeded to speak. Soon I had a large audience, to whom I preached the gospel of Anarchism.

After half an hour of lecturing and taking questions, I closed the discussion and went back to Alfred. He was much impressed, and proposed that I should become co-leader of Bridge in England. Then we went back to Warwick Avenue, where he provided me with an excellent supper – he was a superb cook – and talked about Thomas Mann and Hermann Hesse.

But before I went to work as his recruiting sergeant – after all, the principles of Anarchism were very close to those of Bridge – he suggested that I should attend a few meetings. About two dozen young men and one very pretty young woman gathered in his room, and Alfred would start the evening by playing some music. It was here I made the acquaintance of the superb Brahms first piano concerto, Bruckner's 'Romantic' Symphony and the Mahler Ninth. Then we had a break for coffee and biscuits. Then Alfred talked for half an hour about reason and tolerance, and invited discussion.

It was at this point that I began to experience acute doubt. I was entirely in favour of reason and tolerance. But did Alfred understand the kind of feelings that drove people like Irmgard Huckman and Flax Halliday to look for meaning and adventure in a civilisation that offered no sense of purpose? He was violently anti-religion, and referred to priests as 'black crows'. But did he understand the torments that drove a George Fox or John Bunyan? To dismiss them as religious cranks suggested a lack of the intelligence and insight I had come to expect of Alfred. They revealed him as a fanatic in his own right, as well as a shallow rationalist.

I raised these points, and the meeting turned into an argument between myself and Alfred. And the same thing happened at the next Bridge meeting

I attended, and the next. Finally, Alfred asked me to stop coming, although I would remain welcome as a dinner guest.

It was through Alfred I discovered the music of Berwald, learned to love Brahms, and got to know Beethoven's Hammerklavier and first Rasoumovsky Quartet.

But even at the beginning of our aquaintance, it was clear that an immense gulf lay between us. I had talked to him about Gurdjieff and Ouspensky, and he agreed to read them. I recommended Ouspensky's *In Search Of the Miraculous* as a good introduction, with Kenneth Walker's *Venture With Ideas* as a second choice.

The next time I saw Alfred, he told me he had now read Gurdjieff and decided he was a charlatan. I asked him what he had read. He said *All and Everything*. Appalled, I told him that was the worst possible place to start, that Gurdjieff had deliberately written the book as a kind of obstacle course to deter the intellectually lazy. Alfred said grandly that he believed in going straight to the source and ignoring the disciples, and that *All and Everything* was quite plainly rubbish. It was then I recognised that Alfred and I would not, after all, become soul mates.

The beautiful girl I have mentioned was the wife of a good-looking young man named Stuart Holroyd and, as will be seen, he would play an important part in stimulating me to write *The Outsider*.

I introduced Joy to the group, and Alfred was impressed to learn she had a degree – not many women had in those days. And at a later date, Joy even took Flax Halliday to a Bridge meeting when I was working one evening. Flax caused indignation by arguing in favour of war and militarism.

By all normal standards I had become a bum and a drifter; I had done no regular work for a year, and was living outdoors to avoid paying my wife maintenance. And yet I still had the totally subjective temperament of my childhood; I wanted to be left alone with a pile of books in a room of my own. I hated this business of living outdoors, of never being able to sleep deeply and soundly because some tramp might stagger over me in the dark, or a policeman order me to move on. (A policeman had told me that it is illegal in England to sleep without a roof over your head.)

In the mornings I would wake up to find the sun shining on the damp grass, the sky bright blue, the heath empty. It ought to have been poetic, but I had no capacity for enthusiasm. I saw it all through a grey mist of exhaustion.

In the Reading Room, I had taken note of the Superintendent, the novelist Angus Wilson. In fact, it was impossible not to notice him. He had greying hair that flowed back from his forehead, a purple bow tie, a distinctive nose and a high voice that carried all over the Reading Room when he was on the phone. He was often heard saying things like: 'Can I speak to John Gielgud? . . . Oh, hello, John, this is Angus . . .'

His novel *Hemlock and After* had appeared in 1952, when I was living with Betty in North Finchley. *The Times Literary Supplement* had said that it was one of the wittiest novels since Oscar Wilde, and I had hastened to order it from the library. I was disappointed to find that it was not in the least like Oscar Wilde; the rather bitter satire reminded me of Aldous Huxley's *Point Counterpoint*. But he was the first published writer I had seen in the flesh, and I stared at him with fascination.

One day I spent half an hour trying to find, without success, an article that T. S. Eliot had written about *Ulysses*. I went and asked for guidance at the central desk, and found myself speaking to Wilson. He came back several hours later with the volume, having spent the morning searching through the catalogues for it. We got into conversation, and I told him I was writing a novel. He said that he would like to see it when it was finished, and that if he liked it he would show it to his publisher. I took this very seriously (although, having myself said the same thing to many young authors, I now realise that it may not have been too seriously intended). After that I saw him occasionally, but we never exchanged more than a few words.

I took the opportunity of days in the Reading Room to learn about existentialism. I had discovered Robert Bretall's *Kierkegaard Anthology* in the Holborn Public Library, but knew very little of Sartre or Camus. So I read, in quick succession, Helmut Kuhn's *Encounter With Nothingness*, Guido Ruggiero's *Existentialism* (an attack on it), Blackham's *Six Existentialist Thinkers*, Iris Murdoch's little book on Sartre, Heidegger's *Existence and Being*, and Sartre's *Nausea* and *The Age of Reason*. And I subsequently wrote an article on existentialism for a magazine called the *Intimate Review*, lauched by a Soho friend, John Rety.

I quickly realised that I had always been an existentialist without knowing it. Sartre and Heidegger were exploring the same kind of questions as Dostoevsky and Eliot – or even Graham Greene: whether human existence is as brutal and meaningless as it looks.

But Sartre and Heidegger concluded that the answer was yes. And I had a deep and instinctive conviction that they were wrong. Graham Greene has described how he played Russian roulette with a loaded revolver, and how, when he missed death by merely one chamber, he had experienced an overwhelming sense of joy, a feeling that life is infinitely beautiful and excit-ing. I had felt the same after my suicide bid at sixteen. Even Sartre had commented that he had never felt so free as when he was in the Resistance, and knew he might be arrested and shot at any moment.

Surely that proved that what is wrong with human existence is simply that ordinary consciousness is too feeble? The real question is how we can raise its pressure. Even sleeping out on Hampstead Heath was making me aware that this could be done, for the possible danger of being shaken awake by a policeman, or even attacked by some drunken vagrant, kept me at a high level of alertness, and the result was a sense of being more alive.

Meanwhile, I seemed to have brought Joy some of my own awful luck with landladies. She was sharing a room with a French girl, so I could not spend much time there, but the landlady allowed them to use a basement room to receive visitors. One night, the rain came down in torrents, so I slept on the settee in this visitors' room, promising to leave very early, before the landlady was about. For some odd reason, the French girl came down in the middle of the night, received a shock at the sight of a strange man asleep, and complained to the landlady. Joy was more furious with the French girl than the landlady, and decided to move.

She found a room at the other end of Fellowes Road – which was, in any case, more convenient for the Swiss Cottage underground. (She was now working as a librarian at Stanmore.) I used to cycle down from the Heath in the morning, have coffee in her room, then cycle to the museum. After a few mornings of this, her landlady exploded and gave her notice. The woman was an unpleasant neurotic who screamed at her children all day; Joy moved out to a room in Stanmore with some relief. My opinion of landladies was confirmed.

August was approaching, and I wanted to get out of London for a few weeks. This meant finding another job. I had been borrowing money from a grant that Joy had been given to study as a librarian, but she would have to be repaid shortly. I was told that there were many well-paid temporary jobs in dairies; I made inquiries and was directed to one out on the Great West Road, near Osterley Park. The pay was good, although the work was monotonous and hard, consisting of lifting crates of milk on to a moving belt.

The day started at seven in the morning, and I worked until seven in the evening to make as much money as possible. I found a field only a few minutes away from the dairy, and slept there. On the corner next to the dairy there was a workman's café called The Better 'Ole. (It has now been pulled down to make way for a garage.) I spent most of my evenings there, since it was too far to go into town for a few hours. Joy came out and joined me at weekends, sharing the sleeping bag. I had started to learn Greek, to make the job less boring. I would learn a vocabulary in the coffee break, then go over the words in my head as I worked; if I forgot one of them, the book was open on a nearby crate for a quick glance. I also met a strange woman called Grace, who worked in the canteen and was a student of astrology and occultism. My scientific training had made me a sceptic about such things, but I had to admit that Grace seemed to know things about me that only my mother could know.

It was while I was working in the dairy that I came across Camus's novel *The Outsider* in the Chiswick Public Library. The title instantly caught my attention, for I thought I was the only person who used the word in this sense. The book was short; I read it in an evening, and added it to the list of books about 'outsiders' that I had been accumulating since 1950 in Leicester.

After a few weeks at the dairy, I had enough money to repay Joy and we went off for a week in Cornwall. It was our first holiday together; curiously enough, we had camped in a field that is less than half a mile from the house where we are now living. Cornwall delighted me; we bought Norway's *Highways and Byways in Devon and Cornwall*, and read aloud to each other legends of giants and trolls and pixies, or stories of Drake and the Spanish Armada.

By that time the inevitable had come about and we had become lovers. As soon as that happened, I sent her off to the birth control clinic, for I had no desire to repeat what had happened with Betty. To my surprise she went without protest – for she seemed so demure and passive about sex that I expected a certain hanging-back. She told me much later that it had not been a pleasant experience, for she had to wear her engagement ring and claim she would be marrying in a few days' time. In the prudish 50s, it was felt that to provide contraception without immediate prospect of marriage would have been to encourage immorality.

But in spite of the demureness, she was deeply satisfying as a lover and partner. She had a natural shy sensuality that made my head spin when I kissed her. The shyness was important, for it made it immensely piquant to watch her taking off her clothes. It made her seem like a nun doing a strip-tease.

When I first knew her, she wore rather gauzy blue panties, but somehow these failed to excite me, being too insubstantial, even if they did make her look like the heroine of the Jane comic strip in the *Daily Mirror*, who lost her skirt at least once a week. But I think it must have been some telepathic sympathy – I certainly never dropped the least hint – that led her to start buying the kind of panties whose smoothness was deeply satisfying to the erect penis rubbing against them. And when she occasionally climbed into bed in her panties and bra, with a suspender belt holding up her stockings, I felt – as Apuleius says in *The Golden Ass* – as if the apple bough of love had bent over me so I could help myself.

Years later, when I became a friend of Abraham Maslow, I realised that Joy and I are what he calls 'good choosers'. In a paper on dominance, he mentions an interesting experiment with pigs. Some of the babies in a new litter were shy and nervous, and preferred to stay near the mother. Others were energetic and full of curiosity, and liked to wander. When the most dominant of these was exploring outside the pen, the experimenter closed the door so it could not get back, and it became frantic. Yet at the next opportunity, it was doing it again. Curiosity was greater than fear.

So the experimenter decided to try offering the pigs two types of food. One smelled good but was not particularly nutritious; the other was highly nutritious but smelled awful. The dominant pigs chose the nutritious one and became more dominant than ever. The non-dominant pigs chose the other food, and became even less dominant. The dominant ones obviously had an instinct about what was good for them. And from the beginning, Joy and I had a powerful instinct that we were good for one another.

It struck me then, as it had with Mary and Betty, that the basic sexual stimulus is visual. As you become accustomed to lovemaking, the 'robot' edges over the 'real you', and you find yourself dependent on imagination. A man in the grip of intense sexual excitement is simultaneously lying on top of the girl, and floating several feet above her, looking down on her. Joy's kisses were so sweet, and her body so sensual, that I sometimes joked that she was a combination of every famous concubine in history.

But on that Cornish holiday, something seemed to have gone wrong with the system, and this brought me a moment of insight that has stayed with me ever since. For a few days, we were afraid that Joy was pregnant and I experienced again the old, hunted feeling that I had known four years earlier. The first three days of the holiday dragged, and both of us were thinking of the same thing all the time. I had always been oddly happy about Joy; somehow, I had a feeling that she was a kind of lucky mascot, and that now I knew her, things were bound to go right. Now I wondered if this was another piece of self-deception. If she was pregnant we had to get back to London immediately, and she had better start thinking about hot baths and jumping off tables.

In Teignmouth, she vanished into a ladies' toilet for half an hour. When she came out, we wandered along the sands in the direction of the river bridge. I said: 'Well, I suppose we ought to think of returning to London tomorrow.' 'London?' She looked puzzled for a moment. 'Oh, there's no need for that. It came on an hour ago.' It was typical of Joy; she had forgotten to mention it. I was staring out over the sea toward Exmouth as she said this, and suddenly the sea was transformed and appeared incredibly beautiful.

I found myself thinking: ah, that's just because you're relieved. Then I looked at the sea again and thought: no it's not. It really *is* beautiful.

What struck me so clearly was that what I was seeing – this immense depth of mystery, beauty, magic that seemed to be exhaled from the sea and Exmouth peninsula beyond it – was quite objective. It was really there, all the time. '*Meaning is an objective datum*', as if Nature is actually telling you something. The mechanism of tension and relief had merely pulled aside the veil as the curtains of a theatre part to reveal the opening scene.

But if that was so, then man should be able to induce mystical ecstasy by simply learning to see things as they are. How? By somehow learning to reproduce the mental process that had just removed the blinkers from my own eyes.

My basic insight here was not a new one: it is Blake's recognition that things would be seen as 'infinite' if the doors of perception were cleansed. But at this point, my scientific training took over. What precisely was the nature of the mental act that would clear the doors of perception?

Human beings possess certain curious powers that distinguish them from animals: not only their ability to be raised into a trancelike state of delight by poetry or music, but also the capacity to induce sexual excitement – and even an orgasm – without the actual presence of the sexual object. No animal can masturbate without the presence of some stimulus; only man has this power to build up a complex set of responses in the mind by imagination alone.

In the same way, there is no reason why man should not learn to brush aside these veils of indifference and habit that separate him from reality. It is simply a question of reproducing the mental act.

Why do I feel so happy when a tune or a smell vividly reminds me of some event in my past? Because I become aware of the richness, the multiplicity of life, and I burst out of this narrow room of subjectivity. When I am trapped in that room, nothing seems worth doing; trivial inconveniences throw me into despair. And then some tiny event – like Proust's madeleine dipped in tea – reminds me of 'otherness', and it is like an immense laughter that brushes aside all my own values and feelings and places me in contact with something infinitely more important than the 'me' I know.

Is this not the secret of all poetry? Is this not why Shelley was so exalted by the sheer power of the west wind?

Back in London, I took a job at the Lyons Corner House in Coventry Street, this time as a kitchen porter. It was pleasant enough; I was glad to have my meals supplied, and began to put on weight. The only memory that makes me wince is of an old cockney woman who worked behind the counter and who hated life. She nagged and grumbled all day long, and wore a sour and disgusted expression. I never took her seriously until one day the vile old thing saw me helping myself to a cream cake, and reported me to the manageress. The latter was only mildly reproachful, but my detestation of the old woman – which was so violent that I wanted to hit her – made me decide to leave the job.

It struck me then that no doubt her life was dull and frustrating, but she had chosen to be negative about it, chosen to remain stuck in her sour little subjective values. I was becoming increasingly aware that human beings die inside a prison cell of their own making unless they can find salvation by directing the whole being outwards, towards something impersonal.

I continued to sleep on Hampstead Heath, always choosing the same spot under a tree on a slope, but as the weather became colder, I decided to look for a room again. The trouble with the waterproof bag that encased my sleeping bag was that perspiration was unable to escape, so the inside of the bag was always soaked in the morning, and the inner bag was as wet as if it had been left out in the rain. I usually risked sleeping without the waterproof outer cover, but as the winter came on, this became more risky.

So one Friday evening, I cycled over Blackfriars Bridge to south London, and stopped at every newsagent's shop to look at the cards pinned outside. Finally, I found a room in Brockley, near New Cross station. My landlady was a plump, good-natured cockney with a large family. She was by far the nicest I had encountered, having better things to do than nag her tenants. The address was 31 Endwell Road, and I felt that the name was a good omen.

I told her that Joy and I were married but that Joy was at a librarians' school, so we could only spend weekends together. She knew perfectly well we weren't married, but didn't care. Joy spent every weekend with me.

I was now in the midst of a phase of interest in the mystics, reading St John of the Cross, Jan van Ruysbroeck, Lorenzo Scupoli, William Law, Jakob Böhme and *The Cloud of Unknowing*. Luckily, Brockley Public Library had the best collection of the mystics in London – most of them in the reserve section in the basement, for they were never taken out.

I was becoming more and more obsessed by the question of what one could *do* in a civilisation like ours, which has no real symbol of spiritual values. In the Middle Ages, if you had a temperament like mine, you simply renounced the world and went into a monastery. It was an alternative you could choose; it was there, for anyone to see. But it had taken me ten years and more to understand the essence of religion, as distinguished from its dreary rituals: boring church services on Sunday mornings and even duller Sunday school on Sunday afternoons. I agreed with Eliot that religion ought to be something you could see and touch: the great soaring sweep of the nave of a cathedral, stained-glass windows, the chanting of monks by candlelight, gorgeous processions with purple and silver and the burning of incense.

For this reason, I was strongly inclined to Catholicism. I occasionally warned Joy that one day I might have to leave her and go into a monastery. It was not that I wanted celibacy and a shaven head, only that I felt I had to find a way of life that corresponded to my inner urges. I wanted to get away from this civilisation that forced me to conform to its material standards and tried to make me believe that man was primarily a social animal.

Toward Christmas, I bought a second-hand typewriter from a friend of Bill's for seven pounds, and started to type out the first part of *Ritual*, now completed as far as the end of Part One, the scene where Nunne becomes Nijinsky. Flax Halliday visited me one day, and I read him parts of it. He was impressed by the Nijinsky scene: 'You didn't put a foot wrong.' He had grown tired of Leicester, and decided to become a policeman in the East End of London – anything for colour and challenge. (Later he would join the Canadian Mounties for the same reason.)

It was on this occasion that he told me the story – included later in Chapter Two of *Origins of the Sexual Impulse* – of how he and another policeman spent the night making love to a nymphomaniac art student, one after the other, with the light on, until both had had half a dozen orgasms inside her. Meanwhile, Sybil – unconscious after a birthday party with lots of champagne – slumbered on in the next bed. I was struck by the ending of the story: how Flax, having outperformed his rival, had rolled off the girl when she finally complained of being sore, and had washed his hands and genitals at the sink, looked at the room of prostrate bodies – the policeman had dropped out of the contest after his sixth climax – and 'I felt myself . . . *the Victor*.' I noted this as an interesting example of the will-to-power that drove Flax.

Since Angus Wilson had told me he would be taking a few weeks' holiday at Christmas, I completed typing up the first part of *Ritual*, and gave it to him the day he left.

I gave up the job at Lyons shortly before Christmas 1954 to work in the post office of St Martin le Grand, sorting Christmas mail. I spent Christmas Day alone in my room, writing – Joy had gone home to see her parents. They had become more or less reconciled to me by now, and wanted us to get married – I had not yet explained to them that I was already married.

I felt at a loose end without *Ritual*. That afternoon, after a lunch of egg, bacon and tinned tomatoes, I decided to sketch out the 'Outsider' book that I had planned before I married Betty. Having read Camus's *Outsider*, I was much intrigued by the passive hero – smoking, making love and lounging in the sun. He reminded me of Krebs, the hero of Hemingway's story 'Soldier's Home', who experiences a similar feeling of indifference when he returns to his home town in the mid-west after World War One. And Krebs in turn recalled Oliver in Granville-Barker's play *The Secret Life*.

Something began to take shape in my mind, and I wrote at the top of a page in my journal: 'Notes for a book *The Outsider in Literature*. To show that the "outsider" is evidence of a particular type of moral development that has its finest fruit in the Christian tradition'. I was speaking, of course, of St John of the Cross and Meister Eckhart.

The outline that followed was very substantially *The Outsider* as it was finally written, except that there was a chapter on 'The Weak Outsider' – Oblomov, the Great Gatsby, Ernest Dowson, Hamlet and Villiers de L'Isle Adam's *Axel* – and a section on 'criminal Outsiders', a group in which I included Jack the Ripper and the Düsseldorf sadist Peter Kurten.

As soon as the British Museum opened in the new year, I cycled there to begin the book. I was, of course, anxious to see Angus, but he was away for a month. On the way, I recalled how the introduction to Henri Barbusse's *Under Fire* had mentioned that the novelist's first success was a book called *Hell* (*L'Enfer*), about a man who discovers a small hole in the wall of his room, and spends his days peering through it at the life that comes and goes in the next room. This was obviously the perfect symbol for the 'Outsider'. So as soon as I arrived at the museum, I looked up the novel in the catalogue and ordered it. When it arrived I settled down and read it from beginning to end. Then I copied a paragraph into my notebook:

In the air, on top of a tram, a girl is sitting. Her dress, lifted a little, blows out. But a block in the traffic separates us. The tramcar glides away, fading like a nightmare.

Moving in both directions, the street is full of dresses which sway, offering themselves airily, the skirts lifting; dresses that lift and yet do not lift.

In the tall and narrow shop mirror I see myself approaching, rather pale and heavy-eyed. It is not a woman I want – it is *all* women, and I seek for them in those around me, one by one . . .

It was obvious that Barbusse is talking basically about sex, and about the fact that it contains a frustrating element of illusion. His hero takes a prostitute to bed, but finds it banal and disappointing. For sex, like Yeats's waterfall, proves that:

> Nothing we love overmuch
> Is ponderable to the touch . . .

As I left the museum at five o'clock, I knew I had the beginnings of a book.

I had plenty of material. For years now, I had continued to keep my journal, noting down anything that interested me in the books I read, trying to relate together various works of 'outsider' literature and my own experiences. I have my journal for the period by me as I write. It is full of entries on Rimbaud, Axel, Raskolnikov, Steppenwolf, Rilke, Niebuhr's *Nature and Destiny of Man*, Nietzsche, Meister Eckhart, Ramakrishna and George Fox. Early versions of *Ritual* were full of obscure references to them, until I decided that the kind of novel I wanted to write should not be overweighted with quotations.

Another important insight had come as I was walking along the Embankment past Charing Cross underground, talking to Bill Hopkins about the plot of *Ritual*. I explained that its three main characters represent the three different types of Outsider. The hero, Gerard Sorme, is an intellectual Outsider like Nietzsche – he has great discipline of the intellect, but not of the emotions or the body. The painter Oliver Glasp has great emotional discipline, like Van Gogh, but not of the intellect or the body. And the killer, Austin Nunne, has physical discipline, like Nijinsky, but not of the intellect or the emotions. Combined together they would form a unified human being instead of three incomplete beings.

Dostoevsky had used the three Karamazov brothers to symbolise the same problem: Ivan, the intellect, Mitya, the body, Alyosha, the emotions. This is why *The Brothers Karamazov* came to occupy such a central position in *The Outsider*.

To begin with, the book went slowly. Since I had run out of money I had to find another job – according to my journal I owed Joy two pounds. So I went to the local Labour Exchange, and was directed to a laundry, this time in Deptford. This job was one of the hardest I ever had. We worked in shifts, starting at seven in the morning. Rusty tin baths full of wet clothes came past on a moving belt, and we had to empty these as fast as we could. My hands were soon covered with cuts from the baths. The pace was so hectic that we worked for twenty minutes, and then had a ten-minute break (when I carried on learning my Greek vocabulary).

It had started to snow heavily, so that it was difficult to cycle to work. At six o'clock in the morning, it was too dark to see the snowdrifts, so I frequently cycled into them. It was safer to walk most of the way.

But I liked Deptford, with its cobbled streets, and its cranes against the skyline and great ships in the docks. It had not changed greatly since the days of 1905 when the Stratton brothers were hanged for the murder of an old couple – the case is remarkable because it was the first time in England that men were hanged on fingerprint evidence.

But I soon found myself disliking the job when my journals were stolen from my coat pocket one day. Someone must have opened them at one of the entries on sex, and decided that they would make good bedtime reading. (They were not highly descriptive, but I had mentioned that night Joy and I slept on Maurice Willows's floor, and she had not objected when I slipped my hand up her dress.) I had bound together three or four pocket-sized notebooks, so it covered about a year, and was a considerable loss. I tried offering a reward, but to no effect. Unable to bear the sight of the place, I gave in my notice and left in disgust.

CHAPTER 8

Breakthrough

At the end of January 1955, an acquaintance told me that a new Coffee House was opening in the Haymarket and would need staff. I cycled in and was taken on as a dishwasher. My journal for 4 February contains the entry:

> This morning is the first beautiful day since November – I've been able to sit in bed reading and drinking coffee with the window open, without the gas ring on to warm the room, the sunlight everywhere. The Coffee House job in the evenings suits me well enough – not tiresome yet, and needn't become so if I discipline myself not to let time drag. They give me sandwiches to bring home and I eat them all day and so save myself buying food . . .

By 'disciplining myself' I meant refusing to let myself slip into boredom, no matter how tired I became.

In fact, the job was the most enjoyable I'd ever had. For the first time since I left school I was working mainly with young people of my own age; they were mostly drama students or art students. The surroundings were pleasant – there was an enormous fountain in the centre of the floor made of sheets of coloured glass placed at angles that allowed the water to run down them into a basin. We were allowed to help ourselves to food and drink. The manageress was a bouncy, noisy bohemian lady called Gabriele Grahame-King, who loved her job, and had a tendency to engage queers because she liked them.

I used to cycle there from the British Museum, and carry my bike downstairs to the basement, where I worked. But after a few weeks, they took me off dishwashing and let me serve behind the counter. This was a completely different world for me, civilised and amusing.

Gradually, I relaxed. It was like heaving a huge, slow sigh of relief. I would spend days in the British Museum, writing *The Outsider* at a great speed – for I had been thinking about its subjects for years – and then work in the Coffee House from five thirty until about eleven thirty. When the theatre crowds came out after ten, the job became suddenly hectic, and it needed precise coordination to keep four coffee machines working at the same time. If I forgot to start the coffee percolating the moment a machine was empty, it would mean a ten-minute wait for the queue of customers.

When we all went downstairs at the end of the evening and removed our white jackets, there was a warm feeling of comradeship, of liking everybody – even people you normally found boring.

As I wrote *The Outsider* I had a feeling of enormous excitement. It was pouring out of me like molten lava out of a volcano, and I knew it was good. I was writing about myself, seeing myself mirrored in Van Gogh, Nijinsky, Nietzsche, T. E. Lawrence. I was writing of men who had been half-forgotten – Granville-Barker, Leonid Andreyev, Hermann Hesse. (Significantly, most of Hesse's books came back into print after *The Outsider*, and several books were written about him. I have most of them, and not one of them mentions my book. The reason will appear presently.) The theme of the book was the misfits in modern civilisation, the creative men who feel out of place in the rat race.

There is a sense in which the origin of *The Outsider* lies in a paragraph from Lawrence's *Seven Pillars of Wisdom*. It describes Lawrence's feelings as he set out at dawn with an Arab raiding party:

> We started out on one of those clear dawns that wake up the senses with the sun, while the intellect, tired of the thinking of the night, was yet abed. For an hour or two on such a morning, the sounds, scents and colours of the world struck man individually and directly: they seemed to exist sufficiently by themselves, and the lack of design and carefulness in creation no longer irritated.

I had experienced many such mornings in my teens, when I set out to cycle to Warwick or Stratford or Matlock, and I recognised that feeling of sheer joy, the sense that none of the miseries of the world really mattered. What I was experiencing was what the German writer Gottfried Benn called 'primal perception', when everything looks new and sparkling, and we realise that our basic problem is the tendency of the mind to soil and taint the world with its thoughts, as we would soil a sheet of white paper by handling it with dirty fingers. That is what I wanted to write about: the fact that gloom and despair would be impossible if we could understand the hidden powers of the human mind.

That is why I took care to state that the Outsider is not necessarily creative. His lack of self-understanding may be so complete that he never even begins to achieve the catharsis of creation. Van Gogh and Nietzsche had burst into a definite flame of affirmation; most outsiders only smoulder and produce a black smoke that chokes themselves and everybody around them. I was to become aware of a great deal of this among the younger generation in America, some ten years later.

I was so confident of what I was writing that I noted in my journal: 'This book will be the *Waste Land* of the fifties, and should be the most important book of its generation.'

I was still living at New Cross, but one day a letter came from Betty once again threatening to sue me for maintenance. I had not sent her money since I started sleeping out on Hampstead Heath. I gave my landlady notice – with some regret – and moved.

I found a room in a slum area behind Gray's Inn Road. It cost less than the New Cross room, but to get into my bedroom, I had to pass through the family's sitting room. One night when I had been there for a week, an acquaintance told me he had just been thrown out of his lodgings and had nowhere to go. I took him home with me for the night, and the next morning we had to pass through the family's quarters on the way out. That evening, the landlady gave me notice.

But as usual this turned out to be a blessing in disguise. Gabby – the manageress at the Coffee House – said she knew of a friend with a room to let in Nottingham Place, near Baker Street. It was a pleasant basement flat. Being a friend of Gabby's, my new landlady, Inger, was casual, easy-going and tolerant of visitors, even if they stayed all night. I wrote a lot of *The Outsider* here, on days when I was too lazy to go to the museum. Life was more satisfying than for many years. I had an intuition that fate had at last changed its policy, and decided to stop hounding me.

My life had also changed in another respect. When I came to work at the Coffee House, I found it very pleasant to be surrounded by attractive young drama students, and flirted mildly. Joy, who was now studying to be a librarian in Ealing, was still very much the centre of my world, but she came to stay with me only at weekends. Inevitably, if one is in contact with attractive girls for day after day, week after week, flirtations have a chance to develop. I used to walk home with a sweet and quiet art student named Marina, who shared a room near Victoria station with a girl called Cynthia. Once or twice I accepted her invitation to go up and have tea with them. One evening, for some reason, she came back to my room. She knew about Joy, and she herself had a boyfriend who wanted to marry her, so there was no question of starting an *affaire*. Rather than walk home in the early hours of the morning, she slept in my bed between the sheets, fully clothed, while I slept under the eiderdown.

Nothing happened, except that I felt it would be a pity not to kiss such an attractive girl when she was lying beside me, particularly since she obviously wanted me to. We were both playing with fire, and rather enjoying it.

On the next occasion she again slept fully clothed but this time I joined her between the sheets. And on the occasion after that, she removed most of her clothes. It was still understood that we had no intention of becoming lovers – at least, it was pleasant to tell ourselves so. As a last line of defence for virtue we both wore our underwear. The truth was that it was much more pleasant to play this kind of game than to take off our clothes and have sex. It was another example of Frankl's law of reverse effort.

There came the night when, as I was lying between her thighs, with my erection pushing at the barrier of her cotton panties, it seemed absurd not to go further, and I pulled the barrier aside and entered her. The pleasure was so intense that I had to withdraw immediately. I felt ashamed that I had terminated her pleasure.

We both felt we had spoiled our game. We didn't want to have an *affaire*; we wanted to play with fire. So Marina never came back to my room again. In any case, she met a new male employee of the Coffee House, broke with her previous boyfriend, and started a serious relationship.

I had always known that healthy men and women are interested in sex quite apart from the desire for permanent involvements. I had my permanent involvement with Joy, and nothing would have persuaded me to do anything that might damage it. Ever since that first night in bed together, I had felt in some sense married to her. But the kind of mild sensuality I had enjoyed with Marina was certainly no threat to that.

Behind the coffee counter I was partnered at different times by a number of attractive girls, and two more came back to my room during that summer. With a girl called Hazel nothing happened except that we shared the same bed and exchanged a few kisses. The other, a girl named Jo, came back with the intention of making love, and took off all her clothes before she climbed into bed. And the law of reverse effort saw to it that I had lost all interest in her by the next morning.

Not long after that, I served coffee to a pretty blonde of about seventeen, who introduced herself as Carole Ann. She had a well-developed figure, and was pert, lively and good-natured. Her parents lived in Petts Wood, a middle-class area south of London, and she was a drama student at the polytechnic in Regent Street. She also worked in a record shop in the City, and since the next day was her half-day, she came to the British Museum to see me, and I showed her the Egyptian and Assyrian rooms, after which we sat in the tea shop and exchanged details about ourselves. Carole Ann was remarkably frank. She had met an actor who attracted her, and agreed to spend the night with him in Brighton because she thought it was time she lost her virginity. But that had been frustrated by a train strike . . .

Sensing that she saw me as a substitute for the actor, I told her about Joy, and about how Joy had broken off her engagement to come to London. And when Carole Ann came to the Coffee House the next day, I invited her back to my room on Saturday – to meet Joy. I introduced her to Joy simply as a girl I had met in the Coffee House. But later that evening, after we had all been out for cider and sandwiches, and I was walking Carole Ann back to the underground, she said seriously: 'I was furiously jealous of Joy before I met her, but now I can see why you intend to stay with her.' She hesitated. 'But I'd like you to be my first lover all the same.'

I felt it would have been absurd to reject her invitation. I had concealed nothing from her, and could not be accused of setting out to seduce her. As with Marina, it was a matter of two adult people of opposite sexes deciding to give one another pleasure. So two evenings later, she came back to my room. After a few preliminary kisses I removed her skirt and knickers, and we got into bed. But it was not as simple as she had expected. In *Ritual in the Dark*, in which Carole Ann appears as Caroline, I describe the difficulties of making love to her, but for the sake of dramatic unity I do not mention that it took two evenings.

Carole Ann and I continued to see one another for about a year, and to enjoy a pleasant relationship in which there was no deep commitment on either side.

During that period I drifted into another involvement. Her name was Dorothy, and she appears in my second novel, *Adrift in Soho*, as Doreen. She worked in a theatrical costumier near the Coffee House, and was pretty, dark haired and shy. Because she often came in for coffee, things were again allowed to develop at a gentle pace. I met her one morning in Harrods, and a few evenings later took her out to a pub and introduced her to Bill Hopkins. She came back to my room but, even though she missed her last train, insisted on taking a night bus to Kensington.

On the next occasion she stayed the night, but slept fully clothed. But halfway through the night, her bra felt uncomfortable and she sat up and removed it, not realising that when a man finds himself in bed with a girl with naked breasts – particularly beautifully developed breasts – he assumes it is an invitation to go further. Dorothy was obviously shocked when I tried to remove the rest of her clothes, and I was made to desist.

She showed the same curious innocence when I went to the flat she shared with a beautiful and sophisticated girl called Francesca, whose boyfriends called for her in two-seater sports cars. I was kissing Dorothy on her bed and she was obviously becoming increasingly excited. She sighed and opened her legs wide, and I naturally lost no time in placing my hand between them. She instantly froze, and I realised that the movement had been quite instinctive and automatic.

It sounds as if I was carrying out a planned campaign of seduction, but this was not true. I would not have cared in the least if nothing had happened. I simply found a magic in these relationships: in sitting in a pub and eating a sausage sandwich and drinking cider, or feeding the ducks in Hyde Park, with a pretty girl beside me. If Dorothy had found another boyfriend, like Marina, it would not have made me jealous. I felt that social life ought to be this casual, easy involvement of the sexes, simply enjoying what each has to offer.

In the case of Dorothy there was a gradual drift into physical involvement. When Francesca moved out, a girl named Fenella moved in, and Bill and I often went there for a meal, taking bottles of beer or cider. We flirted with both of them. Sometimes, my Leicester friend David Campton came along. Occasionally, after Fenella had changed into her nightie and climbed into bed, I would lie on the bed beside her, kissing her. Then I noted the truth of Flax's observation that a woman feels it to be quite innocent if a man slips off the shoulder-strap of her nightdress and kisses her breasts, or caresses her nipple between his lips. With a layer of bedclothes between them she feels as secure as if wearing armour.

One evening after Fenella had gone to bed, Dorothy and I lay kissing on the sitting-room carpet. She had been nervous about sex, but was now used to me. She made no objection when I raised her skirt and removed her knickers. I don't think she enjoyed our first attempt at lovemaking, but purely as an operation it was successful.

It was bound to end in tears. One evening I came back late from work and found Joy crying, with a diary of mine on the carpet. It was a bad weekend, and I wince when I recall it. She was not the type of person to fly into a temper and walk out; she was too gentle and dependent. I certainly had no desire to hurt her, and yet obviously I had.

But Joy had one advantage: I had no intention of giving her up – I knew when I was well off. It was Carole Ann and Dorothy who had to be given up. Carole Ann soon found another admirer, and bore me no ill will; we even continued to see one another occasionally. Dorothy eventually went to Spain with an art student who had been pursuing her for months. Bill, whose affairs were mostly conducted on a more casual basis, chuckled at my discomfiture.

Some time later – perhaps a year – I bumped into Dorothy in St Martin's Lane, looking quite beautiful in a powder-blue suit, and she told me she was on her way to get married. She looked so lovely I was almost jealous.

Joy, still studying librarianship in Ealing, came over every weekend. She had joined a friendly group consisting of another female student and two males, as students will, and once when I went to see her in her lodgings, one of the males was there. I was not jealous: he was bearded, with a London accent, and I felt he offered no kind of competition, even though it was clear he had fallen in love with Joy. She told me that he had asked her if she slept with me when she came over for the weekend, and she admitted she did. This apparently threw him into a frenzy of jealousy, and he begged her to go to bed with him. I felt almost sympathetic, for I could put myself in his place.

One evening, when I had cycled over to Ealing, I left him with Joy, and as I was walking up to the Underground, he cycled past and spat at me. This struck me as stupid and boorish, and I told Joy so. She took him to task about it, and told me he looked ashamed.

A few months later, when she was changing her lodgings, Joy left a suitcase in my room. I looked inside it, and found a batch of letters from him, which made it clear that he was not only obsessed with Joy, but that they had been engaging in lovemaking. It was as if a bomb had exploded inside my head, and I felt physically sick. Of course, I had no right to be angry, in view of my own infidelities, but sex is not a matter of reason. I tried to ring Joy. She was out and I left a message. When she rang me back I was packing my belongings in preparation for finding another room. I told her I had discovered the love letters and said I was leaving at once. She begged me to wait for her. An hour later, when she arrived, I was in a worse state than ever.

She swore that she had never given herself to him. I pointed out a passage in which he talked about the pleasure of feeling her tender thighs pressed against his. This, she said, was mere romanticism; they had never done more than kiss.

I was inclined to believe her, remembering my rival's unattractive face and straggly beard. I certainly wanted to believe her, for Joy had become for me a symbol of the eternal feminine, and the thought of her giving herself shocked me deeply, as I had once been shocked to learn that Queen Guinevere gave herself to Sir Lancelot. Besides, I had known Joy long enough to know that she was hardly the unfaithful type. I was aware that in the past few months Flax had been to visit her in her room, and she admitted to me that he had propositioned her, and been promptly turned down. So I allowed myself to be convinced. But the music I had been listening to as I read the letters – D'Indy's *Symphony on a French Mountain Song* – was quite spoiled for me, until I decided that it was stupid to have one of my favourite pieces of music ruined by a boorish lout, and deliberately played it again and again until I had erased its associations. But for many years I would wake up out of a dream that Joy had been unfaithful, and feel again that same torment.

Joy and I continued to spend weekends together, and we occasionally hitch-hiked to places we wanted to see: Cambridge, Stratford (which I knew from my teens), Chichester, Arundel, Brecon. One day, when I was already working on the fourth chapter of *The Outsider*, we decided to hitch-hike to Canterbury, and on the way passed through Tilbury, where we explored a second-hand bookshop. There I came upon an anthology of religious mysticism called *A Year of Grace*, edited by the publisher Victor

Gollancz. I bought it, and it was while Joy and I were wandering around Canterbury Cathedral that it suddenly struck me that Gollancz might be interested in *The Outsider*. He was obviously a man who would agree with my basic theme, the defence of religious values.

The next task was to type out what I had already written, for the book was in manuscript. At this time I was doing a day job as well as my evening one. Maurice Willows had come to London, and found a job sitting by a telephone all day in a builder's office. He was giving it up, and suggested I take over. Since I could go on writing my book there, I found it an excellent suggestion. Besides, as there was a typewriter there, I was able to type out *The Outsider*.

I was soon quarrelling with a thoroughly unpleasant foreman who felt I was being paid for nothing, and objected to my making tea on the gas ring. He would hide the ring; I would find it, and have my tea boiling away whenever he came into the office. He even tried hiding the typewriter, but I would find it again – perhaps hidden in the basement.

One day I told him to go to Hell, and he told me I was fired. But by this time, I had typed out the first four chapters of *The Outsider*. I wrote Gollancz a long letter, and sent him an outline of the book, together with selected pages. He replied almost by return post, saying that he thought it probable that he would want to publish it – would I send him the completed typescript?

In retrospect, I have one major criticism of *The Outsider*: it is too romantic. Its mood of world-rejection, of disgust with civilisation, sprang from my years of struggle, and now seems to me too absolute.

As a child I had always been religious, and used to pray as I walked along the street, particularly if my mother was ill or worried. My period of nihilism put an end to that, but later, as I read my favourite poetry – Shelley, Keats, Eliot – I realised that all true poets are basically religious because they possess a sense of the sheer magic of the universe, which involves a sense of a benevolent force behind creation. So it seemed to me clear that humanism – the feeling that men are alone in an empty universe – is nonsense. *The Outsider* was meant to be an argument for religion and against humanism.

It seems to me now that the distinction I then made between religion and humanism is a false one. I knew that I sympathised with Eliot, and agreed with him that 'civilization cannot survive without religion'. I knew that I had no patience with the anaemic, university-trained humanism of Kathleen Nott in *The Emperor's Clothes*, her attack on Eliot, Greene and other defenders of the religious attitude. But the truth is that the basic position of *The Outsider* is humanistic.

I had been divided for years in my attitude towards religion. I was in total intellectual agreement with the 'dynamic' religion of the saints (to use Henri Bergson's terminology), the religion whose aim is union with God, but I had no sympathy for the 'static' religion that develops from it. By temperament I was not fitted to be a member of any group or congregation. I was irritated by the pessimism of religious intellectuals – Eliot, Greene, Marcel, Bernanos, Kierkegaard, Simone Weil. I was equally irritated by the shallow materialism and intellectual complacency that I found in Bertrand Russell and A. J. Ayer, and felt no hesitation in choosing between them and the religious faction.

My mistake was in supposing the choice was necessary, for I had as little – or as much – in common with Kierkegaard as with Russell. I should have asked myself the question: which would be easier: to deepen philosophy until it includes the insights of religion, or to somehow 'humanise' religion? The answer was obvious: to deepen philosophy. Whitehead – a philosopher I admired enormously – certainly thought so. As it was, I rejected Kierkegaard's dead-end pessimism about philosophy, and stuck to my Shavian evolutionism, without seeing that this made me a humanist. It is a pity that I use the word 'humanism' as a term of opprobrium in *The Outsider*. I should have risked inventing a word like 'Russellism'.

There was one important influence on the writing of *The Outsider* that I have not mentioned: my friend Stuart Holroyd. I have spoken about Alfred Reynolds, the Hungarian Jew who was forced to flee to England from the Nazis. Stuart Holroyd was one of his disciples, and had a ravishingly pretty wife called Anne; they had been married since they were seventeen.

Stuart said very little; he was a quiet bird. But I found him intelligent. One day, I suggested to Alfred that I might give a reading of extracts of my favourite literature at one of his Bridge meetings. This sounded harmless enough to him, so he agreed.

What I then did was to choose extracts that all illustrated my point: that human nature has evolutionary cravings that go beyond 'reason', and that may turn to violence if unexpressed. I selected some of the more horrifying passages from Lawrence's *Seven Pillars*, and from Dostoevsky, Nietzsche, Tolstoy, Van Gogh (the letters), Blake, and so on.

I knew Stuart loved the metaphysical poets, so I asked him if he would read some extracts from Donne, Herbert and Blake for me. He not only agreed, he saw what I was getting at, and felt that I had a point. The reading was a success, although Alfred complained at one point, 'You are twisting a knife in my bowels.' He didn't agree with me, though. And he was naturally unhappy about the defection of one of his favourite disciples.

I discovered that Stuart was trying to write for a living. He produced articles for a little poetry magazine, while his wife kept them going by working as a shorthand typist. Stuart knew a great deal of poetry, but had read very little else. I introduced him to Dostoevsky, to William James's *Varieties of Religious Experience*, to existentialism, to the work of Hesse and Rilke. Stuart became enthusiastic about the latter's *Duino Elegies*, and suggested to the poetry magazine that they allow him to write an aticle comparing them with Eliot's *Four Quartets*. I spent an evening outlining my ideas for such an article, and Stuart finally accumulated so much material that he persuaded the magazine to allow him to expand it into three articles – one on Rilke, one on Eliot, and one comparing the two. In due course, these articles appeared, and I read them.

I must admit that I experienced a kind of jealousy to see so many of my ideas in print under someone else's name. It was shortly after that that Stuart told me he had decided to expand the articles into a book about poetry and religion. This would become *Emergence from Chaos*, which was later published by Gollancz in England, and by Houghton Mifflin in America.

But when I realised that Stuart really meant to write a critical book, I decided it was time I wrote one too. It is true that there is no copyright in ideas, and Stuart had a mind of his own. But by introducing him to so many writers who meant so much to me, I had given him a stake in the same field of ideas. This was one of the reasons that I wrote *The Outsider* at such a speed: I wanted to get it out before *Emergence from Chaos*.

Joy and I saw a lot of Stuart at their flat while I was writing *The Outsider*. I recall a party at their room in Belsize Park when Joy, quite uncharacteristically, drank too much and was sick in the sink. After that she flopped on the divan bed and passed out. Her stocking-clad legs, visible to the knees, looked so delicious that I tugged her skirt halfway up her thighs so the other male guests could admire them. When I told Joy the next day, she said: 'Oh, you swine!' but said it with her usual mildness and tolerance.

My grandmother died when I was writing *The Outsider*. I was sorry, for I had been very fond of her. She was a rather saintly woman who had the same kind and gentle temperament as Joy. When I had been in my mid-teens, I had gone there every Saturday afternoon to write – a volume called 'Essays on the Life Aim' and a book on Shaw (which I called *The Quintessence of Shavianism*), an analysis of the plays that I never finished. It would have given me enormous pleasure to give her the first copy of my first book.

And then, in late May, my mother suddenly became very ill. She had inherited her mother's gentle temperament, and I suppose I felt about her the same deep attachment that D. H. Lawrence felt towards his mother, accompanied by a certain impatience with my father, since he and my mother had as little in common as Lawrence's parents, and I felt he treated her as a household servant – certainly they were about as ill-assorted a couple as I have ever come across. She had developed a stomach pain and the doctor had prescribed Alka-Seltzer. It was actually a rumbling appendix, and when it exploded, she had an operation for peritonitis. This was unsuccessful, and she was operated on again, while still very weak. This was also unsuccessful. It looked as if I might also be losing her before *The Outsider* saw print. So I decided to return to Leicester.

I had written about half the book – which was then called *The Pain Threshold* – and before I caught the train to Leicester I called at Gollancz's office in Covent Garden, and asked a secretary if I could leave the book. She said that Mr Gollancz never looked at unfinished books, and advised me to take it away and send it when it was finished. I explained that I was about to go to Leicester, where my mother was ill, and might be away for months – could I not simply leave the typescript there? If he didn't have time to look at it, I would collect it when I came back. Reluctantly, she agreed.

In Leicester I went immediately to see my mother, who looked very sick and frail. There was not much I could do except visit her regularly, but very slowly, after more operations, she improved, although she suddenly looked ten years older than her forty-three years.

As soon as she was out of danger, I returned to London, and was delighted to find a letter from Victor Gollancz waiting for me. He said he had read my typescript, and would definitely publish it.

I was overwhelmed: it seemed incredible that I was going to be a published author. I rushed to Ealing to tell Joy, and found the bearded type there. But I felt almost benevolent towards him; Gollancz's letter made everything else seem unimportant.

What worried me now was whether I could keep up the same standard for the rest of the book. What if Gollancz didn't like the second half? But I lost no time writing to my mother to tell her my book had been accepted.

It was now mid-June, and Gollancz wanted the completed typescript by mid-September. That meant three months of non-stop work. I could no longer spare the time to write in longhand, then type it out. To begin with, I thought the solution might be to try dictating it to a typist. I found a girl at the Coffee House who could take shorthand, and went to her room in south London to try the experiment. I began by saying: 'This is chapter seven, and it is to be called "The Great Synthesis". Put that in capitals, and follow it with a row of dots.' I meant the dots to go underneath the title, but she misunderstood me, and typed: 'The Great Synthesis . . .' I never bothered to remove the three leader dots, and they are still included in every edition of *The Outsider* in the world.

I dictated the 'Great Synthesis' chapter, then decided that dictating took too long; so – with misgivings – I began to type the book straight on to the typewriter. I found this just as easy as handwriting, and have used this method ever since.

The book continued to flow easily, and I often wrote ten pages (2,500 words) a day. There were distractions. My landlady's mother went insane one morning, smashing milk bottles all over the road, and had to be taken off to an asylum. Bill Hopkins almost got me thrown out of my flat after he had slept on the floor one night. He went home by the first bus, then rang me back at six a.m. to ask if he had left his tobacco behind. My landlady got out of bed to answer the phone, opened the door of my room, and saw two more of my Soho friends asleep on the floor. Her comments were justifiably acid, and I started thinking about moving yet again.

Joy and I returned to the West Country in August, cycling this time. We loved it there, with its old-fashioned pubs that sold draught cider, and views from the tops of cliffs. I can still recall walking with Joy up the hill out of Lyme Regis, and looking at the sea birds nesting on ledges on the face of the cliff, and experiencing a surge of sheer exultation – the feeling that I was with a lovely girl and on holiday and, moreover, didn't have to go back to a factory or office. I felt suddenly that life was entirely good, and that only our habitual mistrust turns it sour. And I could see clearly that it is this sourness that causes misfortune and invites disaster; if we could stay relaxed and affirmative, all life would be good.

We were both full of optimism. Ever since Gollancz had written to say that he would definitely publish *The Pain Threshold*, I had experienced an intoxicating sense of having finally broken through. At last, after eight years during which I had been constantly 'plagued by crowds', I felt I could afford to relax and enjoy life. The days when I feared I would never achieve a break-through now seemed a bad dream. I had found a girl who suited me perfectly, I had a job I enjoyed, a reasonable landlady, and my first book had been accepted. The holiday stays in my mind as having a golden glow about it.

It was pleasant having Joy; she was such a sweet-tempered and good-natured girl that everybody liked her. Men tended to fall in love with her – her fiancé had apparently proposed to her a few hours after meeting her at a dance in Dublin; evidently she had had the same effect on him that she had on me.

Back in the British Museum, I learned that Angus Wilson had read the first part of *Ritual* and liked it. Now, when I told him that Gollancz was interested in my new book, he suggested that I allow his own publisher, Fred Warburg, of Secker and Warburg, to see it. Warburg seemed bored when I took the manuscript in, but twenty-four hours later he rang me up in great excitement to say that he would give me a contract and an advance immediately. I decided to make no instant decision, but this offer seemed to confirm my own feeling that this was a book that could make immediate impact.

Only two years before, I had decided that I was prepared to wait for recognition until I was fifty. My reasoning was that there was no point in waiting for the acceptance of my first book before I began my writing career; I might as well start now, and drop the books into a drawer; then, when success came, I might have a dozen more books to offer for publication. Now it seemed clear that such stoicism would not be necessary after all.

Sometime before Christmas, I began to work part time at the other Coffee House in Northumberland Avenue, and to work on *Ritual* again. Gollancz had accepted my completed book (suggesting I change the title to *The Outsider*) and given me a twenty-five pound advance, with another fifty due on publication.

I had finally decided to let Gollancz have it rather than Secker and Warburg because Fred Warburg wanted me to make several alterations in it. He thought the chapter on Lawrence, Van Gogh and Nijinsky deserved to be enlarged. Gollancz was satisfied with it as it stood, so, being lazy, I accepted Gollancz's offer.

Altogether, it was amusing to have two publishers vying for my work. Gollancz, while in many ways a delightful man, had a tendency to fly into rages of furious self-righteousness, and Warburg's attempt to lure away one of his writers had him spluttering with indignation.

It was Gollancz who took me out to my first expensive meal in a restaurant. We had smoked salmon – which has been a favourite of mine ever since – and some excellent red wine to follow. He was a big man with a large stomach and a booming, Oxford voice. In his office building he was regarded as a demon. One day when I was sitting in the office of my editor, John Rosenberg, there was a furious shout of 'How dahr you? How dahr you?' followed by a crashing down the stairs outside. I asked John: 'What on earth's going on?' and John said lightly: 'Oh, it's only VG kicking Brian downstairs.' Brian was Gollancz's assistant.

As we walked from VG's office to the restaurant – in St Martin's Lane –VG asked: 'How on earth have you succeeded in reading so much at your age?' And after that lunch I wrote and told my mother that Gollancz had told me: 'I think it possible that you may be a man of genius.' It was a conclusion I had reached years before, but it was pleasant to hear it confirmed.

On the evening of Gollancz's definite acceptance of the book, Joy and I went to the Carlton Cinema to see Leslie Caron and Fred Astaire in *Daddy Longlegs*. Astaire's number 'Something's Gotta Give' can still bring back the memory of those exciting days when I play the record. I had always enjoyed reading about early success in biographies of my favourite writers – Wells, Shaw, Chesterton; now I seemed about to experience it, and it was more delightful than I had anticipated.

I delivered the finished *Outsider* to Gollancz in early October, and went back to working on *Ritual*. I experienced misgivings about devoting so much of the book to criminality and sadism, and decided to consult the *I Ching*. The result was hexagram 61, Inner Truth, and my scalp tingled as I read the words:

> Thus the superior man discusses criminal cases
> In order to delay executions.

After that I felt no more qualms about discussing murder. And the appositeness of the quotation dissolved any lingering doubts I had about fate and Jungian synchronicity. How could I not believe that my struggles had been directed by some fate that had my best interests at heart?

In late October, I was surprised to receive a telephone call from a woman called Gwenda David, who explained that she was the representative of the American Viking Press, and wanted to offer them *The Outsider*. The idea delighted me, since I was (as usual) broke, and hoped she might persuade them to give me an advance. I went to have tea with her in her house in Hampstead. She was a small, attractive woman in her forties, whose husband, Eric Mosbacher, worked on *The Times*. We liked one another immediately. I was impressed with the row of the Viking Portable Library on her shelf, and sat reading the Nietzsche so avidly that she gave it to me. I still have the copy, full of my notes.

Alas, nothing came of this. Just before Christmas 1955 – when an advance would have been welcome – Viking finally turned it down.

Over the pre-Christmas period, I again worked in the post office at St Martin-le-Grand. This was always enjoyable, because you met such an interesting cross-section of people. There was a cadaverous sports journalist named John Kerr, who looked like Edgar Allan Poe but had a pleasantly dry sense of humour. There was a smartly-dressed ex-army officer named Goodall, who was sixty-five, and told me that he had been the original inspiration for Noël Coward's song 'Mad Dogs and Englishmen'. In Malaya, he had developed a skin complaint of the scalp, and had been recommended to sit out in the midday sun. Coward had seen him and asked what on earth he was doing; the result was the famous song. Goodall told me how, many years later, he wanted to get into a Noël Coward show in Piccadilly Circus, but there were no seats left. So he sent a note up to Coward's dressing room, and signed it 'Mad dogs and Englishman'. The messenger came back with a ticket.

Christmas came, and I went to Leicester. My mother was home, looking tired and old, but slowly recovering after five operations. I could now go into the Coleman Road Working Men's Club with my father and be introduced as 'an author'. My position was no longer ambiguous.

After Christmas I decided that it was time to change my lodgings again. This time, I had no complaint to make of my landlady. But fifty shillings a week was more than I could afford when I had only a few pounds to last me until publication day the following May. I saw an advertisement on a notice board in Notting Hill, and rang the number. A girl with a pleasant voice invited me to go and see her.

The house was on a corner in Chepstow Villas, and was completely dilapidated. It had stood empty for many years, but its owner had now given it to her daughter, Anne Nichols – the girl with the pleasant voice. She had thought of making a living by renting rooms, but since the house was in appalling condition, with peeling wallpaper and shattered windows, she needed someone to help her get it into a state of repair. I explained my own need – a very cheap room – and she made me an offer: I could have the upstairs bathroom for a pound a week (it had no bath, only a disused lavatory), if I would help her to get the rest of the house into order. I agreed, and moved in.

It was a freezing January, and I had no furniture. I slept in my sleeping bag on the bare floorboards of the bathroom, and cooked on a small electric ring. Joy came over at weekends – she was still studying to be a librarian – and slept on the floor with me. House-decorating was hardly in my line, but I worked hard at it. Anne was a painter, and all kinds of weird Soho characters drifted in and out.

When the proof of *The Outsider* finally arrived, I went to Cheam to show it to Laura's parents. Her mother had made no secret of the fact that she thought me an impractical intellectual whose enthusiasm for ideas would never produce any solid result. I can still remember reading the proof on the train, and turning again and again to the title page to assure myself that my name was at last in print.

I now saw more of Angus Wilson, who lived with his boyfriend Tony in Dolphin Square, a block of flats on the Embankment, facing the Thames. Angus was a delightful, kindly man, and his prominent nose and flying mop of white hair made him a caricaturist's dream. I knew many people in the Reading Room who enjoyed imitating his fluting high voice. One of them told me how Angus had telephoned an RAF station where he was due to go and lecture, to make sure they could put him up for the night, and how, when he got there, he found he had been assigned to the WAAF's quarters.

Angus invited Joy and me to lunch at Dolphin Square. We were both overawed by the fountain in the garden between Angus's ground-floor flat and the restaurant. It seemed miraculous to be hobnobbing with a published writer. He told us delightfully malicious stories about Somerset Maugham, mentioning that Maugham was homosexual, and he dismissed the newly published *Fellowship of the Ring* as 'don's whimsy', and thought that the novels of his next-door neighbour C. P. Snow were a bore.

When he told us he knew Stephen Spender I asked him what he thought of Spender's poetry. 'I've never read it. What I really like about him is that he's such a marvellous malicious gossip.'

Angus asked our advice about leaving the British Museum to become a full-time writer. If I had known as much about the literary life as I soon came to know I would have advised him to stay in the security of the museum at all costs.

What I found so pleasant about Angus, although I agree this sounds an odd thing to say, was that he was one of the first genuinely intelligent and cultured people I'd ever met. My working-class background meant that I had met very few really intelligent people, and although many friends, like Bill and Laura, were highly intelligent, neither was an obsessive reader, as I was. With Angus, it was wonderful to be able to refer to anyone from Homer to Sartre, and know he would understand. It made me wish I had been mixing with people like that all my life.

As I write about Angus I feel a surge of fondness, for he was a kind, generous and genuinely good person. It was not until I saw a television programme after his death that I learned the vital key to his personality: his sadistic obsession. It is a sign of my obtuseness that I had not already guessed, for there are plenty of clues. In *Hemlock and After*, the hero, the aging novelist Bernard Sands, who has developed homosexual tendencies late in life, is sitting in a café in Leicester Square when he witnesses a young man being arrested for soliciting and, as he sees the terror on the young man's face, experiences a savage glow of erotic delight. This deeply undermines Sands's view of himself as a liberal humanist, and initiates his decline. And the story 'Raspberry Jam' is about two sweet old ladies who put out the eyes of a live bird in front of a horrified small boy. In other works Angus displays a certain morbid preoccupation with perverse sexuality: in 'Crazy Crowd' a brother and sister are glimpsed embracing passionately on a bed; in *The Old Men at the Zoo* a woman has sex with an Alsatian dog.

Clearly, Angus felt like Bernard Sands: he was a decent, humane liberal, yet experienced these sadistic compulsions. This, he felt, told us a great deal about the mentality that had given birth to Auschwitz. In 1955 he was planning a novel called *The Goat and Compasses*, the goat being the devil and the compasses God ('God encompasseth'); he was, in his way, as preoccupied with the problem of evil as Dostoevsky, and his favourite character was Alyosha Karamazov.

What would eventually destroy Angus was his love of the literary life and all that it involved – lectures, chairing committees, foreign travel. Brilliant, intelligent novels like Angus's do not become best-sellers or attract film rights, and in her biography of Angus, Margaret Drabble reports that he seldom sold more than 8,000 copies in England, which only represents about £2 a copy. And since it took him several years to write a novel, this kept him close to the poverty line. In an attempt to economise he moved to a flat in France, but in so doing cut himself off from his friends and literary roots. By the time he died in 1991, he was suffering from encephalitis, and his hospital expenses were being paid by the Royal Literary Fund.

In January 1955, Angus offered to lend me his cottage near Bury St Edmunds, so that I could finish *Ritual* undisturbed. Here there was another clue that I failed to register. Angus was obviously fascinated by the work of John Cowper Powys, who makes no secret of his own sadism in books like his *Autobiography* and *Glastonbury Romance*, but at that time I had not read either.

I accepted the offer of the cottage gratefully, and cycled there on a windy day, with a portable typewriter, borrowed from Laura del Rivo, on my bike, and the usual library in my haversack. The cottage stood in the middle of a field, and had no electricity, only gas jets. The day after I arrived it began to snow, and soon it was difficult to get in or out of the place.

I worked hard, and managed to finish *Ritual* in two weeks, but I was dissatisfied with it. This was not the novel I had been trying to write for so many years. It lacked real narrative flow – for a reason that will be immediately apparent to any novelist. I had written and rewritten it all; some pages had been retyped a dozen times. The final manuscript was barely seventy thousand words long, and yet I had probably written half a million words over five years. All this meant that I could not approach the task with a fresh outlook; I had lost my critical sense completely about some of the older passages. It was like trying to rebuild a house that you have pulled down twenty times, using a mixture of old and new bricks.

However, it was finally finished, and submitted to Gollancz, who declared that he could not print it. He said the subject – a sadistic sex killer – was bad enough, but its unending sordidness had a profoundly depressing effect on him. He told me that he suspected I was not a novelist, and advised me to begin another philosophical book.

Angus's opinion of the book was more cheering. It had many faults, he said, but he would certainly recommend Warburg to publish it if I would try to correct its structural faults. Warburg agreed to this, and advanced me a badly needed fifty pounds

When I returned to Chepstow Villas I discovered, to my disgust, that a lavatory in full working order had been installed in my room. My books and other belongings were strewn all over the floor. Anne explained that the sanitary inspector had threatened to throw everyone out unless the house had a second lavatory. I moved all my belongings down to a room on the ground floor, and agreed to pay an extra ten shillings a week for it. On the whole, I doubt whether it was worth it – any more than the bathroom had been worth a pound – but total lack of interference from my landlady made it worthwhile.

The ground-floor room was slightly larger than the bathroom, so Bill Hopkins was able to move in too. He was working as a night editor on the London edition of the *New York Times*, and was well paid; so I borrowed from him while I waited for advances.

In late March 1956, I was invited to my first literary party. It was given by Gwenda David, for the publication of Iris Murdoch's second novel, *The Flight from the Enchanter*. I met Iris, then in her mid-thirties, and immediately liked her. A round-faced, slightly shy woman, she struck me as rather sexually attractive. I recall telling her that my major ambition was to live to be three hundred, as Shaw had suggested in *Back to Methuselah*. She, in turn, asked me whether I would like to go to Oxford and take a degree – an idea she brought up several times after that. Having too many other things to do, I did not even consider it.

At the same party I met a writer called Elias Canetti, who lived just across the road. He was a square-faced man with an ironic, downturned mouth, a bushy moustache and a strong German accent. He and I took to one another immediately; he was one of those urbane, cultivated Europeans, like Alfred Reynolds, and I felt certain we were going to be friends.

There was also the poet Kathleen Raine, a quiet little middle-aged woman, dressed untidily in grey, with whom I talked about Blake. We had a great deal in common and might have become close friends if I had not moved out of London so soon.

Gollancz sent me to get my photograph taken for publicity purposes. I wore a polo-neck sweater – I had been wearing them ever since I was in the Western Hospital because I liked the look of them – and it was not a particularly good photograph, taken at a shop in the Harrow Road. But it appeared in all the original publicity, until I had better ones taken.

This was a pleasant period. I saw many people, spent whole nights talking with Bill, and went to a few parties. I worked at odd jobs spasmodically, when the cash shortage became too serious: a few weeks in the Northumberland Avenue Coffee House, and a few weeks for the Students' Association, making flags for their flag day. Joy, also rather broke at this period (she told me that one evening she had to go without food because she had no money) also took a job as a waitress at another branch of the Coffee House in Kingsway.

Two weeks before publication day, I went to another party at Gwenda David's, and there met a young, good-looking Scot called James Burns Singer, whose fine blond hair and delicate features gave him a girlish appearance. To my surprise, he had read *The Outsider* in proof, and told me he had reviewed it for *The Times Literary Supplement*. He mentioned that he had written an article about the Scottish poet Hugh MacDiarmid, and intended to collect his fee from the *Encounter* office the next day. He invited me to join him and have a drink afterwards.

I met him at eleven, and we went to the office of *Encounter* in Panton Street, where he got an open cheque for £40, then went to a bank around the corner and cashed it. And as it was nearly midday, he dragged me into the nearest pub, and there proceeded to drink the money. This carried on through most of the afternoon, although I took care to drink less than he did, and to eat sandwiches to soak up the whisky.

Although a poet, Burns Singer claimed he was able to make a great deal of money from his work. The secret, he said, was simply to write enough. He explained he had just sold a sequence of a hundred sonnets to a literary magazine called *Bottega Oscura*, edited by an Italian millionairess, and after his fourth whisky, he proceeded to recite some of them. (I was to note in the coming years that this is a habit that seems to be common to Scottish poets.)

That evening I had been invited to the flat of Maurice Cowling, one of the editorial board of a magazine called the *Twentieth Century*, to discuss contributing to a special issue devoted to young writers. The meeting had been arranged by Ian Willison, a friend who worked in the British Museum. John Wain, who had achieved celebrity with his first novel, *Hurry on Down*, was to be there. And since Burns Singer wanted to meet Wain, he came too. But by that time he could scarcely speak, and before Wain arrived, he had fallen asleep on the settee, and only grunted when our host tried to wake him.

Wain himself struck me as a gruff and aggressive person. He had a belligerent gaze and a tight mouth. He had been at university with Kingsley Amis, but Amis's *Lucky Jim* had had a far greater success than Wain's novel, and the two now regarded themselves as rivals. Wain, like Amis, wrote poetry, but he seemed to want to present himself as a bluff and downright person, on no account to be taken for a poet. Angus Wilson had told me about a debate in which he had taken part with Wain and J. B. Priestley, in which the two had vied with one another in trying to show that each was more plain-spoken and down-to-earth than the other. And at Cowling's flat, Wain told me that the three writers he admired most were Arnold Bennett, George Orwell and the American humorist George Ade. There was an irritable and irascible streak about Wain that I found unlikeable.

In due course I left Burns Singer asleep on the settee – he was quite unwakable – and returned home to tell Bill – who had just returned from a stint on the *New York Times* – about my day among London's literati. (In due course, Burns Singer would drink himself to death – he was found dead in bed in September 1964.)

My expected friendship with Elias Canetti failed to develop. I had read his novel *Auto-da-Fé*, and found it disappointingly negative and depressing. But when Gollancz heard I had met him, he suggested that I ask if he would be willing to review *The Outsider*. I accordingly wrote to Canetti, but received a reply from his wife, explaining in shocked tones that Mr Canetti *never* reviewed books, and implying that I had committed an appalling solecism in asking him. And he and I never met again. No doubt this was just as well: Peter Conradi's life of Iris Murdoch makes it clear that Canetti was what we now call something of a 'control freak'. Iris, it seems, had already started an affair with him before that party at Gwenda's, and was his mistress for several years. When she became involved with him, Canetti made her promise not to have sex with John Bayley, the man she eventually married.

Finally, publication day approached. Gollancz told me that a journalist from the *Evening News* wanted to interview me, and I cycled around to see David Wainwright, who had been told about my book by John Connell, the newspaper's reviewer. David, a quiet, rather shy young man – not at all what I expected for a journalist – was delighted when I told him about Hampstead Heath, and said it was a 'natural' for a story. It seemed that Bill had been right about 'building up the legend'.

Saturday May 26 came. Publication day was the following Monday. I saw a notice in one of the evening papers that mentioned that the *Observer* would carry an article 'Are Men of Genius Outsiders?' I bought an *Evening News*, but could see no review. I took Joy to the cinema that evening, and when we came back I discovered that my bicycle had been stolen from outside the house. This seemed inauspicious. That night I woke up and again experienced what I called 'the vastation feeling' (Emanuel Swedenborg's term), a sense of the total absurdity and meaninglessness of life, the possibility that all life is only an escape from the horror of death, and that human relations are a temporary deception to make us forget the horror. It seemed to me that each human being is alone; our human companionship is no more protection than the companionship of sheep against the butcher.

The next morning Joy and I hurried to the corner of Westbourne Grove and bought the two 'literary' Sunday newspapers, the *Observer* and the *Sunday Times*, then rushed back home without opening them. I gave Joy the *Sunday Times* while I read the *Observer*.

This contained a review by their lead reviewer, Philip Toynbee, comparing me to Sartre, and saying that, on the whole, he preferred my style and method.

In the *Sunday Times*, Cyril Connolly described me as 'a young man of twenty-four who has produced one of the most remarkable books I have read for a long time', and went on to say 'he has a quick, dry intelligence, a power of logical analysis which he applies to those states of consciousness that generally defy it', and concluded: 'you should keep an eye on Mr Wilson and hope that his sanity, vitality and typewriter are spared.'

At this point someone from the basement came up to congratulate me on my review in the *Evening News*. Incredulously, we searched through it again, and found a review by John Connell with a headline: 'A MAJOR WRITER, AND HE'S ONLY TWENTY-FOUR'.

The man from the basement shouted that I was wanted on the phone. It was a friend, ringing to congratulate me. No sooner had I returned upstairs than it rang again.

My unfortunate neighbour's phone rang steadily for a week. The following day – Monday – an immense pile of letters arrived for me. It seemed that every friend I had ever had had decided to write and congratulate me. Even the headmaster of my old secondary school wrote to say how thrilled he had been to read Connolly's question 'Who is Colin Wilson?'

I had intended to take the train to Leicester the following day. One of my daydreams had been to visit a book store called The Midland Educational – in which I had spent a great deal of time as a schoolboy – and to look at my book in the window. But the success of *The Outsider* made it impossible to leave London.

Worse still, I had invited Betty to come and use my room while I was in Leicester: she was hoping to find herself a flat. She arrived on publication day – Monday 28 May 1956 – to find me in the midst of this frantic commotion, being interviewed by journalists and called incessantly to the telephone. It was the worst thing that could have happened. She was still my wife, and only a few weeks before had written to say that she continued to hope we could live together again. Now that 'success' had arrived, she felt that she ought to be sharing it. But I had only lived with Betty for eighteen months, and had been with Joy for two and a half years. Was I supposed to tell Joy: 'I'm sorry, but I'm going back to my wife'? So the exhilaration of overnight success was contaminated by the sour taste of guilt.

Soon after Betty arrived, the *Sunday Times* rang and asked if I would like to do regular reviewing for them at forty pounds a time. I gasped at the sum. The BBC and Independent Television rang and asked when I would be available to record programmes. On Monday evening, David Wainwright's article appeared – a full page, with the bad photograph in polo-neck sweater. Reporters were arriving at a rate of four a day. I had my second expensive restaurant meal with Godfrey Smith of the *Sunday Times*. *Life* magazine contacted me to say they wanted to do a profile with photographs.

The BBC organ the *Listener* carried a review of *The Outsider* by the doctor Kenneth Walker, whose *Venture With Ideas* had given me my first clear insight into Gurdjieff's ideas; it contained a marvellous quote: 'The most remarkable book on which the reviewer has ever had to pass judgement.' I went for a drink with Walker – he told me to call him K – in his Harley Street house, and a warm friendship grew up that lasted until his death.

A few days later, a popular tabloid, the *Daily Sketch*, published a gossip paragraph about me that concentrated mainly on Joy, the 'little woman' behind this 'midlands D. H. Lawrence'. Betty was infuriated and upset – apparently her relatives did not know that we were no longer together. And as she left a few days later she said angrily: 'Goodbye – for always!'

By a coincidence John Osborne's play *Look Back in Anger* had opened at the Royal Court theatre the week before. The *Sunday Times* wrote about the two of us in their 'Atticus' column, and J. B. Priestley wrote an article on us in the *New Statesman*. Then *The Times* used the phrase 'angry young men' about us, and suddenly the newspapers had invented a new cult. It lasted the rest of the summer, until everybody was sick of it.

All this furore was due to the fact that the critics had been complaining for years that no new generation of writers had appeared since the war. After World War One there had been Joyce, Eliot, Pound, Hemingway, Faulkner, Dos Passos, Wyndham Lewis, Scott Fitzgerald, Aldous Huxley, and half a dozen more. But since World War Two, there had been no comparable explosion of talent. There had been Angus Wilson – but he belonged to the same generation as Auden and Spender. And there had been, of course, Amis, Wain and Iris Murdoch.

And then, suddenly, *The Outsider* and *Look Back in Anger* had appeared in the same week. That was all the press needed to start talking about a new generation.

Now Osborne was, in fact, a special case. A young actor with a natural tendency to irritation and impatience, he detested his mother, and came to feel much the same about his wife, who was an actress. He had a natural gift for invective – he once told me that a girl he disliked 'needed to be fucked by a syphilitic gorilla' – but a fairly low level of self-control and self-criticism. Joy and I were taken by a friend – Dan Farson – to see *Look Back in Anger* in its second week, and I hated it. It seemed to me an outpouring of self-pity and bad temper. Under different circumstances, I think most critics would have dismissed it as muddled, undisciplined and poorly constructed.

But it so happened that a brilliant young critic named Kenneth Tynan, who had come down from Oxford and was determined to make a name for himself, saw it as an opportunity to express his own intense dislike of capitalist civilisation. (Tynan was a passionate admirer of Bertold Brecht, and – although he was discreet about this – regarded himself as a Communist revolutionary.) So Tynan chose to praise *Look Back in Anger* in extravagant terms.

Representing the older generation, Harold Hobson, the theatre critic of the *Sunday Times*, said polite things about the play, but made it clear he felt it was all much ado about nothing. But Tynan's extravagant praise carried the day. To express reservations about *Look Back in Anger* was to identify yourself as a boring old reactionary. So most of the critics fell into line, and Osborne found himself famous.

The *Daily Express* had approached John Osborne, myself, and an eighteen-year-old playwright named Michael Hastings – whose first play had been presented at a club theatre in Notting Hill – to contribute to a series called 'Angry Young Men' and explain what we were angry about. I wasn't in the least angry – except about my years of struggle; and now that I was recognised, even this hardly applied. But the *Express* was paying well, so I agreed to write for them – and, of course, helped to establish the 'Angry Young Man' myth.

I had no idea how much I would come to hate this label.

CHAPTER 9

Backlash

It sounds wonderful – overnight fame, money, television appearances with celebrities, literary parties, invitations to lecture at public schools and universities . . . In fact, I soon began to find it bewildering and rather repetitive. It all seemed to have nothing to do with me, or with the book I had written.

The problem was simple. Ever since my early teens, I had spent most of my time in a world of books. I had been deeply influenced by the spirit of Romanticism – by Goethe, Blake, Shelley, Hoffmann, and by those *fin-de-siècle* poets that Yeats called 'the tragic generation' – Yeats himself, Ernest Dowson, Lionel Johnson, James Thompson. The starting point of *The Outsider* had been why so many men of genius in the nineteenth century had committed suicide, like Thomas Lovell Beddoes and Van Gogh, or died insane, like Hölderlin and Nietzsche.

The answer I had suggested in the book was that these man of genius were too subjective and romantic, and found themselves unable to cope with the trivial problems of the everyday world. They wanted to turn their backs on it and devote their lives to realising 'the eternal longing'.

But running away was no solution. The urge that drove them was the craving to evolve a more intense form of consciousness. So what was the good of blaming fate and sinking into misery and defeat?

I had lived through these problems myself. By the age of sixteen I had been thoroughly indoctrinated with Romanticism, and had often quoted Yeats's lines:

> . . . what the world's million lips are searching for
> Must be substantial somewhere . . .

My decision to kill myself with cyanide had been the result of the conviction that 'real life' and its triviality will always prevent us from satisfying 'the eternal longing'. But what I had seen, as I raised the poison to my lips, was that such a solution was absurd. I had realised, obscurely, that I was causing my own problems by allowing myself to become discouraged. Faced with the prospect of dying in a few seconds, I had realised that the answer lies in our power of *focusing attention*.

Imagine a balloon that has been dragged underwater and is held there. It seems obvious that if the water pressure increases, the balloon gets smaller. But human beings can defy this 'law of nature' and increase their own inner pressure by concentration.

What does that mean? It means that as soon as we concentrate the attention, something begins to happen inside us; a curious spring of warmth arises from our depths, and fills us with that sense of sheer joy that Proust experienced after tasting the madeleine. 'I had ceased to feel mediocre, accidental, mortal . . .'

So what had all this silly publicity about 'Angry Young Men' got to do with me? I was a hermit by nature, a recluse. Being the author of a best-seller was certainly better than working in a factory. But I felt just as uncomfortable, just as alienated. Instead of becoming more fulfilled, my life had turned into a kind of gossip column.

I lectured extensively. One of the first was at the Institute of Contemporary Arts, in Piccadilly. It was pleasant to be able to introduce Joy to Stephen Spender, knowing that the last time she had seen him was when he was lecturing to the Literary Society at Trinity. I noticed in the audience the bearded character who had been with Joy at library school in Ealing, and who had spat at me as I rode past. It was also at this meeting that I met Laurie Lee, a man whose good looks and charm were even then reputed to be irresistible to women.

Of course, it was interesting to meet literary celebrities whose books you had read – Stephen Spender, Christopher Isherwood, Edith Sitwell, Herbert Read, Louis MacNeice – and painters like Francis Bacon, Lucian Freud and L. S. Lowry. But I soon felt I had had enough of literary parties.

I gave a couple of parties myself, one in honour of Angus's latest novel, *Anglo-Saxon Attitudes*, and one for *The Outsider*. John Osborne came to the latter – I had met him at the Royal Court when its director George Devine had asked me there to think about writing a play for him. John came with his wife, Mary Ure, who had played the wife in *Look Back in Anger*. Mary got thoroughly drunk on brandy, and began telling me that John was the greatest English playwright since Sheridan, and that *The Outsider* was just an anthology of other people's ideas. I took care not to betray my own opinion about *Look Back in Anger*.

My new celebrity brought occasional pleasant surprises. A copy of Groucho Marx's autobiography *Groucho* arrived one day from Gollancz, and since I knew VG was not a person to give things away, I wrote to ask him why. He replied that he had asked Groucho who should be sent free copies, and Groucho had telegraphed back: 'Winston Churchill, Somerset Maugham and Colin Wilson'.

I wrote to Groucho to thank him, and mentioned that I was writing a novel based on Jack the Ripper. Groucho replied with a charming letter in which he said: 'Jack the Ripper was always a hero of mine. Unfortunately, physical limitations have prevented me from following in his footsteps.'

At the Royal Court I met Samuel Beckett, and was tempted to challenge him about whether he really thought life was totally meaningless, but he was obviously such an amiable and unaggressive person that I couldn't bring myself to do it. But I *did* challenge another playwright, Eugène Ionesco, about the assumption of meaninglessness that seems to underlie his own plays. Ionesco gestured at the rain outside the window. 'Look, the rain is falling – what is the meaning of that?'

One of my chief problems was the inane publicity I seemed to attract. One evening, Joy and I attended a party at Faber and Faber. We had been invited by Geoffrey Faber, whom I came to know and like, and were hoping to meet T. S. Eliot. Eliot failed to appear, but we met William Golding – then virtually unknown – and Laurie Lee, also unknown, and the novelist Phyllis Bottome.

On our way home – rather the worse for champagne – we passed a theatre off the Haymarket with huge crowds outside. We asked the driver to let us off, and enquired what was happening. It seemed that it was the first night of Arthur Miller's play *A View from the Bridge*, and the crowds were hoping to glimpse Marilyn Monroe.

When I saw the name of Anthony Quayle on the posters (I had met him at a party) I walked up to the stage door – between two rows of policemen – and asked: 'Mr Quayle's dressing room?' 'Number one,' said the door-keeper. 'Down the corridor and first left.'

It was crowded, but we recognised Laurence Olivier and Vivien Leigh and numerous other celebrities, including Marilyn Monroe, who was standing in front of the mirror, trying to heave up a tight strapless dress that had obviously been sewn on, and that was slipping down towards her nipples. Since she was alone, I went and introduced myself – I had been told that she was bookish – and then introduced Joy. Then I went off to say hello to Anthony Quayle. He introduced me to Vivien Leigh and Olivier, and I asked Olivier if it was true that John Osborne was writing a play for him. He said it was, and invited me to write one too.

Vivien Leigh was obviously slightly drunk, and rather flirtatious; when I found myself alone with her, I felt embarrassed by the way she gazed into my eyes. When I told her how much I admired her performance as Cleopatra in Shakespeare's play, which I had seen recently, she said: 'Come and see me, and we'll talk about it.' It was only much later that I discovered – from a book about her – that at this time she was showing signs of alcoholism and nymphomania, and sometimes went to bed with taxi drivers.

I remember little else of that evening, except that a gossip columnist came up to me and asked me what I was doing there. I told him that I had been to a party hoping to meet T. S. Eliot, and instead had ended up meeting Marilyn Monroe. The next day, this item duly appeared in the gossip column, together with the comment that I intended to write a play for Olivier.

This kind of publicity helps to explain why critics like Cyril Connolly and Philip Toynbee felt increasingly that I was squandering my credentials as a serious writer.

The success of *The Outsider* seemed to cause a great deal of hostility. On a personal level I often tried to defuse this. After a newspaper interview had quoted me as saying I would like my name to become a household word, a provincial journalist wrote to say: 'You are a household word, Mr Wilson, and the word is phoney.' Curious as to whether he had actually read *The Outsider*, I wrote back asking him to explain why he thought so. He replied with a long letter, detailing his own disappointments as a writer, and soon we were exchanging perfectly friendly letters. It made me recognise that there was no point in getting upset at hostility, since it usually had nothing to do with me, but was due to some hang-up of the individual.

The same kind of thing happened with a writer called Correlli Barnett, who later became a fine military historian. He lauched his career with an amusing but savage novel called *The Hump Organisation*, and then attacked myself and Bill Hopkins in a popular newspaper. I bought and read his novel, thought it excellent, although I disliked the undertone of cruelty, and wrote to tell him so. He replied with an invitation to dinner somewhere in the stockbroker belt of Surrey, and proved to be good-looking and charming, with a beautiful wife. He asked me to call him Bill, and we parted the best of friends. But Bill Hopkins thoroughly disapproved of this policy of turning the other cheek, and firmly declined to meet him or hear any good of him.

As the hostile publicity increased, I began to get a sensation that I find hard to describe; it was as if these absurd misunderstandings were somehow 'fated'. It felt as if I had fallen into a mill race, and was being swept along, unable to get a grip on the bank. I had no underlying doubt that fate meant well by me – my consultations of the *I Ching* had convinced me that there is no such thing as chance – but in the meantime, some of the bruises made me wince.

At a party given by Melvin Lasky, the associate editor of *Encounter*, I met Christopher Logue again. I was delighted to see him, and shook his hand. 'Chris, how are you? What are you doing in London?' To my surprise, he looked at me coldly and said: 'Hello, Wilson. My name is Christopher, if you please.' And for the next few minutes, our conversation made it clear that he no longer regarded me as a friend. Yet he had been so kind and helpful in Paris that I found this hostility incomprehensible. It was only afterwards that I came to the conclusion that the *succès fou* of *The Outsider* had caused the resentment.

Part of the problem was that Logue had become a close friend of Kenneth Tynan, who professed to regard me as a Fascist. And both Logue and Tynan were involved in an incident that garnered a lot of unpleasant publicity.

Stuart Holroyd had written a play called *The Tenth Chance*, based on the diary of an RAF pilot who had been shot down and kept in solitary confinement by the Nazis. The diary describes how torture and solitude finally led to a religious conversion.

George Devine had offered to give the play a Sunday evening performance at the Royal Court. Naturally, all Stuart's friends and supporters came, including Victor Gollancz and his wife Ruth. Stuart's ex-wife Anne was there with Michael Hastings, and Stuart was accompanied by a beautiful American girl he had picked up when he lectured in Oxford. Bill Hopkins was also there, and so was the Leicester playwright David Campton, a friend of my teens.

The Tenth Chance was not a good play – religious conversion is not an ideal subject for the theatre. Towards the end of the play, as Peter Moen prays aloud, there was a loud shout of 'Rubbish!' and Logue strode up the aisle and went out banging the door. A few moments later, Kenneth Tynan followed him. As he passed me – I was at the end of a row – I grabbed him by the arm and said: 'Can't you control your noisy friends?' Tynan shook himself free and shouted: 'G-g-g-get out of my life, Wilson' (he had a bad stammer). A few minutes later the curtain came down, but the ending had been spoiled.

Outside I saw Gollancz and Ruth, and used some heated language about Tynan and Logue. I felt embarrassed later when I recollected that I had referred to Logue as a fucking bastard. Then Bill and I and Stuart went into the pub next door. Logue and Tynan were sitting there, and I went up to Logue and asked him whether he did not consider it a dirty trick to interrupt someone else's play, and why he didn't write his own. Logue was sitting with his chair tilted on its back legs. As I was speaking to him, someone hurtled past me and grabbed him by the throat – it was Stuart's ex-wife Anne. His chair went over backwards on to the floor with a crash. For a moment Logue looked up into my face and flinched, and I saw he thought I might kick him in the head.

Moments later, the landlord had come out from behind the counter, and the brawl was over.

David Campton's agent, Jimmy Wax, lived a few hundred yards away in Sloane Street, and we all adjourned there. Bill asked if he could use the phone. A few minutes later I made my way to the bathroom, and heard Bill's voice saying: 'Is that the *Daily Express*? Have you heard about this brawl with the Angry Young Men at the Royal Court? . . . Well, there was Stuart Holroyd, Colin Wilson, Bill Hopkins . . .'

Bill told me later that he had started by ringing his brother Ted, who worked on the *News Chronicle*, then decided he might as well pass it on to the rest of Fleet Street.

The next morning, several newspapers carried the story on their front pages: ANGRY YOUNG MEN IN PUB BRAWL. And once again, it did nothing but harm, giving the impression that we were brash publicity seekers.

As I have said, I often felt that Bill was still living in the nineteenth century, identifying with Victor Hugo and the famous clash between Romantics and Classicists. But I feel that Bill failed to grasp the difference between nineteenth-century journalism and its sensation-seeking modern equivalent.

The hostility I aroused often seemed out of all proportion to its cause. One evening I joined a group of new acquaintances in a restaurant for supper. We had all been at a party given by Margot Warmesley, the business manager of *Encounter*. Opposite me was the novelist Constantine Fitzgibbon. Margot asked me my opinion of Dylan Thomas, and I replied that I disliked most of his work intensely – that it struck me as all sound and no meaning. To my amazement Fitzgibbon went purple in the face, and began to shout at me and invite me outside for a fight. 'You bloody young upstarts who think you own the world because you've had a lot of publicity . . .'

Margot finally calmed him down, but he glowered sullenly at me for the rest of the evening. I gathered that he had known Thomas, but this was hardly relevant to my criticism of Thomas's poetry. (Even now, when I am willing to concede that Thomas was a great poet, I still feel he often elevates sound above meaning.) Two evenings later Fitzgibbon poured a pint of beer over the head of a friend of mine who was defending me in a Soho pub.

This friend, Dan Farson, was to cause me a lot of trouble. I met him for the first time in the Soho bookshop owned by a charming and generous homosexual named David Archer, a few days before publication of *The Outsider*. Dan was the son of the travel writer Negley Farson, and was a journalist and an excellent photographer. He had heard rumours about *The Outsider* before publication, and said he would like to interview me for the *Daily Mail*. He came to my flat in Notting Hill – by this time I had moved into a room overlooking the back garden – and brought his friend Francis Bacon, who had achieved recognition with his paintings of Screaming

Popes. Dan and Francis were both homosexual masochists who enjoyed picking up drunken sailors and getting beaten up. Francis, with his huge round face, looked like a good-tempered farm labourer. Dan went on to write an amusing article about me in a series on modern writers.

A few weeks later, when I told him that Joy and I were thinking of taking a holiday in the West Country, he invited us to join him and journalist Kenneth Allsop. Allsop, who was going to interview Dan's father, drove us down in an open-topped sports car. It seemed a marvellously glamorous way of travelling.

Negley Farson was an American. He lived, with his wife Eve, in a house on a cliff top in North Devon. When we arrived he was sitting outside in the sunlight, wearing only a pair of shorts and a shirt open to the waist. His leg, which had been injured in a flying accident in the First World War, had a gaping hole in the shin. He had a deep, powerful voice and an American accent. Sitting there in the sunlight he reminded me of Gorky's description of Tolstoy sitting under a tree and looking like a nature god.

Dan's mother, Eve, had been a nurse when Negley met her during the war, and was a model of practical efficiency. After years as a journalist, Negley had achieved fame in the mid-1930s with an autobiography called *The Way of a Transgressor*. But celebrity had increased the tendency to alcoholism that he had picked up as a newspaper man, so that he had now given up drink entirely – except when he fell off the wagon, and went on drinking until he collapsed in a coma. After that he had to stay in bed for a week.

Negley, whose publisher was also Victor Gollancz, already knew about me, and was warm and friendly. Nothing gave him so much pleasure as to talk about his past, and his meetings with famous men like Roosevelt, Gandhi and Smuts.

He told me of how he had gone to interview F. Scott Fitzgerald, and found him standing upright at a tall writing desk. He asked why Fitzgerald preferred to stand while writing. Fitzgerald said: 'Because when I sit down I want to do this' – pointing at a gin bottle beside the settee. Then he laid down his pen. 'Come on – let's sit down.'

Negley also told me about how he had gone to the morgue to see Dillinger's body, after the gangster had been shot. The corpse was covered from the waist down with a sheet. The morgue keeper raised this, and said: 'Look, he's well-hung, ain't he?'

Joy and I slept in a 'chalet' that they had built for guests, and the following morning, Dan produced a new tape recorder, and asked me if he could test it out by doing an interview with me. As a journalist, Dan loved asking provocative questions, and he soon brought the interview around to the question of my 'genius'. The *Sketch*, as already noted, had called me 'a new D. H. Lawrence', presumably because we were both midlanders and working-class; another tabloid had even compared me to Plato. But then, I had been telling myself I was a genius since I was a teenager; it was a necessary bulwark against discouragement, as well as being in the best Shavian tradition. Shakespeare obviously had no doubt about his own genius when he wrote that 'not marble nor the gilded monuments of princes/Shall outlive this powerful rhyme'. T. E. Lawrence, on the other hand, had never achieved self-belief, and this was largely responsible for his destruction.

All this I explained to Dan, in answer to his question. But when he blandly asked me whether there were any other geniuses around, I rose to the bait and answered: 'Bill Hopkins.'

A few months later, the interview appeared in a new Beaverbrook magazine called *Books and Art*, under the headline: 'Colin Wilson talks about: MY GENIUS'.

This did me no good – nor Bill, for that matter. And the silly interview added to the increasing groundswell of irritation that was now being directed at the 'Angry Young Men'. Within a few weeks of *The Outsider* and *Look Back in Anger*, most of the press stories about us were either satirical or hostile.

In all this, Bill Hopkins played something of the part of a Machiavelli. He had always admired the combative older generation of writers, from Hugo and Zola to Wells and Shaw. He believed, as they did, that a writer ought to be prepared to be a national influence. He was even more contemptuous than Milton of 'cloistered virtue'; his ideal was a kind of writer–politician, foreshadowed by Shaw in Undershaft. One day a female journalist came to see me when Bill was present; he joined in the arguments with enthusiasm, and expressed a violently anti-feminist point of view. Her article, when it appeared, was scathing; but it quoted all Bill's opinions as if they were mine, and made no mention of Bill.

Bill was surprisingly unenvious of my success; it only filled him with determination to join in the battle. He began writing like a steam engine on his novel *The Divine and the Decay*, which was immediately accepted by the publisher Howard Samuel, whose editor-in-chief was a brilliant young self-publicist called Tom Maschler. Tom saw all this publicity about Angry Young Men as a heaven-sent opportunity of stirring up further controversy and making a name for himself in the process. So he proceeded to organise a book called *Declaration*, a series of essays by 'Angry Young Men'. Of course, there were not enough of us, and Kingsley Amis and Iris Murdoch wisely refused to have any part of it. So Tom was forced to make do with myself, Osborne, Wain, Tynan, Bill Hopkins, Stuart Holroyd, film director Lindsay Anderson, and novelist Doris Lessing.

Stuart Holroyd had recently published his *Emergence from Chaos*, which had been accepted by Gollancz, who explained on the dust jacket that it had 'a similar message' to *The Outsider*, and added – quite inaccurately – that Stuart had not been influenced by me. The book had achieved a great deal of attention in the wake of the Angry Young Man mania.

But the newspaper critics, who were already regretting their praise of *The Outsider*, were determined not to allow another 'angry' upstart to achieve overnight celebrity, and one of them even denounced Stuart as a new 'messiah of the milk bars'. Typically, this happened after a long and apparently friendly interview.

Stuart, like Bill, was a victim of the *succès fou* of *The Outsider*. Swept up in the publicity, they failed to understand that the end result would be a backlash. They also took advantage of the party circuit, and the girls who wanted to share the limelight, so Stuart's marriage to Anne failed to survive. Stuart had a number of *affaires* in quick succession with a number of girls, including Carole Ann. The non-stop party atmosphere made me think of the 1920s.

My own financial success had been considerable. Gollancz had printed a first edition of five thousand copies, but this sold out within a few days of publication. After that, impression followed impression in quick succession. The book went on to sell forty thousand copies in its guinea edition. An American publisher – Houghton Mifflin – accepted it, and published it in September. *Time* magazine brought out a full-page interview with me shortly before publication, and the book quickly became a best-seller in America too. *Life* even photographed me on Hampstead Heath in my sleeping bag, wearing the polo-necked sweater that I had become identified with.

It was soon after this that I finally met T. S. Eliot. It started when someone in my club – the Dionysus, which was actually the bar of the Mercury Theatre in Notting Hill – told me that Eliot went to church every Sunday morning at St Augustine's, in Queen's Gate. My informant – a playwright named Ashley Dukes – added that Eliot was a church warden, which meant that if anyone brawled in church, it was his duty to take them by the scruff of the neck and eject them. Joy and I decided to go to church the next morning to see if Eliot would really be there.

He was. As soon as we went into church, we saw him sitting at the end of a pew at the back, dressed in his neat black suit and a shirt with a starched collar. We went and sat opposite him across the aisle.

As the sermon began, there was a loud crash of broken glass that made everyone jump. It came from outside the rear church door facing Queen's Gardens. A moment later there was another appalling crash, then another. I had noticed the milk bottles outside this door as we passed it; evidently some urchins had decided to throw stones at them. Eliot, whose job it was to go and investigate, looked embarrassed. Finally, when there was another mighty crash, I strode down the aisle, went outside, and caught two scruffy children running away. I said: 'Listen, you little bastards, if you don't stop this I'll bang your heads together,' and let them go. As I went back to my seat, I got a grateful nod from Eliot.

The following week I had to go and see Eliot in his office. I was collaborating with the poet Ronald Duncan to get Ezra Pound out of jail, where he had been incarcerated for treason, and wanted to get Eliot's signature on a petition. I went to Eliot's office at Faber and Faber, behind Russell Square, and was shown in by his secretary (who later became his wife). I was struck by an umbrella in the hat stand with the largest handle I have ever seen. Eliot looked much as he had in church – he always dressed like a business executive. When I said: 'I saw you in church last Sunday,' Eliot said: 'I know. I recognised you.' I was astonished. 'How?' 'No one else would come to church in a polo-neck sweater.'

As it happened, Eliot was unable to help us. He explained that he and Pound's lawyer had already set the wheels in motion to try and get the poet released. And a few months later, during the lunch hour, when all the journalists were in the pub, a judge quietly signed Pound's release.

Negley had an amusing anecdote about Eliot's wife Valerie. At a dinner party, a little dog jumped up and began to lick her bare shoulders. Eliot smiled and said: 'I know exactly how he feels.'

Another literary pundit I met at this time was C. P. Snow, whose work Angus had dismissed as dull and overrated. I had read a novel by Snow called *The New Men*, about Cambridge scientists, and thought it was one of the most intelligent novels I had ever read. Since Snow, like myself, was a 'Leicester lad', I wrote to him to tell him how much I liked it. He replied, inviting me to meet him in a pub south of Hyde Park for a drink. It was a beautiful day, and we sat outside on the pavement under a lime tree, and talked about Leicester. Snow, I was glad to note, still had a faint Leicester accent.

We took a great liking to one another. And as we separated, he said: 'Let me give you a piece of advice. You have a likeable, friendly personality. If I were you, I'd mix more with people. Go to more parties. Half these people who attack you would be won over.'

He was obviously right, but I was already suffering from what I called 'people poisoning' in London, and the thought of more parties made me shudder. But the advice was typical of Snow; he was known in Whitehall as a master 'fixer'.

Although I was not enjoying the success much, I was at least enjoying having enough money to live as I liked. This was altogether the pleasantest part of the furore. I had bought a cheap gramophone (for £10) from Dan Farson, and I could walk into the Gate Book Shop, five minutes away from Chepstow Villas, and browse through second-hand records and books, then write a cheque for twenty pounds or so to pay for them. I can still recall the gloating delight with which I would go through my new purchases when I got home.

I bought a new *Encyclopaedia Britannica* and the set of Toynbee's *Study of History*. What was most pleasant of all was to walk into the delicatessen in Pembridge Villas and be able to afford to buy a cold chicken, already cooked, quantities of olives, gherkins, and delicacies wrapped in vine leaves, then get a bottle of burgundy from the wine shop next door, and provide Joy with a cold lunch or supper.

It was also pleasant to be able to take her to good Soho restaurants, or to a pub opposite Hyde Park, where one could sit on the terrace in the sun and eat excellent cold lunches and drink beer. For years, I had eaten tinned beans and bread and cheese without a complaint, honestly believing that I was not interested in food. Now I discovered that I enjoyed good food as much as any gourmet.

Joy had got herself a job as a librarian for a naval institute in Surrey. We were living together in Chepstow Villas, and she went off to work every morning. Her family thought we were living apart, and she kept a rented room to receive her mail.

Her former fiancé had naturally been devastated by her decision to break it off, particularly since he had gone to Canada to set up a home. He now wrote to her to ask her to meet him in London, and she agreed. I don't think she enjoyed the meeting: she said he was bitter and angry about being jilted, and she didn't blame him. I also quite understood and felt sad and guilty about it, although Joy had told me that the two of them had grown apart in the two years since they were at college.

Another immense pleasure was getting to know wine in the civilised manner – by drinking it every day, and trying out every variety in the shop. To begin with, I used to drink a sparkling red Italian wine called Nebiolo d'Asti; later, I drank mostly Nuits Saint-Georges or other Beaunes.

I even allowed myself to be persuaded to join a club, the Savage. Negley had been a member before they threw him out for being persistently drunk and disorderly; so had Dylan Thomas. I remembered the Savage Club from John Buchan's *The Thirty-nine Steps* – the hero had been a member – and felt rather overawed at the thought of joining such distinguished company. In fact, the club had been founded by the actor Henry Irving, and most of its members were distinctly raffish actors, musicians or writers, so I felt very much at home there. But I never quite overcame a feeling of incongruity at walking up its huge marble staircase, or going to urinate in a toilet the size of a small banqueting hall.

This was the pleasant side of success: this, and not having to get up in the mornings. Its other aspect was something I would have avoided if I had known about it in advance.

One evening at the Royal Court Theatre I took part in a debate on the modern theatre. Kenneth Tynan was the chairman, and others on the panel were Arthur Miller, John Whiting and Wolf Mankowitz. (Marilyn Monroe sat in the front row.) Mankowitz was a novelist who specialised in cockney humour and pathos. Within a few minutes of the start of the discussion, Mankowitz suddenly described *The Outsider* as an anthology of quotations. This raised a laugh. Encouraged, Mankowitz kept up this line of attack throughout the evening. The following day, an unsigned report in a London evening paper declared: 'Mankowitz played with Wilson like a good-natured lion with a mouse.'

The next day, I was asked to appear on television to argue the point with Mankowitz. I did, and the discussion was heated but not downright rude. Afterwards I asked Mankowitz who had written the report in the evening paper; he reddened, then scowled defiantly and snapped: 'I did.'

I was asked to address some kind of a spiritualist society at a Knightsbridge hotel. When I arrived, I discovered they were mostly mild old ladies. A gossip columnist from the *Daily Express* approached me, winked at me, and asked me to come and have a quiet drink. He intimated that we were fellow-conspirators among a lot of old tabby cats, and asked me to 'have a go at the old bitches'. I said I couldn't do that – they were my hostesses – but we went on drinking on friendly terms. In my speech after the meal, I said that I was tired of being described as a spokesman of the younger generation; I represented no one but myself. *The Outsider* was a personal statement, and I felt a fraud when it was taken to be an expression of a new anti-Establishment attitude.

The next day, the *Daily Express* appeared with a headline: 'Colin Wilson Admits He Is a Fraud'. I was quoted as saying 'The Outsider was written with completely false intent . . .' Gollancz was immediately on the phone to me, roaring with rage, and two days later his solicitor managed to induce the newspaper to print an apology, but I got the feeling that many people would be only too happy to dismiss the book as a fraud.

When the *Observer* published, in its Christmas issue, a page by well-known writers stating what they thought to be the most interesting books of the year, *The Outsider* received only one mention, by Arthur Koestler. It read: 'Bubble of the year: *The Outsider*. In which a young man discovers that men of genius are prone to *Weltschmerz*.'

The attacks went on. They were provoked by the non-stop barrage of publicity. My friend John Rety asked me to write an article for his magazine the *Intimate Review*, then plastered advertisements for it all over the London Underground, so I found my face staring at me every time I travelled on the tube.

This infuriated the serious critics. Angus Wilson asked me to lunch, and told me that the hostility towards me was growing – most people seemed to think I was orchestrating the publicity. I told him that I had no more notion of how to generate publicity than a football has of scoring goals. He urged me to get as far as possible from London, and stay there.

And why did I allow myself to become the subject of so much silly publicity? In retrospect I can see that it was a mixture of innocence and stupidity. I had been unknown all my life, then suddenly, I was a 'celebrity'. Every time I appeared on television, or my name appeared in a newspaper, I felt that this was one more guarantee that I would never again disappear into oblivion. If I had been less naïve, I would have seen that I was simply arousing the kind of irritation that would rebound on me and invite the devaluation I was so anxious to escape. I mistook celebrity for fame.

What this meant was that, six months after the book's publication, it was the general opinion among English intellectuals that *The Outsider* had been a craze that had died a natural death, and that I should now be returned to the obscurity from which I had accidentally emerged.

I subscribed to a press-cutting bureau, but the cuttings were becoming almost uniformly hostile. I got the feeling that every journalist in England wanted to throw his stone on the cairn that covered my dead reputation. The Americans also joined in the fun. No country is more eager to hail celebrity; none more delighted to see its downfall. At a party in London I had met a fat and pleasant-voiced American called Dwight Macdonald, blessed with an attractive wife and a pretty daughter. We got on excellently. One morning, my press cuttings brought me a copy of a review from the *New Yorker* that amounted to a long and vigorous attack on *The Outsider*, signed by Dwight Macdonald. I remained friendly with Macdonald, but I didn't like the way his review was taken as a signal for a radical re-estimation of *The Outsider* by his countrymen.

I decided that the answer was to get out of London. A correspondent called Hugh Heckstall Smith offered me the use of two rooms in his house near Totnes, Devon, and this seemed a reasonable solution. I had never met Heckstall Smith and knew nothing about him, except that he had been the headmaster of Stowe, and had written textbooks on physics for schools. Bill Hopkins decided that he would come with me for a few weeks, and we set off in November.

But although Hugh Heckstall Smith turned out to be the soul of amiability, and one of the most interesting and original minds I had encountered, the idea didn't work out. Perhaps it was the cold and damp of November; perhaps it was living away from Joy – not to mention books and music. After a week or so Bill and I returned to London. At least I had managed to get well into *Spiritual Reformers* (the original title of *Religion and the Rebel*) in a fortnight, and Bill had written a chapter of *The Divine and the Decay*.

In retrospect I can see that I should have stayed out of London. What was about to happen was the worst piece of publicity so far.

In February 1957 Joy went home to Bedford to have her tonsils removed. I went up to see her, and while I was at the hospital her sister Fay picked up a diary I had left on the hall table and opened it casually. Some impatient remarks about her parents aroused her interest, and she read on. There was an entry about a homosexual friend who had talked to me about his problems, and a great deal of discussion of the sexual deviations that are the main theme of my *Ritual in the Dark*. Altogether, I think she had an interesting half-hour. When I returned I thought she looked at me oddly, but I paid no attention.

When Joy finally returned to Notting Hill, she was exhausted and in tears. Her mother had been pestering her for days, ever since she came out of hospital. Her parents knew by now that I was married, and wanted me to get a divorce, which Betty was not even prepared to discuss. Joy's mother wanted me to go to Las Vegas. So when Fay happened to ring in the early evening, I told her that if her mother didn't stop nagging Joy, I would tell Joy to stop going home for weekends.

Later that evening – it was Tuesday 19 February 1957 – the storm broke. Joy and I were giving dinner in my flat to a corpulent, plausible old rogue named Gerald Hamilton (the original of Isherwood's Mr Norris in the Berlin novel *Mr Norris Changes Trains*). Suddenly, the door burst open, and in strode Joy's mother, father, brother and sister. Joy's father was a gentle, grey-haired man, but her mother was dominant and self-assertive. Her brother Neil was, like his father, a gentle and rather shy person, but her sister Fay – a dazzlingly pretty girl – was capable of becoming hysterical.

I assumed this incursion meant they had discovered I was living with Joy – but then, Fay had known this for a long time, and even stayed with us. So I could only look bewildered.

Her father shouted: 'The game is up, Wilson!'

'What game?'

'We've read your filthy diary!'

Then at last I began to understand. The notes for *Ritual in the Dark* included a sketch of the Polly Nichols murder site in Whitechapel. Fay must have got the idea that I was at least a sadistic pervert.

Her father turned to Joy. 'Did you know he's a homosexual and has six mistresses?' I am not sure how he reconciled these statements.

I took my diary out of a drawer. 'Here. Take it away and read it.'

He snatched it from me and thrust it into his pocket. Then, from his briefcase, he took a horsewhip, and raised it above his head. I pushed him in the chest and he fell down, whereupon Joy's mother hurled herself on me, shouting: 'How dare you hit an old man?' and proceeded to belabour me with her umbrella. I tried to say: 'But he was going to hit *me*,' but it all seemed so funny that I rolled on the floor, shrieking with laughter. Someone kicked me but I still couldn't stop laughing.

By this time several other tenants, attracted by the uproar, had come in to see what was happening. Joy's family had grabbed her arms and were dragging her out. I grabbed one of her hands and heaved in the opposite direction. But four against one was too much, and it looked as if they would succeed in dragging her off. Fortunately, the other tenants helped me to pull until it looked as if Joy was going to come apart down the middle.

Finally, I managed to get to the phone in the kitchen, and rang the police.

They arrived surprisingly quickly: a sergeant and police constable. They demanded to know what it was all about. Joy's father waved the diary.

'Look, he's a sexual pervert, and he's living with our daughter.'

The sergeant ignored it. He asked Joy: 'How old are you?'

'Twenty-three.'

He turned to Joy's parents. 'Then I'm afraid you'll have to leave. She's over twenty-one.'

'But he's a pervert!' said Joy's father, evidently believing this would lead to my immediate arrest.

'But this is his residence, and if he asks you to go, I'm afraid you have to go.'

He looked sympathetic, as if saying: 'I agree he looks like a pervert. And if I had my way we'd put them all in jail. But I'm afraid that's the law.'

I tried to ease the situation, and asked Joy: 'Why not go with them, and come back when you've talked it over?'

For a moment Joy looked as if she might be persuaded; then I think she wondered whether Carole Ann might seize the opportunity to come and console me, and shook her head.

Eventually everyone left except the two of us, but even the peace seemed ominous.

Five minutes later, there was a ring at the doorbell. I went to the kitchen window, which overlooked the front door. The two men on the doorstep were obviously reporters, for one of them carried a flash camera. It was only then that I noticed that Gerald Hamilton was no longer with us. I decided to let them in, feeling that a little publicity might keep Joy's parents at bay. I told them the story briefly, and allowed them to take a photograph.

Ten minutes later, there was another ring at the doorbell. I looked out and saw a crowd of reporters with several cameramen.

We rang up Tom Maschler, who lived nearby, and asked him if we could come and stay at his flat. Then we sneaked out of the back door, looking guiltily over our shoulders. But the pressmen had not seen us.

Tom put us up overnight, and gave us a chance to discuss the problem quietly. What bothered us most was that Joy's parents might make another attempt to drag her off, perhaps meeting her on her way back from work. She kept repeating: 'They're so innocent.' We decided that it might be best to leave London for a few days. So the next morning we rang Eve Farson, and asked if we could come and stay. We took the next train to Devon.

We had rung Bill Hopkins to tell him what had happened, and the next morning he went out and bought the newspapers. Several of them carried the story – what made it irresistible was the touch about the horsewhip. Bill also told us that one newspaper quoted extracts from the diary that I had handed to Joy's father, and which he in turn had handed to the *Daily Mail* reporter.

Safely in Devon, we rang Bill again, and learned that the *Daily Express* was bidding to publish extracts from the diary. They were offering £50, so I asked Negley's advice. It was uncompromising: 'Never sell your private life to a newspaper.' The result was that Bill told the *Express* that they could publish the extracts for nothing, provided he was allowed to choose and edit them. And the next day, the *Express* came out with a double page spread: THE DIARY OF COLIN WILSON, with a cartoon of me, in polo-neck sweater, being chased by an angry father wielding a horsewhip.

On another page, there was a drawing by Osbert Lancaster, the famous cartoonist, showing a bespectacled young man in a polo-neck sweater, looking over a banister at a tweedy-looking lesbian marching upstairs with a horsewhip. He is saying nervously: 'I think it's your mother come to pay us a visit.'

I now recognise that fleeing London was the worst thing we could have done. The story would otherwise have died a natural death in a day or so. As it was, the press had a marvellous story about runaway lovers, straight out of *Look Back in Anger*, and were determined to play it for all it was worth.

Within a few hours, a crowd of reporters and cameramen arrived outside Negley's house. The phone rang non-stop. And then halfway through the morning, Negley told me that he had just talked with the *Daily Express*, and they had an offer for me. If I would allow them to take just one photograph of the two of us together, they would drive us to any place in England and allow us to go.

This was too good to refuse, and I agreed. Negley's house overlooked a long beach, and his next-door neighbour was a friendly and cultured American. I could easily sneak along the beach to his house, and the *Express* reporters would meet me there. Then we would have to go and collect Joy – she was staying at a pub on Exmoor, in case her parents made another attempt to drag her away.

The *Express* reporters met me outside the house of Negley's neighbour and I clambered into their car. Behind us, a few hundred yards away, waited the reporters with their cameramen, unaware that their prey was escaping.

The senior reporter, Jim Brady, was from Bristol. He and his assistant drove me to Exmoor, where we collected Joy, then we drove off to Taunton station, where the photographer took his photograph on a deserted platform. After that, Jim Brady went to telephone his editor to report the success of the assignment. But he came back looking upset and embarrassed. His editor had told him to stay with us, wherever we went. He was very apologetic about it. He said that if we would promise not to try to escape, they wouldn't bother us. But if we managed to lose him, it would be more than his job was worth. We promised, and again we climbed into his car.

We had already decided where we wanted to go – Dublin, where Joy had been at university. So Jim drove us to Ilfracombe, where we caught a ferry across to Swansea. I remember that Franck's Symphony was being played through the loudspeaker as we looked back at the receding Devon coastline. The symphony still brings back that trip across the Bristol Channel, and the sense of happiness and adventure.

In Swansea, we found a hotel, then rang Kingsley Amis. Joy and I had met him soon after *The Outsider* came out, in that pub in Charing Cross Road near the statue of Henry Irving, whom Amis typically referred to as 'old nonsense'. Amis was a good-looking man, whose voice had a peculiarly pleasant timbre. Dan Farson had introduced us, and I had found Amis amusing and likeable. He had already published a vaguely mocking review of *The Outsider* in the *Spectator*, entitled 'The Legion of the Lost', which began: 'Here they come – tramp, tramp, tramp – all those characters you thought were discredited, or had never read, or (if you are like me) had never heard of: Barbusse, Sartre, Camus . . .'

Incensed by his remark about T. E. Lawrence: 'who, whatever his claims as a man, was surely a sonorous fake as a writer', I had written Amis a rather irritable note, and received a good-natured reply. But in a letter to Robert Conquest of June 1956, Amis quotes my letter to him at some length, and adds: 'Good stuff, eh? I give him 2 years before paranoia closes over his head.'

But we spent a pleasant evening with Amis and his wife Hilly, who was pretty and blonde. It was Hilly's birthday, and the Amises were sitting on either side of a table full of spirits and liqueurs. (I remember he said he much preferred Irish to Scotch.) When we left, we were both slightly unsteady on our feet.

The following day we took the boat from Fishguard to Dun Laoghaire. After we had settled in a hotel in Dublin, it was time for work: the reporters insisted on taking us to Sandymount Strand and taking photographs of us posed on a rock. It appeared in the *Express* with a caption 'Colin and Joy in the south of England'. I have a borrowed portable typewriter on my knee, and Joy is having problems controlling her dress, which is lifting in the breeze. (It can be found in Sidney Campion's 1962 book about me, still with the wrong caption.)

That evening we wandered around Trinity, then went to the Pearl Bar. There we fell into conversation with a professor of Irish literature named Con Leventhal, who knew about *The Outsider*. (We had seen a copy on the hotel bookstall as we arrived.) We told him our story, and were soon surrounded by a crowd of literary Irishmen and being plied with whiskey. Con, it seemed, was an old friend of Samuel Beckett, and when I said I couldn't stand Beckett's dreary pessimism, he said that he was nevertheless a delightful man and a marvellous drinking companion.

Con invited us for dinner the next day, cooked by his wife Eithne, a doctor. I got the feeling that Con and Eithne regarded us as incredibly lucky, rather like Scott and Zelda Fitzgerald, and there in Dublin, surrounded by happy drinkers, I must admit that I *felt* incredibly lucky. In a pub on the quays we ate magnificent ham sandwiches and drank Guinness, and had salmon in Jammet's restaurant, in the days when salmon was still an expensive rarity. I found it hard to remember that, only the previous year, I had been struggling to raise the money for the rent. There was a marvellous feeling that life had suddenly stopped hounding me.

A few days later, Joy and I decided to leave Dublin and go to look at the west coast. By now, the *Express* was willing to let us go unhindered. Money had arrived from my bank (care of Con Leventhal), so we took a train to Tipperary, then to Tralee, where we found a pleasant, old-fashioned hotel (as most hotels in Ireland were in those days). Because of the newspapers, we registered under a false name – in the 50s, the Irish would have frowned on an unmarried couple sleeping together.

In the bar, we made the acquaintance of a pleasant woman in her thirties, to whom we told our story. It seemed she owned a run-down house not far away, in Dingle, and she offered to sell it to us at a remarkably low price. Since we were already thinking seriously about moving out of London, we went to look at it, but decided it would cost too much to repair.

The next day she came to our room with a copy of *Time* magazine. There was a photograph of myself and Joy, and an account of the 'horse-whipping'. We decided to check out of the hotel right away, and caught the next train back to Dublin. But even there, as we sat in an O'Connell Street bar, a stranger leaned across to me and said: 'Why don't you sue *Time* magazine?'

By the following day we were back in Chepstow Villas. Within hours, the *Daily Mail* learned we were back, and rang up to ask if they could come and interview me. Joy, who had by now developed a phobia about the press, made sure she was not there when they arrived. The photographer set up a camera and took a picture of me sitting in a battered armchair. When the photograph appeared in the newspaper it covered the whole back page. There were white circles all over it, and underneath was a key explaining what they referred to: (1) bare floorboards, (2) lamp without lamp shade, (3) armchair missing an arm. And so on.

My father was furious. Since *The Outsider* came out he had basked in his son's celebrity, and probably boasted too much. Now, suddenly, his friends at the Coleman Road club were saying: 'Why does your son live in such a rat hole?' He cared far more about what the newspapers wrote than I did.

Gollancz asked me to go around and see him. When I did, he advised me – as Angus Wilson had – to get out of London as soon as I could, while I still had a few shreds of reputation left. He told me that there was an impression that I was a publicity seeker, and that this would undoubtedly draw hostile reviews when I wrote my next book.

I had a hankering to go and live in the Hebrides, which sounded romantic. (When I visited them a few years later I was glad I hadn't – they were too wet.) But a friend who lived in the next room had an interesting alternative to offer. He was a poet called Louis Adeane, who worked in London for a publisher, but longed to return to Cornwall, where he rented a farm cottage. For this he paid twenty-five shillings a week. But he saw no prospect of returning for at least two years. If, in the meantime, I rented the cottage for thirty shillings a week, it would not only save him rent, but give him a small profit.

Joy and I went down to look at it one weekend in early March. We stayed at a boarding house in Mevagissey, run by the poet and critic D. S. Savage. The next morning we took a taxi over to the farm, and walked half a mile down a long dirt-track with pools of cow dung.

It was a sparkling, bright morning, and when I saw the cottage I could hardly believe our luck. It stood at the head of a valley, at the end of which we could see the sea. Just below the cottage there was a wooden shed with a desk and bookshelves, and below the shed ran a stream that made a continuous sound like heavy rain. The cottage was Elizabethan, and was called Old Walls because its whitewashed walls, about two feet thick, were made of cob. There was no elecricity – only oil lamps – and the stove ran on Calor gas. The lavatory had to be flushed with buckets of water. But it all looked so beautiful that I began to worry in case Louis changed his mind. I could see why he was so attached to the place.

We agreed to take it, and paid rent in advance. But before we moved down, we had to get electricity installed – otherwise there would be no music – which meant a generator in the shed next door. For hot water we had to keep a stove burning in the bathroom, but since it was next to the lavatory, it was a pleasure to sit there reading. Drinking water had to be fetched from a well down the garden.

I bought a generator for about a hundred pounds, and a friend named Mike Whyatt – a highly intelligent would-be writer – came down and installed electric wiring. The generator charged a dozen twelve-volt car batteries, and these had to be recharged every day. A device called a vibrator-pack – which made a loud hum – stepped up the voltage so it would work the record player. There was no television, of course, but in those days we had no desire to watch it, since there was almost no choice of programmes.

That first evening, as I relaxed in my armchair in front of the fire and shared a bottle of hock with Mike Whyatt, I felt that Joy and I had found our paradise.

CHAPTER 10

Getting Away

It was probably just as well we decided to move to the country. For at every London party I had attended, I had met attractive girls who were obviously willing to have an *affaire*. Being fairly susceptible and full of romanticism, I would have been glad to avail myself of some of these opportunities, but since I was now settled with Joy, this was out of the question. My exploits in the Coffee House had made her miserable, and I was determined not to do it again. Ever since I had met Joy, I had been quite certain that she was the girl I had always been looking for, my own embodiment of the eternal feminine. But, like Shelley, I felt it was a pity to have to consign the rest of womankind to 'cold oblivion'.

Other writers – like H. G. Wells and Bertrand Russell – had solved the problem by having affairs, and leaving their wives to cope as best they could. I knew from gossip that Philip Toynbee, Cyril Connolly and A. J. Ayer kept half a dozen affairs going at a time. This would have struck me as downright heartless, since I adored Joy, and had taken her away from a safe conventional marriage. But I must admit that being forced to reject the temptation of pretty and compliant girls was as painful as having an arm amputated. At least living in Cornwall placed me at arm's length from temptation.

Living in the country was like a wish-fulfilment fantasy. We would wake up to the sound of the stream, and the sunlight on the opposite hillside (our bedroom faced west). After breakfast I would walk up to the farm to collect my mail, which was delivered to a shed in the farmyard. But if I saw a brown envelope with press cuttings, I opened it with a sinking feeling. Almost everything written about me in the British press was now hostile.

I was in a strange situation. One year ago, no one had heard of me. Then I became 'famous'. And now, ten months later, it seemed it had all evaporated like fairy gold. Had it really gone for good? There was no way of telling. Meanwhile, at least it was a lovely spring, and I was 300 miles from London, and Cornwall was pleasant and peaceful.

Most of the pubs were old-fashioned, with horse brasses on the beams and huge oak settles. The locals were friendly, and I soon got into a habit of playing darts with them. On the quay you could buy fish and crabs straight out of the sea. Our village, Mevagissey, was so picturesque that it looked like a stage set, and the view from the hill above it was spectacular, with Plymouth almost visible across the bay to the east and Falmouth to the south-west.

We bought an ancient car for £40, and as we were returning from the garage, Joy showed me the rudiments of using the clutch and the gears. That same afternoon, I drove it for the first time. Joy had gone for a walk to Mevagissey with Bill Hopkins, and when they were not back by late afternoon, I thought they might be grateful if I drove down to save them the walk. I got into the car and started it as Joy had shown me – by turning the key and pressing the starter. Then I depressed the clutch and drove it up the hill as far as the first farm gate. There it stalled because I forgot to put it in neutral. So I started it again, opened the gate, and got it as far as the second farm gate, where I stalled it once more.

Driving down Bodrugan Hill, the steepest in the district, was so hair-raising that I wished I had stayed at home. Fortunately I met nothing on the right-angle bend. And I drove unsteadily the two miles to Mevagissey, where Joy and Bill stared in disbelief at the sight of me driving down Polkirt Hill towards them. It was a huge relief to let Joy take over, and when we arrived home we opened a bottle of wine to celebrate and put *Guys and Dolls* on the record player.

During the next week or so we drove all over Cornwall – Looe, Polperro, St Agnes, Perranporth – eating fish and chips or Cornish pasties, and drinking beer. I would work all morning on the sequel to *The Outsider* (now retitled *The Rebel*), then we would walk down the valley for a swim, or look at the map and decide where to drive today. It was like a holiday that went on and on. When I had worked in factories or offices, I could not have believed that life could be so pleasant.

The Suez crisis had caused a fuel shortage, but our local garage would usually give us a fill of petrol. For some reason, the government also decided that during the crisis, learner drivers did not need a qualified driver in the car, so I learned fast – so fast that when Stuart Holroyd came to stay with us, I was able to teach him to drive. When we took him back to London, he drove most of the way.

However, the old Ford was too rickety for such long journeys, and broke down in Hammersmith. A garage told us it would cost more to repair than the car was worth, so we sold it for scrap, and took the train back to Cornwall, where we bought our first new car, a Ford Anglia, on hire purchase.

The sales representative, John Cookson, brought a photographer over with him to take a photograph of me taking delivery of my new car, for use in the Ford trade magazine. Then he took us to his favourite pub, the General Wolfe in St Austell, where we were introduced to the small back room where the regulars congregated – the local optician, the ex-Police Superintendent, the fire chief, and various shop owners. It proved to be a seductively pleasant place, and when they told us that the pubs were open all day on Fridays because it was a market day, we made a habit of going in on Friday mornings; and while Joy did the shopping, I would join the crowd in the back room. I seldom drank too much – confining myself to halves of bitter – although if I allowed myself to be persuaded to move on to whisky, I usually left the worse for wear. I recall one occasion when I fell into Joy's flower bed while relieving my bladder. And Joy, instead of being annoyed, found it all very amusing. But then, I was very seldom drunk, unlike many of my friends in the back room. One of these, Ralph Goodenough, who had inherited a shoe shop, often fell down in the street and had to be carried home.

I noted again that sense of relaxation and happiness that convivial drinkers share, the feeling that life is wonderful and will go on being wonderful. For me, its nearest equivalent was the feeling I used to experience at Christmas as a child, when the whole world seemed transformed into a kind of fairyland. Now, for the first time, I could see why my father had spent most of his leisure in the Coleman Road club. I could also see why so many writers, from Rabelais to G. K. Chesterton, had elevated drinkers into a kind of mystical brotherhood.

My second book, now called *Religion and the Rebel* (Gollancz finally chose the title), came out on 21 October that year. I had prepared myself for a hammering, although I still hoped that some miracle might persuade the critics that I had something worth saying. That hope soon evaporated as I read Philip Toynbee in the *Observer* describing it as a rubbish bin, while in the *Sunday Times*, Raymond Mortimer explained that *The Outsider* had never been much to his taste, so that he was not surprised to find the sequel disappointing. Without exception, other critics took a hostile line. And under the headline SCRAMBLED EGGHEAD, *Time* magazine lost no time informing American readers that the book had been universally damned.

Oddly enough, I experienced a sense of relief. Being 'famous' had been no fun at all, even before the press turned hostile. And now I had time to relax and think quietly about it all, I could see that, as strange as this sounds, this was what I wanted. I had tried fame and found it exhausting. And I could see that now I was in the 'fast lane', it was going to be hard to escape. I wanted to lead the kind of relaxed life that Wordsworth had led in the Lake District. But even Wordsworth had to submit to being lionised and fêted.

I had read of literary celebrities who had been killed by success – Ross

Lockridge Jnr, who had written *Raintree County*, and Thomas Heggan, who had written the play *Mr Roberts*. Both had committed suicide. They had to think about the next success, and then the one after that. But if that was what success cost, I didn't want it. I wanted to be allowed to read all the great novels I had not read and listen to all the music I wanted to hear, and be allowed to study philosophy from morning till night. Like De L'Isle Adam's Axel, I didn't want to 'live'.

Then what did I want?

To spend my life thinking about the question that really interested me: how to transform my consciousness at will. Wells had expressed it clearly at the beginning of his *Experiment in Autobiography*, when he complained that trivial problems were eating away his life. And he explained: 'The originative intellectual worker is not a normal human being and does not desire to lead a normal human life. He wants to lead a supernormal life.'

I suddenly grasped the full implications of this a few years later when I was driving home from Torquay with Joy and our two sons. I was talking about philosophy, and it suddenly struck me that I was living on two levels at once. The 'everyday me' was driving a car – perfectly safely but automatically – while another level of me was engaged in 'originative intellectual work'. My body was inhabiting the 'first stream' of physical existence; my mind was inhabiting a *second stream* of ideas and insights. Wells had said: 'I have no wish to live unless I can get on with what I consider to be my proper business.' I could see that our proper business is this second stream.

So now I felt I was off my pedestal and back on solid ground again, I could get on with my real work. The next task was to finish *Ritual in the Dark*.

But first I had agreed to go and lecture in Europe. Before the *Religion and the Rebel* fiasco, I had been invited by the British Council to lecture in Oslo, and at the end of November Joy and I took our first flight in an aeroplane. It was a marvellous experience to see the snow-capped mountains below us. But when we climbed out of the plane, the cold took my breath away. We were driven to our hotel – the Continental – through falling snow by the British Council representative, Brian Swingler, a charming man who looked after us well for the next six days. At the hotel, I found a woman journalist from *Dagsblatter* waiting for me, and was surprised and pleased to be asked serious questions – about my opinion of the existentialism of Sartre and Camus – instead of about my sex life.

For the first time I recognised that I had been born in the wrong country. The British are incurably trivial-minded. And this, I concluded, was because Britain has been a secure little island for so long. We have not been invaded since 1066. So it is simply not in the British temperament to produce a Dostoevsky or a Goethe, or even a Sartre. In England, it is not fashionable to deal with the kind of questions I had written about in *The Outsider* and *Religion and the Rebel* – questions about what Reinhold Niebuhr called 'the nature and destiny of man'. People who do so are regarded as cranks.

So it was exciting to be in a country that treated such matters as important. The gloomy Scandinavian winter induces a certain seriousness of temperament, which I found congenial. Our hotel was opposite the theatre, with its statues of Ibsen and Bjørnson, and in discussions with journalists, I felt that literature was here a subject for excitement, and that ideas might be a real influence on the future.

On the second evening, a Saturday, I lectured in a vast hall, and the students sat at tables and drank beer as they listened. Everyone seemed to speak English. When I had finished there was an interval, during which a string quartet played Brahms and Nielsen. Then question time began – which was completely unlike anything I had experienced in England. The students went up on to the stage and each delivered his own short address – if it became too long, the chairman cut them short, but most of them were remarkably disciplined.

What I wanted to explain was why, in an age of pessimism, I was possessed by an absolutely absurd optimism. I began by speaking about existentialism, particularly Heidegger and Sartre, and explained why their view of human existence is so negative. But, I went on, my own experience of the world seems to contradict this pessimistic attitude. This is not simply because I have a naturally cheerful disposition, but because when I go out on a spring morning, or listen to music, I am clearly conscious of a sense of *meaning*, which seems to me to be inherent in the universe itself, the product of some external intelligence, not just a 'feeling'. Great music and poetry seem to *widen* my consciousness in some way, and when that happens, I get a sense that it lets in more meaning. Sometimes, when overwhelmed with this sense of meaning, I feel almost afraid to open the gates any wider, in case it floods in and drowns me. That experience leaves me in no doubt that I am seeing something that is really out there, in the world itself, not just inside me. This is why I feel the need to create a new form of existentialism that is not limited by pessimism . . .

Many of the students obviously found it hard to share my optimism – but then, to the young, the world often seems a difficult place because they are full of self-dissatisfaction. Yet I felt that if I could have stayed there in Oslo, engaging in more discussions like this, most of them would end by agreeing with me.

A party that went on until 3 am left us worn-out, and by the next morning a sore throat had developed into a heavy cold. Stuck in bed in my hotel room, drinking potions of hot lemon and aspirin, I read James Jones's *From Here to Eternity* (which I had found in a bookshop next door), and was much impressed. This American wrote like a master. If I wanted *Ritual in the Dark* to be equally powerful, I had to treat it as a story, a narrative, and forget James Joyce and *The Egyptian Book of the Dead*. And since the novel was about a sadistic killer based on Jack the Ripper, it obviously had to be written as a kind of detective story.

In spite of a sore throat that reduced my voice to a croak, I lectured that evening at the Anglo-Norse Society, although by the end of the lecture I had virtually no voice left. It took another day in bed to restore me to something like normality. A strong Norwegian beer called Julol, brewed only in the Christmas season, proved to be a powerful restorative.

Heavy fog closed the airport and kept us in Oslo an extra day. That morning we received a telegram from Bill Hopkins, saying that he was going to Hamburg, and asking us to join him. We decided we would. Bill had gone to work on his second novel *Time of Totality*. *The Divine and the Decay* had been published the day we left England, and at the airport we had bought a copy of *Books and Bookmen* because Bill had learned there would be a review. There was more – a whole double centre page devoted to a long extract from the novel, together with a warm review. I was delighted, and commented to Joy: 'Well, it looks as though Bill got through . . .'

It was just as well we decided to break our journey in Hamburg. When the taxi dropped us off at the address Bill had given us – his ex-landlady – we found Bill sitting on the doorstep. His publisher had promised to send him a weekly allowance, but it had not arrived, so he hadn't eaten for twenty-four hours. We were able to lend him money, and we found a small hotel nearby – the Haus Heimhude, in the Heimhuderstrasse – and then walked down to the nearest bar. It was as freezing cold in Hamburg as in Oslo, and Bill advised us to try the hot rum punch. We did, and found it just what we needed. Then we ate an enormous German meal of eisbein and sauerkraut. And as we sat listening to the German popular music that filled the bar, we experienced one of those surges of delight and optimism, and Joy and I decided on the spot that we would remain with Bill until he returned to London at Christmas, in four weeks' time.

Bill's girlfriend Gret had not yet sent him any reviews, and I had only seen *Books and Bookmen*. The morning after we arrived, Bill came into our room for tea, and told me that I had let the attacks on *Religion and the Rebel* affect me too much. It was to be expected in an age when success had become associated with film stars and pop stars. No one had had my kind of overnight success since Byron woke up on the morning he published *Childe Harold* – and look what they did to Byron . . .

Letters had arrived for him that morning, but he had decided not to open them until we got to the café in the Stephansplatz where we intended to breakfast. On the way there Bill continued in the same vein. One should be strong enough to laugh at attacks . . . As we sat down, he opened a letter, and pulled out some press clippings. For a moment or two, he read in silence, then his face darkened, his eyes opened wide, and he suddenly exclaimed, in a voice that startled everyone in the café: 'The BASTARDS.' A moment later, he saw our smiles, and joined in the laughter.

But the reviews certainly were not funny. Kenneth Allsop later remarked in *The Angry Decade* that in this case the critics seemed to have ignored the tacitly recognised rule that an author's first book should be treated with a certain amount of gentleness. All this was very clearly the result of the 'England's Other Genius' publicity. The critics went in with knives and knuckledusters.

But then, *The Divine and the Decay* was the kind of novel that was bound to infuriate left-wing critics. It was about a politician who has founded a breakaway right-wing party, and who goes to the island of Sark to give himself an alibi while his closest political ally is murdered. Bill's obvious lack of disapproval of his Machiavellian hero was bound to cause outrage, and it did.

At all events, Hamburg was a good place to take refuge from hostile critics; a foreign city fosters a natural sense of detachment. When I told Bill I was beginning *Ritual* yet again, he had an excellent suggestion: I should open the book in the Diaghilev exhibition, which I had seen several times. It had been presented in semi-dark rooms, to simulate backstage at the ballet, and the scent of Diaghilev's favourite perfume, Mitsouko, hung in the air. In the exhibition I had been particularly impressed by the bust of Nijinsky by Una Troubridge. Now I wondered why I had not thought of Bill's suggestion myself.

So during the next three weeks we lived in Hamburg, ate breakfast (with lager) at midday in Ribow's, in the Collenaden, and then Bill and I went back to the pension and worked on our books, while Joy read or did some sightseeing. Sometimes we ate in a students' restaurant in the Schluterstrasse, and engaged in discussion with students about politics and the divided Germany, which enraged everyone. Nevertheless, there was a great deal of leftism among the students, and many approved of Mao's 'Great Leap Forward' in which the peasants were organised into communes.

Bill had been in Hamburg immediately after the war, when he was doing his National Service. It had then been in ruins from the heavy allied bombing, and its lake, the Alster, so full of corpses that the place stank of rotting flesh. The hero of Bill's *Time of Totality* was an ex-RAF man, and Bill had wanted to return to remind himself of the atmosphere.

He took us down the street devoted to brothels, near the Reeperbahn. It had a kind of narrow gate at either end, with a notice that declared in English that it was forbidden to foreign troops (who were then still in Germany). We walked, with Joy between us, past windows in which women sat half-naked, like dummies dressed in underwear. They resented the presence of other women: some scowled at Joy and one made a rude sign. As to me, I found the situation amusing – this shy, ultra-respectable accountant's daughter walking between two men down the street of sin.

Bill's first book had already been sold to a German publisher, Rowalt, although it was not yet out. Nevertheless, he contacted his publisher, Henry Ledig, a charming and cultured man who took us out on the town accompanied by his beautiful girlfriend Paula, wearing an obviously expensive fur wrap.

He took us first to a club where we had a drink, and a troupe of pretty girls in Bavarian costume performed a folk dance. Then one of the most attractive of them did a solo dance that we might have seen in the Highlands of Scotland. I was looking at this delicious creature in her checked dress, and wondering what she would look like without it when, as if reading my mind, she proceeded to unzip the back and remove it.

She was within a few yards of me, and my heart was beating fast as she went on to cast off her underskirt. Then she came over to me, and asked me to unhook the back of her bra. My fingers were trembling so much that I could scarcely undo the catch. She turned to thank me and I tried not to look at her firm breasts. Finally, she climbed out of her panties and tossed them aside. She was wearing a silver star over her pubis. And I, feeling as if a bomb had exploded underneath me, watched with fascination as she picked up her clothes and danced out to applause. I took a long drink of my beer, and hoped no one had noticed how shaken I felt.

Later, Ledig took us to a nightclub where women wrestled in mud, and where horses were brought into a sawdust ring. I protested as Ledig pushed me forward, since I had never been on a horse in my life, but Paula whispered in my ear: 'Grip tight with your knees.' Joy mounted her horse – but then, she had learned to ride as a teenager – and I held on tight as the half dozen or so horses trotted around the ring, wondering if I was going to end up under the horse's belly. I had been slightly drunk when I mounted the horse, but by the time I got off I was completely sober.

Finally, after dinner in another club, we took a taxi back to Heimhuderstrasse, and I slept off too much strong beer.

The next morning, Bill woke us up. He had received a phone call from Paula – she had left her fur behind at our final stop. Could we recall the name of the restaurant? Ledig had gone to the country for the weekend, and she had no way of contacting him.

Here my curiously associative memory came to the rescue. As I tried to remember the name of the restaurant, the only word that came into my head was 'Dostoevsky'. One by one, I ran through the novels of Dostoevsky, and when I came to *The Possessed*, a kind of buzzer sounded in my brain. I began to go through the characters one by one: Stavrogin, Shatov, Kirilov,

Peter Verkhovensky . . . Then I remembered. The name of the restaurant was Peter something.

Still my memory insisted we had not finished with *The Possessed*, and I began to go through the names of the minor characters. And when I got to the governor, von Lembke, it suddenly came to me: the name of the restaurant was Peter Lembke.

We met Paula, jumped into a taxi, and shouted: 'Peter Lembke.' In twenty minutes, Paula had her fur wrap back again.

We had meant to stay until the New Year, but a week before Christmas we were beginning to feel homesick. Joy and I flew back to London just before Christmas. Bill, who disliked flying, travelled by train, and later told us he had had a terrible journey of freezing cold and mishaps.

At Old Walls, nothing had changed, except that damp had penetrated the rear wall and ruined the covers of my set of *Britannica*: having taken bookbinding classes at school, I rebound them myself. That night we were awakened by a tremendous banging noise downstairs, and I rushed down expecting to find burglars. But everything looked normal until I opened the vegetable cupboard under the stairs and found that a sack of potatoes had been gnawed open by rats, which had then played football with its contents. We sent for the 'rodent operator' (rat catcher), who discovered that they had entered through a pipe under the sink. He left a pile of bran there, and the next morning it had disappeared completely. So the following day he mixed it with arsenic. We had no further trouble from rats.

This episode had an amusing sequel. A few weeks later we noticed an unpleasant smell in the spare bedroom, but were unable to trace its source – we finally decided that a rat must have died inside the thick cob walls. One day, Kenneth Allsop came down to interview me, and stayed in the spare bedroom. The smell had now almost vanished, but could be detected if the window was kept closed; so we advised him to keep it wide open. When his article appeared in the *Daily Mail*, it referred to my 'rat infested cottage'. Again, my father was furious as his workmates pulled his leg about Old Walls.

The solution to the mystery came two years later, after we had left Old Walls. The next tenant removed a huge pile of mattresses from the corner of the spare bedroom, and found the skeleton of a rat near the bottom. It had crawled there to die, but the mattresses looked so tight-packed that we had never thought of investigating them.

My parents came to Cornwall at least twice a year, and my father revelled in it. He loved the countryside, and was a keen fisherman. But he had spent his whole life working in factories, and I found it poignant that he was enjoying it all as if he had been let out of prison. He was so happy that it was impossible to hold any grudge about the past.

There was only one problem: holidays in Cornwall made him deeply dissatisfied with Leicester. He loved the sound of seagulls and the noise of the stream below the cottage. He loved to get up before anyone else was awake, and light fires in the kitchen and the sitting room – even in midsummer. Then he went off to fish in the sea, or set traps for rabbits, or helped himself to apples from the farmer's orchard. As a young man he had been a swimming champion, but now he never even put on bathing trunks.

Joy had by now become reconciled with her parents, and often went home for weekends, but they never came to stay.

In 1958, I was invited by the British Council to do a lecture tour of German universities, and we decided to follow this with a trip down the Rhine, taking my parents abroad for the first time.

We decided to drive, for the pleasure of seeing something of Europe – and also to save money by camping. My journal records that I was highly reluctant to leave Old Walls – as a typical Cancer, I become deeply attached to my home. Joy and I crossed to Ostend on 9 July, drove to Bruges and Ghent, and stayed on a camping site in the middle of Ghent. We had bought a double air mattress in London, a double sleeping bag, and two nylon and tube camp beds (for my parents, who would be joining us later.)

We crossed the Rhine at Aachen, then went on to Bonn, where we met a friend we knew in London, Alphons Hilgers. The next day we went on to Düsseldorf, and camped on the banks of the Düssel. While we were out at dinner, there was a tremendous storm, and we returned to find that our tent had been flattened. Fortunately, our possessions had been under the waterproof car cover, so nothing was damaged. But the crisis meant that there was no time to go and look at the flat of the Düsseldorf murderer Peter Kürten, the equivalent of London's Jack the Riper (and the inspiration of Fritz Lang's film *M*), who was also the inspiration for the final version of *Ritual in the Dark*.

We drove on to Winningen, on the Moselle, where we camped on an island in the river, irritated by midges. The next day we drove down the Rhine, enchanted by the scenery and by memories of Wagner, and stayed in Heidelberg, at a hotel called the Hollander Hof, near the old bridge. We drank beer in an inn that looked like a set from *The Student Prince*, and felt we were back in the eighteenth century.

The next day I gave my first lecture. Since I never use notes, I began slowly, feeling my way, before I got into my stride. The literature professor there, Heinrich Walz, was one of those charming and cultivated Germans that I love, and he admitted to me afterwards that his heart sank during the first five minutes of my talk, thinking it was going to be a disaster, then cheered up as my old Hyde Park training began to take over.

In my journal I record that I was dazzled by the attractive girl students, and was envious of Walz when I learned that he used to be Heidelberg's best known rake until a year ago, when he married a girl thirty years his junior. ('A slim and dark, Charles-Adams-type wife.') That same afternoon we drove to Neustadt, where I lectured to an audience of teachers, and praised Bill's novel. The following day I lectured again in Heidelberg, 'stunned by delicious little sweeties who stare with the eyes of bobby-soxers'.

This, I must admit, I found disturbing. More than forty years later, I can see that if I hadn't had Joy, I would have wasted an appalling amount of time chasing the sexual will o' the wisp, which leaves nothing behind – not even experience.

The following day we had lunch with Walz at a restaurant on the top of the mountain overlooking Heidelberg, the Königstuhl, and I was again overpowered by a feeling of how incredibly interesting life had become; this, I realised, was what I had really wanted before *The Outsider* came out – not literary parties and gossip columnists.

We went on to Besigheim for the weekend to see Irmgard Huckmann, the pretty girl I had taken out when I was at the Western Hospital, and she showed us around the incredibly old walled town, and guided us around a children's festival at Dinkelsbuhl.

In Tübingen, we spent much time with a charming Englishman called Peter, an incorrigible flirt with a roving eye for his prettier students. Later, we went to a party where I record that his wife almost raped me, possibly in revenge for Peter's interest in a pretty girl named Herlynt. What happened was that while we were alone, waiting for Peter and Joy to return from driving some guests home, she came over and kissed me, then unzipped my fly and caressed my erection, but she declined to go any further – as I later told Joy.

We went on to Freiburg, where I lectured to large audiences, and read *Gentleman Prefer Blondes*. I had been hoping to meet Heidegger, but was told that he had retired to his hut in the mountains.

We drove back to Paris, where we found a camp site, and I went into Gallimard's to see my editor, M. Mascolo – *The Outsider* had been published in French by Gallimard, who had also accepted *Religion and the Rebel*. The next day Joy and I called on Raymond Duncan at his 'Akademia' in the rue de Seine, and I was delighted to find him completely unchanged – and was also gratified to be able to present myself to him as a successful author. (A few years later he returned the visit, calling unexpectedly at our house in Cornwall with Mme Bertrand.)

Two days later I flew back to England – alone – to pick up my mother and father and my ten-year-old sister Susan. My father was worried about flying, but all went well, and Joy met us at Le Bourget – to tell me that our car had been broken into. She had been staying with a delightful woman called Odile de Lalain – a friend of Camus's – who was married to an English businessman called Michael Tweedie, and Joy had made the mistake of leaving the car parked in the street with our luggage visible through the window. Fortunately, only a travelling clock had been taken.

That afternoon, August 1st, I went to Gallimard's to meet Albert Camus, while Joy took the family off to exchange traveller's cheques and see Paris. Before leaving England I had written to Camus to tell him I would be in Paris, and he had invited me to call at his office, in rue Sebastian-Bottin. Like T. S. Eliot, Camus supplemented his income by working as a publisher.

In terms of reputation, Camus was then probably the world's most successful writer, and had received the Nobel Prize the previous year, at the age of forty-four. During the war, he had been in the Resistance, and had edited the Resistance newspaper, *Combat*, so when the war ended, he was treated as a hero. His novel *The Plague* (1947) sold a quarter of a million copies in France because the French saw the plague as a symbol of the German occupation. A young film critic once made an impromptu speech in a nightclub in which he said that Camus was a walking injustice, because he had 'everything it takes to seduce women, to be happy, to be famous, and in addition he dares to have all the virtues! Against this injustice we can do nothing.'

In view of his reputation as a moralist, I had expected Camus to remind me of T. S. Eliot, so I was surprised to meet an extremely young-looking man. Most of his photographs make him appear serious, as if brooding on questions of eternal justice. In fact, I would have guessed his age to be about thirty, and his brown eyes seemed to dance with liveliness and good humour. He had a touch of the urchin about him, as if he was capable of knocking on doors and running away.

Unfortunately, he spoke no English, but his French was clear and easy to understand. During the afternoon I spent with him, we discussed many subjects, including my own books – he was complimented by my treatment of his ideas in *The Outsider*, and said nice things about it.

He also told me he intended to write an introduction to *Religion and the Rebel*, an idea that surprised me, since Camus made no secret of his rejection of organised religion. But the reason became clearer when he told me about the novel he was working on. It was to be called *The First Man*, and was about a man who begins by rejecting education, morality and religion, but ends up having to construct all three for himself.

As he explained it, the novel sounded like an interesting extension of the theme of *L'Homme Revolté*, a critique of the 'politics of revolt'. The revolutionary feels that society wants to tie him in a strait jacket, cramming his head full of useless facts (education), forcing him to pay constant attention to the wishes of other people (morality), and to accept its notion of what he ought to do with his life (religion). He begins by rejecting all three and living according to his own natural sense of fitness. He feels, for example, that if a girl attracts him, the natural thing to do is to sleep with her, and ignore the parents and relatives who feel he ought to get engaged, then marry her in the proper manner.

But even a simple situation like this is set with traps. What if, after sleeping with her, he wants to move on, and the girl wants him to stay? – a situation Camus often encountered. The natural rebel would ignore her wishes and leave her – and then wonder why it makes him feel like a bastard. At which point, it may strike him (if he is capable of thinking) that 'morality' is not really an invention of the bourgeoisie; it is inherent in human relations. And if you become involved with a group of other people in some mutually advantageous relation, you soon discover that there is also such a thing as social morality which, when projected into the field of social organisation, becomes political morality.

All this struck me as a fascinating and important advance on the position of *L'Étranger* and *The Myth of Sisyphus*. These start from the 'rebel' assumption that religion and morality are human inventions – lies designed to make us feel comfortable. From what Camus told me, the hero of *The First Man* would begin as another 'outsider', like the hero of *L'Étranger* and end as . . . as what? Presumably another Albert Camus, since the novel was to be basically autobiographical.

All this made me aware of the question I really wanted to put to Camus. Where was he going now? To me, it looked as if he had reached a kind of dead end, a cul-de-sac in which man must make the best of a meaningless universe – although I was not rude enough to say so.

L'Étranger and *The Myth of Sisyphus* are basically pessimistic books, whose starting point is that man finds himself in a world that is empty and futile, and that he must live 'without appeal' to religion. Meursault, the hero of *L'Étranger*, is condemned to death for a crime he did not commit, and the implication is that the universe is quite likely to play such tricks on us. This can again be seen in a play, *Le Malentendu*, which is even more Hardyesque: it is about peasants who unintentionally murder their son for his money, failing to recognise him when he returns home after years at sea.

In *The Plague*, Camus is still concerned to attack the 'false assumptions' of religion. But when, I wanted to know, would he stop attacking, and attempt to be more constructive? It sounded to me as if this is what he was aiming at in *The First Man*.

And at this point I said what I had always wanted to say to him – that my own conviction was that meaning is a reality that exists outside us. And surely this is a solution that is hinted at in several places in his own work, where he seems to come close to a kind of mysticism. One occurs in the early essay on the wind at Djemila (in *Nuptials*), where he explains why he rejects expressions like 'future', 'good job', 'self-improvement'. All these things, he says, seek to deprive man of 'the weight of his own life'. 'But as I watch the great birds flying heavily through the sky at Djemila, it is precisely a certain weight of life that I ask for and receive.' Again, at the end of *L'Étranger*, after shaking a priest by the throat, Meursault receives a kind of mystical illumination, when he becomes reconciled to the indifference of the universe, and recognises that 'I had been happy and I was happy still'. The story 'The Woman Taken in Adultery' (in *Exile and the Kingdom*) again deals with something like a mystical illumination: a woman who experiences a kind of orgasm as she feels total unity with the African night. I compared the latter story with the work of D. H. Lawrence, and Camus remarked that I was the first person to see the connection with Lawrence; he had, in fact, been thinking of that author when he wrote the tale.

But were not these experiences, I asked, in a sense the answer to Meursault's sense of the absurd – just as Alyosha Karamazov's mystical illumination, his sense of unity with the stars, is the answer to Ivan's determination to 'give God back his entrance ticket'?

The idea seemed to worry Camus. He gestured out the window, at a Parisian teddy boy slouching along the other side of the street, and said: 'No, what is good for him must be good for me also.' What he meant was clear enough: that any solution to this problem of 'absurdity' must be a solution that would be valid for the man in the street as well as for mystics and intellectuals.

I became excited, and said that this seemed to me to be a mistake. Although a problem might be comprehensible to the man in the street, this does not mean that the answer must also be understandable to him. Anybody can understand the problem implied by the question: 'Where does the universe end? Does space go on for ever?' Einstein's answer involves such concepts as space-time curvature, and seems to be understood fully only by mathematical physicists. The same thing, I suspect, may be true of the question of the meaning of human existence. Mystics who claim to have glimpsed the answer say that it is too simple to be expressed in words. They seem to imply that our basic method of approaching the question is mistaken. But the basic method is the only thing which seems to make sense to the ordinary man. So we may well have to begin by forgetting the ordinary man, and thinking in terms of the non-ordinary.

Or, to put it as simply as possible: if the answer lies outside the normal range of everyday human life, in some paradoxical glimpse of freedom or intensity, then it is no use trying to translate it into terms of normal consciousness. The result would be bound to be a complete falsification.

To explain this would have been beyond the capacity of my rather limited French: I contented myself with saying that his assertion was equivalent to holding that Einstein should never have created the theory of relativity, because it was beyond the understanding of a Parisian teddy boy. Camus clearly disagreed: his basic premise seemed to be that all human beings are in the same boat, and that one of these days, if God condescends to explain to us what life is all about, we shall all groan with exasperation and say: 'Of course!'

I see from my journal that I spent two hours talking with him, but I have no further notes of what we said. I left with a sense of frustration and intellectual deadlock.

Although we later exchanged some letters, and he sent me two of his early books in French, we never met again.

One evening more than a year later, my phone rang. A strongly accented voice identified itself as a journalist from a French news agency, and told me Camus was dead. I said: 'I'm delighted to hear it,' for I thought it was Bill Hopkins playing a joke on me, and trying to convince me that another literary rival was no longer in the running. (Bill often rang me up pretending to be a Chinese laundry or a Russian agent trying to recruit beautiful girls to the KGB.) It took a while to convince me that this call was genuine.

Camus had apparently been driving back to Paris with Michel Gallimard, when the car skidded off the road and hit a tree. If Camus had been wearing a seatbelt he would have survived; as it was, he was catapulted through the rear window and died immediately. His death was as 'absurd' as anything in his own work.

It was not until the American critic Herbert Lottman published a biography of Camus in 1979 that I understood why Camus was unable to escape this *cul-de-sac* of pessimism. Yet I had been handed the clues in 1958. When I asked Odile de Lalain where Camus lived, she said that he was elusive because he moved from room to room. In fact, he was married with children, but was unable to resist the temptation to take full advantage of the fact that women wanted to fling themselves at him. So Camus, said Odile, had many *affaires*.

I could understand perfectly. It seemed Camus was a victim of the sexual delusion that was still costing me a certain amount of self-division. It seems clear that Camus loved his wife. But, like Wells and Russell, he felt it would be a sheer waste of opportunity to turn down all the admiring females who were dying to share his bed. Wells's wife did her best to put up with it, convinced by her fast-talking mate that sexual freedom was everyone's birthright. But she wilted away and, after her death, Wells was racked with conscience.

But Camus set himself up as some kind of a moralist; the question is fundamental to his work. His wife was an eminently good and intelligent woman of considerable character. There can be no doubt that the moralist in him told him to treat his wife as she deserved. The satyr contented itself with an occasional insincere prayer: 'O Lord, make me good – but not yet.'

This, I think, explains why Camus regarded himself as a kind of 'light-weight', a kind of fake.

This becomes clear in the novel that won him the Nobel Prize, *The Fall*, which is about a lawyer who regards himself as a generous and altruistic individual until he begins to see through his own self-complacency. His relations with women in particular fill him with guilt, for he is a highly successful Don Juan. Self-knowledge finally drives him to abandon his flourishing practice, and become a kind of penitent in a run-down quarter of Amsterdam.

As far as Camus's peace of mind went, the Nobel Prize was in some ways the worst thing that could have happened to him. All those who felt he had been far too successful turned on him. Even the visit to Stockholm for the Nobel Prize was marred by attacks from political militants who implied that Camus was a hypocrite. When he heard the news that he had won the award, Camus declared: 'I am castrated.' And, in effect, this turned out to be true.

CHAPTER 11

John Braine in Leningrad

The poet Louis Adeane, from whom we rented Old Walls, had hinted that he might want to return in 1959. Early that year we wrote to ask him exactly when he wanted to move back to Cornwall, but he was too lazy to reply. So in February, while I worked hard on *Ritual in the Dark*, Joy went off looking for a house. She saw one advertised in the next village, Gorran Haven, but the price was high – £4,900. (Most properties around here could be had for £2,500.) It proved to be up a long private drive – in fact, a muddy dirt track – and when she peered at it from the entrance, decided it was far too big for us. But just as she was about to leave, she saw someone looking at her out of the window, and felt it would be bad manners to go away. She knocked on the door, and was invited inside for a cup of tea.

When she came home she told me it was too expensive and too big. I said: 'Good – lots of room for books and records.' So we drove over to see it.

It had been built six years earlier by a couple named Davis. They came from Brighton, and had intended to run the place as a market garden – it had two acres of land. But Mrs Davis had become homesick for old friends, and wanted to return to Brighton.

The house was called Tetherdown, which we decided to change. But thinking of something better was more difficult than we thought, so we ended by keeping the name. The long lane – five hundred yards of it – was certainly impressive. The house itself was less so, being a bungalow built of Cornish blocks – large hollow blocks cast in concrete – and painted a greenish colour with waterproof cement paint. There was a huge greenhouse, about twenty yards long, and a large back garden. The rest of the two acres was uncultivated field. But its front windows had an enormous view of the sea. I decided that if we could raise the money, we would take it.

It seemed to me that it would be an excellent idea to ask my mother and father (and sister Sue) to come and live with us. My father had loved his holidays at Old Walls, and was always saying that he wished he lived in the country. He could carry on Mr Davis's market garden, growing tomatoes in the greenhouse. And in the garden below the house there was a small two-room 'chalet' which the Davises had rented to summer visitors. Dad could also take on the task of maintaining this, and collect the rent for pocket money.

The legal formalities all took far longer than expected. My family moved down to Old Walls in early April 1959, but it was mid-May before we were able to move. On my father, the effect of this long wait was disastrous. Having worked all his life, he was in the habit of regarding every day either as a working day or a holiday. That long wait allowed him to slip into the insidious habit of thinking of life in Cornwall as a holiday. Since he had always spent most of his spare time in the pub, he quickly reverted to habit.

He would get up – as usual – at seven in the morning, light two huge fires, then go off fishing. He was back home by eleven, and wanted to be taken to the pub, either in Gorran or in Mevagissey. (In those days there was no pub in Gorran Haven.) At two o'clock he needed to be picked up again. He dozed in the afternoon, then started glancing at the clock towards opening time. He liked me to go and join him, but I soon became bored with wasting my evenings drinking beer and playing darts, and began to make excuses. So at ten o'clock, he needed to be fetched from the pub again.

We had very little money. In order to buy furniture we had raised a second mortgage on the house. Gollancz had finally accepted *Ritual in the Dark* (Fred Warburg had dropped out of the running a long time ago), and given me an advance of £500. And I told my American agent to try to persuade my publisher there – Houghton Mifflin – to give me an advance of $5,000 – a large amount for me (they had paid $1,500 on my previous books). It was a huge relief when they agreed, for we were up to our over-draft limit.

All the same, it was wonderful to be in our own home – to be able to have a bath by turning on the hot tap instead of having to light a fire under a boiler. But every time I took a bath I wondered how long we would be able to afford to live here, with two £125 mortgage payments a year. (Our income was about £140 a week, but it came in piecemeal.)

My father's boredom and dissatisfaction made things worse. When the summer was over, and visitors had stopped renting the chalet, he suggested that he and my mother should move in there, and that she should cook for the two of them. He wanted to be able to return from the pub at any hour and expect a meal. My mother understandably objected; she preferred living in the house and eating her meals with us. Finally, when they had lived in Cornwall for six months, she announced she was going back to

Leicester. She said that if my father continued to spend his days in the pub, he would drink himself to death. They returned in late November 1959. I was sad to see my parents go, but must admit that it was a relief to have the house to ourselves.

Dad, of course, had to return to work in a factory. And although he had become frustrated and dissatisfied with Cornwall, he hated Leicester even more. I suspect that his frustration was the cause of the cancer that eventually killed him.

That spring, Joy had an accident that made me suddenly aware of the strength of my feeling about her. We were returning to Old Walls, and Joy got out of the Land-Rover and went to open the gate. There were a number of cows waiting to return from milking, but Joy was used to cows, and pushed her way through. Suddenly I was aware of one of the cows charging at her, and butting her against the stone gatepost. As I watched, she sank to the ground, and the cow went on trying to get its horn into her.

I jumped out of the Land-Rover, ran up to the cow, and pounded its ribs, shrieking curses. It backed away, and I picked Joy up – she was very light – and carried her back to the car. The cow had taken a chip out of the flesh on her nose and the blood was running down her face.

I got her back home and into bed, then called the doctor. He came quickly, examined her, and concluded that she had a broken rib (in fact, there were two). But there was nothing he could do – putting the ribs in plaster would cause her more trouble than it was worth. She simply had to stay in bed, and make sure she did no heavy lifting.

As Joy lay there, with the piece out of her nose, I was suddenly aware of how much I loved her. This may sound surprising; but Joy had always been a rather cool and detached girl, who never expressed strong feeling, so I had never really felt close to her. She had always seemed oddly 'non-reactive'. This was why I had never felt guilty about Carole Ann or Dorothy. But seeing her like this made me feel intensely protective, and it was as if some invisible obstacle between us disappeared, and allowed me to feel close to her, as I had towards my brother Barry, and as I now do towards my children.

The cow, we discovered, was suffering from milk fever, and died a few days later.

In January, Joy announced that she was pregnant. I recall that I was filling in a crack in the ceiling at the time, and playing a record of Shostakovich's newly issued fourth symphony. My reaction was less ecstatic than it might have been. I had already tried being a father once, and had not particularly enjoyed the experience. But at twenty-eight, Joy obviously felt it was time she had a baby.

In late February 1960, *Ritual in the Dark* was finally published, and

(*Right*) Me, aged two

(*Below left*) My father,
Arthur Wilson, 1930

(*Below right*) My mother,
Anetta Wilson, aged 17

(*Above*) A birthday party for Grandad. I am on the extreme right, a writing pad sticking out from my pocket
(*Below*) Visiting my family in Leicester at 5, the Littleway, in 1956. Right to left: back row, brother Barry, me, brother Rod, front row, my father Arthur, sister Sue and mother Anetta

THE
OUTSIDER

*An inquiry into the nature
of the sickness of mankind
in the mid-twentieth century*

by

COLIN WILSON

(*Above*) At home in London
at Chepstow Villas. *Harper's
Bazaar*, 1956

(*Right*) At Old Walls cottage,
Mevagissey, 1957

(*Above*) London, East End.
Investigating the Jack the Ripper
murder sites, 1960

(*Left*) Me

(*Left*) On a trip to the Soviet Union, July 1960. At a Leningrad tram stop, with author John Braine, Robert Pitman, literary editor of the London *Daily Express*, and Pat Pitman, my co-author of *The Encyclopedia of Murder*, 1961

(*Below*) Teaching in the USA, 1961

(*Above*) Bill Hopkins and me in Gorran Haven, 1959

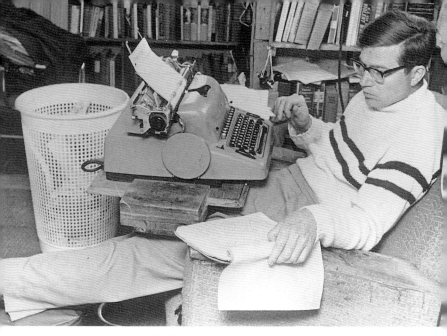

(*Above*) Working at home in Gorran Haven, 1960s

(*Below*) Living in a cottage can sometimes have its advantages...

(*Above left*) With my children, Sally and Damon, 1967

(*Above right*) Portrait in Los Angeles, 1989

(*Left*) Portrait, 1970s

(*Below*) Dowsing in Merry Maidens
stone circle, Cornwall, 1990s

(*Top left*) Joy (*Above*) Walking with my dogs

Edith Sitwell launched it with an excellent review in the *Sunday Times*, although Karl Miller, an old enemy, gave it a vicious review in the *Observer* in which he referred to 'the odious *Outsider*'. It appeared in America at the same time, and did almost as well as *The Outsider*, selling around 25,000 copies. I felt that the eleven years I had spent on it had been worthwhile. And Robert Pitman, a friend who was a book critic on the *Sunday Express*, gave it an admirable review, in which he said: 'Not since Dickens had anyone dealt with murder in a novel of this size and seriousness.'

We had met Robert Pitman through the novelist John Braine. And since Braine will play a central part in the events that follow, this is the place to say more about him.

Room at the Top appeared in March 1957, and a review by John Metcalfe in the *Sunday Times* launched it with the comment: 'Remember the name. John Braine. You'll be hearing quite a lot about him.' But the reviews made me feel it was not my kind of book. The hero, Joe Lampton, was described as a ruthless go-getter who tramples on other people's faces to get to the top – not the kind of person I wanted to read about. But a year later I saw a second-hand book-club edition and bought it. It was probably another six months before I opened it. But when I did get around to it, I read on with fascination until I got to the end. It struck me as very nearly a great novel.

It was quite obvious the critics had got it wrong. This was not a novel about a heartless social climber, but about a romantic young Yorkshireman who takes a job in a strange town, far less grimy and depressing than his own, and knows from the moment he arrives that he is going to enjoy it. So the book had a sparkling atmosphere of expectation that made it a delight to read. When the hero joins the local drama group, and is attracted to the mill-owner's pretty daughter, he doesn't feel he stands a chance with a well-educated middle-class girl. So the reader enjoys Joe's pursuit of her – and ultimate success – as much as Joe does himself. (Perhaps I enjoyed it so much because it reminded me of my own pursuit of Joy.)

The novel was completely free from the cynicism I expected – on the contrary it has an atmosphere rather like a fairy story. Moreover, there was an honesty about it that reminded me of Hemingway. I felt a twinge of the kind of anxiety that I had never experienced reading Amis or Wain or Sillitoe: that this man might be a real contender for the literary heavy-weight title.

I wrote to Braine, care of his publisher, telling him how much I admired the book, and received an amiable reply. And in October 1958, Joy and I drove up to Bingley to meet him.

The man who came to open the door was not in the least like Hemingway. I described him in my journal as 'a beefy man with a large tummy, horn rimmed specs, a strong Yorkshire accent – giving the impression of being bear-like, slow-thinking (though by no means thick-witted) and good tempered.' Nine years my senior, he made me think of an overgrown school-boy, swaying back and forth from heel to toe as he talked in the centre of the rug, with his hands clasped in front of him.

His wife Pat was an attractive, slim girl with a lovely transparent complexion. She had been a schoolteacher when they married.

Before dinner, Braine took me to the local pub in his small car. He was a learner driver, and the ride was hair-raising. He kept apologising for being a bad driver, and I would politely reassure him, then have to bite back a gasp of alarm as he took a corner too fast or missed another car by inches. There was something endearingly incompetent about him. When we came out of the pub – where he was treated as the local celebrity – he dropped his car key among a pile of autumn leaves, and we had to switch on the headlights, and crawl on all fours searching for it.

Again, I made the mistake of reassuring him about his driving. 'Tell you what,' John said brightly, 'I'll just take you on a little run up to the edge of the moor.' And we hurtled along a narrow road between stone walls, occasionally plunging into darkness as he switched off the headlights in an attempt to dip them. When I staggered out of the car half an hour later, I was nervously exhausted.

John enjoyed playing the bluff Yorkshireman, and referring to himself as 't'Master'. It was obvious that he was basically a shy and sensitive person who had taught himself to present a bold face to the world by laying down the law. 'Truman's a bluddy murderer!' he pronounced, on the subject of the atom bomb, and glared aggressively round the table. Predictably, no one contradicted him, feeling that a person of such strong convictions deserved respect – which, I came to feel, was part of his method.

When Joy and I were about to go to bed, John winked and said: 'By the way, there's no sex allowed here. We try to run a decent house.'

The next day, while he was driving us on a tour of the area, he told us how *Room at the Top* had come to be written. A few years earlier, John had been in an amateur dramatic society, and had met a beautiful young girl – the model for Susan Brown. John could hardly believe it when she made it clear that she found him attractive. She had an odd masochistic streak and, when John took her virginity, was obviously excited by the pain, and even fascinated by the sight of blood on her thighs.

Enraptured by this enchanting embodiment of femininity, John felt the need to be something more than a local librarian. He had had some art-icles accepted by *Tribune* and the *New Statesman*, so now decided to go to London and become a writer. But his £150 in savings soon ran out, and the occasional piece for the *New Statesman* would not even pay the rent of his bedsit. When a bout of laryngitis turned into tuberculosis, he went back to Yorkshire (he told me he was 'shipped back on the train') and into a sanatorium. During the eighteen months he spent there, the girl he adored broke off the relationship and married someone of 'her own class'. John was shattered, but finally wrote it out of his system in *Room at the Top*.

The novel was a commercial success, and was made into one of the best British films of the 50s. Unfortunately, the film rights had been sold before publication for a mere £5,000. The Penguin paperback went on to sell a million copies, but since John received only about a penny a copy, the royalties came to less than £5,000.

Typically, when he was invited on to the film set to meet the cast, John made a speech, telling them: 'Do you realise you're all figments of my imagination?'

The following year, when Joy and I had moved into the house in Gorran Haven, John and Pat came to stay with us, with their small son Anthony. (John insisted on pronouncing the 'th' as in 'thorough'.) When a bat flew in through our window at dusk, John went berserk, assuring us that if it bit Anthony, he would die of blood poisoning.

He also spent much of the week in Cornwall sighing and complaining about an article he had to write for a Sunday newspaper, on the theme of the 'wet hero' who is so prominent in modern fiction, his groans implying that he faced a major creative task on a level with *Room at the Top*. But it was also typical of his style that, as I was about to drive him to the station, he flourished my copy of Brendan Behan's *Borstal Boy* and said: 'I'll take this' (not 'May I borrow this?'). Later he admitted, also without apology, that he had somehow lost it out of the window of the railway carriage.

Interestingly enough, one of the writers he admired most was John O'Hara, who shared his obsession with social distinctions and class symbols like expensive cars and girls with a Riviera suntan. At that time I think John's ambition was to become a kind of British O'Hara, carefully researching the social and historical backgrounds of his characters, and producing vast documentary novels. When we first met him, he told us that his next major project was going to be a novel about Bradford, and about the whole 'missing generation' of young men who were killed in the First World War. But John somehow lacked that kind of talent. Unlike J. B. Priestley, whom he also admired enormously, he had no ability to create large canvases or larger-than-life characters. His own work was essentially personal and autobiographical.

A few months after his visit to Cornwall, Braine, Stuart Holroyd and I came to an agreement to share the rent of a room in the house where Bill lived, at 25 Chepstow Road (just around the corner from my former address at Chepstow Villas). It was owned by Peter Rachman, a notorious slum landlord of the time, whose name was later associated with the Christine Keeler scandal. We were allowed to live there for a minimal rent (about £5 a week) because so long as the house had a few 'respectable' tenants, the police could not close it down as a brothel. But it was often hard to sleep, for car doors slammed all night as clients came and went. The lady who lived on the ground floor, opposite the only lavatory, had a clothes line strung outside the door, on which dangled a most amazing array of brightly coloured panties – red, purple, green and bright yellow.

In a large room on the third floor lived Tom Greenwell, a gossip columnist on the *Evening News*, and one of the kindest and most good-tempered men I have ever known. He was tall, thin and elegant, sported fancy waistcoats and bow ties, and spent his evenings at first nights and cocktail parties. Tom seldom came home before three in the morning, and when he did, he usually found his room crowded with friends like Bill, Stuart, Braine, myself, and various attractive young ladies who had become groupies of this Notting Hill branch of the 'Angry Young Men'. If he was tired or dismayed, he never showed it.

I have to confess that I often felt a certain envy of Bill, Stuart and Tom, since they were free to take advantage of the pretty groupies, while John Braine and I were married and therefore out of the running. But then, a week in London always left me exhausted and suffering from 'people poisoning'. I always heaved a sigh of relief when I was back in my secure retreat in Cornwall.

When John Braine introduced me to Robert Pitman of the *Sunday Express*, I established an immediate rapport with his wife, Pat, because she was as interested in murder as I was. And it was this shared interest that led us to decide to compile an encyclopedia of murder – something that no one had so far attempted.

This came about because Dan Farson had invited various friends to his flat overlooking the river in Limehouse. These included Pat and Bob Pitman, Joy, the American 'Beat' poet Gregory Corso, the playwright Frank Norman, and one of Dan's beefy young men. I was talking to someone about the Crippen murder case, and could not remember where he lived. I called to Pat – in the next room – 'What was Crippen's address?' and she called back instantly: 'Thirty-nine Hilldrop Crescent.' It was in that moment that I decided that Pat would make an ideal collaborator.

I should explain that Dan had now achieved fame as a television celebrity, and that I was partly responsible. In 1956 he had applied to Associated Rediffusion for a job, and they asked him who he knew. He mentioned Francis Bacon and myself. They told him that he could have the job if he could get me to do an interview. I, of course, agreed, and Dan arrived at my room with a camera crew. I was just finishing a meal, and as we talked, I picked up a pear and bit into it. When the show was broadcast this exhibition of sangfroid created widespread comment, most of it hostile, and Dan went on to become a television interviewer, specialising in asking brutal and probing questions. He became so successful that he bought himself a pub on the Isle of Dogs.

Dan's downfall would come about, as he himself admitted to me, through hubris. His popularity was enormous, and he felt that he was not being given enough creative freedom. So he resigned, convinced that they would lose no time in conceding his demands. But they didn't – possibly, as he admits in his autobiography, because of his heavy drinking and bizarre sex life – and Dan became a freelance interviewer and writer, never regaining his former position. The pub on the Isle of Dogs went bankrupt, probably because Dan gave away too many free drinks. In any case, being a pub landlord was the worst possible occupation for someone of his temperament, since he was already as confirmed an alcoholic as his father.

Negley himself was dead by that time. On 13 December 1960, his bags packed for another journey, he pointed at the breaking surf, and said to Eve: 'This is the perfect place for a journey's end.' Then he sat in his armchair and died quietly.

Eve was shattered. After being married to such a dynamo, she found life without him intolerable. She drove down to stay with us for a weekend, and when I offered to play her a tape I had made of Negley, said: 'No don't – I couldn't bear it.' And that same evening she commented: 'I don't care how soon I die – the sooner the better.' I shook my head and warned her that that kind of pronouncement was tempting fate, and she said: 'I don't care.' But when, on her way home, her car broke down in Launceston and she had to spend the night in a hotel, I had a feeling that she had brought it on herself.

Not long after that, she tripped at the top of a flight of stairs after lunch with a friend, and broke her neck.

My visit to Dan's Limehouse flat was the beginning of a year-long collaboration with Pat on the *Encyclopedia of Murder*. I offered the book to Victor Gollancz, but he turned it down, explaining that he had once published a novel that described a particularly subtle method of murder, and that subsequently someone had copied it in real life. Apparently the suspicions of the police were aroused by a copy of the book in the killer's room.

So I offered the *Encyclopedia* to the publisher George Weidenfeld, whom I met at a party, and he accepted it.

Pat and I began by making a list of famous murder cases and dividing them up between us. In general, Pat preferred domestic crimes and poisoning cases, while I dealt with mass murderers and sex crimes.

In the spring Bob Pitman suggested that Joy and I should join him on a trip to Leningrad. A new Russian boat called the *Bore II* was sailing from Tilbury, and the fare was absurdly low. So although Joy was now seven and a half months pregnant, we joined the rest of the party – which included Pat, their ten-year-old son Jonathan, and John Braine – on 6 July 1960.

I had not seen John for some time, but Bob had told me that he was drinking far too heavily. After *Room at the Top*, he had written a novel called *The Vodi*, in which he continued the story of the unhappy love affair that had made him write *Room at the Top*. The hero is in a nursing home suffering from tuberculosis, and suspects that the girl he is engaged to is getting tired of him. The Vodi of the title are unpleasant little creatures whose purpose is to see that the good fail and the wicked succeed, and the hero invents a fantasy in which they are responsible for all his misfortunes.

It was not a good novel. I had read it in typescript with a sinking heart, wondering how the author of *Room at the Top* had convinced himself that this depressing rubbish, with its thoroughly 'wet' hero, was worth writing. The reviews, predictably, had been unenthusiastic and the sales poor. I was not surprised that John was drinking too much.

But when we met at Tilbury, I thought he looked cheerful enough. He told us that his doctor, who was also his best friend, had warned him that unless he stopped drinking he would ruin his liver. So John was now on the wagon. Pat was staying at home to look after Anthony.

The Russian ship smelled of fresh paint and the pungent pink soap in the toilets. On the wall opposite the gangplank was a cartoon-like painting of a rocket heading for the moon – the Russians had recently taken the lead in the space race. Bob and I made our way to the bar, and ordered vodka. It was very cheap, and smelled and tasted quite different from the vodka we drank in England, having a curious oily flavour that reminded me of the taste that comes up in your throat when you have heartburn. But after two or three you got used to it and noticed only the warm glow.

John came and joined us and stuck to lemonade, preaching the virtues of abstinence. As always when he was sober, he was serious and subdued. He told us he was thinking of writing a sequel to *Room at the Top*, but at the moment had no ideas about a plot.

Dinner was filling, but was certainly not haute cuisine – red cabbage, potatoes, well-cooked meat and dumplings. We ordered red wine with it, and were disconcerted when it proved to be sweet. The Russians, apparently, preferred their wine sweet – even their champagne.

That night the sea was rough, and the boat surged crazily up and down. At breakfast the next morning, Joy and I were almost alone in the dining room. Joy recalls that we were given porridge with a layer of floating butter on it. I have always been a good sailor, perhaps because I used to bite my nails; I have been told that nail-biters are not prone to sea-sickness.

My problem was that travel bored me. As soon as we landed in a city like Copenhagen or Stockholm, I made straight for the nearest bookshop – they all had a good selection of American paperbacks. It was in Stockholm that I discovered Friedrich Dürrenmatt through his novel *The Pledge*, and decided that he was one of the best writers of his generation.

I finally became so indifferent to the sight of foreign cities that when the rest of the party went ashore at Gdansk, in Poland, I stayed on board reading the Faber volume *Best SF*.

John stuck to his vow of teetotalism until we went ashore in Stockholm. There we stopped at a café at mid-morning and drank some of the local schnapps. John decided to allow himself just one, but after the first, drank two or three more. It was then I saw that John had become a genuine alcoholic – after drinking just one glass, he had to carry on until he was incapable of standing up. We went back on to the boat for lunch, and he had vodka. Then he came along to my cabin, and asked me if I had anything to drink. In fact, he knew I had, since he had seen me buy a bottle of cherry brandy that morning. John then sat and drank all of it. He did not appear for supper that evening.

The result was that during the rest of the trip he became the noisy and self-assertive drunk that I had often seen in Notting Hill, laying down the law and talking obsessively. When John was drunk, the Yorkshire accent would become stronger, and he enjoyed saying: 'Now you listen to me . . .' wagging his finger or striking the table.

In this state, he was suddenly possessed with a desire to show you how much he knew about everything, particularly material goods. *Room at the Top* is full of acute observation of wealth-symbols: expensive cars, Rolex watches, Savile Row suits. He was capable of saying, at two o'clock in the morning, when everyone was yawning: 'Have you ever thought about kitchen stoves?' (Pronounced 'storves'.) 'Doan't say that stoves are not important – any housewife will tell you different. Now there are six main types of stove . . .' And on and on until his audience was glassy-eyed with boredom. Pat Pitman liked to refer to our ship as Bore Two and John as Bore One.

In Helsinki we called on my Finnish publisher, who took us to a restaurant overlooking the harbour, and bought us an excellent meal of reindeer meat. It was also in Helsinki that we changed on to a Finnish ship which was more spacious and well-lit than the Russian vessel, and blessedly free of the smell of pungent soap. We sailed at sunset, and the red sky behind those tiny islands in the bay was breathtaking, one of those moments in which I experienced an upsurge of sheer wellbeing. And as the ship turned west towards Leningrad, we went down to the dining room to a buffet supper that was like a royal feast – vast plates of sliced smoked salmon, smoked eel, trout, a huge joint of ham, another of rare beef, quails in aspic, asparagus and pickled herring in cream. It was even possible to buy wine that did not taste as if someone had poured the sugar bowl into it.

In Leningrad we used the boat as a floating hotel, and went back every evening. It was half an hour's walk through the docks into the city, and there were no taxis. I was impressed by the size of the great square drainpipes on the side of the buildings, and the fact that they stopped a few inches above the pavement, so that when it rained, the pavement below them turned into a swollen river.

Joy was wearing bright red tights – tights had recently become fashionable in London – and they created a sensation as we walked down the Nevsky Prospect, as did Pat's orange slacks. People actually turned and stared at us. The Russian women all looked depressingly drab, rather as British women used to during the Second World War.

But I was much impressed by the dishes of caviar on sale at green metal tables in the Park of Peace – great pointed mounds of it, as big as a large ice cream, and all for a few roubles. Otherwise, the food was as atrocious as on the Russian boat. In a run-down restaurant in the Nevsky, we had to wait an hour before our food appeared, but at least they set on the table two huge fat carafes of vodka – unbelievably cheap as usual – and dishes of sour pickles that made the eyes water until you flushed away the taste with vodka that tasted like fusel-oil.

It was in this restaurant that there were not enough chairs at our table, and we were directed to a back room to find some for ourselves. The place was full of broken chairs – chairs without a leg, chairs without a back, chairs with a hole in the seat – and we had to do our best with what we could find.

I was also struck by the sheer inefficiency of the waiters, who looked as if they had walked straight out of the pages of *Oblomov* or *Dead Souls*. Before we left for Russia, I had read a life of Peter the Great that emphasised his brutality. But after a little experience of Russian waiters and tradesmen, I began to sympathise with him, and saw that the knout might be the solution.

Most of the time, we were followed around by a KGB man, although I cannot imagine why he bothered, since there seemed to be nothing worth spying on. One day we went out to the Peterhof Park – near the royal palace – and Bob went up and engaged him in conversation. He proved to be perfectly amiable and polite, and Bob did not embarrass him by asking why he was following us.

On the visit to the Peterhof I was much amused by the Russian sanitary arrangements. I wanted to urinate, and went into a wooden structure. Inside there was a long board with round holes in it, and below these holes the grassy hillside descended steeply into what looked like a ravine. As I stood there watching my urine cascade down the slope, a fat woman came in, heaved up her dress, sat down on one of the holes, and proceeded to relieve her bowels.

Joy and I managed to find our way across Leningrad to the palace of Prince Felix Yussupov, and went in the courtyard where Rasputin had been gunned down, and looked down a flight of stairs that led to the basement where he was poisoned with cyanide-filled cakes. The Intourist guide from whom we had enquired the way was reluctant to encourage our morbid interest in the days before the Glorious Revolution that had freed Russia of such scum, and also strongly discouraged us from trying to find Dostoevsky's house. He told us that Dostoevsky was no longer read.

On our last evening, we were invited to a reception at the Astoria, Leningrad's major hotel, and introduced to Russian writers and literary bureaucrats. John's *Room at the Top* had been published with immense success there, and had made him a rouble millionaire. (The Russians published editions of fifty thousand as a matter of course.) The book was regarded as an attack on capitalist civilisation, and John took care not to disillusion them.

I overheard Pat asking a stern-faced lady who spoke good English whether there were any important Soviet murder cases we ought to include in our encyclopedia. Snorting contemptuously, the lady told her that such crimes were virtually unknown under Communism.

In most cities we had visited so far – Copenhagen, Stockholm, Helsinki – John and I had been interviewed jointly as representatives of England's 'Angry Young Men'. But here in Leningrad, no one seemed interested in me, and I spent most of the reception talking to Joy and Pat. The few Russian writers I was introduced to smiled politely, shook my hand, then drifted off. I assumed that this was because no one in Russia had ever heard of me or of *The Outsider*.

It was not until several years later that I discovered the facts, when I reviewed a book about Khrushchev's Russia by Alexander Werth. It turned out that, on the day before we landed in Leningrad, *Pravda* had published an attack on Camus and myself, denouncing us as decadent Western writers. The article had been written by Alexei Surkov, head of the Union of Soviet Writers – I had met him at the Astoria – but, according to Werth, had been inspired by Khrushchev himself.

John enjoyed himself playing the celebrity in Leningrad, and spent his roubles freely. (He was not allowed to take them out of Russia.) And finally, he was invited to go on to Moscow as the guest of the Writers' Union, while the rest of us travelled back to England without him.

Instead, we were joined on the boat by John Wain, a man, as I say, I had always found oddly lacking in charm. He seemed to be driven by a kind of will-to-power, possibly exacerbated by his feeling that the novels of Kingsley Amis were better received than his own. He had no doubt that he was a far better and more serious writer than Amis – and I am inclined to agree – but I always found that his novels had a curiously unpleasant, bitter flavour, an offputting taste of egotism and selfishness. His heroes are determined to get the girl into bed, but seem to have no personal feeling towards her – just a desire to remove her clothes. It struck me as a little like the attitude of a rapist to his victim.

This aspect of his character was illustrated by an anecdote told me by Richard Adams, the author of *Watership Down*. He had been at a writers' conference with Wain, who was accompanied by an awful, loud American girl who made everybody cringe. Finally, when whisky had warmed them into a sense of intimacy, Adams asked what Wain saw in her. Wain replied: 'Well I'll tell you. When this evening's over, we'll go to the room, and I'll lock the door, then I'll fuck her till the pictures fall off the walls.'

Wain took a certain pleasure in being rude and abrupt. When I first met him he had given me a copy of the paperback of *Hurry on Down*, but I had left it behind somewhere. When Joy and I called in to see Wain at Reading University I mentioned that I had mislaid the book, and Wain immediately snapped: 'Well I'm not giving you another,' although he knew perfectly well that this was far from my thoughts. He enjoyed playing the gruff curmudgeon.

Wain also had no doubt of his own genius, and I remember him remarking casually: 'When I get the Nobel Prize . . .' A few years later I heard that he had moved to Wales to write a big, serious novel, and when *A Winter in the Hills* came out in 1970, I hastened to read it. But within fifty pages I was put off by the same bitter flavour of obsessive egoism, and inability to treat women as anything but objects of conquest.

Wain had an interesting story to tell me about Amis. A year or two earlier, Bill Hopkins and I had been at a party at the house of the publisher Anthony Blond, and had taken our drinks to the flat roof, and stood there looking at the view. Wain told me that he and Kingsley – now drunk – came up to the roof, and Amis said: 'Look, there's that bugger Wilson – I'm going to push him over.' As he lurched towards me, Wain grabbed his arm and stopped him.

It seemed that ever since my combative letter about his facetious review of *The Outsider*, Amis had always regarded me with a kind of defensive caution. I liked him, and always assumed he liked me. We met several times and seemed to be on friendly terms – including that evening at his home in Swansea when we were on the run from the press. Yet in his *Memoirs*, he tells that story and makes it appear that we gatecrashed rather than being invited. And in a letter he tells Philip Larkin that I had brought a bottle of whisky with me, but that my morbid interest in murder had made him afraid to drink it in case it was poisoned, and that he had finally given it away to someone, who had survived.

It is true that Joy and I took a bottle of whisky with us when we called on him. But I had not at that point published the *Encyclopedia of Murder*, which came out in 1961. Amis clearly invented any story that sounded amusing. In the mid-60s, when I happened to see him in London, I suggested we meet the following lunchtime for a drink. Brady and Hindley had recently been arrested for the Moors Murders, and Amis brought up the subject, and told me that he had talked with a policeman on the case, who had been present when the body of twelve-year-old John Kilbride had been dug up. He lowered his voice and looked grave. 'His trousers were round his knees and there was evidence of sexual assault.' In fact, the body had been in the ground so long that sexual assault would have been impossible to determine.

If someone had asked me during Amis's lifetime I would have said that we were friends, for we got on well and enjoyed talking about our favourite jazz. His references to me in his *Collected Letters*, however, published after his death, reveal a continuous vein of hostility. For example, he tells Larkin that I refused to grant a journalist an interview unless it was 'me, Shaw and Dante – OK?' It does not seem to have struck him that any worthwhile journalist would have told me to go to hell. The story had been invented by an over-imaginative friend of mine, Wilfred De' Ath, but even Amis should have been able to see that it was too illogical to be true.

I had always suspected that Amis, under the façade of nonchalance and humour, concealed the same deep lack of self-belief as Braine, a suspicion that had first dawned on me when I read that he was afraid of the dark. He did a rather better job of concealing it than Braine, but as he became older, increasing alcoholism revealed the depth of the problem.

Braine's deterioration became apparent when he arrived back from Russia. He arrived at Pat's home after a bender that had obviously lasted for days, and made straight for the drinks cupboard. His ravings so upset Pat's mother in law, who was on a visit, that she wanted to call the police. Pat wrote to me: 'we both quailed in the basement, whilst drunken shouts from above resounded through the house, along with the crashes of glasses against the fireplace'.

When Pat's daughter Katie came home from school, John calmed down. Pat heard him say: 'Eeeh, Katie, when you're a bit older, will you come to look after me?', to which Katie responded promptly: 'No fear!'

On two subsequent occasions, Pat recalls, he arrived to take them out to dinner so drunk that he could hardly stand, and the second time the taxi driver refused to allow him to get in the cab.

At least Braine had one consolation: in spite of the alcoholic crisis – or perhaps because of it – he had succeeded in inventing a key episode for a sequel to *Room at the Top*, in which Joe Lampton arrives home unexpectedly to find his wife in bed with another man, and comes close to a total breakdown. The marriage is saved when he decides to stay with her for the sake of the children.

After the Russian trip I began to feel increasingly exasperated with John because I sensed an element of play-acting about him. He *played* the part of the bluff Yorkshireman to impress people, but anyone who knew him felt he was trying to convince you of something that wasn't true.

Our relations broke down not long after the Russian trip, and this came about when he quarrelled with Bill Hopkins.

Bill and a businessman named Bob Guccione decided to launch a magazine that would appeal to the same audience as Hugh Hefner's *Playboy*. To me the idea sounded like a non-starter. London already had a number of men's magazines with titles like *King* and *Mayfair*, and most of them had folded. Bill and Guccione nevertheless succeeded in raising about a thousand pounds between them, enough to print a small glossy advertising pamphlet that described *Penthouse* as a freewheeling magazine for intelligent males with a taste for sexy ladies. I was mentioned among those who would write for it; so was John Braine; so was Bertrand Russell – who threatened to sue them unless they removed his name.

The pamphlet went out with a subscription form, and to Bill's delight and my astonishment, subscriptions began to roll in – more than enough to print the first issue.

Bill, as editor, decided to imitate a typical *Playboy* feature, the Playboy Forum, a kind of rolling dialogue that went on for issue after issue, in which the participants argued about the meaning of sexual freedom. Hefner, I believe, actually invited his celebrities to sit around a restaurant table for the 'forum', but Bill and Guccione decided to reduce costs by doing it over the phone.

One day Bill rang me and asked me what I thought about sex. Echoing Groucho Marx, I said I thought it was here to stay. And so we went on talking for half an hour or so, while I expressed many of the views that I would later put into my *Origins of the Sexual Impulse*. Finally, Bill explained that he had been taping the conversation, to use in the first *Penthouse* forum. I chuckled at this example of his Machiavellianism, and gave my permission to use it.

Next Bill rang John Braine, and repeated the procedure. But John's reaction on being told that he had been taped was explosive. He called Bill a 'dirty little guttersnipe', and hung up after more scathing comments of the same nature.

Bill rang me back, told me what had happened, and asked if I would ring John and try and talk him round. I did, but it was no use. John was furious at what he considered an underhand trick.

'I've got a wife and child to support – I doan't do things for nuthing.'

Bill had told me to assure him that he would be well paid, but it made no difference. John was now into his hard-headed Yorkshireman act, and carried away by the kind of moral indignation he could summon at a moment's notice. So I had to ring Bill back and confess failure.

Unfazed, Bill rang Stuart Holroyd, and asked his views on sex – then, half an hour later, admitted it had all been taped, and asked permission to use it. Stuart, of course, gave it at once. But when Bill reread it, he decided that Stuart was not controversial enough. So he simply put Stuart's name to John Braine's remarks, and printed them in the first *Penthouse* forum.

I felt thoroughly irritable with John. It seemed typical of him to refuse to let Bill print his comments on the grounds that he had a wife and child to support, and then decline to accept payment. What really worried him, I suspect, was having his name in a 'girly' magazine.

Sadly, *Penthouse* failed to realise Bill's expectations of providing us all with an income. He omitted to get the partnership agreement in writing, and in due course was forced out.

I, naturally, took Bill's side in the argument with Braine, and for a long time, John and I ceased to communicate. But many years later I was asked to lecture to the Society of Authors, and met John there. Naturally, neither of us raised the matter of the estrangement. John introduced me to his new lady – he and Pat had long since separated – and we had a friendly conversation. She was pleasantly ordinary and, like John and myself, middle aged.

After my lecture, there was a question period, and John immediately rose to his feet, stuck his thumbs in the pockets of his cardigan, and told the audience that he was delighted to see his old friend Colin Wilson, whom he had known since the days when we were both labelled Angry Young Men . . . He went on for a quarter of an hour, while the audience, obviously accustomed to John hogging the floor, waited resignedly for him to finish. John was perfectly sober – he told me he no longer touched alcohol – but it was apparent that he was still unable to resist the temptation to launch into monologue.

This was the last time I saw him. We occasionally exchanged books, but I found John's later novels virtually unreadable. For years now, since he had moved to Woking, he had been writing about suburban couples who are members of the local golf club and have adulterous affairs with other suburban couples. Now he turned to writing about an aging novelist who has left his nagging wife and found happiness with a mistress of his own age, his 'one and last love'. But John had failed to recognise that even a mere two hundred pages about a blissful relationship are boring unless something happens. I said complimentary things about both books, but could not, in fact, finish either.

In 1986, a girl I knew rang me to say that John was in hospital with a burst stomach ulcer. I rang the hospital to ask how he was, but they refused to give me information on the grounds that I was not a relative. Shortly thereafter, Joy and I had to travel to Japan, where I was lecturing. We were sitting in a Tokyo restaurant, when my agent asked me if I had heard that John Braine had died that day. It struck me as ironic that I should be so far from home when I heard of the death of an old friend, and wished that I had had a chance to see him at least once again. It seemed so long ago since I had read *Room at the Top*, and experienced that twinge of alarm in case this new writer would prove to be a second Hemingway, who would give all of us a run for our money.

I have often asked myself what exactly went wrong for John as a writer. And I suspect that the answer lies in the parallel with Hemingway. Like Hemingway, John created a kind of alter ego that was completely unlike his real self. One critic caused deep offence by asking when Hemingway was going to come out from behind the hairs on his chest. But John's problem was not a question of virility. It was that he was a shy and sensitive person who was inclined to take a poor view of himself. Even when I first knew him, he often referred wryly to the size of his midriff. I think he saw himself as someone rather like the frog prince in the fairy tale, unattractive to women, unimpressive to men. But he wanted to be seen as sensible, hard-headed and assertive. So this was the part he chose to play. The trouble is that no one who is taken in by his own play-acting can survive as a serious writer.

As his political opinions swung from left to right, John took pleasure in proclaiming himself a believer in flogging and capital punishment. And he failed to see that even his right-wing friends – like Kingsley Amis, Anthony Burgess and Bernard Levin – had no desire to sit and listen while he went on laying down the law and flogging dead horses.

He once told us that his most important piece of literary advice was given to him by his father, who advised him to write only about what he knew well. He stuck to this advice, and paid for it with an increasing narrowness of range that finally strangled his literary talent.

In retrospect, I can see that John was a kind of dual personality. Part of him was intelligent, sensitive, and had a genuinely deep human understanding. But his alter ego was entirely concerned with how other people saw him. I think he rather envied Priestley the universal respect he earned during 1940, when he was giving those remarkable war postscripts on the BBC. The sensitive, human Braine once remarked: 'Even a spoilt rich lady with a fat Pekinese needs love as much as anybody.' But the Braine, who longed to be admired as a Yorkshire sage, would go on talking reactionary politics until his audience was crying for mercy. Self-division is not supposed to be a mortal illness, but I think John died of it.

CHAPTER 12

America

Sally was a pretty and lively child, and from the beginning I adored her.

The day Joy returned with her from hospital brought me another important insight. Before I set out to pick them up from Redruth Hospital, the *Daily Mail* rang me, and asked if they could send a photographer over to get a picture of the baby. When I told Joy this, she exploded. She had disliked the press ever since the horsewhipping scandal. Now she said indignantly: 'You might have spared me this!' And we quarrelled.

But when we got home, the journalists had still not arrived. The house was clean and tidy, and the sun was streaming in the windows. Joy relaxed and, by the time the photographer arrived, had become her usual serene and good-tempered self. She refused to be photographed, but left me holding the baby, who had so far been fast asleep. At that moment, Sally woke up and gave me a delightful smile. Joy assured me later that babies at ten days old do not smile, and that it must have been wind. But it was not wind – my daughter smiled at me. And the picture appeared the next day under the heading: 'Angry Young Man holds placid young girl'.

In other words, Joy's anger had been a merely superficial reaction, and when she found herself back home on a sunny morning, she responded with a sense of 'Aren't I lucky?'

What I liked about Joy was that this happened so infrequently; her calm and serenity never ceased to make me feel ashamed of my own explosiveness.

I found fatherhood a marvellous experience. When Joy had told me she was pregnant – that day when I was on a stepladder – I had not been at all sure that I was pleased. I had been a father once before, and although I had found Roderick a nice little boy, had not felt very 'fatherly' – perhaps at nineteen I was too young. With Sally it was quite different; I adored her from the moment she appeared. I was inclined to suspect that this was because she was a girl, but when Joy went on to produce two boys, I found I adored them just as much. I was undoubtedly made for family life.

Shaw once asked: is there a father's heart as well as a mother's? Sadly, he never had a chance to find out. But in my own case the answer was definitely yes. I am an abnormally affectionate person, periodically overcome by the need to hug someone. (On one overdemonstrative occasion I cracked two of Joy's ribs.) But with Joy and three children (Damon in 1965 and Rowan in 1971), even I had enough outlet for my explosions of affection.

It was just as well I had this warm and secure family background, for the 1960s was a decade of unremitting work to stay out of debt. When, ten years or so later, someone asked me to write a piece about the 1960s, I had to admit that I had not noticed them – I had been too busy working to keep my bank manager happy.

The problem was fairly simple. The £40,000 or so I had made on *The Outsider* was soon spent since a sudden change in lifestyle always makes costs mount. Joy worked out that we needed roughly £5,000 a year for basic expenses: mortgage, electricity, petrol, telephone, and so on. If Gollancz gave me an advance of £500 on a book, it had to sell 2,500 copies to cover its advance, and most of my books sold two or three times that amount. The American edition would, with luck, make about the same. Foreign publishers usually paid an advance of £25 or £50; that was all I saw. So my basic income from books was about £4,000 a year. Journalism might bring another £1,000. But when the time came to pay the mortgage there was usually a panic and a plunge deeper into overdraft. So this new life of being a 'famous writer' was rather less glamorous than it sounds.

This must be qualified by saying that I had some wonderfully interesting times, and met some fascinating people. America was particularly rewarding.

One day in Spring 1961, an American poet named John Brinnin rang me up. He was in Cornwall on holiday, and I invited him round for a drink. Brinnin had been responsible for Dylan Thomas's lecture tours of America. And in the course of the conversation, I asked him how I could arrange such a tour. He told me that the best way was to contact the Institute of Contemporary Arts in Washington D.C.

Of course, America had killed Dylan Thomas – or rather, he had killed himself by drinking too much. And Negley Farson had gone to America for a lecture tour in 1937, but did not even start it – he had just stayed drunk in New York. But although I loved wine, I had no inclination to alcoholism, so this did not worry me.

The ICA in Washington said they would be happy to arrange a tour for me, and I set out in September 1961. Whilst staying at the Algonquin, as I was dropping off my key at the desk, I heard a messenger boy say: 'A letter for Mr Graham Greene.' This reminded me that a journalist who had interviewed me had told me that Greene was staying in the hotel.

It seemed a pity not to take advantage of a chance to meet an important contemporary. It was true that I had mixed feelings about Greene – even in the days when my interest in the Christian mystics had made me sympathetic to Catholicism, I had disliked what seemed to me a kind of melodramatic pessimism, a deliberate attempt to paint the world black, in an attempt to convince the reader that the only answer lies in the Catholic Church. On the other hand, I had quoted the Russian roulette episode again and again, and the sudden insight of his 'whiskey priest' in *The Power and the Glory* who, facing a firing squad, knows 'it would have been so easy to be a saint'. So I wrote Greene a note and asked the desk clerk to put it in his box.

A few hours later, after eating a solitary steak supper in a Broadway bar, I was back in my room, and preparing to go to bed, when my phone rang, and a voice said: 'This is Graham Greene. Do you feel like coming down to my room for a drink?'

It was only when I was in the lift that it occurred to me that I had said some rather unfavourable things about Greene in the book I had just finished, *The Strength to Dream*. Therefore, as soon as I walked into his suite, I said: 'Look, I'd better tell you, I've made some critical comments about you in my latest book. I'd be glad to send you a proof, and include any comments you want to make.' Greene shook his head. 'Quite unnecessary. Just send me the book when it's published.'

In a letter to Joy, written the following morning, I summarised my impressions:

> I was surprised by his appearance – a rather lanky man with a nervous, shy manner and a faint lisp. Bulgy eyes, like a tired headmaster, and a rather over-cultured, reedy, public-school voice. Altogether, he makes an impression of weakness, and perhaps a defensive kind of shiftiness. His voice was precious, very nervous and tense. But his face also gives an impression of meanness – one could easily imagine him saying bitchy things.

After more than forty years, I had forgotten that my first impression was so unfavourable.

Apparently I made some attempt to outline some of my misgivings about his work, and this may explain why I tell Joy: 'Although we had an interesting conversation for an hour and a half, he doesn't relax and get friendly, like Charles Snow.'

I had not expected Greene to be so much the British public schoolboy. Cyril Connolly once claimed that no one who has been to an English public school ever gets over the trauma; it leaves him slightly unsure of himself for the rest of his life. This is how Greene struck me. For example, he referred to himself as 'one': 'Of course, when one wrote *Brighton Rock* one felt completely different . . .'

In spite of which, I spent an interesting time with him. The main thing I recall was his account of souvenir shops where they sold ghastly relics – that afternoon he had seen the hand of a dead airman. This reminded me of a passage from *The Lawless Roads*, in which Greene speaks of a teenage boy and girl who had committed suicide by putting their heads on a railway line – she was pregnant for the second time, and had had her first child at thirteen; her parents had been unable to fix responsibility among fourteen youths. The double suicide and the dead airman's hand could be seen as effective symbols of Greene's view of reality.

Back in my own room, kept awake by heat and the New York traffic, I reflected that Greene was much the kind of person I had expected. I had always felt that the gloom of his novels seemed to betoken low self-esteem: the kind of thing experienced by so many of my 'Outsiders' – Barbusse's hero in *L'Enfer* says: 'I am nothing and I deserve nothing.' I had felt like that in my mid-teens – the desire to 'give God back his entrance ticket'. But years of struggle had toughened me until I realised that the 'life-rejection' of the Romantics was no solution. Talking to Greene I could not help feeling that his pessimism sprang out of low vitality.

The trouble was that I did not believe in Greene's pessimism. I felt he was using it to build up a view of life whose gloom was slightly bogus. It justified the grim atmosphere of *Brighton Rock* and *The Power and the Glory*, but made me think of the comment Tolstoy made about the work of Leonid Andreyev: 'He keeps on shouting "Boo!" but he doesn't scare me.' I suspected that the truth was that Greene rather enjoyed life, particularly sex, and that his Jansenist view of adultery only made 'sinning' more enjoyable.

I had also noted a touch of paedophilia in Greene. In 1937, reviewing a Shirley Temple film for the magazine *Night and Day*, he caused outrage by implying that the sight of the nine-year-old child star, whose knickers showed under her short frock, was intended to titillate dirty old men in grubby raincoats. Twentieth Century Fox sued the magazine and won £3,500. By the time of the trial, *Night and Day* had gone bankrupt.

Again, in 1956, Greene recommended Nabokov's *Lolita* as one of the best books of the year. *Lolita* was at that time only published in Paris by Olympia Press, which specialised in 'dirty books', and no one in England knew what Greene was talking about. It was Bob Pitman who read the book, realised it was about a middle-aged man having sex with a ten-year-old girl, and passed on this information to John Gordon, editor of the *Sunday Express*, who denounced it in his column. The result was a scandal that turned *Lolita* into a bestseller and made Nabokov famous.

When a writer sees paedophilia in a Shirley Temple film in 1937, and twenty years later recommends *Lolita* as his book of the year, one might be forgiven for suspecting that he has a touch of paedophilia in his own makeup.

Equally interesting is the fact that, at a certain point in his life, Greene decided that he no longer wanted to be a married man with a family – it was much more fun taking advantage of his fame to have love affairs – rather like having an enormous harem. This he continued to do for the rest of his life.

Any writer can understand this, and many have done much the same as Greene: H. G. Wells, for example. I have already described how, when *The Outsider* was published, I felt some frustration at being unable to take sexual advantage of my 'fame'; given the opportunity, I might well have settled for a lifetime of *affaires*. But I knew that leaving Joy would be unforgivable, a kind of insult to fate. More importantly, I knew I had no right to wreck Joy's life merely for the pleasure of sleeping with strange girls. And I knew too that she was far more important than any casual *affaire*, and that having a wife and children was, for me, the way of life for which I was intended.

When *The Strength to Dream* was published the following year, I sent Greene a copy as I had promised. As I expected, I never heard from him.

I made another interesting acquaintance at the Algonquin. After lunch the following day I was interviewed in the foyer by a columnist called Leonard Lyons. After Lyons had finished and gone, a good-looking, big-chinned young man came across to me and asked if I was Colin Wilson. He, it seemed, was Robert Shaw, who was in New York acting in Harold Pinter's play *The Caretaker*, which was opening off Broadway.

When Shaw said he had acted at the Royal Court, I asked him if he knew John Osborne. He looked at me in an odd way and said: 'He's citing me as co-respondent.' It seemed that one day when Osborne and Mary Ure had been bickering in his presence, he had said to her: 'If you ever decide to leave him, come to me.' And one night a month or so later, there had been a knock on his door, and it was Mary.

Recalling her quarrelsomeness after she had been drinking, I did not envy him.

Shaw had to go to a rehearsal, but we arranged to meet later. In a liquor shop opposite the hotel I saw that vodka was an absurdly low price – about two dollars a bottle. I bought a bottle, and when Shaw returned he came to my room and we drank some of it, which was by no means bad. And Shaw brought me a copy of a novel he had just published, *The Sun Doctor*. I read its first chapter – all I had time for with my hectic schedule – and was impressed. Stylistically, it was as good as Graham Greene.

Like so many fine actors, Shaw was dissatisfied with interpreting other people's words, and would have preferred to be a professional writer. When he told me that he had written a play, I suggested that we might collaborate. He seemed to be interested in the idea, but it was never to come about. His acting career took off. Two years later he played the part of the KGB killer in *From Russia With Love*, and two years after that, the Panzer general in *The Battle of the Bulge*. By the time he played the shark fisherman in Spielberg's *Jaws* he had put on a great deal of weight.

Mary Ure died on the opening night of a new play by Shaw, in 1975, at the age of forty-two, from a mixture of whisky and tranquillisers. Robert himself died of a heart attack in 1978, at the age of fifty-one.

I had been looking forward to this American tour. In fact, it proved to be so gruelling that I was in a state of exhaustion long before it was over. But to begin with I had no cause to complain. I enjoyed getting to know New York and being interviewed by literary columnists. And I proved to be fairly well-known there – I went into a public lavatory in Greenwich Village, and a stranger asked: 'Aren't you Colin Wilson?'

A few days later I took the night train to Washington – I had a broadcast early in the morning – and found the city full of the colours of autumn, with squirrels running up and down the trees outside my hotel, the Brighton. I lost no time in asking the way to the nearest record shop, for I had seen the Schwann record catalogue, and it had made my mouth water: it was full of records that were not available in England, particularly the symphonies of Bruckner and Mahler. (The long-playing record had been invented only about ten years earlier, so there were still many gaps in the catalogue.) The proprietor of the Disc Shop in Connecticut Avenue, a warm, enthusiastic man named Dan Danziger, took personal charge of me, answered my queries, and invited me back to his home for dinner. It was the beginning of a friendship that has lasted to this day.

I had a few lecture engagements at colleges and universities around Washington. *The Outsider* had reached the best-seller list and been something of a sensation in the United States. And since most students see themselves as rebels and outsiders, I received a warm reception on the lecture platform. I enjoy lecturing, and always do it without notes, which makes it easier to establish a rapport with audiences. The enthusiasm would have gone to my head if I had not already experienced this kind of thing when *The Outsider* came out. As it was, I soon began to feel rather like a literary Elvis Presley, surrounded by enthusiastic admirers.

Without exception, the professor with the task of introducing me began by explaining that I was a 'high-school dropout', and then went on to say that my books were now published in twenty languages and my name known all over the world. I did not mind these pardonable exaggerations, for I knew the Americans loved success stories, and were only doing their best to make their students feel I was a worthy role model. As to me, I found it pleasant to bask in all this acclaim and admiration, and to be a 'college professor' (an honorary rank I was granted in every place I visited).

But I took care not to allow myself to become too self-satisfied. I always had an underlying feeling that my real job was to write books. Being surrounded by admirers certainly creates a delightful feeling of warmth, but good writing requires an essentially cool environment. Besides, I actively dislike being treated as a guru; it embarrasses me.

There was another disadvantage to becoming an instant cult figure on every campus – it meant that I had little time to myself. If I went for a meal after a two-hour lecture and question period, a crowd of students trooped along too – even the occasional professor. This meant talking non-stop, until I longed to be allowed to eat a meal alone.

Partly to get some time to myself, I attended one of the lectures of the Protestant theologian Paul Tillich, at Georgetown University; his work had always interested me, with its emphasis on existentialism. The lecture theatre was crammed, but it was hard to understand why, for Tillich was an extremely poor lecturer, who expressed himself in a highly abstract Germanic English. (He had been driven out of Germany by the Nazis.) I concluded that the Americans are simply fascinated by celebrity, and enjoy merely looking at someone they know to be famous, whether or not they can understand what he is talking about.

It was only much later, after Tillich's death in 1965, that a book by his wife Hannah revealed that he was a kind of sex maniac, who obsessively seduced his female students, and was often caught by his wife reading a pornographic magazine concealed inside his Bible.

The tour proper began after my stay in Washington. In Richmond, Virginia, I checked into a pleasantly old-fashioned hotel, the Jefferson, which probably looked much as it had during Jefferson's lifetime. I arrived at 5.30, had a martini in the bar, then went to find the dining room. I was shown to a seat on a kind of great balcony that looked down on the hotel lobby (there was a poster advertising a Victor Borge concert), where a black waiter of ancient appearance lit two candles in silver candlesticks, then took my order. I had a dozen oysters – a delicacy I had learned to enjoy in London – followed by turkey, and half a bottle of good burgundy. And sitting there, listening to soft music, and now slightly drunk, I had a strange feeling, as if taking part in a play, or a film about my own life.

The following day the professor who had left me to myself the previous evening drove me to Lexington, a hundred and thirty miles away, through lovely autumn countryside, with mist over the Blue Ridge mountains. At one point, there was a stench so overpowering and sickening that he hastily closed the window – apparently a skunk had been hit by a car. I had not realised just how bad a skunk smells.

My lecture that evening at the university was a great success. Unfortunately, it was followed by the usual party, in which I had to stand with a glass in my hand, being introduced to professors and their wives, and answering over and over again where I had been so far, where I was going next, and how I liked America. This was the really depressing part of the American tour – dozens of faculty parties that finally all seemed to blend into one, so that it was hard to tell the difference. These, I can now see, were the real problem, for they caused me to groan and switch on to 'the automatic pilot', which causes our energies to 'leak'.

So was a trip I made not long after to Los Angeles. I was lecturing at Long Beach College, and looked forward to seeing Christopher Isherwood and Aldous Huxley.

I had met Chris – no one ever called him Christopher – at Stephen Spender's not long after *The Outsider* came out. It had been a remarkable evening. A writer named Jon Rose had been there, the 'partner' of Sandy Wilson, the author of *The Boy Friend*, whom I had come to know well. Sandy was shy and reserved; Jon was assertive and combative. He came from Australia, and liked to tell people that he had been 'the most fuckable dish in Sydney'. Volatile and insecure, Jon had a huge chip on his shoulder.

On the evening I met Chris, Jon had taken the centre of the floor – as he was prone to – and was holding forth in an aggrieved tone, arguing with an attractive woman whose name I had not caught. He became indignant, and asked: 'Who do you think I am? *Who* do you think I am?' The lady on the settee replied snappily: 'A fucking self-assertive little queer.' In a room with Stephen Spender, Chris Isherwood and Chris's boyfriend Don, this was hardly a tactful thing to say. I found myself looking at her admiringly. Jon retired into hurt silence for at least two minutes.

The discussion turned to Angus Wilson, to whom I had dedicated *The Outsider*. I told the story of how Angus had sent me a short story called 'A Bit off the Map', explaining that some people thought the polo-neck-sweatered hero was supposed to be me. Nothing, he said, had been further from his thoughts. If I objected to anything in it, would I please make any changes I liked?

I replied that I wouldn't dream of demanding changes, although I made a couple of suggestions for improving the story, which I considered less than his best.

In due course, the story appeared in a volume called *A Bit off the Map*. And various friends told me that Angus had been going around saying that the central character was based on me.

I added that Angus himself had told me that an overpowering female in his *Anglo-Saxon Attitudes* was based on Sonia Orwell – but had apparently denied this to Sonia Orwell herself.

Stephen Spender looked distinctly embarrassed. One or two other people coughed. Then the lady on the settee said: 'I'm Sonia Orwell.'

She turned out to be charming, if forthright, and Joy and I later gave her a lift home to Soho, and talked to her for half an hour in the car.

I had liked Chris immediately, and kept in touch with him – he lived in Santa Monica. Good-looking and boyish, he looked twenty years younger than his actual fifty-three. Unlike Stephen, with whom there was always a residue of shyness and awkwardness, Chris seemed a well-groomed, confident ex-public schoolboy, with a natural gift of inspiring affection. I never thought of him – as I thought of Spender and Auden – as a member of the older generation; he was like a contemporary.

Now I looked forward to seeing him again, and had written to say I was coming to L.A.

At Long Beach College I became friendly with a lecturer in the English department named Hugh Smith who, like me, enjoyed modern jazz. On my second day at Long Beach, Hugh told me there had been a phone call for me from Christopher Isherwood, asking me to ring him back. I did, and arranged to go over to see him that afternoon at Santa Monica.

Half an hour later, there was another message for me, this time from Henry Miller. He said he would like to meet me, and was willing to come to Long Beach. He would ring back later. When I heard that Miller lived at Pacific Palisades, not far from Santa Monica, I left a message suggesting that he should come to Isherwood's, and save himself a long journey.

Hugh offered to drive me up to Santa Monica. So we set out around lunchtime.

As soon as I walked into Chris's house, he said: 'I've had a phone call from that dreadful bore Henry Miller. He's coming over here shortly.'

I asked: 'Don't you like him?'

'I've never met him. But I don't like his books.'

Tropic of Cancer had recently been published in America, after two decades as a 'banned book', and had become a best-seller. I had read it years before in Paris, as well as its sequel, *Tropic of Capricorn*, and concluded that Miller was not really to my taste.

This had been confirmed when I found a copy of his book *Sexus* lying on a park bench in London, and had not been surprised that its owner had abandoned it. It opens with Miller falling in love with a 'ten cents a dance' girl he meets in a dance hall, and becoming frantically enamoured. He pursues her and bombards her with letters for days, until they meet and he takes her out for a meal. And then, as soon as they climb into a taxicab, she pulls up her skirt and plunges on to his erection. 'We went into a blind fuck, with the cab lurching and careening, our teeth knocking, tongues bitten, and the juice pouring out from her like hot soup.'

My feeling was that Miller seemed to revel in making sex sound coarse and nasty. I suspected that if he thought it would titillate the reader to describe having sex with an elephant, he would have done it without hesitation. So I could understand why Chris was not enthusiastic.

The problem, it seemed, was that Chris had arranged to take me over to see Aldous Huxley that afternoon, and then later, to have tea with his next-door neighbour Charles Laughton.

The doorbell rang, and Hugh said he would take his leave. A moment later, Miller and his son Tony were shown in.

Miller was shorter than I'd expected, but otherwise exactly like his photographs, with the almost completely bald head, the thin, almost ascetic face not unlike Henry Ford, and heavy, sensual lips. He spoke with a Brooklyn accent, and you might have taken him for a cab driver or street sweeper.

Tony was an intelligent, good-looking boy of about fourteen. We all shook hands, then stood around feeling awkward. Finally, plunging in head first, I asked Miller if he felt his books to be entirely serious, or whether the dirty bits hadn't been inserted to please the foreign tourists.

Miller looked irritated, and said (with his broad Brooklyn voice): 'All you critics are the same. You all write from here [tapping his head] instead of from down here [striking his solar plexus]. It's just head knowledge.'

This annoyed me so I said: 'Come off it, Henry. I'm a writer too, and I've read D. H. Lawrence as well. You're not among professors here.'

After this, it looked as if my afternoon with Miller was going to be a definite flop.

In fact, he had a natural, easygoing charm that disarmed criticism. On the way over to Huxley's, in the back of Chris's car, we talked generally about writing. He had never read any of my work, and seemed to have an idea that I'd written slightingly of him somewhere (which I hadn't – even the mild criticisms of *Origins of the Sexual Impulse* were then unpublished).

He mentioned that he was now, for the first time in his life, able to stop worrying about money, since *Tropic of Cancer* was a best-seller: on the other hand, he said, he hadn't yet seen much of the immense amount of money it was supposed to have made. He seemed to feel that it might never materialise – the outcome, I suppose, of sixty years of being permanently broke. In fact, as I learned later from a biography of him, he quickly spent most of it, and was soon as broke as ever.

Huxley lived in a rented house in the hills behind Hollywood Boulevard – not his own house, which had been destroyed in a brush fire the year before, together with most of his books and manuscripts. (I had been told that he was on an LSD trip at the time, and had found the flames so beautiful that he made no attempt to save his possessions.)

I had met him a few years earlier in London, when he had taken me to lunch at his club, the Athenaeum. He was very tall, almost blind, with a rather thin, slow voice. I remember saying to him, as we stood side by side in the urinal: 'I never thought I'd be having a pee at the side of Aldous

Huxley,' and Huxley replied: 'Yes, that's what I thought when I was standing beside George V.'

It is worth mentioning that Huxley had an amusing peculiarity: he did not know how to say goodbye on the phone. It was not that he was an obsessive phone-talker – simply that he was unable to end a conversation. I had noticed this the first time I rang him, when he was staying with his brother Julian in Hampstead – he talked for half an hour. I suspect that this tendency was connected with his gentle and kindly nature; in his latter years he struck many people as virtually a saint. But this inability to end a phone conversation also brings to mind the social ineptitude of so many of his heroes.

And that, I should explain, is why my attitude to Huxley's writing was ambivalent. I had first read him at the age of seventeen, urged on by Millicent, my colleague in the tax office, who regarded him with passionate admiration. I had plodded my way through *Point Counterpoint* and *Eyeless in Gaza*, detesting their feeble heroes, who seemed to be trapped in permanent self-doubt. *Brave New World* struck me as wickedly clever, but suffered from the same fault. On the other hand, *Antic Hay*, which brightened my days when I was in the RAF training camp, dazzled me with its brilliance, and still seems to me his best novel. So I regarded Huxley with a mixture of respect and exasperation.

Our misgiving about taking Miller to meet Huxley proved unnecessary. It turned out that they had met long before, and (to my relief) seemed glad to see one another again. It was strange to see them together: Miller was then seventy, Huxley was three years younger, but it was Huxley who seemed the old man; Miller gave the impression of being about fifty. Huxley was so short sighted as to be almost blind; his voice was slow and precise, like a professor lecturing, and he walked with his shoulders bent. Miller had something very youthful about him – a ready enthusiasm, a lack of dignity, bouncing with a kind of happy vitality, like a friendly puppy. I have met many famous writers, but never one who seemed so unconscious of his position. I am sure that if a shop assistant told him to stop shoving, he would have looked crestfallen and guilty. No doubt this was one of the results of not achieving fame until he was in his fifties.

They made an odd pair – Huxley using the occasional Latin tag or quoting something in French, Miller listening like a schoolboy and occasionally shouting, 'Sure!'

Although Huxley had come to accept the basic principle of religion in recent years, and there was something almost saint-like in his mildness, there was still more than a touch of the amusing malice that can be found in *Point Counterpoint*. He mentioned a block of government offices that Le Corbusier had been asked to design in Delhi; the architect decided to make them mostly of glass, forgetting that the Indian sun would turn it into an enormous hothouse. Huxley chuckled like a saturnine headmaster as he described the clerks being slowly roasted by this huge magnifying glass.

At one point, Isherwood mentioned Lope de Vega. Huxley asked if he had read him, and Chris said yes, one or two plays. 'Is he any good?' Chris said no. Huxley smiled happily. 'I'm so glad, I've always felt guilty about not reading him, and now I don't feel guilty any more.'

I had a lot to talk to Huxley about, so after a while I rather monopolised the conversation. Since I had been lecturing for weeks on my 'new existentialism', my mind was full of ideas, and new ways of expressing them. Since we were only there for an hour or so, I felt I had to get these over as briefly as possible – Huxley and I had been corresponding then for two or three years, but oddly at cross purposes. So I talked like a machine – fast, but with all the precision I could muster. Huxley didn't respond much – it struck me that he didn't seem to want to wrench his mind off the problems of world population (which he had been writing about when we came) to think about existentialism.

I never saw Huxley again; he was to die on 22 November 1963 of cancer of the mouth. But since he died on the same day Kennedy was assassinated, his death was completely overshadowed by that of the president.

As we left Huxley's house, I realised that I had at least 'come across' to Miller. He grasped my hand and said, 'Gaad, I never heard anybody talk like that before!' (Knowing that he was a friend of Lawrence Durrell, I didn't take this compliment too seriously.) Miller had the faculty of making people like him by seeming to like and admire them; both Chris and I noticed this.

After dropping off Henry and Tony at Pacific Palisades, and meeting his Japanese wife and pretty daughter Val, Isherwood and I drove back to Santa Monica agreeing that Miller was one of the nicest men we'd ever met, and that he'd have no hostile critics if he could meet and talk with them all.

Later that evening, Chris took me to see Charles Laughton – who was already suffering from the illness that was to kill him in the following year – and his wife, Elsa Lanchester.

This proved to be as amusing and memorable in its way as the meeting with Huxley and Miller. Laughton was a big man with a large stomach, and that superbly modulated voice that everyone remembers from *Mutiny on the Bounty*. He was making the film of *Advise and Consent*, in which he was playing a southern senator, and he performed one of his major speeches for us. It was amazing to see him transformed from the suave English actor to an earnest native of Georgia.

Laughton proved to be that exceptional rarity, a highly intelligent and well-read actor, and told amusing anecdotes about Brecht (in whose *Galileo* he had created the title role), Thomas Mann and H. G. Wells.

Wells, of course, had been a well-known womaniser, and I enjoyed collecting anecdotes about him. I had become a friend of the pianist Harriet Cohen (who had been the mistress of the composer Arnold Bax), and she had once shown me her twenty-first birthday book, with the signatures of all the guests who had come to the party, including Wells, Shaw and D. H. Lawrence. I noted that Wells's signature was at the top of the list and Harriet confirmed that he had been the first to arrive. Knowing that Harriet had been incredibly beautiful, I asked her: 'Did Wells make a pass at you?' 'Oh yes.' 'What happened?' She said: 'He gazed into my eyes, and said: "I'm gonna have you . . ."' I asked: 'And what did you say?' Harriet said: 'Oh yeah?'

When Elsa Lanchester told me she had known Wells, I asked: 'Did he make a pass at you?' 'Yes'. 'What happened?'

She told me that they had met at Garsington, the home of Lady Ottoline Morrell, the society hostess. Elsa and Wells had been standing on a small hump-backed bridge over a stream, and Wells had gazed into her eyes and said: 'I'm gonna have you.' 'And what did you say?' Elsa replied: 'Oh yeah?' I roared with laughter at the coincidence.

Laughton had read about the horsewhipping episode with Joy's parents, and when I told him about how we had been pursued by the press, he made the interesting comment: 'The British press is the dirtiest in the world. American journalists have a bad reputation, but they're not nearly as bad as in England.' And he told a story of how he had recently been in England, and a journalist had asked him about his part in *Advise and Consent*. The journalist had said: 'Of course, we can understand why they cast you in the film. But why did they choose an old has-been like Franchot Tone?'

Whatever he replied would have been wrong. Even if he had said: 'I don't agree that Tone is a has-been', the remark would have sounded as if he was defending a down-and-out actor. So he simply turned and walked away.

I was charmed by Laughton, who told me to call him Charles, called me 'Young Wilson', and put his arm round my shoulder. A fleeting suspicion crossed my mind that he might be homosexual, then I dismissed it – he had been married to Elsa Lanchester since the 1930s. It was only after his death that I learned that not only was he homosexual, but that Elsa Lanchester was lesbian, and that their marriage was a kind of smokescreen.

The next day, back at Long Beach, I saw Hugh Smith, who said: 'I could hardly believe my ears – Henry Miller, Aldous Huxley, Charles Laughton and Elsa Lanchester. It was like hearing someone say: "We're going over to see Shakespeare, then calling on Ben Jonson, and after that I'm taking you for a drink with Sir Walter Raleigh and Queen Elizabeth . . ."'

* * *

Long before the end of the tour, I was becoming very tired. In Winston Salem, where I was lecturing at the Baptist College, I discovered that I had a day free, and decided to spend it in bed, resting. Someone had lent me a copy of *Esquire* which contained a complete novel by Dürrenmatt – *The Quarry*, the sequel to *The Judge and his Hangman*. But although I spent the whole day relaxing and reading, it left me feeling even more tired – and taught me that mere relaxation is not the best way of restoring depleted energies. Doing something with interest and enthusiasm is the right way. But when you have been talking non-stop for weeks it is hard to think of anything that would restore the feeling of 'absorption'.

On the day I was due to fly out from Washington, the accountant of the Institute of Contemporary Arts asked me into his office, studied the record of my earnings, and told me that I owed the US government several hundred dollars in income tax. This was a blow I had not expected, for I had thought my American income would be taxed, like American book royalties, by the British government. I had to write him a cheque, then accompany him to the tax office to have my visa stamped before I was allowed to leave the country. That meant, in effect, that I was leaving as broke as when I arrived. Now I could begin to understand what Stephen Spender meant when he said that Dylan Thomas was the first poet who had been killed by the tax man.

CHAPTER 13

The Peak Experience

Back in England in early December, I realised how much the ten-week tour had taken out of me – I felt exhausted and bad-tempered for weeks, and it was two months before I began to feel normal again. This is clearly because giving lectures and meeting people never seizes my interest in the way that writing and thinking do, and the resulting boredom and lack of inner pressure leads to a continual leakage of vitality.

But at least the tour had one important result: it had brought me some fundamental insights. Repeating my ideas over and over again to lecture audiences had made me really begin to understand what I was trying to say.

To begin with, I realised that what I was talking about was a leap forward in human evolution.

This in itself was not new; in fact, it had first dawned on me one day in 1960 when I had been lecturing to the Shaw Society in London. At the end of my talk I heard myself saying that I believed that man was on the point of an evolutionary leap to a higher stage. I thought about this afterwards, wondering if I really meant it, or whether it was merely one of those things we sometimes say in the excitement of the moment. But the more I thought about it, the more I realised I did really mean it.

In retrospect, I can see that one of the major factors that led to this conviction was the work of the American psychologist Abraham Maslow.

Four years after the American publication of my book *The Age of Defeat* – under the title *The Stature of Man* – I had received a letter from Maslow, who was a professor at Brandeis University. He explained that he had been impressed by the optimism of *The Stature of Man*, and about the way I had pinpointed the sense of defeat the permeates our culture.

Maslow had begun to have certain doubts about Freudian psychology, feeling that it 'sold human nature short'. This was something I had felt strongly for years: Freud's view that all our deepest urges are sexual seemed to me to leave out some of the most important members of the human race, from Leonardo to Bernard Shaw. I had come close to quarrelling with

Freud's grandson Lucian after I had written a newspaper article attacking Freud for his sexual obsession – but then, Lucian himself struck me as something of a sexual obsessive.

One of Maslow's basic insights had come when he was studying monkey psychology in the Bronx zoo. The monkeys were given simple puzzles to solve and, when they solved them, were given a banana as a reward. Next Maslow tried substituting a wooden banana, which would be exchanged for a real banana, and the monkeys worked just as well. Finally he tried offering them no reward, and still the monkeys went on trying to solve the puzzles. This was completely contrary to the various motivation theories of the time. We know that humans enjoy solving crossword puzzles 'for fun', but monkeys were supposed to be interested only in food.

Yet here were Maslow's monkeys solving problems because they clearly enjoyed it. Could it be, Maslow wondered, that all living things share a fundamental evolutionary urge – the craving to *learn*?

What fascinated me most about the Maslow material was his remark that, as a psychologist, he had got tired of studying sick people because they talked about nothing but their sickness. So he looked around for the healthiest human beings he could find, and studied them instead. And he quickly made an interesting discovery: all his healthy subjects had, with a fair degree of frequency, moments of sudden immense happiness. He came to call these 'peak experiences' (or PEs). The peak experience was not necessarily 'mystical' in the religious sense – just a sudden overflowing of sheer joy and vitality.

He noted the case of a young mother who was preparing breakfast for her husband and children. Suddenly a beam of sunlight came in through the window, and a surge of happiness lifted her into the peak experience.

Again, he described the case of an American marine who had been on a remote island in the Pacific for years without seeing a woman. When he got back to base, he saw a nurse, and instantly had a peak experience – not because he felt sexually aroused, but because he suddenly realised that *women are different from men*. Habit causes us to think of them both as types of human being, when they are actually as different as horses are from cows.

Maslow's observations impressed me deeply. *The Outsider* had been about poets and artists who had peak experiences looking at nature. But most of them felt that such experiences are incompatible with the triviality and boredom of everyday life, and retreated into a gloomy world of subjectivity. What I now knew was that there is no point in retreating from life. It is important to be strong enough to cope with it.

But Maslow's most important observation was that when he talked to his students about peak experiences, they began remembering peak experiences they had half-forgotten, and *began having peak experiences all the time*.

I began thinking about the example of the mother at breakfast. Her peak experience sprang from the feeling: 'Aren't I lucky?' But she was lucky *before* she had the peak experience. What made her aware of it was the sudden flood of vitality that came from *being reminded* that she was lucky. (The philosopher Fichte said: 'To *be* free is nothing; to *become* free is heavenly.')

The mother's experience made me recall something that had happened when I was a schoolboy. I was sitting in the cinema, and as the film came to an end, I realised I was feeling very happy about something. Then I remembered. That afternoon we had broken up from school for the long August holiday. I had forgotten exactly what I was feeling happy about, but the happiness remained as a kind of pleasant glow. Later I came to label this glow 'underfloor lighting'.

It happened in my teens, when I had been working as a navvy for the Leicester corporation. I had been sent to a dreary place called Stocking Farm, where we were laying electricity cables. It was a wet, cold day, and the place was deep in mud. But that evening, I was taking out a girl called Bobbie, and because that was at the back of my mind, the mud and the rain lost their power to depress me.

So, in fact, *thought itself* was acting as a counterweight to the mud and rain.

I also recalled how I used to return home from the wool factory, feeling exhausted and depressed, and then go to bed and read poetry. And after soaking myself in a bath of gloom, reading Poe and Eliot and Thomson's 'The City of Dreadful Night', I would become steadily more cheerful, and turn to Shelley's 'Ode to the West Wind' and Milton's 'L'Allegro', and end up bubbling with energy and happiness. Again, *thought* had dispelled the negative feelings.

Now here again, as I read Maslow, I was glimpsing a new possibility in human evolution. It was the intuitive recognition that human beings can control their feelings through thought. We wake up on a rainy day, remember that we have to pay a large bill, and allow a kind of gloom to settle on us like grime on a car windscreen. We are forgetting that we have the equivalent of windscreen wipers and a windscreen washer: it is stupid to allow the negative feelings to influence us for hours. We are simply *forgetting* powers we actually possess.

The implications are tremendous. We all possess the ability to switch on 'underfloor lighting' at will. Maslow's young mother was reminded that she was lucky by a beam of sunlight. All she had to do to renew the experience was to sit down and reflect on her good fortune for a few minutes, until it had been 'saved' in her unconscious mind as I can 'save' this text by hitting a key on my computer. That may sound easier said than done – until we recall that Maslow's students began to have peak experiences all the time when they began to talk about peak experiences.

The conclusion seems to be that we all have a layer of happiness just below the surface of the mind, and that the problem is how to penetrate down to it. After all, we are all lucky to be alive, as Dostoevsky realised as he stood in front of the firing squad. Hans Keller, the former music director of the BBC, tells how, when he was in Germany in the 1930s, and fellow-Jews were vanishing into concentration camps, he thought: if only I could get out of Germany I would never be unhappy for the rest of my life. In other words, he felt he merely had to hit the 'save' key.

I could soon distinguish two levels of peak experience. In its simplest form, it was simply a matter of 'feeling good', which acted as a kind of windscreen wiper that swept away negative feelings, and restored a sense of the reality of the future.

But there was a second level that carries a definite sense of meaning. Chesterton, after all, had talked about 'absurd good news', and news is bound to be *about* something. This 'news' was about human life, and my own life in particular, and brought an absolute certainty that, in spite of practical problems, I had no cause for doubt or anxiety. All I had to do was grind on, like a tractor ploughing a field, and the rest would be taken care of. I had a strong feeling that some power apart from myself was in charge of my life.

There was obviously a third level – of meaning made visible and over-whelming, a feeling that the outside world and everything in it is communicating with you as clearly as if speaking in your ear. Aldous Huxley experienced the same effect under mescalin, although my own mescalin experience – which I shall describe – was quite unlike this. The closest I came to 'the third level' was when I was driving back from the Lake District, and felt the sensation of intensified awareness, as though I could see through mountains to the other side.

But Huxley also noted that our senses are filters, designed to keep things out as much as to let them in. We can adjust them, like drawing the curtains on a hot day. To me it seems clear that being able to achieve the third level would be like standing on the top of Everest when you already know what it is like to stand on top of the Matterhorn. What is really important is the intellectual conviction that 'absurd good news' is a reality.

Maslow was by no means the first psychologist to recognise that the most remarkable thing about human beings is that we possess free will. Probably that honour goes to an eighteenth-century French philosopher called Maine de Biran. At that time, thinkers like Cabanis and La Mettrie argued that man is a machine – in fact, La Mettrie wrote a book of that title. At first Maine de Biran was inclined to agree – until he recognised one day that when I make some effort, I have a clear feeling that it is *I* who am making it not a machine. I may feel mechanical when I am doing something that is boring and automatic, but the moment I exert my will, I become aware that I possess an *active power*.

However, Maine de Biran's insights were unfashionable; the French preferred to believe that man is a machine and nothing but. And even today, very little has changed: the major French thinkers – Derrida, Baudrillard, Lyotard, Deleuze – remain mechanists.

Soon after my return from America I also stumbled on another vitally important idea: that precisely 5 per cent – or one in twenty – of any animal group – including humans – is 'dominant'.

This came about when I discovered a book called *African Genesis*, by the American playwright and film scriptwriter Robert Ardrey. In fact, I bought the book for Joy, because it looked the kind of thing she would enjoy, then read it and was overwhelmed by it. Ardrey was arguing that human beings originated on the African savannas about two million years ago, and that they learned to walk upright to leave their hands free for the use of weapons – like bone clubs.

I was not particularly concerned about why man had decided to walk upright. What excited me was the idea that human beings had come into existence through *an evolutionary leap*.

I wrote to Ardrey care of his publisher, and he replied. We were soon engaged in a regular correspondence, and when he came to England – he lived in Rome – he took the trouble to travel to Cornwall to see me.

Ardrey told me that 'the dominant 5 per cent' had been discovered during the Korean war, when the Americans were puzzled that there were no escapes by American prisoners of war. Eventually, they discovered the reason. The Chinese had studied their prisoners carefully until they established which of them was 'dominant' – which had leadership qualities. They took these prisoners and placed them under heavy guard in a separate compound. And the other prisoners, deprived of the 'troublemakers', became so passive that the Chinese could leave them with almost no guard at all. The number of 'troublemakers' was always the same – 5 per cent.

Bernard Shaw had known about this. At the beginning of the twentieth century, he had asked the explorer H. M. Stanley: 'If you were sick, how many other members of your party could take over from you?' and Stanley had replied: 'One in twenty – five per cent.'

And, Maslow also knew about the 5 per cent. In his days as an experimental psychologist, he had decided to undertake a study of dominance in women. He deliberately chose women because they tended to be more honest than men (who were inclined to stretch the facts in the interest of self-esteem). He quickly discovered that women fell into three distinct 'dominance groups': high, medium and low.

High-dominance women – 5 per cent – tended to be sexually aggressive, and liked high-dominance males – the kind of man who would tear off their clothes and fling them on a bed. They were sexually experimental, promiscuous, masturbated frequently and often enjoyed lesbian activity. They regarded the male sexual member as beautiful.

Medium-dominance women – by far the largest group – were romantics who were looking for Mr Right. They liked being given flowers and taken to restaurants with soft lights. They were capable of mild promiscuity, but really wanted a home, children and the other advantages of a stable marriage. Their feeling about the male sexual member tended to be neutral.

Low-dominance women were afraid of men. They liked the kind of man who would admire them from a distance without speaking. And they thought the male sexual member was downright ugly.

Maslow made the interesting discovery that all women wanted a male who was slightly more dominant than they were, but not too much more. Maslow even devised tests that would show whether the 'dominance gap' between a male and female contemplating marriage was too great, not great enough, or just the right size.

Relationships in which the woman was dominant were seldom happy. One highly dominant woman spent years looking for a more dominant male, but was never successful. Finally, she found a man who *was* more dominant, but not enough: So she would cause quarrels that made him lose his temper. He would then slap her around, hurl her on a bed and virtually rape her. These she found the only truly satisfying sexual experiences.

Both men and women wanted a partner within their own dominance group. Medium-dominance women were afraid of high-dominance males, while low-dominance women were afraid of medium-dominance males. As to high-dominance males, they would have sex with any woman who was available – 'prick fodder' – but could not get personally involved with someone who did not belong to their own dominance group.

I could see at once that my relationship with Joy was something of an anomaly. I was obviously high-dominance; she was obviously medium-dominance. From the beginning, I liked her sweetness and her intelligence and her conscientiousness. But what cemented our relationship was her sexual shyness and reserve, the fact that we did not become lovers for many months. Men tend to devalue what they get too easily. And by the time we became lovers, I had become completely addicted to her.

This also explained why her parents had tried so hard to separate us. They had recognised instinctively that the dominance gap was too wide and that their daughter was likely to end up hurt – or worse still, pregnant and abandoned. Fortunately, for the reasons explained, they turned out to be wrong – I write this when we have been together almost fifty years.

This insight into the role of dominance was a revelation. I realised that this was the vital clue to the problem of 'Outsiders'. They were not – as I had said in my book – simply frustrated men of genius. Barbusse's hero says: 'I am nothing and I deserve nothing.' But they all belonged to the 'dominant 5 per cent', and it was their natural dominance that made them dissatisfied. Before he became an actor, the great Henry Irving was a bank clerk. But imagine what would have happened if he had remained a bank clerk and never tried to become an actor. He would have been deeply unhappy and frustrated, yet would not have been able to find out what was wrong with him. A dominant person remains dissatisfied and thwarted until he has placed himself in a position in which he can exercise his dominance.

Two or three centuries ago, such a person would find it far easier to find his place in society, because life was less competitive. To begin with, in a small population, the dominant ones would have less rivals. In our overpopulated world, there are millions of dominant individuals, and establishing their position is far more difficult.

I could see, for example, that Sandy Wilson's boyfriend Jon Rose – the one Sonia Orwell dismissed as a 'fucking self-assertive little queer' – was a dominant person, and that this was his problem. The publicity director of Houghton Mifflin, Pat McManus, who had looked after me in New York, had been in charge of Jon and Sandy when they came over for the Broadway production of *The Boy Friend*, and said that Jon had soon made himself detested by his assertiveness. At press conferences, he kept interrupting and answering questions intended for Sandy. He could not get used to the idea that it was the gentle Sandy that journalists wanted to speak to, and not Sandy's abrasive and opinionated partner. Jon died a few years later of some minor illness; but undoubtedly he really died of frustration.

What does this mean for 'Outsider theory'? That 'Outsiders' are members of the dominant 5 per cent, and that they remain Outsiders until they have found some way of expressing their dominance.

It is important to understand that 5 per cent is a huge number of people. Every factory foreman, every sergeant in the army, every supermarket manager, belongs to the dominant 5 per cent.

John Calhoun, a scientist at the Institute of Mental Health in Bethesda, Maryland, performed an experiment with rats that led to some astonishing insights. Calhoun wanted to study the effect of overcrowding in rats, so he placed a large number of them in two interconnected cages. A highly dominant rat, a 'king rat', took over one of the two cages for himself and his harem, so that the remaining rats were now grossly overcrowded in the remaining cage. And what then happened was that the dominant 5 per cent became a criminal 5 per cent. They did things that rats do not normally do, like raping female rats (rats, in fact have an extremely elaborate courting ritual), and becoming cannibals and eating babies. In other words, when the dominant 5 per cent has no outlet for its dominance, it becomes a criminal 5 per cent. This explains why so many human criminals emerge from slums, or deprived backgrounds.

But the really interesting point here is that there are a very small number of rats who are so dominant that they are 'king rats'. These are not ordinary members of the 5 per cent; they are probably more like .005 per cent.

There is another important observation to be made here. Most of the dominant 5 per cent need other people to express their dominance: the actor needs his audience, the politician needs his electorate. But there are a very small number of dominant human beings – maybe .005 per cent who do not need other people to express their dominance. For a tiny percentage of artists or poets, the need to create works of art and literature is of more importance than being 'recognised'. These are what Wells called 'Originative intellectual workers.'

But here again there is an interesting corollary. The latest research on Albert Einstein shows that he was driven by strong sexual urges, particularly towards cleaning women. Richard Feynman, the great quantum physicist, made a habit of seducing his female students and even the wives of his male students. John von Neumann, the father of computers, could never enter a room with a pretty girl without dropping a pencil on the floor and trying to peer up her dress. The psychologist Jung often seduced his female patients. And the theologian Paul Tillich, as already noted, was an obsessive seducer of his students and any other woman who would cooperate. Obviously, this does not imply that he was an insincere Christian or a bad theologian – merely that, like most men of high dominance, he was a Jekyll and Hyde.

These people were undoubtedly members of the .005 per cent. Yet in spite of their track record as seducers, they did not need other people to express their dominance. They were driven by a basically *impersonal* urge, the evolutionary urge to create. As Shaw said, such men create new mind as surely as any woman creates new men.

'Outsiders', then, are the evolutionary spearhead of the human race. In which case, how is it that so many of them have gone insane or committed suicide? Why have so many concluded that human life is meaningless and pointless?

When my daughter Sally was four years old, I had an experience that showed me the answer.

Joy and I had spent a few days in Leicester with my parents. On our way home, we intended to stop in Bristol to see a remarkable painter called Bill Arkle.

We set out at about two in the afternoon, after I had drunk two pints of beer with my father in the Coleman Road Working Men's Club. That was a mistake. Within an hour I was yawning and fighting off a feeling of sleepiness.

Our route lay through Cheltenham, where there was an excellent second-hand bookshop run by my friend Alan Hancox. I looked forward to browsing there for half an hour before driving on to Bristol.

We were able to park almost in front of the shop, and I went in with Sally, while Joy rearranged luggage in the boot of the car to make way for books.

After about ten minutes, Sally said: 'Where's mummy?' I took her to the door and pointed to Joy, and Sally trotted off towards her. I went back and continued to browse. Five minutes later, Joy came into the shop alone, and I naturally assumed that Sally was in the car. Another five minutes passed before I asked casually: 'Where's Sally?' and Joy said: 'I don't know – she was with you.'

There was instant panic. We rushed to the door and looked into the crowded street. There was no sign of Sally. She must have trotted straight past Joy.

I went one way and Joy went the other. I was in a state of panic. Since she had been born, Sally had never been out of our sight. And now she had disappeared. My head filled with lurid fantasies. What if someone had lured her into a car and kidnapped her? What if she stepped off the pavement and was killed by a bus? It was the rush hour in Cheltenham, and the street was crowded with traffic.

I reached a traffic light, and a barrier at the edge of the pavement. She had obviously not gone this way. I hurried back and met Joy, who had obviously had no luck either. Off we went again in opposite directions. I found it impossible to believe that we had lost my daughter, and that this disaster had descended so suddenly.

When I went back a second time, Joy had found her. She had walked around the corner and to the other side of the block. But fortunately she had stayed on the pavement.

We took her back in the shop with us, and bought the books I had piled up at the side of the till. I was dizzy with relief. And as we drove away, I experienced an immense delight. I was thinking: 'Aren't buses beautiful objects? And isn't exhaust smoke a pleasant smell?'

It began to rain as we got on to the Bristol road, and road works meant we had to crawl along in a traffic queue. But I felt no impatience. I had the window wide open, and everything seemed beautiful. When we arrived at Bill Arkle's an hour later, I was still in a state of euphoria.

What had happened, of course, was basically what had happened to Greene after playing Russian roulette. I had been sunk in a kind of indifference and boredom. Then the crisis of losing Sally had galvanised me into a kind of frenzy. The subsequent relief transformed the world into a paradise.

Now Edmund Husserl – the philosopher on whose 'phenomenology' Heidegger and Sartre based their existentialism – had one tremendous basic insight: that consciousness is *intentional*. When you look at something, you direct your attention at it like a light beam. Without this effort of attention, you would be hardly aware of what you were seeing. Think of what happens when you look at your watch with your mind on something else. You have to look at it again to see what time it is. You could compare your act of perception to a whaler throwing a harpoon at a whale. When you 'see' things, your attention has harpooned them.

Then why is it that we usually see things as so dull and boring? We do not throw the harpoon hard enough. Where 'intentionality' is concerned, human consciousness is habitually lazy.

Why? Here I must mention another of my central ideas: the 'robot'. We all have a kind of robot in our unconscious minds which does things for us, like a servant. You learn to type slowly and painfully, but at a certain point, your robot takes over and does it far more efficiently than you could. He drives your car and talks French for you.

But there is a problem. This excellent servant often does things that we would prefer to do ourselves. You hear a piece of music that moves you deeply. But after the tenth time, the robot is listening instead of you. You go for a favourite country walk, but the robot somehow takes away half the pleasure.

The problem is simple. The robot takes over when we are tired, cutting in like a thermostat. He can drive you home from work, and you cannot even remember the journey.

Clearly, 'robotic' consciousness is far less intense than 'wideawake' consciousness. What Greene did when he pointed the gun at his head and pulled the trigger was to wake himself up, to make his consciousness twice as 'intentional'.

Losing Sally in Cheltenham had also acted as an 'alarm clock', and made me twice as awake. And suddenly I saw the world with the intensity that Van Gogh had seen it when he painted 'The Starry Night'.

Obviously, 'normal consciousness' is half-asleep, and we have to learn how to persuade it to wake up. At first I was inclined to think that the answer lies in the sudden shock, the sudden crisis. But as a method of inducing peak experiences, Russian roulette would be rather dangerous.

And then I began to see the answer. Before Greene played Russian roulette, his mind was slack and bored. When he pulled the trigger, his consciousness was suddenly galvanised by the expectation of death, and *contracted*. And when there was just a click, he breathed a sigh of relief, and his consciousness was able to expand again. So the movement is one of concentration, followed by relaxation.

I began trying, just as an exercise, to make this work by imagination alone. I concentrated hard, then relaxed and allowed myself to 'expand'. And I soon discovered that if I kept on doing this, the effect was a feeling of strain, as if I was expanding and contracting some muscle behind the eyes. But as this 'muscle' began to feel tired, further effort would produce the peak experience. I was, as it were, producing Greene's Russian roulette effect *in slow motion*.

The simplest way to do it, I discovered, is to hold up a pen against a blank wall, then concentrate hard until you see nothing but the pen. Then relax the attention so you become aware of the wall. Then concentrate again. I usually find that ten or twelve efforts of concentration release the peak experience.

And then I saw that this is the answer to creating a new form of existentialism which avoids the pessimism of Sartre and Camus and the nihilism that so many 'Outsiders' suffer from. If consciousness is 'intentional', you can simply make it more intentional by that act of focusing.

But how? Are you supposed to sit and concentrate until you go red in the face?

The answer came to me one day when I was about to travel to London on the night train. As a typical Cancer, I love my home and hate travel, and the thought of the effort involved depressed me.

Moreover, Joy and I had been invited out to dinner that evening. Our host was the owner of a house at nearby Porthpean, where a spectacular murder had taken place. In November 1952, 26-year-old Miles Giffard, the son of well-off middle-class parents (his father was the clerk of the court) had become angry and frustrated when his father had refused to let him borrow the car to drive to London to see his girlfriend. When his father came home, Miles went down to the garage and hit him on the head with an iron pipe, battering in his skull. Then he went to the kitchen and killed his mother in the same way. He lifted their bodies into a wheelbarrow, took them to the top of the cliff, and threw them off, hoping they would be carried out by the tide. Then he drove to London and spent the weekend with his girlfriend. The bodies were soon found, and Miles was arrested. The jury found him guilty and he was hanged.

The current owner of the murder house, which was now called Blue Waters, had asked us to dinner. After that, Joy had to drive me to the night train.

As I was thinking gloomily about this prospect, it suddenly occurred to me that this was absurd. Before *The Outsider* had been published, I would have regarded myself as very fortunate to go to dinner to look at a murder scene then to go to London by sleeper.

As soon as I recognised this, I saw the answer: that I had to stop feeling unwilling and *reluctant*, and put a certain effort and enthusiasm into going to dinner, then to London. And that is precisely what I did. As we left our house to go to Blue Waters, I summoned energy and prepared to enjoy myself – which I did. Then I went to London in the same frame of mind. Everything went well, and I returned the following evening feeling as if I had been on holiday. I had made the trip enjoyable by simply doubling the effort I put into it.

This was, of course, a logical extension of what I had been doing all my life, since the 'suicide' attempt at sixteen. This had obviously been my own version of Greene's Russian roulette experience, looking 'into the pit' and being suddenly overwhelmed with the ecstasy of being alive. As I stood there, holding the cyanide bottle, I became two people, the 'real me' and the frustrated adolescent. The problem, I then saw, was to learn to transfer my centre of consciousness to the 'real me', and to recognise the adolescent as an imposter. Thereafter, I never took my miseries too seriously, aware that my 'sufferings' were basically a kind of confidence trick.

I had grasped that same insight when I was thrown out of the RAF – the sheer joy of walking along that sunlit 'Roman road to Wendover, by Tring and Lilly Hoo', and knowing then that if it was a choice between Rabelais and Eliot's 'Hollow Men', I would choose Rabelais every time.

The same thing happened when my first wife, Betty, told me she was not pregnant; and again when Joy told me she was not pregnant in Teignmouth. And as soon as I grasped what Husserl meant by saying that consciousness is 'intentional', I understood that there is something absurd in waiting for 'peak experiences' to arrive; they could be induced by an act of concentration and reflection. This is what I grasped so clearly after we lost Sally in Cheltenham. Indeed, a few years later, I happened to be describing this incident to my literary agent as we walked on a Cornish beach, and as I reached the conclusion of the story, my scalp suddenly tingled with a sense of pure joy as if I was re-living the experience of finding her.

The principle involved here is an interesting one, and I recognised it again when I was next in California. I had been invited to lecture at a place called the Esalen Institute, which was on the coast near Big Sur, and which had hot and cold springs. These ran into two huge stone tubs, each about five feet high. One was full of steaming hot mineral water, the other of ice-cold water.

As I came in, I saw a man heaving himself out of the hot tub, and then lowering himself, without apparent discomfort, into the cold tub.

I said: 'My God, how do you manage to do that?'

He said: 'It's a perfectly simple trick. Your body can't really tell the difference between very hot water and very cold water. So as you lower yourself into the cold tub, you *tell yourself* that this is deliciously hot.'

I tried it and it worked. As I lowered myself into the cold tub, I told myself that this was as hot as the other. And my body was convinced, and relaxed in the cold water as happily as in the hot.

This is not some form of confidence trick. That experience of losing Sally in Cheltenham had taught me that we always have a thousand reasons for happiness, and that misery and depression are basically a form of self-indulgence. If some god had offered to return Sally on condition I walked to the North Pole and back, I would have agreed without hesitation, feeling it was a good bargain.

Several decades later, I learned that a remarkable man of genius called Syd Banks had stumbled upon these insights, and that they had become the basis of a new psychology created by an American psychiatrist named George Pransky.

Banks is neither an academic nor a psychiatrist; he is an ordinary working man. And the dazzling insight that struck him one day happened in the following manner. He had remarked to a friend that he was feeling unhappy, and the friend replied: 'You're not unhappy, Syd – you just think you are.' Banks stared at him in amazement and said: 'Do you realise what you've just said?'

The insight that had dazzled him was that all our psychological problems arise from our *thoughts*, and that we can make them go away by changing our thoughts. Maslow would have said that pessimists do not have peak experiences because they are pessimists. Optimists *do* have peak experiences because they are optimists.

Banks was so stunned by this insight that he began giving lectures about it. Soon, he was giving seminars that were crowded with professional men – doctors, businessmen, psychiatrists.

George Pransky, who like Maslow had begun to feel disillusioned about Freud, went along to a weekend seminar, and at first could not understand what Syd Banks meant when he said that all our problems are caused by our thoughts. But he observed that the people at the conference all seemed full of energy and optimism – that they were all 'copers' who were in charge of their lives. And when he understood what Banks was saying, he suddenly began to share the feeling. He went on to apply these insights to his patients, and found that they worked. Pransky has created a psychology that is based on the peak experience.

This is Husserl's 'intentionality' in action. It is the recognition that *the mind itself* dictates most of our feelings and responses. We induce most of our own misery.

Intentionality can be used to create what I have labelled 'holiday consciousness', that wide-awake sense of reality that is of the same nature as Proust's '*moments bienheureux*' and Chesterton's 'absurd good news', the sudden joyful recognition that the mind itself can transform and control all our feelings and reactions.

Gurdjieff aimed at inducing this high level of control in his followers, as can be seen from a story told by J. B. Bennett in his autobiography, *Witness* (1974).

In the autumn of 1923, Bennett went to stay at the Prieuré at Fontainebleau, where Gurdjieff had set up his Institute for the Harmonious Development of Man. Everyone was expected to work extremely hard: building walls, digging the garden, and performing the incredibly complex 'movements' devised by Gurdjieff.

One morning Bennett woke up shaking with fever. Just as he was telling himself, 'I will stay in bed today,' he found himself impelled to get up, 'with a queer sense of being held together by a superior will'. In spite of exhaustion – due to dysentery – he joined a group being directed by Gurdjieff in some new and very complicated exercises. One by one, the others dropped out, but Bennett felt he was being willed to continue by Gurdjieff, even if it killed him.

Then, quite suddenly, 'I was filled with an influx of an immense power. My body seemed to have turned into light.' All weariness and pain had vanished.

To test this power he went into the fierce afternoon sun and began to dig at a pace he could not normally have maintained for more than a few minutes, and continued for more than an hour. 'My weak, rebellious, suffering body had become strong and obedient.'

He recalled something that Ouspensky had once said: some people believe they can be angry or pleased at will, but to grasp our limitations we only have to try to be astonished. 'Instantly, I was overwhelmed with amazement . . . Each tree was so uniquely itself that I felt I could walk in the forest forever and never cease from wonderment. Then the thought of "fear" came to me. At once I was shaking with terror . . . I thought of joy, and I felt that my heart would burst from rapture . . . The word "love" came to me, and I was pervaded with such fine shades of tenderness and compassion that I saw that I had not the remotest idea of the depth and range of love . . . After a time it became too much for me . . . I wanted to be free from this power to feel whatever I chose, and at once it left me.'

But I have left to the end one of the most important parts of the story. On his walk in the forest Bennet meet Gurdjieff, who told him that what he was experiencing was 'Higher Emotional Energy'. And he added that 'there are some people . . . who are connected to a Great Reservoir or Accumulator of this energy.' And such people – Gurdjieff implied he was one of them – can connect others to the Great Reservoir.

I suspect I achieved some very slight contact with this reservoir on my drive back from Sheepwash.

CHAPTER 14

Philosophy and Dirty Books

The years between my return from America in late 1961 and my next trip there in January 1966 were a period of non-stop work. We were living off an overdraft all that time, and I wrote hard to keep the bank manager from bouncing cheques.

Apart from chronic shortage of cash, I had no real cause for complaint. I adored my family, and was living in a pleasant home overlooking the sea. I could spend the morning working, then go to the beach and sunbathe and swim, then return home and open a bottle of wine.

As I have watched other writers' marriages fall apart, I have realised that meeting Joy was perhaps the best piece of luck of my life. Her gentle, easygoing nature made me feel immensely protective towards her, just as I was protective towards Sally – and, later, towards my sons. We had a record about the Flopsy Bunnies with a song that went:

> We're a happy family
> Yes, a happy family
> And we live at the foot
> Of the big fir tree . . .

and I never heard it without thinking: Yes, we *are* a happy family. So I wasted no time in worrying about why we were always so broke, although I sometimes suspected fate did it to me to thwart my natural laziness. As long as we could scrape along, being in perpetual overdraft didn't seem to matter much.

On Blackpool pier, a fortune teller looked at my palm and said: 'You'll never be rich, but you'll never be really short of money.' So far, she has proved right.

One day Gollancz wrote to me, suggesting that the only way to disarm the hostility of the critics (who continued to pan my books) was to stop writing for a few years. He suggested that I should find myself a job –

perhaps with a publisher, or perhaps an academic post – and learn to live on a lower income. The thought made my heart sink – I had spent years working at jobs I hated, and was determined not to become a wage slave again. As I re-read the letter, my spirits plunging deeper into depression, Sally laughed from the next bedroom, and my gloom vanished. So long as I had my wife and my daughter, nothing could worry me deeply.

Of course, the greatest blessing was the sense of freedom. This would descend quite suddenly, and fill me with a wild feeling of delight. I recall driving back from London with Joy, and stopping off at a pub near Stonehenge to have a sandwich and a glass of beer (in those days, pubs did not sell wine by the glass). Sitting outside at a wooden table in the sunlight, I realised how immensely lucky I was to be there instead of in a factory or office. Since I had expected to spend my whole life working for someone else, mere lack of money seemed a triviality.

Of course, I spent far too much on books and records. In July 1961 I note that I had 5,000 books and 1,500 records in the house. By 1963, I had 10,000 books and 4,000 records. Today I have about 25,000 books and the same number of records. This probably goes a long way towards explaining why we never had any money.

It also explains why I wrote so much. For example, in 1960 I wrote in record time a novel that appeared as *Adrift in Soho*. This had started as a collaboration with an old Soho friend named Charles Belchier, a good-looking actor with a voice so seductive that he could charm a girl into bed in half an hour.

We had not been close friends in my Soho days, for Charles, like so many actors, was uninterested in ideas, so we had little in common. But after *The Outsider* came out, he contacted me, and came to stay with us on several occasions. And he asked my help finding a publisher for an unfinished autobiographical book called *The Other Side of Town*.

As soon as I read it I saw that it was unpublishable in its present form – it was too short, and had no development. But the fragment fascinated me.

Charles described waking at nine o'clock on a rainy morning in a disused cinema where he has spent the night sleeping on the floor with a girl, going outside and watching the people hurrying past to work, and feeling a delighted superiority in the fact that he is free, and can spend the day as he likes. He steals a bottle of milk from a doorstep and drinks it instead of breakfast, then goes off in search of enough money to buy himself lunch . . .

For about a week I tried to rewrite it as a novel, then suddenly realised that I could not write the book from behind Charles's eyes, so to speak; I had to put myself into it. So it turned into a story about a provincial youth who, like myself, has worked as a navvy in an attempt to avoid office work, and who goes to London in search of a more interesting life. There he makes the acquaintance of this handsome, smooth-talking actor, who makes a living by sketching people in Soho pubs and entertaining theatre queues.

I soon used up all Charles's plot, and decided to extend it with bits of my play *The Metal Flower Blossom*. But even so, I ran out of inspiration after another ten thousand words. I finally sent it to Gollancz and asked his advice. To my delight – and Charles's – he decided to publish it exactly as it stood, without bothering with an ending. I gave Charles a third of the advance, and *Adrift in Soho* came out in September 1961. Since it seemed an unpretentious little book, most critics gave it good reviews.

The remainder of Charles's story is sad. In the summer of 1968, he wrote to me from some island in the Mediterranean, telling me that he had found the perfect way of life, beach-combing, dozing in the sun and smoking pot. Six months or so later, I received a press cutting from his girlfriend: it is from the *Daily Express* of 6 December 1968:

> A 43-year-old Englishman arrested for peddling dangerous drugs in West Germany committed suicide in his cell in Heilbronn today. He was named as Charles Belchier of no fixed address.
>
> He and two associates were arrested after they were found with hashish worth £1,500 on the black market.

Apparently Charles had hanged himself. His girlfriend was convinced that he had been murdered by other smugglers to keep him from talking, and I have to agree that this is plausible – I feel Charles loved life too much to kill himself.

The following year, 1962, saw the publication of the first book about me, *The World of Colin Wilson* by Sidney Campion. The author was a Leicester man whom I had once regarded as a hero and role model.

In about 1943, when I was twelve, my father brought home from work a book called *Towards the Mountains* by Sidney R. Campion, describing how he had been born in a slum, and worked as a newspaper seller from the age of eleven. When he was selling newspapers outside the London Road station he had fallen into conversation with the Labour politician Ramsay MacDonald, who had recognised his quality, and helped him find work on a local newspaper. Burning with ambition, Sidney was determined to become a great man, and the Prime Minister of England. And although he failed in his political ambitions, he became a barrister and a high-ranking civil servant, and was at one point given the OBE and awarded the freedom of the city of Leicester at a banquet in the Town Hall.

It was an amazing story of self-help, and I was thrilled by it. So was my mother; after reading Sidney's description of how he had obtained a copy of *Lady Chatterley's Lover* when it was first published, and written a passionate defence of the book, she immediately borrowed *Sons and Lovers* from the local library, and became one of Lawrence's devoted admirers. I also read Lawrence and admired him; but I did not think he was half as good as Sidney Campion.

About a month after *The Outsider* came out, my phone rang, and the man on the other end identified himself as Sidney Campion. 'Not *the* Sidney Campion?' I asked incredulously. And indeed it was. It seemed that the great Leicester firebrand was now retired in Wimbledon, carving sculptures as a hobby, and wanted to know if I would sit for him. Naturally, I said yes, and immediately wrote to my mother to tell her that Sidney Campion, the *great* Sidney Campion, wanted to carve a bust of me. I think that this was the first time that my mother realised that her son had really 'arrived'.

I made my way down to Wimbledon on the underground, and was mildly surprised to find that the great Leicester writer was living in an ordinary semi-detached, and was a mild, kindly and deaf old man (in fact, he was younger than I am now) with a perceptible Leicester accent. (I had got rid of mine years before.)

He introduced me to his wife, Clare, a plump, grey-haired lady in her sixties, and it took me some time to reconcile her with the woman I remembered so clearly from Sidney's first volume of autobiography, *Sunlight on the Foothills*. For Sidney's description of her had haunted my adolescent fantasies, particularly a phrase about 'our warm naked bodies entwined in one another's arms', and his admission that his desire for her was so urgent in those early days of marriage that he often used to make some excuse to break off work and hurry home during the day.

Sidney seemed to greatly admire me, and it did not take me long to understand why. He felt he had never achieved his lifetime ambition to 'reach the top'; he had never become famous. And apparently I had done it with a single book. And as we sat in his studio on that first occasion, he confided in me that his ambition was to write one more book – a biography of me.

The idea struck me as slightly absurd – after all, I was only twenty-five. But Sidney had taken to heart Edith Sitwell's comment that I would one day be a 'truly great writer', and was determined to be my first chronicler. So he went up to Leicester, met my mother and father, and returned with a briefcase packed with my letters home. (He also developed a definite sexual interest in my mother – Sidney was nothing if not young at heart.)

But when his typescript finally arrived in the post, I was appalled. Sidney had written the book as if it was a kind of heroic continuation of his own story, and I was portrayed as a cross between Wagner's Siegfried and Scott's Young Lochinvar. One sentence described how the teenage Colin Wilson used to cycle around the lanes of Leicestershire, 'his long blond hair flying in the wind, his beautiful blue eyes blazing with madness'.

I had lent Sidney my early journals, written from the age of seventeen to about twenty-one. He had devoted a whole chapter to extracts from them, and had chosen with unerring instinct every bit of overwritten juvenile romanticism.

There was another problem: Sidney was no intellectual, and existentialism was frankly beyond him. The writers he admired most were Thomas Hardy and D. H. Lawrence, and Sartre was well beyond his range. So his comments on my books were on a level with a sixth-form essay.

I could see there was only one thing to do: settle down and rewrite the whole thing. And this I did in a few months of hard work. I carefully kept Sidney's original copy, in case he was tempted to restore some of the purple passages. I was unaware that he had a carbon copy.

It hardly seemed to matter, since the book was turned down by every publisher to whom he submitted it. But, not to be defeated, Sidney placed an advertisement in *The Times*, saying that he had written a biography of me, and it was accepted by the publisher Frederick Muller. When I saw it in print, I realised that, indeed, Sidney had restored some of the worst purple passages, although fortunately not the one about my long blond hair flying in the wind.

Predictably, it received some harsh reviews. One writer compared Sidney to a dog that raises its back leg against every lamppost. If I had any serious reputation left by 1962, *The World of Colin Wilson* certainly did nothing to improve it.

Meanwhile, in the three months after my return from America I had written two books – *Origins of the Sexual Impulse* and a first version of *Beyond the Outsider*. I worked fast because my brain was seething with ideas.

The sex book had been in my head a long time, but I had delayed because I knew that Gollancz would turn it down, as he had turned down the *Encyclopedia of Murder*. He did, but fortunately Arthur Barker publishers, which was a subsidiary of Weidenfeld and Nicolson, accepted both.

The paradoxes of sex had always fascinated me, and the reason becomes obvious on the first page of *The Outsider*. Barbusse's hero looks at the women on top of a tramcar, with their skirts lifting gently in the breeze, and realises: 'It is not a woman I want – it is *all* women.' Every male can understand what he means. Yet when he takes a prostitute back to her room, it feels like a 'sudden hurtling-down'. He has recognised that purely physical sex is a kind of confidence trick.

The point had been brought home to me even more clearly by a South African poet called Philip de Bruyn. He had sent me the typescript of an autobiography called *A Pagan's Hosanna*, describing his wanderings around the world – San Francisco, Hong Kong, Johannesburg – in search of an elusive ideal of freedom. Like Charles Belchier, Philip felt that taking a job and settling down is a profoundly unsatisfying way of life, so he spent years as a kind of tramp – as I had been prepared to do in my teens.

What fascinated me was his search for a sexual ideal. In his book he described how he had been lying on an empty beach when a beautiful girl came and changed into her bikini. Philip lay there, pretending to doze, but actually watching her in a state of wild lust. At the same time, he recognised the element of absurdity in his desire. What he wanted was to possess her immediately, without preliminaries. But he knew that this was impossible unless he raped her – and that even that would have been equally unsatisfying.

So he went through the social ritual: engaged her in conversation, took her out for a meal, and ended by marrying her. I later met his wife; they came and stayed with us, and she was a pretty and agreeable girl. (Philip was lucky to get her, for he was fat and bald headed.) But I could see what he meant. There was no way of satisfying that *original* desire, that craving he had experienced when he first saw her taking off her clothes and changing into her bikini.

Now the Marquis de Sade, who had started out in life as a young army officer with enough money to keep several mistresses, nevertheless recognised that he was subject to this same 'metaphysical' frustration: that there seemed to be something unattainable about the object of male desire. In the quest for satisfaction, he soon became addicted to flogging and being flogged, and even persuaded women to allow him to make small cuts with a razor and drip hot sealing wax into them.

As we read the preposterous sadistic fantasies Sade committed to paper in the Bastille (to which he had been consigned by a vengeful mother-in-law) under the title of *120 Days of Sodom*, we can see that he had become hopelessly lost and confused. The sexual will o' the wisp continued to elude him.

That is what I wanted to write about in *Origins*: the attempt to achieve 'what the world's million lips are searching for' through sex.

What was perfectly clear was that sex tends to drag us off in the wrong direction. I had been greatly taken with a story told to me by a young television producer who had come to stay with us. He was upset and miserable because the girl he had been living with was a nymphomaniac. She was not only unfaithful, but enjoyed telling him about her infidelities.

A few days earlier, after a party, she had gone into the cloakroom to collect her coat, and had bent down to adjust the suspenders holding up her stockings. (This was the time when tights were only just coming into fashion.) The door behind her opened, but she ignored it and went on adjusting her suspender. The man who came in raised her dress from behind and pushed his erect penis into her, then, after he had achieved a climax, withdrew and went out again. And she made no attempt to look round and see who it was. She preferred not knowing; it satisfied her craving for 'sex with a stranger'.

Where my producer friend was concerned, this was the final straw, and he had broken off with her just before he came down to see me. But what struck me about his story was its absurdity. The girl might have found herself pregnant, or suffering from some sexual disease, without even knowing who was responsible. And all because she found ordinary sex, with its social preliminaries, ultimately unsatisfying. She was expressing the same frustration as Philip de Bruyn.

It was obvious to me that most sex murderers, from Jack the Ripper to the Boston Strangler (who was operating in the early 60s), were driven by this same illogical impulse, and this also explains why I have written so much about sex crime. This was not – as hostile reviewers assumed – because I wanted to make money from writing near-pornography, but because it was a logical extension of the theme of *The Outsider*.

While I was writing *Origins of the Sexual Impulse*, I received a letter from Maurice Girodias, the Paris publisher who specialised in obscene books. When I was in Paris in 1953, many British writers – like Alexander Trocchi and Christopher Logue – were eking out a living by writing 'dirty books' for Girodias – Trocchi even wrote a fifth volume of Frank Harris's *My Life and Loves*. Now Girodias was proposing that I should write a 'dirty book' for his Olympia Press imprint.

The idea appealed to me. In 1962, the police were still liable to seize any book they considered indecent. And I liked to be allowed to write frankly about sex.

I wanted, for example, to be allowed to tell the story of how, when I was about seventeen, I had gone to help an acquaintance set up his market stall in a town near Leicester. His name was Morrie, and he was a master of the art of manipulating a crowd. 'I'm not going to ask you ten pounds for this watch, or even five pounds – no, not even three pounds. All I want is thirty bob, one pound ten shillings. How about you, sir?'

I was standing at the front of the stall, pushed against it by the crowd behind me. And the woman who was pressed against my buttocks was wearing a thin dress, so that I could feel the contours of her thighs and pubis. Naturally, I became excited. I cautiously adjusted my erection so it was pressed against the edge of the stall, until her slight movements brought me to a climax.

In today's climate of sexual frankness, such an anecdote would not even cause a raised eyebrow. But in 1962, it would have been regarded as obscene. These were the days before *Portnoy's Complaint* had broken the taboo about masturbation.

So I settled down and wrote a sequel to *Ritual in the Dark* called *The Man Without a Shadow* – this referred to the novel *Peter Schlemihl* by Chamisso, whose hero loses his shadow. It was a pleasure to write, for I enjoyed telling the story of my own sex life in a slightly fictionalised form.

I liked above all talking about the paradoxes of the sexual impulse. The hero describes, for example, how he is on his way to spend the night with a girlfriend, and stops at a shop in Kensington High Street to buy her a pair of stockings. He turns around from the counter, and sees a woman standing in one of the changing rooms. She has forgotten to draw the curtain, and is pulling a dress over her head. He experiences a surge of sexual desire that makes him gasp. But as he leaves the shop he sees the absurdity of his sexual excitement. The woman is middle-aged, yet he has experienced an intensity of desire that is stronger than anything he will experience watching his girlfriend get undressed. This experience – which had actually happened to me on my way to spend the night with Dorothy – was one of many I wanted to be allowed to describe.

When I told my publisher, Jim Reynolds of Arthur Barker Ltd, that I was writing a dirty book for Girodias, he asked to be allowed to see it. I sent it to him and, to my surprise, he said he could see no good reason not to publish it in England. I was, of course, delighted, since he would give me a far larger advance than Girodias (who was notoriously mean with his authors).

Jim insisted on cutting out only one story. This was something that had happened to a friend of mine named Austin Pauley, who had worked with me in the Post Office over Christmas 1955. Pauley, who was unmarried and permanently sex-starved, had answered one of those advertisements pinned outside a newsagent in Notting Hill – for the kind of lady who advertises herself as an 'erection and demolition expert'.

When he saw her, he was disappointed; she was completely unattractive. He undressed and climbed into bed with her, hoping that being at close quarters would enable him to forget what she looked like. But it was no use; his sexual energies remained dormant.

At that point, she went to a cupboard and removed an apparatus with a large wheel and two long wires. The wires were attached to his penis with adhesive tape. When she turned the wheel, he experienced a series of mild electric shocks that were pleasantly stimulating. Slowly he reached a state of erection, and she quickly unharnessed him. But the moment he was disconnected, the erection subsided. They tried again and again, but each time the hesitant response failed to survive the stimulus, until Pauley was shamefacedly forced to admit defeat.

When the book was published, I talked about it on a television programme recorded in Birmingham. During a camera rehearsal I told the story of Pauley's fiasco, and the crew roared with laughter, but when we came to make the final recording, the producer decided not to risk it.

The American publisher who accepted the book preferred to call it *The Sex Diary of Gerard Sorme*. Unfortunately, he decided to try to bring it out before the American edition of *Origins of the Sexual Impulse*, with the result that the two books were published in the same month, and were reviewed together, so they killed one another.

After the publication of Philip Roth's *Portnoy's Complaint* in 1967, all inhibitions vanished, and publishers vied with one another to see who could provoke a prosecution under the obscene publications act, and so make a fortune. My friend Philip de Bruyn contacted me again, having decided to try and emulate the example of the *Sex Diary*.

He sent me the result – an obviously autobiographical novel with the curious title *You Owe me a Tickey, Arona Cronje*, Arona Cronje being a girlfriend who had bet him that he would never dare to tell the whole truth about his sex life. Philip won, and the novel was probably the most appallingly frank confession I have ever read. I thought my own sex drive was fairly strong, but Philip made me feel like a eunuch. His life had been a non-stop pursuit of sex whose objects ranged from six to sixty, the six-year-old being someone whose parents assumed he was a trustworthy babysitter.

Philip had also been, like me, a devoted underwear fetishist, but his quest of satisfaction had been rather more determined than my own. He described how he had once crawled on all fours into a bedroom where two men and two women were asleep, picked up a pair of panties in his teeth, and had been crawling out again when one of the women woke up and screamed. Philip was beaten up by the two men.

Philip wanted me to help him find him a publisher, and I wrote him an Introduction. I asked my secretary to read the novel and give me her opinion on whether it could be published. She said she thought it was the filthiest book she had ever read, and that no publisher would dare risk it. My American agent agreed with her. And when I recently reread my Introduction, I suddenly remembered what was wrong with the novel: the relentless sexual obsession, continuing for chapter after chapter, finally makes the reader feel physically soiled, as if he has been rolling in a pig sty.

Since I wrote the Introduction, in 1975, I had often wondered what became of Philip. I learned the answer from a correspondent a year ago, who told me Philip had died in the mid-90s.

Reading Philip's 'novel' had again made me aware of this fundamental problem of human sexuality. Why do most of us find sex the most fascinating thing in the world? Clearly because it can cause a state of *focused attention* that seems to free us from the domination of the robot. But Philip made the mistake of thinking that the more sex you got, the more freedom you experienced; and this is simply untrue. Without that obsessive concentration, sex can become as unexciting as eating egg and bacon. The mind relapses into its familiar state of sleep.

When Ouspensky asked Gurdjieff how we can cease to be machines, Gurdjieff told him:

'If you *understood* everything you have read in your life, you would already know what you are looking for now. If you understood everything you have written in your own book [he meant *Tertium Organum*], I should come and bow to you and beg you to teach me. But you do not understand . . .'

And now, as I was struggling with a final version of *Beyond the Outsider*, I wondered if this was true of me. Did I understand everything I had written in my own book?

Aldous Huxley had described his own experiment with the drug mescalin, and the stunning sense of reality he experienced. Now I was writing a chapter about Sartre's experience of the drug – when he had the hallucination of being followed by a gigantic lobster – and comparing it with Aldous Huxley's semi-mystical experience. When I had first met Huxley in the Athenaeum, he had advised me to try mescalin. Now, three years later, I decided to follow his advice.

Mescalin was not, at that time, a banned substance, but I had no idea of how to go about buying some. Fortunately, a psychologist friend, John Comley, wrote me out a prescription for a gram of mescalin sulphate, and told me where to obtain it.

It came in the post a week later, a tiny quantity of white powder in a sealed tube; I think it cost me £5. I decided to try it the following day.

The evening before, I read Huxley's *The Doors of Perception* again, and had a strong intuition that taking mescalin would be pointless for me. My own most powerful 'peak experiences' had been moods of intense optimism, the feeling that the basic answer to the problem of human existence lies in will and determination.

All the same, it seemed absurd to buy the drug and then not use it. So at about half past nine on the morning of 18 July 1963, I took about a quarter of a gram dissolved in water. It tasted like Epsom salts.

An hour later, nothing had happened, so I took about another quarter of a gram. Still no effect, except that I began to feel rather hot and oppressed. So I decided to take a walk. It was a dull morning with rain in the air, and I soon began to feel more oppressed. I stopped to talk to a friend who said she was suffering from a hangover, and I felt much the same.

When I came home the world seemed oddly distant, and I made myself sick by pushing my fingers down my throat. I could taste the mescalin as it came up. I sat with sweat on my forehead, cursing myself for a fool and feeling as if I had taken poison. I drank a glass of water, lay down on the bed, and made myself sick again. All I wanted now was for the filthy stuff to wear off.

For half an hour I lay there, feeling feverish. Joy came in several times to see if I was all right, but I asked her to go away because I simply felt ill. I had to suppress panic, and to tell myself that no one had ever been harmed by mescalin, but as the room seemed to shrink and become hotter, it was hard to stay calm.

I dozed, and felt better when I woke up. Now I could tell something was happening inside me. The varnished door seemed to glow prismatically and arrange itself in patterns. But this was the only visual effect. I did not, like Huxley, see everything as immensely real. (He had said that a deckchair with red and green stripes looked as if it was made of red and green fire.)

I felt hugely weary, and out of control. Then I noticed there was a wonderful sweetness flowing through my body, erotic and yet very innocent. (I actually tried, as an experiment, giving myself an erection, but could only manage it briefly, as if I had been drinking heavily.) It was like kissing Joy or Sally. I could also see why Marilyn Monroe exerts such an attraction on males – because she exudes the same mixture of eroticism and innocence. I felt rather like a mother breastfeeding a baby, or a sow feeding a whole farrow. It was like being in bed with a very loving – and insatiable – female, who is also an idiot.

As a child I disliked being kissed and petted, and now I reacted in the same away. I had always tended to be attracted by rather innocent girls, and now it felt as though I was in bed with all of them at once, and they were all saying, 'We love you.' And it was as if I was replying: 'I know. But now let me alone. I want to *think*.'

I felt guilty about my present situation. It was true that I now knew the world to be basically good. But I was a husband and a father; I had to protect Joy and Sally. Therefore I couldn't simply relax into the mescalin experience. I had to keep my wits about me. This feeling of being lapped in a sea of universal love was debilitating, rather like an orgasm that tricked on indefinitely. It was as if I was lying on a floating bed on a gently undulating sea. All this love was rather like having a large dog putting its paws on my shoulders and licking my face, and I wanted to grimace and push it away.

Joy brought me some soup, and I asked her to cook me a lamb chop. But I was unable to eat more than a mouthful. It was underdone, and I was too aware that it had been a lamb.

This triggered a bad phase of the experience. I recalled the scene in *The Magic Mountain* where Hans Castorp falls asleep in the snow and dreams of a beautiful island like one of those glowing paintings of Claude Lorraine; then this gives way to a vision of two horrible old crones tearing a baby apart. I remember feeling: drugs are all very well, but who is going to stop things like this happening unless I do it? The curious rhythm running through my head and down my body made me think that this is how Joy must have felt when she was having Sally: the need to *push*.

I was seething with peculiar psychic forces, and I recalled a psychic friend telling me that she was invaded by strange insights when she was in a state of nervous exhaustion. She had once stopped outside a fish-monger's hung with dead rabbits, and suddenly felt the panic of the rabbits as they were killed. It made her feel sick.

I now felt rather the same – as if I was in a telephone exchange with messages coming from all around me, as if I had accidentally got into telepathic contact with the whole district. Oddly enough, I felt that this part of Cornwall is strongly connected with witchcraft. (I have never tried to find if this is true.)

It was mid-afternoon, and Joy told me she was taking Sally to the vicarage fête. I decided to go with her to try to throw off the effects of the mescalin. And gradually, to my immense relief, the sensations started to wear off. At the fête, in a garden, I noticed that the scent of flowers was intensified, and that when I drank some water, it tasted thick and slimy, almost like glycerine.

By the time I went to bed, I was feeling normal again. But for weeks afterwards, it could come back in a brief flash, like a door being opened and fairground music coming out. Eating radishes could also bring it back – a sinking feeling, as if I was walking on a frozen pond and the ice suddenly broke.

When I looked back on it later, I could see that I had been right in thinking that I didn't need the mescalin vision. I already accepted that the universe is basically good. To be flooded with this feeling seemed unnecessary. It was like placing your hands under a tap for a drink of water, and being knocked off your feet by a tremendous gush.

Huxley had mentioned Henri Bergson's theory that our senses are not intended to let things in so much as to keep them out. They are filters. And mescalin had removed the filters.

When I am working, my mind is like a searchlight beam that can pick out and illuminate ideas. When I am very interested or excited, the beam seems to narrow until it has the power of a laser. Mescalin had caused my beam to widen, rather like those torches where you can control the beam by twisting the lens.

To use another analogy, my mind is like a radio with a VHF system, so I can tune in to stations that are difficult to obtain. Mescalin had destroyed this system, so I was receiving half a dozen stations at the same time.

Now I could understand why Sartre had had such a bad trip, and Huxley such a good one. Mescalin immobilises the filters that keep reality at arm's length. The effect is rather like waking up on a train and finding a stranger with his face within an inch of your own. The effect is one of shock. If, like Sartre, you basically mistrust the universe, your response is to scream. If, like Huxley, you trust the universe, then your response is one of wonder and delight.

Mescalin had made me aware of my own basic trust. And it had the same effect on Charles Belchier, who ingested the remains of my mescalin sulphate when he came down on a visit. He spent the next few hours repeating, 'I feel wonderful!' Evidently he had enjoyed the feeling of universal love which I had found rather stifling, like being embraced by an affectionate fat lady. When I put on a record of Wagner's *Tristan*, he burst into tears of joy.

Laura del Rivo, on the other hand, had a mescalin experience that was more like Sartre's. 'I was eating a pear, and suddenly noticed that its flesh was composed of granules. Where I had bitten, the granules were writhing like bisected maggots and bleeding pus. The whole thing was organic; it revolted me. I turned the pear and regarded it from an oblique angle; now it heaved and writhed like larvae. I could not stop looking at it; I was hypnotised by disgust.'

Laura's novel *The Furnished Room* reveals this same negative feeling about reality, a sense of depression. But then, Laura had always struck me as slightly depressive. When I once spoke to her about my own sense of underlying meaning, she replied that it was surely self-evident that reality was meaningless.

Her attitude fascinates me, for it raises the question of how one can *learn* to 'see' meaning. She admits that the mescalin experience had a long-term effect on her by way of general depression and abnormal behaviour. 'I did not like writing this account . . . I do not like thinking of those years at all; the ice is so thin; it is easy to fall again into the terrible depression.'

This is the place to say something about Laura's subsequent career. I was curious to see how she would develop after *The Furnished Room*, which is brilliant, dark-coloured, and full of almost Sartrean negativity. Her second novel was called *Animals* – although her publisher insisted on changing it to the irritatingly sentimental *Daffodil on the Pavement*. The heroine, Maggie, is more than a touch autobiographical; the hero, Jacob, 'talks like an ideas machine'. (Laura admitted that it is a partial portrait of me.)

Although full of ironic observation and striking images ('A blizzard of gulls wheeled'), it is depressingly static, like a series of still-lifes. The reader wants something to happen, to be told a story, but the writer obviously has no story to tell. So the end seems to peter out.

In the 1980s, after more than a decade of silence, she wrote one more striking work, a novella called *Speedy and Queen Kong*, stylistically her most brilliant so far. 'Speedy was poor but dishonest . . . A changeling, he could only imperfectly mimic human behaviour. He sent another charge of electricity through the uneven tufts of the hair that were wired to his skull. Small horns of smoke rose from his temples. Then he extinguished; went out. His tongue lolled on his lip. He was disconnected.'

Speedy is a schizophrenic youth, the lover of a vast lady called Queen Kong, who lounges around all day in her underwear, watching television, eating chocolate biscuits and custard-pie cakes, and waiting for her lover to arrive and provide sexual satisfaction. At the end of the book he escapes from a mental home and drops dead in a field. Queen Kong expresses her grief by wrecking the café where Speedy used to spend most of his time, and no one dares to stop her. The book has a strange, manic nihilism reminiscent of the American Nathanael West, whose Hollywood novel *The Day of the Locust* seems to be driven by the same boredom and disgust.

By the time she wrote it, Laura was supporting herself running a second-hand clothes stall in Portobello market, and the book is full of the bustle and vitality of market traders and con-men, and the grotesque antics of drug addicts, bums and layabouts. But even this cannot save it from conveying an ultimate sense of futility.

Laura's problem is analogous to Graham Greene's. In the account of his Russian roulette experience, he says of his teens: 'For years . . . I could take no aesthetic interest in anything visual at all; staring at a sight that others assured me was beautiful, I would feel nothing. I was fixed in my boredom.' But the Russian roulette galvanised his consciousness out of this passivity, and made him aware that 'the world is infinitely exciting' – an insight he apparently forgot immediately. He would have found the mescalin experience as horrifying as Laura did.

My own mescalin experience brought me an insight into the solution. It lies in my concept of the 'robot'.

You might say that, for everyday purposes, we are all 50 per cent 'robot', and 50 per cent what you might call 'real you'. When we become tired, we become 51 per cent robot and only 49 per cent 'real you'. If I become run-down and depressed, I become 52 per cent or 53 per cent robot.

More than that is extremely dangerous, for if you slip down to a level at which you become 55 per cent robot, and only 45 per cent 'real you', the real you is so immobilised by automatism that it is very difficult to fight back and recover some degree of freedom.

Now Maslow's 'peakers' were energetic people who found it easy to become 51 per cent 'real them'. When I was driving back from Sheepwash through the snow, sheer concentration and urgency led me to push myself into a state of 52 per cent or 53 per cent 'real me'.

Once you have had peak experiences, they are easy to recover because you only have to recall that curious sense of optimism to suddenly *feel* it. You realise that half the peak experience lies in the intentionality of consciousness, in a basically *active* attitude towards the world.

One of Maslow's students was working his way through college as a drummer in a jazz band, and described how, at two o'clock one morning, he found himself drumming so perfectly that he went into the peak experience. He had, so to speak, contacted some profoundly natural rhythm of his body, which enabled him to become aware of great powers in his own depths. And the memory of these powers, the recognition of their reality, would trigger a sense of optimism – and more peak experiences.

So by the mid-60s, I was aware that the chief danger for 'Outsiders' is to surrender to a sense of passivity. And that, I could see, had been the main problem of my American lecture tour: allowing fatigue and a sense of repetition to undermine my vitality and allow me to slip into a state in which I became more 'robot' than 'real me'.

My second lecture tour of America in 1966 gave me a chance to put this insight into practice.

CHAPTER 15

On the Road

When I left for America in early January 1966, I was thoroughly depressed. The thought of leaving Joy and Sally – and our new baby, John Damon – made my heart sink. As a result, I had drunk rather too much the evening before I left, and climbed on to the train suffering from a hangover.

The weather was unseasonably warm for January, and British Rail had turned on the heating, so I sat in the carriage perspiring and trying to catch the breeze from the wide open window.

Ninety minutes into the journey we passed through Teignmouth, and I recalled – as I always did – how Joy had thought she might be pregnant on our holiday in 1954, and how she had told me in Teignmouth that her period had started. And I recalled my enormous relief, and how I had thought: the sea is beautiful, then thought: no it's not – you're just relieved, and then suddenly realised that this was not true – that the sea and the Exmouth peninsula *were* beautiful, and my relief had simply drawn back the veils from my perceptions and enabled me to see what was actually there.

And now, sitting alone in an overheated carriage, I felt a kind of rage. If the sea *was* beautiful, why could I not see this now? I twisted my face into a grimace of concentration, and exerted all my will power. If anyone had been watching me, they would have thought I was having an epileptic seizure.

After a few minutes there was an odd feeling inside my head, as if heavy doors were being pulled back, and the sea suddenly exploded into beauty. I know precisely how long this took, for since then I have often timed the distance from Teignmouth station to Dawlish, and it is about two minutes.

During the rest of that journey to London, all my tiredness had vanished, and I felt wide awake, with the feeling that I could draw upon immense reserves of vitality. I decided that I would give up drinking for a few weeks. It seemed important to try to preserve this sense of mental clarity.

A few hours later I caught my plane at Heathrow, and landed in New

York at Idlewild – now John F. Kennedy – airport which was covered in snow. I took a cab to Grand Central Station, and there caught a train to a place called Hastings-on-Hudson, where I was going to see a mathematician named Martin Gardner, who wrote the Mathematical Recreations column for the *Scientific American*.

I had written to him about a geometrical problem involving a triangle inscribed in a circle, and we had corresponded ever since. I knew him as the author of an amusing book called *Fads and Fallacies in the Name of Science*, which takes a savagely sceptical view of rebels like Wilhelm Reich, and anyone else who questions strict scientific orthodoxy. I had, I must admit, been a little irritated by its tone of omniscience, and wondered if the author would be as intolerant as he sounded. In fact, he proved to be charming – I described him to Joy as 'a cross between Sidney Campion and old Raymond Duncan' – and something of a mystic. I would have found it hard to credit that within a year or two he would be attacking me violently as a woolly-minded enemy of science.

Waiting for me at Martin Gardner's was a letter from my lecture agency, Colston Leigh. It stated that I would have guaranteed earnings of $7,500 in ten weeks, a substantial amount since I was glad to get a $5,000 advance on a book. This greatly cheered me, since I had left Joy with a pile of debts.

A few hours later I arrived at the first stop on my itinerary, the University of Bridgewater. As I strolled out to the post office the following morning, in an icy wind that made my face feel like rubber, I was charmed by the quiet American town, with its wide roads, white clapboard houses, and Christmas trees on the lawns. (It would have interested me deeply to know that the Bridgewater State mental institution at present housed Albert DeSalvo, the Boston Strangler; DeSalvo had only just confessed his murders to the lawyer F. Lee Bayley.)

I lectured at 10.30 that morning to a flatteringly enthusiastic audience, which led me to consider whether I might not be better off making a living as a lecturer. I was still thinking about this as I caught a bus to my next port of call, New Hampton College in New Hampshire.

My first impressions of this place were unfavourable. I learned that I was being paid only $350 for two days, and that I was expected to teach class for five hours as well as lecture in the evening. Since my lecture agent was taking half the fee, this was far from generous.

In fact, my hosts were charming, and when I enquired if there was a local barber's shop, the wife of one of the professors offered to cut my hair for me. As I was sitting in her home with a towel round my neck, I commented on the volumes of C. S. Lewis on the bookshelf, whereupon she told me an anecdote about him. In 1952, her closest friend was a woman named Joy Davidman, and when Joy's marriage broke up, she had announced: 'I'm going to England to marry C. S. Lewis.' The astonished lady asked: 'When did he ask you?' 'He hasn't,' said Joy, 'but he will.' 'But do you know him?' 'No, but we've exchanged a couple of letters.'

So Joy called on Lewis in Oxford – a bachelor and confirmed misogynist – and married him just as she said she would. Telling Joy (my Joy) about this in a letter, I commented that it just shows that a determined woman can get anything she sets her mind on.

The professor's wife also made a comment that I took care not to report to Joy – that I was getting fat. Indeed, that thought had occurred to me. Ever since I had stopped growing, I had weighed eleven stone – 154 pounds – and that continued for year after year. I was six feet tall, and had a thin face with high cheekbones – rather like Una Troubridge's bust of Nijinsky. Joy told me this was one of the reasons she was attracted to me – the slavic cheekbones. For a year or so after *The Outsider* came out, my weight remained unchanged, in spite of good food and a daily intake of wine. Then, slowly, it increased to twelve, then thirteen, stones – 182 pounds. My increasing girth disturbed me, but I was tall enough to carry it without looking podgy. No one had ever remarked on it in England, but the professor's wife, as a health-conscious American, felt she ought to warn me. I resolved to give it some thought when I returned to England.

But it was not for this reason that the little Connecticut town of New Hampton became literally a turning point in my life.

That evening, after my lecture, I was invited to a party at the house of one of the professors, and there was introduced to a thin, sandy-haired man with a southern accent and a flamboyant personality. You could not be in a room with him, no matter how large and crowded, without knowing he was there. He was a writer named Calder Willingham and, apart from Grace Metalious, he was the best-known literary celebrity of the area. Calder had become famous in 1947, when he was twenty-five, for a novel called *End as a Man*. Mailer's *Naked and the Dead* had appeared in the same year, and both authors had become instant celebrities.

Calder's novel was about a military academy, with emphasis on brutal bullying and homosexuality, and a film version ten years later had been equally successful. Since then, Calder had made a good living as a screen writer. (His later credits would include *The Graduate* and *Little Big Man*.) In 1962, his novel *Eternal Fire* had been denounced by some critics as obscene.

The antihero of this work was apparently a sexual athlete called Harry Diadem, who seduces and rapes his way through the novel with the panache of a Casanova. And naturally, the book was one of the main subjects of discussion that evening. As I arrived, Calder was telling the story of how a nymphomaniac Hollywood agent had read *Eternal Fire*, and told Calder's agent – while Calder listened in over an extension – that the book should be burned and the author castrated. (His agent later told Calder of how he had been in a restaurant with the lady, and how she had proposed that they return to her flat, meanwhile reaching under the tablecloth and removing his penis from his trousers.)

Later that evening, as he drove me back to my guest room, our host told me that Calder had recently turned down a job as Writer-in-Residence at a girls' college. Since I had promised to drop in on Calder before I caught my plane the next day, I decided to mention it. When I told him that I was trying to find myself a job as Writer-in-Residence, Calder immediately picked up the phone, and rang Hollins College in Virginia. 'I've got a British writer called Colin Wilson here with me. Is that job still open?' He put his hand over the phone and said: 'Did you write *Hemlock and After*?' Ignoring my disclaimer he said: 'Yes, he did.' He handed the phone to me. 'You speak to him.'

The professor at the other end asked: 'Are you married?' I said I was. 'Do you expect to publish anything next year?' I said I had about four books in the works. 'Fine. Can you start in September? We pay $12,000 for the year, and travelling expenses for you and your family. You get a house on campus.'

When I hung up a moment later I was a professor at $6,000 a semester.

I shook hands warmly with Calder, and went off to my eleven o'clock class. At lunchtime I telegraphed Joy to tell her that we would be travelling to America in August.

Later that day, as I travelled through the snow-bound New England countryside, I was bubbling with euphoria. It seemed marvellous that I would be bringing Joy to live in America. After the non-stop grind of the past five years, life seemed to be opening up.

I picked up a copy of Calder's *Eternal Fire* at the first opportunity. It came as quite a shock. The nymphomaniac Hollywood agent was by no means entirely wrong. This was a pretty nasty book.

Its sixth chapter had been printed in *Playboy*, and describes a bus journey in which Harry Diadem seduces a teenage girl. She is an innocent virgin, but as they spend the night petting on the back seat, he ends with her panties in his pocket, and the girl has several orgasms. She is on her way to a religious convention, but feels there is no harm in petting. And when Harry tells her that he is deeply religious, and is at that moment praying for his sick grandmother, the girl is ready to trust him with her life.

Harry skilfully lures her into a bedroom at a coach stop – telling the hotel proprietor that his pregnant wife needs to lie down – and then rapes her. And having done it once, he makes her strip, takes off his own clothes, and does it again. Then they board the bus, with the girl in tears, asking him if he will keep his promise to marry her.

I could see why the nymphomaniac lady was outraged. There is something cold and brutal about the whole chapter, the implication that Harry is merely exercising his rights as a healthy male to seduce teenage girls. And the male reader is expected to sympathise. Calder had described how, at a local party, a respectable academic had asserted drunkenly: 'I am Harry Diadem. You are Harry Diadem. We're *all*' – gesturing drunkenly round the room – 'Harry Diadem.'

Now as far as I was concerned, this was definitely untrue. Harry Diadem was a disgusting male chauvinist pig, and revealed an unpleasant sadistic streak in his creator. (In that respect, his next novel, *Providence Island*, was just as bad, about a man who is shipwrecked on a desert island with a clergyman's wife and a butch lesbian, and persuades both of them to surrender to his irresistible male dominance.)

Later, I would ask my boss at Hollins College: 'What were you thinking of, asking Calder Willingham to be Writer-in-Residence? You'd have had half the parents withdrawing their daughters,' to which he replied: 'Oh no, parents don't read.'

I left New Hampton in a state of euphoria. The thought of bringing Joy and Sally to America filled me with delight, and the future had become a golden glow. As we drove through the snowy landscape, everything seemed beautiful. We passed a signpost pointing to Danbury, where my favourite American composer, Charles Ives, had been born, and another pointing to Concord, associated with Thoreau (whose *Walden* had been a kind of bible of my teens), and I had the feeling that they were still alive and I could go and meet them.

Two weeks later – on 30 January – I would experience the same feeling in Washington, on my way to Dan Danziger's house. The snow was deep, and I was reflecting on the feeling I had experienced driving from New Hampton – the sense of *reality of the past*. Of course, we know the past was as real as the present, but somehow, we don't 'believe' it. G. K. Chesterton had made the same point when he had said: 'You say thankyou when someone passes you the salt, but you don't mean it. You say the earth is round, but you don't mean it . . .' But there are sudden moments when the mind seems to wake up, and then you can say things and *mean* them. The psychologist Pierre Janet called it 'the reality function', the part of the mind that gives you a sense of being wide awake and in touch with reality.

But then, there are those sudden moments when the whole world seems marvellously real – Proust's '*moments bienheureux*', when Marcel 'ceases to feel mediocre, accidental, mortal'. In that moment, he can say: 'Yes, I was a child in Combray', and *mean* it, just as an astronaut in space can say 'The earth is round' and mean it.

This struck me as one of the most exciting ideas I had ever had, and in an attempt to give it a name, I decided to call it 'Faculty X'. It would become the centre of gravity of books like *The Occult*, *Mysteries* and *Beyond the Occult*. The basic aim of human evolution, I decided, is to achieve Faculty X.

The weekend after meeting Calder Willingham, I stayed in Brooklyn Heights with a minister called the Reverend Bill Glenesk. He had come to call on me in England and had invited me to stay with him when I came to New York.

He lived in Remsen Street, and was certainly the most flamboyant clergyman I had ever met. I suspect he became a clergyman because of its histrionic possibilities, for his greatest interest in life was the theatre and ballet, and his walls were covered with signed photographs of Nureyev, Margot Fonteyn and other celebrities. He introduced me to a man we bumped into on the street as Judge Samuel S. Liebowitz of the US Supreme Court – I had actually read a book about him.

Bill preached like a man on stage, and accompanied the hymns by crashing cymbals together. In England, there would have been complaints to his bishop, but his congregation loved him. He certainly kept things lively for them – I attended a Robert Frost evening in his church, in which the poems were read by two actors and I joined in the discussion that followed.

Bill was also a friend of Norman Mailer, who lived just down the street near Brooklyn Bridge, and when I said I'd like to meet Mailer, he gave me his telephone number.

Mailer had a tough voice with a Brooklyn accent, so that he sounded like a nightclub bouncer, but he was amiable enough on the phone, and invited me round for lunch.

His flat was up several flights of stairs in an old Brooklyn building, and had a magnificent view of the river. On his walls there were a number of framed reviews of his books – not, as one might expect, complimentary, but violently hostile. One of his novel *The Deer Park* announced: 'THE DEER PARK IS GETTING NOTHING BUT RAVES', then had a selection of quotes: 'sordid – crummy', 'moronic mindlessness', 'disgusting', 'exasperating', 'unsavory junk', and many more, to which Mailer had added the comment 'A BUNCH OF BUMS'. Others, of his most recent novel, *An American Dream*, were even worse.

Mailer had the physical presence of a prize fighter, a notion that would have pleased him, since he obviously placed great store in male self-assertion; he would not have been out of place in a 1930s gangster movie. You felt that, like Hemingway, he would like to beat up his most persistent critics. Yet far from being an assertive egoist – most stories about him involved getting drunk and starting fights – he struck me as intelligent and sensitive.

His latest wife, Beverley, was taller than he was, and had shoulder-length blonde hair. She provided an excellent lunch, and meanwhile, Norman offered me a vodka. I explained that I was not drinking at present, but accepted a tomato juice, while Norman poured himself a bloody Mary with what must have been a quadruple vodka. Then we stood and admired an enormous model of a futuristic city that Norman had built out of Lego blocks and looked like a surrealistic cathedral.

We talked about writing – not about its literary aspect but – as most writers do when they get together – about advances and royalties. He had received an advance of $125,000 for *An American Dream*, and I wondered how any publisher could justify this. He explained that when a publisher offers that much for the hardcover edition, he then has to make sure that he will make it back on the paperback, which may have to sell half a million. Everything then depends on his advertising.

The agent who had got Mailer this large advance was Scott Meredith, and Norman recommended that I should move to him. (My own American agent had been the more conservative firm of Harold Ober, who had been Scott Fitzgerald's agent.) Naturally, I was enthusiastic – anything that would increase my American earnings was welcome.

Oddly enough, we devoted some time to discussing dogs. Back in England, Joy had been left with an irritating problem. One of our two dogs, a collie named Badger, had been bought for Sally as a birthday present (selected by herself at a church bazaar). But he had developed an unfortunate habit of killing chickens – not even for food, but simply for the fun of killing. The day before I left for America, he had killed half a dozen ducks on a local farm, and I had paid for them.

When I told Norman about the problem, he said that he had once owned a dog that ate chickens, and had solved it by tying a chicken round its neck and leaving it there until it rotted and fell off. 'It cured it,' said Norman, 'the only problem being that if it got into the house it drove everybody else out.'

Joy had tried a less radical method. She placed an advertisement in my home-town newspaper, the *Leicester Mercury*, that said: 'Large and amiable dog, excellent with children, urgently needs a new home, or will have to be destroyed', and added our phone number.

The day after I had lunched with the Mailers, Joy received dozens of phone calls. She explained the difficulty to each caller, until one of them said: 'That's no problem – we live in the middle of a town with no chickens for miles.' So Joy put Badger on a train from Leicester, with a label on his collar, and we saw the last of him. (The new owner later wrote to say he had settled down and was excellent with the children.) But Joy continued to receive phone calls from anxious dog lovers for days.

When we talked about lecturing, Mailer made a useful comment that I have since often quoted. He said that in the question period, someone always asks a two-cent question that requires a ten-dollar answer. Example: 'What do you think are our social responsibilities?' or 'What do you think of religion?' I have mentioned Mailer's observation when someone has posed a question that requires a ten-minute answer, and asked them to rephrase it so I end up less out-of-pocket.

I decided to risk my own two-cent question. In 1960, Mailer had run for mayor of New York as candidate of the Existentialist Party. I asked him what he meant by existentialism. He waved his hand vaguely; 'Oh, kinda playing things by ear.'

After lunch he asked me if I would like to go to a wedding reception. This proved to be a bore – standing with a hundred or so people packed into an airless room, and I made my escape as soon as I could. It was only later that I learned from Mailer's second wife Adele's book *The Last Party* that he was an obsessive partygoer, who had once been to eight in one evening.

I saw Norman again nearly twenty years later in London, when he was in England publicising a novel called *Tough Guys Don't Dance*. I was asked to appear with him on a television programme – the other guest being Beryl Bainbridge, with whom Joy had been at school in Liverpool. Norman's most recent literary exploit had been to praise a condemned killer named Jack Henry Abbott, who had written to Mailer from prison and, due to Mailer's efforts, finally been released. Abbott had found freedom and celebrity hard to handle, and had finally stabbed a waiter after some trivial quarrel in front of women Abbott was anxious to impress. The waiter – a student working his way through college – was killed instantly, and Abbott, after a few months on the run, returned to jail, this time for good.

As we sat waiting for the cameras to roll, I asked Norman whether he didn't feel he had made an appalling mistake in helping to secure Abbott's release, but he denied this, saying that Abbott could have gone on to become a fine writer. He then suggested that perhaps I ought to get into correspondence with Abbott, a suggestion I turned down.

(Abbott would hang himself with a bedsheet in Buffalo jail on 10 February 1992, aged fifty-eight.)

Mailer had told me that Auden was in New York. I had never met him, but decided to give him a ring. Norman warned me that I probably wouldn't like him. 'He's very cold and distant.' I assumed this might be because Auden was typically English, lacking American warmth. Auden answered the phone himself, and invited me for lunch.

I had always been rather ambivalent about Auden's poetry, no doubt because I was reading him as if he was an inheritor of T. S. Eliot's mantle, and of course, the two have very little in common. Auden, while probably a great poet, is somehow more lightweight than Eliot. I have occasionally wondered if this was something to do with his homosexuality, for Humphrey Carpenter mentions in his biography that Auden felt ashamed of his homosexuality, as if it was a slightly discreditable indulgence, like schoolboys smoking behind the toilet. And my friend Alan Hancox, the Cheltenham bookseller, had showed me some manuscript poetry of Auden's that was a very precise description of two males engaged in sodomy.

But I became an addict of Auden's verse when I picked up an American edition and came upon that remarkable poem 'The Maze', which begins:

> *Anthropos apteros* for days
> Walked whistling round and round the maze,
> Relying happily upon
> His temperament for getting on . . .

I was so impressed by this that I learned it by heart.

Auden lived near Washington Square, in a flat that faced the street. He came down himself to answer the door. A few years before, when he became Oxford Professor of Poetry, I had seen a picture of him in the *Sunday Times*, with the face covered in so many lines and wrinkles that it looked as if Boris Karloff's make-up man had been practising on it. Now I saw that this effect was not due to special lighting. Auden really did look like something from *Famous Monsters of Film-land*.

His partner, Chester Kallman, was away, and the place seemed empty and uncomfortable. I accepted the martini he offered, and talked to him while he cooked lunch. I could see what Norman Mailer meant: there was something dry and distant about Auden. He had a conventional public-school accent, except that he pronounced the a's short -- for example, in grass -- in the American manner. I was inclined to wonder if this lack of warmth was due to shyness, or to the fact that I was not homosexual. But then, Isherwood and Spender were both homosexual, and were warm and friendly with me.

I drank a glass of beer with lunch. And at some point, Auden asked me what I thought of Tolkien. I said I thought *The Lord of the Rings* was one of the great novels of the twentieth century and that I had read it twice. Instantly, Auden's manner thawed, and we talked about Tolkien – whom he knew – for the rest of the meal. It was clear to me that a man who loved Tolkien must be at heart a romantic.

After lunch we crossed Washington Square together, but none of the crowds of students seemed to notice Auden. I reflected that this was because he looked as little like a poet as T. S. Eliot did. By then we were talking about Romantic poetry, and I can remember making the comment that man responds to mountains because they remind him of his own inner mountain landscape. Whatever Auden replied did not stick in my mind.

I also asked him why he had decided to exclude 'The Maze' from the English edition of his poems. He said he didn't think it good enough – a judgment that demonstrated to me that poets are not necessarily the best judges of their own work.

I concluded that the coolness of his manner was, in fact, shyness, and this was confirmed by an incident that took place seven years later, on the only other occasion I met him. Auden was appearing at the Cheltenham Literary Festival to give a lecture about religion, and I was then a member of the board of Southwest Arts, who helped finance the festival. When I went up to the canteen an hour before his lecture, Auden was eating alone at a bleak table without a tablecloth. I asked if he would mind if I joined him, and we ate together. I asked him about Tolkien, and he told me that Tolkien was ill, and he intended to go and visit him. I told Auden about the problem I was having with the Tolkien trustees: I had written an essay called *Tree by Tolkien* (echoing Tolkien's own story *Leaf by Niggle*) and it had been printed in a booklet. But when I sent a copy to Tolkien, it was promptly impounded by the family lawyer, who told me that the title seemed to imply that Tolkien had written it, and asked me to change it. This seemed to me absurd – like saying that *Fanny by Gaslight* sounds as if it is written by someone called Gaslight. Auden promised he would see what he could do about it when he saw Tolkien.

From the point of view of delivery, Auden's lecture was one of the worst I have ever heard. Perhaps he should have had his two or three martinis with dinner. At all events, he read it aloud, and read it as if he had never seen the script before. And at one point, he dropped the pages and they went all over the place. He had to pick them up and sort them out.

Yet the lecture itself was extremely interesting. Like T. S. Eliot, Auden believed that religion is of basic importance to man, and that the modern lack of intellectual interest in it is a sign of the deterioration of our standards. So what he was actually saying struck me as being of primary importance. It certainly chimed closely with what I had argued in *Religion and the Rebel*.

So when the fiasco was over, I slipped backstage, walked to his dressing room with him, and told him I thought it was an excellent lecture. He brightened up immediately. 'Do you really think so?' And as I talked about what he had said, he relaxed and became obviously more cheerful. As he left to return to Oxford (where he was living) I felt glad I had gone backstage, for it *had* been a good lecture, spoiled only by that odd lack of warmth in delivery.

I later wrote to ask him if he could smuggle a letter from me in to Tolkien when he went to see him, and he said he would try. But one evening a few weeks later, in early September 1973, I switched on the radio, and heard that Tolkien had died. A few weeks later, Auden also died, at the age of sixty-six.

The day before my lunch with Auden, I had preached in Bill Glenesk's church, and I described it to Joy: 'It was a huge success, and they clapped me as I sat down – very unusual for church, especially as I said I think Christianity a waste of time.' After my 'sermon' we had a two-hour discussion over coffee.

At Bill Glenesk's I was reading the latest American best-seller, Truman Capote's *In Cold Blood*. On the whole, I was disappointed: I had been hoping for a *Crime and Punishment*, and this commonplace murder by two commonplace thugs struck me as lacking in any quality of interest. There was only one page where the book came alive for me: where we learn that the more intelligent of the two killers, Perry Smith, began to take an interest in philosophy while he was awaiting execution. It made me think of Dr Johnson's remark: 'When a man knows he is to be hanged in a fortnight, it concentrates his mind wonderfully.' If Perry Smith had tried concentrating his mind before he killed the Clutters, he would not have ended on the gallows.

I had asked Mailer what he thought of *In Cold Blood*, and he had said he thought it was a very fine novel. I said I couldn't agree, and that the prose struck me as undistinguished. Norman picked up a copy of the novel, flipped through it, then read aloud a passage in which the two killers are in a bedroom in a cheap boarding house, and Capote mentions the 'violet-tinted glass' of the mirror. That, he thought, showed brilliant observation. I said that I thought it was just the kind of thing a queer would notice, and Norman laughed and conceded the point. I should add that in retrospect I have come to greatly admire the novel.

The following weekend I stayed again in Washington, where I was lecturing at the Library of Congress. I was staying with a woman called Marion Leiter, whom I had met in New York at dinner with Alan Pryce Jones, the editor of *The Times Literary Supplement*. She was universally known as 'Oatsey', but I really felt I couldn't address any woman as Oatsey, and stuck to 'Marion'. An attractive woman in her mid-forties, she told me I could stay at her house when I came to Washington. And since this would save hotel bills, and enable me to send more money home, I accepted with gratitude.

When I told Dan Danziger I was staying with Marion Leiter, he looked impressed and told me she was a famous Washington hostess who had been a friend of President Kennedy. Her husband had worked for the CIA and been a friend of Ian Fleming, who had put him into the James Bond novels as Bond's American counterpart, Felix Leiter. It was Leiter who had introduced Kennedy to the Bond novels, and Kennedy had said something complimentary about them that had helped turn them into best-sellers in America. (Fleming had repaid the compliment by making Bond read Kennedy's *Profiles in Courage*.)

So when I arrived in Washington I went to Marion's house in Georgetown. It was not huge, but was very beautiful, and full of rare antiques. I felt slightly out of place in this magnificent house, with its black servants – worried in case I knocked over some Ming vase.

I bumped into Stephen Spender at Georgetown University. It had been ten years since I had first met him, and it made me realise that I had become far more self-confident in that time – perhaps Stephen's own slightly diffident manner made me more aware of it. When I told Marion that I had seen Stephen, she asked me to invite him around the following evening, when she was giving a dinner party.

So we all sat around the table in Marion's lovely dining room. Most of the guests seemed to have political connections. Stephen and I, sitting next to one another, talked literature, and I described my meeting with Auden. (Stephen thought Auden still wrote beautifully, but had less and less to say.)

I was talking quietly to Stephen about the Kennedy assassination, and the current doubts about whether Oswald was the assassin. I said that my own feeling was that Oswald was guilty, but that the puzzling thing was that it seemed to be generally agreed that his marksmanship was appalling. I had said in an account of the assassination that Oswald was the worst shot in the world, while Kennedy was one of the world's most accident-prone men. So it was a question of which would win out – Oswald's bad marksmanship or Kennedy's bad luck. In the event, Kennedy had lost.

As I was saying this, there fell one of those silences that happens by chance at parties, so my last sentence was perfectly audible. I felt a little embarrassed as I remembered that Kennedy was regarded as an American icon, but it was too late to take it back. And once the conversation had turned to Kennedy, I thought I might as well clear up a question I was curious about – whether it was true that Kennedy was a satyr who slept with dozens of women. This time I really felt I had said the wrong thing. People stared at me disapprovingly and assured me that it was totally untrue that Kennedy was promiscuous. Stephen looked embarrassed that a fellow-Englishman should commit such a solecism (probably remembering the episode with Sonia Orwell).

It was only a few years later that one of Kennedy's mistresses, Judith Campbell Exner, wrote a book revealing that Kennedy had shared her favours with the Chicago mobster Sam Giancana. Then, of course, the dam burst, and the full extent of Kennedy's obsessive philandering became public knowledge.

Marion, at any rate, seemed to bear me no ill-will, telling the black chauffeur who drove us to my lecture: 'You see, Robert, Mr Wilson had no more education than you did, and here he is lecturing in the Library of Congress.'

Meanwhile, my lectures were making me feel more strongly than ever that perhaps the solution to my financial problems lay in this rather than in writing books. What worried me was that I was being forced to write too many books simply to support my family. Robert Ardrey had said to me: 'Brother, you write too much!' I was not afraid of becoming a hack, because I had never written a book merely for money. But if I could make $20,000 a year lecturing, it might permit me to write one book every two years instead of two a year.

One student of Hiram College in Ohio told the professor in charge of arranging lectures: 'If they were all as good as Colin Wilson, you'd always have record attendances.' And at my next stop, in Oxford, Ohio, the audiences continued to grow bigger and bigger over three days until the last one was packed to capacity. All this cheered me greatly, since I had just received a newspaper report of a court case in Boston where *The Sex Diary of Gerard Sorme* had been described as obscene. The judge had disagreed, saying that it was no worse than Henry Miller or *Lady Chatterley*, but then added that he could not imagine how the author of this drivel had ever been described by London critics as a man of genius. This, I could see, was the direct result of writing too much.

A visit to Hollins College in Virginia – my future home – increased my hope of a less strenuous life. The campus was beautiful, with green rolling countryside, and mountains in the background. The faculty houses were pleasant and spacious bungalows. My future boss, Louis Rubin, proved to be charming, and told me that Hollins would pay for the transport of our household goods from England.

The present Writer-in-Residence was a poet named William Jay Smith, but before him it had been my old acquaintance William Golding, whom I had met in 1956 when he was best known as the author of *Lord of the Flies*. While he was at Hollins he had written a book called *The Spire*. And the Americans had suddenly decided that he was a great writer, so that his books were now to be seen on every airport bookstall.

I personally hated his work, finding it as gloomy as Graham Greene, with its implication that human beings are hopelessly trapped in original sin. (I think that, at the time of the Vietnam war, college kids found this view of human nature fashionably pessimistic.) But Golding's novel about children on a desert island reverting to barbarism proves nothing of the sort. A zoologist named W. R. Carpenter had noted that when monkeys were transported on a ship to a remote island, so they could no longer defend 'territory', they seemed to lose all their values; males allowed other males to attack their wives and females ceased to defend their children. As soon as they were on the island, and could choose their own territory, they reverted to normal. So apparently monkeys also suffer from Original Sin.

When, decades later, Golding became my neighbour in Cornwall and invited us to lunch, I felt diffident about putting these criticisms to him, somehow inhibited by the protocol of guest and host.

Hollins certainly looked a perfect place to spend a year. The only thing that bothered me slightly was whether they might discover that Joy and I were not married (Betty was still refusing to give me a divorce). Joy finally solved this by writing to ask the passport office if they would give her a new one in the name of Mrs Wilson (she had already changed her name to Wilson), and after some hesitation, they obliged. (I often felt that Joy – that sweet, middle-class girl so obviously made for a respectable marriage, got rather a kick out of the feeling that she was living in sin.)

After Hollins, the daily grind of colleges and universities continued. But I bore in mind my resolution to keep up a high level of drive and purpose, preventing the creeping boredom that had exhausted me on my first trip. Besides, there were pleasant diversions, like the few days I spent in San Francisco (lecturing at Pacific College), where I was able to renew my acquaintance with the poet Kenneth Rexroth, and spent an inordinate amount of my fees in Lawrence Ferlinghetti's City Lights bookshop.

I had met Rexroth in the late 1950s, when he was staying in our local village, Mevagissey, with his wife Marthe and three daughters. I described him to Joy as looking like a mixture of Mark Twain and Hugh M'Diarmid, with his large moustache. At that time he was working for a San Francisco radio station, and I recorded an interview with him.

Rexroth was then in his mid-fifties, and was a lifelong anarchist and rebel who had attacked Senator McCarthy on his radio programme. (He told me he had called him a crook and a homosexual: when I asked: 'Weren't you afraid he'd sue you?' he explained that the negative publicity would make it counter-productive.) After a lifetime of obscurity as a poet and literary essayist, it amused Rexroth to be regarded as the founding father of the Beat Generation. He told me that in London a stranger had said to him: 'Hello Frankenstein, what are you doing in Europe – trying to hide from your monster?'

Rexroth had become the guru of a group of San Francisco poets, including Allen Ginsberg, Michael McClure, Philip Whalen and Gary Snyder, and it was at a reading of these poets, organised by Rexroth in 1955, that the 'Beat Generation' was born. In fact, it would be no exaggeration to say that Rexroth was responsible for turning San Francisco into a literary centre.

The beginning of the public success of the Beat Generation can be dated to 21 March 1957, when the San Francisco police bought a copy of Ginsberg's *Howl* in the City Lights bookshop and issued a warrant for the arrest of Lawrence Ferlinghetti for publishing it. The case made Ginsberg famous. A few months later, Kerouac's *On the Road* received a rave review in the *New York Times*, and everyone was talking about Rexroth's 'monster'.

He invited me to dinner at his flat – it was cooked by his teenage daughter Mary who, a year or two later, would become a star in pornographic movies. He and Marthe, he explained, had separated. Their relationship had deteriorated in Europe, and when they returned, she had gone to consult a marriage counsellor. 'What happened?' I asked. 'She went to bed with the marriage counsellor.' I shrieked with laughter.

Oddly enough, Laura del Rivo had spent some time staying with Rexroth in San Francisco. She had gone there after selling the film rights of *The Furnished Room*, which had appeared in 1961.

By pure chance, I had been able to play a small part in launching the book, for the *Observer* had asked me to review a batch of novels – something they did about once a year – and Laura's happened to be among them. I gave it a warm welcome – while trying not to overstep the bounds of critical objectivity. And in due course, a young film director named Michael Winner had bought the rights and turned it into his first major film, *West Eleven*.

Laura had met Rexroth in Cornwall, and gave him a ring in San Francisco. Since Marthe had just left him, Laura ended by spending four months there and helping with the housework and cooking. Rexroth said that everyone who met her had become fond of her, and – although they had not been lovers – obviously felt the same himself.

Rexroth was an amazing raconteur, although one had the feeling that he permitted himself a certain embellishment. It is typical that he called his autobiography, which he gave me that evening, *An Autobiographical Novel*, as if to permit himself free rein.

Here is a typical Rexroth story, taken from a letter to Joy:

. . . he told me that he was at a party when a pretty but naïve girl approached him and said: 'Who is that fascinating man who looks like the Mad Hatter?' Rexroth said: 'There is only one man in the world who looks like the Mad Hatter – Bertie Russell. I didn't know he was here.' She said: 'Oh, won't you introduce me – I admire him so much.' Rexroth replied: 'I'll introduce you if you like, but first I ought to utter a word of warning. Russell is incapable of talking to a girl without trying to get his hand inside her panties. And he doesn't just fondle – he sticks two fingers up her cunt and two up her ass. If you want to be treated like a bowling ball, I'll introduce you.' The girl apparently said: 'I ought to slap your face,' but was still keen on being introduced. So Rexroth took her over and introduced her to Russell, who took her in a corner and proceeded to talk to her very intimately, leaning across her. Suddenly Rexroth saw her turn bright pink. After a few minutes she got up hastily, smoothing down her dress, and rushed over to Rexroth saying: 'You were quite right.'

The same letter contains another Rexroth anecdote – this one vouched for by his daughter:

Rexroth said he was on a train from Oxford to London when into his carriage got the dirtiest girl he had ever seen. She had on a kind of black dress of some shiny material, but absolutely covered with food stains and (lower down) sperm stains; her breasts bounced in a way that indicated she had no bra on, and he came to suspect she also had no pants. She had a dead-white face and jet-black hair. She lay down at full length on the opposite seat, her knees well apart, and proceeded to read the *Phaedo* in Greek. At some intervening station, a very respectable man got in, then a well-dressed woman who looked like the wife of a rich businessman on an afternoon shopping trip to Harrods. The man glanced at the girl, winced, and hurried on, but the woman was affronted by the parted knees and general dirt, and said patronisingly: 'Are you feeling well, young woman?' The girl glanced up casually, surveyed her coldly, and said: 'Bugger off, bitch.' The woman gave a shriek of horror and strode off indignantly.

Rexroth said he was talking with his daughter about whether they would stay at the Russell Hotel when the girl glanced over at him and said casually: 'You can stay in my pad if you like, Rexroth.' Rexroth refused politely because he had other arrangements, and he said the girl simply went back to her reading, quite uninterested, and didn't try to open a conversation.

Two days later, a Member of Parliament said: 'I want you to meet the most intelligent girl in London.' It turned out to be the same one (called Diane something), but now looking quite well-dressed and self-possessed. She must lead a kind of double life . . .

But Rexroth was not enthusiastic about the 'beat' way of life, and was scathing about Kerouac. This was because he felt the beats were too self-centred to care about other people. He told me a story (which I later verified elsewhere) of how Kerouac and a group of friends, including his 'blood brother' Neal Cassady, had been smoking pot and talking ideas throughout the night when a girl stood up and said: 'I've had enough. I'm going to kill myself.' The others ignored her as she went out. She climbed up to the roof but, being stoned, tripped and fell through the skylight, then staggered back on to the roof, bleeding badly, and threw herself off just as Kerouac and his friends were emerging into the street. Rexroth felt the girl's death was Kerouac's fault.

Those few days in San Francisco were a welcome change from the grind of one-night stands on campuses, and I looked forward to taking Joy there. I also saw something of Ferlinghetti, a small, bearded man with very blue eyes and a self-effacing manner. He also had a typical story to tell me about Kerouac. While Henry Miller was still living down the coast at Big Sur, Kerouac decided one day to go and introduce himself. He ordered a taxi to drive the hundred or so miles, but when the cab arrived, he was drinking and talking in a bar next door to the City Lights (where Laurence was telling me the story), and asked the driver to wait. Two hours later, at about six in the evening, they set out, Kerouac now drunk and even more talkative. But when they arrived at Big Sur, Kerouac had no idea of the way to Miller's cabin, which was halfway up a mountain. So he went into a field, lay down, and fell asleep. The next morning he made his way to the nearest bar, rang a taxi, and went back to San Francisco.

The story reminded me of my own experience of Kerouac, which had taken place only two weeks earlier, in Florida. I had been lecturing at the University of South Florida in Tampa, and the professor in charge of me, a man named Jack Moore, told me that Kerouac was living with his mother in nearby St Petersburg and would like to meet me. But after my lecture and question period, I was approached by an amiable little man named Cliff, who told me that he and Kerouac had set out earlier in the day to come and hear me, but Kerouac had stopped at every bar en route – Petersburg was thirty miles away – and was finally so drunk that Cliff decided to drive him home.

I said that I would be in St Petersburg the next day, lecturing at a girls' college. Why didn't they come to that, and we could go and have a meal afterwards?

The following evening, Cliff again came up to me after the lecture. The same thing had happened. Kerouac had been sober when they set out, but was so drunk an hour before my lecture that Cliff took him home.

I asked what sort of a person Kerouac was. Cliff said he was very kind and gentle, and had a theory that it was important to love everyone. So he spent a lot of his time in bars, simply talking to strangers, and was mostly drunk.

What Ferlinghetti told me about Kerouac confirmed this. Kerouac seemed to have given up all attempt to control his life and had become a drifter. The success of *On the Road* had destroyed him. Three years later, he was dead at the age of thirty-seven.

By that time, his 'blood brother' Neal Casssady, who appears in *On the Road* as the swinging beatnik Dean Moriarty, had already been gone a year – dead at the age of thirty-two. He had collapsed from a mixture of alcohol and seconals, ingested just before he tried to walk fifteen miles along a Mexican railroad track counting the ties for a bet. In *On the Road*, Kerouac has a scene in which one of the female characters tells Moriarty just what is wrong with him: 'All you think about is what's hanging between your legs and how much money or fun you can get out of people . . . Not only that, but you're silly about it. It never occurs to you that life is serious and there are people trying to make something decent out of it instead of just goofing off all the time.'

This also expresses clearly why Rexroth became so disillusioned about his 'monster'.

During most of that lecture tour I had stuck to my resolution not to allow my mind to become bored and slack. When I had long waits on airports, I plugged in my electric typewriter to the nearest power point and began another letter to Joy. But towards the end of the tour – in late March – sheer travel fatigue began to catch up with me. And as soon as I allowed my will to slacken, everything went wrong. I missed planes, lost my air tickets, and became accident-prone. It was as if I had been keeping problems at bay by sheer will-power, and as soon as I allowed it to relax, all the misfortunes I had so far avoided landed on me at once.

It was an unspeakable relief to stagger on to the plane back to Heathrow. And although most of my American earnings had gone back to England to pay bills, I at least had the delightful prospect of a year on a professor's salary.

CHAPTER 16

Writer-in-Residence

I arrived back in Cornwall a few hours after Joy, who had driven up to St Albans to see her parents. It seemed they were now quite reconciled to me – particularly since I had become a householder and a father.

Although I was tired of travel, I decided that Joy needed a holiday, and since I had been invited to lecture at her alma mater, Trinity College, Dublin, I decided to take her on a trip to Ireland. We had not been there since the time of the 'horsewhipping scandal'; and when she tried entering Trinity with Damon in a pushchair, she was startled to learn that she was not allowed in with children – in all her years there, she had not even noticed that no children were allowed.

When I was halfway through my Trinity lecture, the lights failed. But after three months of lecturing in America, I knew precisely what I meant to say, and simply went on talking in the dark. When, a quarter of an hour later, the lights went on again, the students cheered.

The experience made me think again about a spy novel I had been intending to write since 1963, when I had read a book about sensory deprivation called *Inside the Black Room* by Jack Vincent. It seemed that a 'black room' – a completely dark and silent chamber into which no sound could penetrate – was ideal for relaxing overworked students before they sat exams. In the black room, they would often sleep for fifteen hours, and awake totally refreshed. In that state, they could recall everything they had learned in the past weeks. And if at that point they pressed the button to ask to be released, they could guarantee excellent exam results.

But if they remained in the black room, they became bored, then increasingly desperate. Finally, they might begin to experience hallucinations, or slip into depression and mental breakdown.

There was a rumour that the Chinese had used black rooms to brainwash American prisoners during the Korean war, and convert them to Communist ideology. And I intended to use this idea as the basis for my novel. Suppose some undercover organisation was kidnapping spies from both sides, then brainwashing them in a black room, and using them as double agents . . .

The question I had set myself was this: how could you *train* a spy to build up resistance to sensory deprivation? It is not difficult to train someone to cope with increasingly difficult challenges – commandos do it every day. But how do you train someone to do the opposite – to cope with complete *lack* of challenge? Anyone who could devise such a method would, in effect, have discovered the secret of turning men into gods. A spy who could resist the effects of the black room would be a kind of superman.

Yet if three months of lecturing in America could enable me to go on lecturing in the dark, surely this argued that such a technique was possible?

So in the spring of 1966, I began a first version of the novel that would become *The Black Room*, and to which I had given the working title *Night Without Eyes*. And although I worked on it at Hollins, it would be another three years before it was published.

In late August Joy finally began packing for the trip to Virginia. We weren't sorry to escape because during July and August our house had been full of guests – one of the penalties of living near the sea. And on a stiflingly hot day in early September, we left two neighbours in charge of our house, and travelled to London on a train called the Riviera, which left at 10.30 and arrived at Paddington in mid-afternoon.

We stayed at the huge Great Western Hotel on Paddington station – when built in 1854, it had been the largest hotel in England, with over a hundred bedrooms. (Over the years, our children have used its vast corridors as a playground.) We had taken two bedrooms, for my wife Betty had arranged to come and see me with our son Roderick (now fifteen), and since Betty flatly refused to meet Joy, whom she regarded as a scheming tart, we needed the extra room. So I had to leave Joy and my children for the evening to take Betty and Roderick out with Bill Hopkins and his German girlfriend Carla. Fortunately, it never occurred to Joy to be resentful about being abandoned like this.

Twenty-four hours later we were in New York, which was just as hot as London. The driver of the cab that took us to the Saint George's Hotel in Brooklyn had to point out that if I opened the window we would lose the advantage of the air-conditioning.

The Saint George's Hotel was a vast barn of a place, rather like the Paddington Hotel, and its air conditioning was not up to modern standards. But I wanted to stay in Brooklyn to show Joy and Sally that spectacular view of New York from Brooklyn Bridge – the view that James Cagney admires in *City for Conquest*. And indeed, we walked across Brooklyn Bridge, with Damon in his pushchair, then continued all the way uptown to the Algonquin, where we had tea.

In spite of the heat, I was light-headed with delight at being with my family in New York. For, as odd as this sounds, this was the first time I really appreciated being a successful writer. When *The Outsider* came out in 1956, everything had been too hectic to be able to enjoy it. Then the tide had turned, and I had years of being attacked. And while life in Cornwall was very pleasant, we had too many money worries – and too many casual visitors – to be able to sigh and relax. But walking across Brooklyn Bridge that afternoon in the sunlight was different. Suddenly I was really *there*, instead of half-elsewhere, and there was that marvellous sense of setting out on a new adventure.

I also felt as if I was redeeming a promise I had made twelve years ago, when I had persuaded Joy to break off her engagement and come to London with me. For her, living with a writer had not been all that different from living with a bank manager, since it mostly involved doing the housework and looking after children. And now she was, in effect, on a year's holiday.

On the airport I had found a glossy magazine with a long condensation of Gerold Frank's book on the Boston Strangler – I was not even aware he had been caught – and I read it from beginning to end, lounging on the bed in the stifling hotel room, before we found our way downstairs and drank cold Budweiser, savouring the pleasure of being able to take our children into a bar.

Two days later we were in Hollins. We were assigned a roomy and pleasantly furnished bungalow on a hilltop overlooking the college buildings; our 'street' was known as Faculty Row. The campus itself has an almost chocolate-box prettiness, all southern colonial architecture, white colonnades, emerald-green lawns, immense trees.

I was allowed to teach the girls what I liked – in fact, I devoted one class to explaining the ideas of Karl Marx. No one minded. But since I enjoy teaching, I spent most of my time explaining my own ideas, or giving them a grounding in philosophy.

One thing had bothered me from the beginning. Although perfectly happy with Joy, and not more susceptible than the next man, I couldn't help wondering what it would be like to be surrounded by so many specimens of teenage girlhood. I expected to feel like Mr Bloom among a thousand Gertie MacDowells. On my earlier visit, Louis Rubin had mentioned that I could do anything I liked except have the girls, and I enjoyed telling an apocryphal version of the story in which I replied: 'What, not ONE?' and Louis replied, after reflection: 'Well, perhaps just *one*.'

I need not have worried. A girl is never more attractive than among a crowd of men, and never less attractive than when she is among a crowd of females. Girls in canvas skirts, ankle socks and canvas shoes were no more tempting than a crowd of boys. I even formed a kind of flirtatious relation with my class on this understanding, rather as you might flirt with the twelve-year-old daughter of a friend.

My students used to take a certain pleasure in putting me off my lecture stride by crossing and uncrossing their legs at crucial moments, until they discovered I tried to stare brazenly up their skirts. They then waited until I took sips from a mug of water before uncrossing their knees: I countered by buying a mug with a glass bottom. (In fact, it was impossible to see anything but a blur, but they didn't realise this.)

The mini-skirt had then just come in, and the Hollins version was minier than anything I had ever seen. This made me aware of a paradox. Teenage girls are naturally sentimental; sex is not a physical act but a corollary of romance. Logically, they should go in for concealment and rosy blushes. But male attention has to be attracted in the first place, and the mini-skirt is ideal for that purpose. So my students raised their hem lines until they came an inch below the crotch, then tried to counteract the effect by looking as demure as if posing for a picture of the Lady of Shalott.

I think most male teachers have this problem: no matter how paternal their attitude to their students, they find it hard to restrain the normal reflex of glancing up a skirt as the legs change position – although the Hollins girls made it easier by wearing dreadful knee-length panties made of a fabric like armour plating. One colleague told me a story of a dilemma in which this placed him. He was overseeing an exam and idly glancing at uncrossed knees when he realised that one girl had a sheaf of papers tucked into the leg of her panty-girdle, which she could consult by casually pulling back her skirt. For half an hour he struggled with his conscience, but ended by deciding to forget it.

The same colleague, who had a delightful, dry sense of humour, told me how, when he applied for the job, he had to fill in a form that included the question: 'Do you wish to overthrow the state by force or violence?' and answered: 'Force.'

It was my increasing accumulation of gramophone records that brought me one of my most interesting flashes of insight.

In our local supermarket, the inner envelope that contained the record was made of paper. I greatly preferred polythene, because paper envelopes sucked in dust like a vacuum cleaner. So I ordered a hundred or so polythene envelopes from a record shop in Philadelphia.

The day they arrived, I chuckled with satisfaction, and seated myself in the middle of the carpet, with a pile of fifty or so records beside me, and a damp sponge. Then I proceeded to remove each record from its sleeve and paper envelope, and wipe it clean with the sponge. After that, I inserted it in a polythene envelope, then into the record sleeve, and placed it in a pile on the other side of me.

As I was doing this, it occurred to me that anyone watching would regard it as the most tedious task in the world. And since I myself have always disliked repetitive jobs, why was I actually enjoying it?

Hesse puts his finger on it when he remarks (in *Journey to the East*) that 'a long time devoted to small details exalts us and increases our strength'. But why?

This struck me as the kind of question that takes us to the heart of the mystery of human consciousness.

Clearly when we are deeply absorbed in anything, the beam of consciousness becomes narrow and focused, and therefore more intense.

The calm autumn days and the beauty of the red leaves could not blind me to the darker side of this paradise. Every morning as I drove Sally to school I would listen to the car radio. Roanoke was a small town with a population of a hundred thousand. Every other morning, the announcer would mention that there had been a robbery at some gas station or drug store. One day a woman's body was found in a field near the college. She was a young Catholic, helping to take a census of co-religionists. Her killer had cut open her body and stuffed her with paraffin-soaked rags, which he set alight. She was the third victim of similar crimes in two years. Near a girls' school where I lectured, two youths had walked into an ice cream parlour, taken the two girl assistants into the back room, and shot them both to death.

I found the violence hard to understand until one day I took my walk through the village behind the campus, inhabited mainly by blacks who worked in the college as maintenance men and cleaning women. It had a school, but every window in it was broken. The houses were rickety wooden shacks, and one was leaning at an angle of forty-five degrees, and propped up with poles. There was no glass in any window – only cardboard or linoleum. The stench was atrocious, but this may have been because some houses had pigs in their back yards. The ditches were full of broken glass, rusty sheets of galvanised tin, discarded shoes, twisted bits of pram, and dead animals (an enormous pregnant rat among them). A professor's wife who helped run the school told me there was little furniture in the overcrowded houses. The odd thing was that some of the houses had TV aerials, and a great yellow Cadillac stood outside one of them.

As I came back from my walk, the girls were making the most of the sun, stretched out all over the slope below our house, a hundred or so sunburned bodies in bright bikinis. The contrast was a symbol of the two Americas, Scott Fitzgerald's and Booker T. Washington's. Suddenly, the local crime rate became understandable.

A curious incident reinforced my increasing conviction about the powers of the unconscious mind. I was due to lecture at a Los Angeles college in the morning, and had agreed to meet Joy at Disneyland later. What I had forgotten until I arrived there was that the theme park covered dozens of acres, and that I might easily spend the rest of the day searching. Yet because I had given an exceptionally good lecture, and was full of euphoria, I felt a curious sense of inner confidence. I relaxed and asked my feet to take me to my family. I moved a few hundred yards down the road, then turned left towards a stall that sold Mexican food, and there were Joy and the children. The incident confirmed something I had known for a long time – that we possess a sixth sense that operates best when we are feeling relaxed and optimistic.

One of the most memorable events of that year at Hollins was a trip to Brandeis University to meet Abraham Maslow, who was the head of the Psychology Department.

I went alone, since Joy had to look after the children. It was 1 November 1966, and I was met off the plane at Boston by Abe's assistant, Mike Arons, an intelligent, humorous man – we talked psychology and philosophy all the way to Waltham.

I had seen photographs of Abe, with his small grey moustache and hair combed straight back, so it looked almost like a crew cut. Somehow a crew cut would have suited him, since he seemed so young. (He was fifty-eight at the time.) Photographs gave no impression of his main characteristic – his immense warmth and kindness. He was one of the few people I have met who struck me as genuinely *good*.

His story was an interesting one. He was born in a cold-water flat in a Brooklyn slum, the son of a Jewish immigrant from Kiev. His father was a cooper, whose business slowly improved until he could finally – when Abe was nine – afford a comfortable middle-class home. Abe told me later: 'My mother is the type that's called schizophrenogenic – she's the one who makes crazy people.' Because she was such a self-hating depressive, Abe's upbringing was taken over by her brother, an immensely kind man. Abe was skinny, shy, and looked very Jewish, so he soon encountered anti-Semitism from Italian and Irish kids. This made him deeply introverted, and he spent all his time reading. The New York public library later became his university.

He was a brilliant student, but his teachers were inclined to react against his Jewishness, and it was not until the Latin teacher praised him, and the rest of the class joined in and showed their admiration, that 'the happy time began'.

He was less happy at NYCC – New York City College – where he followed his father's wishes and studied law. He hated it. Throughout his life it was always the same: if he tried to apply his mind to something that bored him, it went blank. One day he simply walked out of law class leaving his books behind.

He had another problem – he was in love with his cousin Bertha but was far too shy to express it. Since he was highly sexed, this was hard on him. So he fled to Cornell University, but only stayed a semester. Then, back in New York, his sister gave the romance a shove by pushing Abe into her arms. 'I kissed her, and nothing terrible happened – the heavens didn't fall, and Bertha accepted it, and that was the beginning of a new life.' The result was a tremendous accession of self-belief. He studied philosophy, went to concerts, and became a socialist.

He married Bertha at Christmas 1928, and both of them decided to study at the University of Wisconsin. It was there he became interested in psychology.

First he launched himself into behaviourism, and the study of cats and dogs. He even did an experiment which verified that dogs would not eat dog meat.

When he graduated, he found a job at Brooklyn College, and remained there for fourteen years. There he worked mostly with underprivileged children, which gave him deep satisfaction. At one point he felt that this dead-end job was unfair to Bertha, and he asked her whether she felt he should aim more determinedly for promotion or a better job. Bertha said no – he should do what he enjoyed most. And from that moment, Abe said, everything suddenly started to go right.

I could empathise, for the same thing had happened to me, when I decided to stop trying to get published, and simply write books and put them in a cupboard. The first result of that decision was *The Outsider*.

His brilliance as a research psychologist became recognised, and his interest in 'higher reaches of human nature' began to attract increasing sympathy in the psychological community, dominated for so many years by a narrow Freudian obsession with sexual neurosis. Maslow had decided at an earlier stage that he felt closer to Alfred Adler, who recognised the role of feelings of inferiority in neurosis, and invented the term 'inferiority complex'. Maslow continued to proclaim his admiration for Freud as the greatest of psychologists, but I felt that this was out of a desire not to upset the Freudian establishment.

In 1951 his brilliance was rewarded by the job at Brandeis, and it was there, fifteen years later, that I spent three days with him. And the warmth and mildness made me understand why his psychology was so non-Freudian. That early shyness and hunger for affection meant that his psychology *had* to have room for love and optimism and creativity.

His preference for Adler over Freud obviously had its root in the feelings of inferiority that he suffered in childhood and adolescence. And those feelings also explained his kindness and gentleness. In that respect he reminded me of Alfred Reynolds – his brush with anti-Semitism had made him doubly sympathetic to his fellow human beings.

His conversion to Adler happened when he was studying apes in the Bronx Zoo. He said he noticed that they screwed all the time. Then he noticed that males often mounted other males, and females other females. That seemed to prove Freud's theory that sex is the most basic drive. Then he noticed something that caused the veils to fall from his eyes. The monkeys who did the mounting were always the dominant ones. All this sex was a display of dominance or inferiority. From then on, he knew Adler was right.

Given that Abe was so people-oriented, it was natural that he would find me too logical and rational, and he says so in his journals, in which he describes my visit. He complains that I am 'not at all interested in visual aesthetics, in beauty of the surroundings, etc., or in emotion experienced, or in affection, etc., even tho he philosophizes about all these. For instance, he derogates the cosmic-consciousness in favour of the laser, narrowing-down type. Indeed, he sees no use at all in peak experience as emotion – only as perception of truth & as helps in solving problems. Very active, pragmatic, & rejects altogether, & even with a certain contempt, the Taoist, the receptive, the passive. Very phallic and active throughout his thinking, & doesn't really feel or accept or build into his system the feminine.' But he adds that, since I am only thirty-five, I would eventually change as I got older 'and less sexy'. (On that point he was right.)

Abe himself had a real sexual problem, and explained to me that it is frustrating to have to hold back on sex in case it gives you a heart attack.

He also complains about the preoccupation with dominance in my thinking and that of Bob Ardrey, which he describes as 'a kind of elitism, to hell with the weak'. I think that neither myself nor Ardrey would accept that criticism; both of us were interested in dominance primarily because it is a key to social problems such as war and crime.

Abe's mildness and kindness meant that people grew very fond of him, and I was no exception. So in 1968, when an American publisher suggested I should write a book about him, I accepted instantly. Abe cooperated by sending me many tapes and unpublished papers. And I was working hard on the book when I received a letter from his secretary saying he had died on 8 June 1972.

In the New Year 1967, there was good news. My novel *The Glass Cage*, based on 'Jack the Stripper', had appeared in England and been a critical success. Not long after that. *The Mind Parasites*, written for August Derleth, came out in England. This had been written in the autumn of 1965, before *The Glass Cage*, but my publisher thought *The Glass Cage* had better commercial prospects, and decided to publish this first. His doubts proved groundless, and *The Mind Parasites* received such good reviews that it began to look as if the years of hostility – created by the 'Angry Young Man' hysteria – might be drawing to an end.

Moreover, my *Introduction to the New Existentialism*, which appeared in America in the spring, sold unexpectedly well on campuses. I have no idea whether this was because my lectures in America were creating a new audience; but after years of hostile reviews, it was marvellous to stop feeling harassed by critics.

After we had been at Hollins six months, I began to feel that this was the ideal way of life for a writer – no money worries, plenty of leisure, and periodic lecture trips to other parts of the country. I started to wonder whether Hollins might be willing to take me on as a permanent faculty member. But then I began to have second thoughts. The trouble with a place like Hollins was that it was too comfortable and too small. It was like living in a delightful village, where everyone knows everyone else's business.

It struck me that a large university might be the answer. So I wrote to the English Department at the University of Washington, in Seattle, asking them if they needed a Writer-in-Residence. (Two years earlier, I had met a professor from Seattle at a party in London, and he had suggested the idea.) And when they wrote back to say they would like me there the following year, I was glad I had not pursued the idea of staying on at Hollins. All writers have this craving for security, but too much security can induce a kind of hypnotic drowsiness that easily turns into sterility. (Since then I have come to suspect that this is why my guardian angel has always kept me so broke.)

I had one more extremely important insight at Hollins, which sprang out of the recognition about 'leakage'.

I had bought a copy of Ardrey's sequel to *African Genesis*, *The Territorial Imperative*. In this I found a story that fascinated me. Two zoologists named Rubinstein and Best were studying planarian worms, which are among the simplest creatures on the earth. Because they are so simple – no brain, no nervous system, no sexual organs – they are ideal for breeding experiments over several generations. Rubinstein and Best were investigating their learning capacity.

The worms were placed in a plastic tube full of water, which had a Y-shaped division. Then the experimenter turned a tap that drained off all the water. And the worms, which need water to live, would rush off down the tube looking for water. Soon they came to the fork. One way was lighted, and led to water; the other way was dark, and didn't. Most of the worms quickly mastered the trick, and could find their way to the water every time.

As Rubinstein and Best kept demonstrating their performing worms to colleagues, a puzzling thing happened: the planaria began to take the *wrong* turning. And finally, some of them would just lie still when the water was drained off, as if saying: 'Oh God, not *again* . . .' They would prefer to die rather than move.

That baffled the scientists, and one of them made the bizarre suggestion: 'Perhaps they're bored.' 'Don't be silly,' said the other. 'How can creatures without a brain or nervous system get bored?'

Nevertheless, they devised an experiment to test the hypothesis. They took two tubes, one made of rough plastic and one made of smooth plastic, so the worms could feel the difference with their stomachs. In the rough plastic tube, the water was down the dark alleyway; in the smooth plastic tube, it was down the lighted one.

Now taking a new lot of planaria, the scientists would transfer them from one tube to the other, draining off the water and seeing if the worms could find more – either down the dark tube or the lighted one. This was obviously far more complicated, and only one third of the worms mastered this double-ambiguity problem.

But that third never regressed. They could repeat the experiment a thousand times, and never start making the wrong choice.

In short, the first lot of planaria *had* been bored. And being forced to *put twice as much effort into the learning experience* meant the second lot ceased to get bored.

This explained why I had enjoyed cleaning records and putting them in plastic envelopes: I was putting a certain *effort* into the process. I developed this insight in a long essay called 'Shake the Mind Awake', written on Christmas Day 1966, and dedicated it to Robert Ardrey and Abraham Maslow. It has since vanished and, unless a copy exists among their posthumous papers, has ceased to exist. (Abe died of a heart attack in 1972, Bob of lung cancer – he was a chain smoker – in 1980.)

In what seemed an absurdly short time, our year at Hollins was over. By mid-May the girls were leaving for the long summer holiday, and it was time for us to pack. We had to decide what to send back to England, and what to leave in America.

A friend I had made in North Carolina on my first lecture tour – a professor of philosophy named Pat Murphy – was now teaching at the C. W. Post University on Long Island, and offered to store our trunks in his basement. We drove up to New York with all our household goods packed in a marvellous contraption called a U-Haul trailer, and unloaded them in Pat's basement, then returned the trailer to a local depot. After a day or two lounging on the beaches and taking Pat and his wife to the best fish restaurants on Long Island, we made our way to Idlewild, and by early June were back in Cornwall.

CHAPTER 17

Seattle

We returned to find England in the midst of one of its periodic credit squeezes, and a letter from our bank manager demanding that we reduce our £2,000 overdraft.

As I look back on the continual cash crises of the 1960s I am amazed that I took it all so casually. But on reflection I can understand why. I had spent my childhood in a house where the total income was £3 a week. And I had worked for years in factories and offices for very little more. So now our lifestyle seemed affluent, with enough money to travel and buy wine and books. Even to have a nagging bank manager was a sign of my new middle-class status.

The only time I occasionally succumbed to anxiety was in the middle of the night, when I woke and began to think about our debts, and what would happen if I ran out of ideas for books. One of my drinking companions liked to quote a line about a writer 'whose works predeceased him'. What if I was forgotten by the time I was fifty? What would happen to Joy and the children? But moods like this had always vanished by the time I opened my eyes in the morning.

In that summer of 1967 there were at least some encouraging prospects. Hollywood was interested in buying an option on my novel *The Glass Cage*.

The novel – my fourth since *Ritual in the Dark* – was a return to the theme of the mass murderer. And as *Ritual* was based on the crimes of Jack the Ripper, *The Glass Cage* took as its starting point the crimes of the 'Thames nude murderer' nicknamed 'Jack the Stripper'.

Between February 1964 and February 1965, eight prostitutes had been found naked and dead, most of them along the foreshore of the Thames. All had been killed by a rather peculiar method (although this was not revealed at the time): the killer had induced them to perform oral sex, then forced down their heads on to his erection, choking them to death.

Jack the Stripper was never caught – there is reason to think he committed suicide as the police cordon closed round him, for they had located the place – on a trading estate – where he kept the bodies before disposing of them.

The case had intrigued me because several of the prostitutes came from the Notting Hill area – where Bill Hopkins and Laura del Rivo still lived – and had used the same pub on a corner in Portobello Road, not more than a hundred yards from Laura's room. I had occasionally had a drink there myself.

As in *Ritual*, I had broadened my scope by borrowing some details from a second murder case: this time the Cleveland Torso murders, which had taken place in the mid-1930s. The 'Mad Butcher of Kingsbury Run' killed a dozen men and women, cutting off their heads. At the time, the Safety Director of Cleveland was Eliot Ness, the man who had destroyed so many of Al Capone's bootlegging operations in Chicago, and who became the subject of the book *The Untouchables*. Its author, Oscar Fraley, went on to write an account of Ness's later period in Cleveland, under the title *Four Against the Mob* and included an account of the Torso Killer. According to Ness, this man was a psychotic homosexual (most of the victims were male vagrants) who was able to escape arrest by having himself committed to a mental hospital. According to Ness, the Butcher (whom he called Gaylord Sundheim) was a big man who came from a wealthy family.

I used Sundheim's name and description for my killer. The man who tracks him down, Damon Reade, is a Blake scholar whose name I borrowed from my son's godfather, Foster Damon.

The Glass Cage went on to sell 10,000 copies in England, and a similar number in America. And soon after we returned from Hollins, we heard that a Hollywood director, John Schlesinger, wanted to take an option on it for Paramount. This would amount to £10,000, half payable immediately and half in a year's time. £5,000 represented about half my yearly income at the time.

There was also some prospect of turning *Ritual in the Dark* into a film. In America in 1961 I had met a brilliant young creative writing student named Steve Geller, who was far ahead of the rest of his class. He went on to write a remarkable first novel called *She Let Him Continue*, which had been optioned by Hollywood (and would be made into a film called *Pretty Poison*, with Anthony Perkins and Tuesday Weld). Now he had formed his own film company, Pequod Productions, and *Ritual* was to be its first venture. I had written a first draft of the script while at Hollins.

No money had, of course, changed hands – this would be paid if – and when – Steve raised the finance.

We were hoping for the first £5,000 on *The Glass Cage* before we left for America, but there were all the usual delays – some underling at my American agent's sending the contracts by surface mail instead of airmail, and a postal delay that made them take four days to arrive from London by first-class post. But at least I was then able to show them to my bank manager, who thereupon agreed to allow us to increase the overdraft by another £1,000. This enabled us to pay our £300 fares to America. (Damon was now two, old enough to have to pay half-fare.)

We left Cornwall in late August. The weather over New York was so bad that our plane was unable to land, and was diverted to Hartford, Connecticut. That seemed a marvellous piece of serendipity, for we had lent the car to some people in Hartford, and it looked as if this would save us a long journey to collect it. But after a night in a Hartford motel, we were unable to get an answer to our phone calls. We hired a car, and located the house – only to learn from a next-door neighbour that they were away on holiday. Our car was in an old barn, but we had no ignition key. Eventually, we had to remove the lock from the car door to find its number, take it to a locksmith, and get a new key cut. We finally arrived at Pat Murphy's, on Long Island, forty-eight hours late.

I went to see my New York agent, and collected a cheque for *The Glass Cage* – $15,000, minus 10 per cent commission. At the current exchange rate, this represented over £4,000, probably the largest single sum I had ever received. About half of that had to go back to England to reduce my overdraft. But the remaining £2,000 made us feel we could relax and enjoy the drive to Seattle.

The trip from the east to the west coast took three weeks, at a rate of about two hundred miles a day, and it enabled me to understand why Kerouac was so mystically obsessed by the vast spaces of America. Its sheer size created a sense of awe. After those industrial cities of the east – like Buffalo, which left our car covered with a fine layer of soot – the country suddenly opened out into those endless flat plains of the midwest, then into the real west, the Badlands of South Dakota, with red, flat-topped mesas rising out of the desert. Finally, up over the Cascade Mountains, then down the rich green slopes towards Puget Sound and the Pacific.

The next day, after three weeks of travel, we located our bungalow in Seattle, two miles from the university. It was not as attractive as our home in Hollins, and rather sparsely furnished. Damon saw a small boy of about his own age playing outside, and immediately went and punched him. He turned out to be the son of the couple with whom we shared the duplex, and we hastened to apologise and explain that Damon was not normally violent.

Joy went off shopping for our dinner, and returned with a strange fish called red snapper, which proved to be as good as anything we could have found in Cornwall.

My new boss, Robert Heilman, was as amiable and helpful as Louis Rubin. He showed me to my office, at the top of the English Department building, and told me that I would be teaching four mornings and two afternoons a week – a heavier schedule than Hollins. But I had no reason to complain, for I was writing a book on Shaw, and could use it as a textbook for my class on Shaw. As to the afternoon classes, I taught existential philosophy and my own ideas. These were a great success, and within a week my class sizes had more than doubled.

Within a day or so of arriving, we were invited to a faculty party in my honour – and that of the other writer-in-residence, the Welsh poet Vernon Watkins, who had been a friend of Dylan Thomas. A few days later, Robert Heilman came to our home to announce that Vernon had died of a heart attack. He had been playing tennis when his wife Gwen had dropped by and said; 'Isn't it time you stopped? You look hot.' 'Just one more game,' said Vernon – and never finished it.

I took this as a warning, and began an intensive diet that reduced my weight by two stone.

Like Hollins, the University of Washington encouraged me to go to other colleges and universities. I spent an interesting week lecturing in San Francisco, staying in a cheap hotel on Sutter Street, seeing something of Kenneth Rexroth, Lawrence Ferlinghetti and other friends I had made on my previous visit. I was alone there – Joy would have liked to come, but it seemed pointless to spend the fees I was earning on hotel bills.

1967 was, of course, the era of the Flower Children, and 'love-ins' in the Golden Gate Park. Rexroth lived around the corner from Haight-Ashbury, and we strolled among the hippies who wore cut-off jeans and shoulder-length hair and anti-Vietnam badges. We may well have passed Charles Manson, who had just been released from prison that year, and was recruiting mistresses and disciples along Haight-Ashbury. But it would be two more years before Manson's family embarked on murder.

In fact, I saw rather less of the San Francisco drug culture than of the poets and occultists who spent their evenings in a British-style pub called the Edinburgh Castle, where you could buy draft beer and eat fish and chips.

I spent much of that week with a friend named Dick Roberts, a longshoreman who earned remarkably high wages because the trade unions in San Francisco were so powerful that their members were paid top rates whether they were working or not. The days of starvation, which had turned Jack London into a social rebel, were long over. Dick had been able to afford to buy his own house, and build up a remarkable collection of the works of Jung, whom he regarded as the greatest man of the twentieth century.

In San Francisco I also saw something of a professor and his wife I had met in Virginia. He was working at a university near San Francisco, and was finding life on the west coast far more entertaining than Virginia. He smoked pot, and attended all-night parties that turned into sexual orgies. I shall disguise his identity by calling him Terry.

Terry told me a story that was typical of his temperament, which was sceptical and detached. At one of these orgies, he had been lying naked on the floor among a tangle of male and female bodies. He had been lying on his side, while a girl sucked his erection, and he performed oral sex on another. Suddenly, the situation struck him as so absurd and grotesque that he went into hysterical laughter – to the astonishment of both sexual partners.

His wife Jane, who was a friend of Joy's, was not of an experimental disposition, and when I saw them, the strain was beginning to tell.

It was a year later, when she came to visit us in Cornwall, that I heard the sequel to the story.

Jane's brother had found himself a teaching job in Oregon, and Jane agreed to go and become his housekeeper. But when she told Terry she was leaving him, he vowed to turn over a new leaf. He found himself a teaching job in Ohio, and tried to persuade her to join him. She agonised for days: 'Oregon or Ohio?' And then, like a revelation, it struck her: 'I don't have to go to Oregon or Ohio. I'm *free*.' She was suddenly flooded with an enormous sense of wellbeing. For days, she felt as if she was walking on air. She said that even her tennis improved.

When she came to see us, she was in Ohio with Terry. But she said she could still bring back that insight by simply thinking: I'm *free*.

This fascinated me. Obviously, what had happened was basically the same thing that happened to Maslow's young mother, watching her husband and children eating breakfast. She had literally 'awakened' to something, and had learned the trick of waking up whenever she felt inclined.

It reminded me of something that had happened when I was lecturing at a girls' college in 1961. One of the teachers was a very good-looking young man, and it was obvious that the girls adored him. Perhaps out of envy, I assumed he was rather empty-headed. But as I was talking about the peak experience in his class, he said: 'Yes, I can do that.' I looked at him in astonishment; 'You can do it? How?'

He explained that when he was a young boy, his mother became very irritable if he fidgeted in church. And one day his mother said: 'If you do that once more, you're not going to get any dinner.' As he sat there in church he began to itch, and was tempted to scratch. But he knew that if he did, there would be no dinner. The itch became agonising; he longed to scratch, but didn't dare. And then, as he concentrated on the itch, it suddenly turned into a peak experience. And ever since that time, he said, he could do it at will.

He gave a sudden wiggle, and beamed at us. 'There, I did it then!'

Joy and I also spent some time in Vancouver, which was an afternoon's drive over the Canadian border, and had two universities, Simon Frazer and the University of British Columbia. Both of them invited me to lecture. And it was at the end of a week lecturing at Simon Frazer that I achieved another vital flash of insight.

Simon Frazer University is on top of a mountain, and I spent most afternoons there, driving back to Joy and the children in the early evening. My class, whose composition included teenagers and middle-aged men and women, often kept me talking long after the class was over.

My last day there was a Friday, and I was beginning to tire. I had been explaining to them how to induce the peak experience using the 'pen trick': repeatedly concentrating hard on a pen against a blank wall, then relaxing. Eventually attention becomes fatigued, at which point a final burst of concentration will give access to the peak experience.

I illustrated my meaning to the class by talking about a friend of mine who used to climb Nelson's Column in Trafalgar Square. His name was Bill Powell, and he achieved it with the aid of a wide leather belt that stretched all the way around the column.

Bill would brace his feet again the column and walk upwards. When his feet were on the same level as his shoulders, he would relax his knees momentarily, and hitch up the belt. Then another walk upwards.

The problem, Bill said, was that when you were nearly at the top, your knees began to hurt so badly that it was difficult to go on. But of course, relaxation was impossible because he would have slipped all the way down again. You had to go on.

This, I explained, also applied to achieving the peak experience with methods like the 'pen trick'. The mind becomes tired, and it is a temptation to relax – a temptation that must be avoided unless you want to throw away the results of your effort.

By the time I left Simon Frazer on the final afternoon I was exhausted, and simply wanted to get back to the motel and have a martini. As I drove down the mountain in the dusk, lights were reflected all over Vancouver Bay, producing a fairytale effect. I thought: isn't it absurd – it all looks so beautiful, and I'm too bloody tired to enjoy it.

This thought seemed to shake me awake, and I felt like swearing aloud. I had been telling my students that when the attention was fatigued, they were close to the peak experience. And yet here was I, failing to put my advice into practice . . .

I made a tremendous effort of will that was actually painful, like stretching tired muscles. And as I did so, the whole bay seemed to explode into light, and I felt a surge of sheer exultation. And, like the effort I had made on the train on my way to America, it lasted all the way back to the motel as a glow of 'absurd good news'.

All I had done, of course, was to achieve what William James calls 'second wind', pushing myself beyond fatigue, beyond my mechanical reactions.

There was a difference, I found, between teaching older students – often middle-aged men and women – and girls like my class at Hollins. The girls were there because their parents were paying for their education; these older students were there because they felt a hunger to learn. Their lives were already half-over, and they wanted to start searching for meaning before it was too late. Jung had noted how many of his patients were middle-aged men who were suffering from a sense of meaninglessness.

The lecture trip to Vancouver finished just before we embarked for England on a ship called the *Chusan*. We decided that this would be the most restful way of going home.

I can still remember my feeling of delight as we steamed out of Seattle harbour, bound for the Panama Canal and the Atlantic – the same feeling of almost ecstatic wellbeing I had experienced nine years earlier as we sailed out of Helsinki and looked at the islands in the sunset. This was the most powerful experience so far of what I called 'holiday consciousness'.

In Long Beach, a strange American girl named Kathie came on board to have a drink with us. She was schizophrenic, and had been writing to me since the days of *The Outsider*, strange letters written in many coloured inks, often with the sentences scrawled on top of one another. Kathie had first come to visit us at Hollins, escorted by a travelling salesman who looked twice her age; it was obvious that she had once been pretty before mental strain had wrecked her looks.

Kathie was obsessed by me, and responded strongly to my optimism, becoming cheerful and normal after I had been talking to her for half an hour. She obviously saw me as the solution to her mental problems, and may have been right. But then, I would simply have turned into her psychiatrist. All the same, she made me aware that, if all else failed, I could always make a living in psychiatry.

Kathie brought her sister Amy on board with her, and we took them to the bar. But Kathie drank her martinis so fast that she was drunk within half an hour, and I decided to take her down to Joy's cabin, leaving Joy with Amy.

In the cabin, Kathie flopped on the bed face downward, and the Spanish shawl she was wearing tangled round her shoulders, uncovering an enormous hole in the back of her skirt, which revealed that she was wearing nothing underneath but her knickers. When I told her that her dress seemed to be torn, she mumbled something about tearing it in the lavatory. Soon after that, Joy came in – obviously worried in case Kathie seduced me – and I told her that Kathie seemed to have torn her skirt.

Half an hour later, Kathie and Amy had to leave. Kathie was now sober enough to walk, and she kissed me passionately as if Joy was not there. As we watched the dock receding, I said I found it hard to understand how she had torn such an enormous hole. Joy said: 'It wasn't torn – didn't you notice that it had been cut with a pair of scissors?'

Was it Kathie's intention to try and seduce me in the cabin? If so, she lost her opportunity when Joy came in.

The children enjoyed the voyage. They loved to float in the open-air swimming pool when the sea was rough, bobbing up and down like corks in their water wings, while Joy and I dozed in deck chairs. Forty years earlier, all long-distance travel had been like this, and it struck me as a far more civilised method than spending nine hours confined to an aeroplane seat.

In Kingston, Jamaica, we had absurdly overpriced drinks in a downtown bar. And on our way back to the *Chusan*, as our coach passed through some miserable shantytown made of rusty corrugated iron, the blacks came out and shook their fists at us, shouting, 'Whitey go home!', reminding me that here, as at Hollins, the world was divided into the very poor and the comfortably-off – among whom, at least for the time being, we could count ourselves.

Joy's younger brother Neil met us at Southampton, four weeks after we had boarded the *Chusan*: he was driving a second-hand Jaguar which Joy had commissioned him to buy for us, and we drove back to Cornwall in style.

Our house had been transformed in our absence. A local builder named Mr Charles – who was also the taxi-man – had offered to start building an extension while we were away. Joy's kitchen was too small, and Mr Charles extended it to more than twice its length. He was also in the process of building an extra room where the children could play – or watch television – in the evenings. Mr Charles had told us optimistically that all this could be done for £1,000, and we had been sending him dollars from America. But he had underestimated, and the extensions finally cost us three times that amount.

Of course, now we were back home, I could no longer count on making a thousand dollars a month lecturing, and had to rely again on my pen. I was nervous about ringing the bank manager, afraid that the account would be badly overdrawn. So it was very pleasant to be told that, on the contrary, we were in credit to the sum of £700 – the first time we had been in credit in ten years. We were even more delighted when, a few weeks later, Paramount paid the remaining £5,000 on *The Glass Cage* option.

I continued to write the book I had started in Seattle, which I referred to as 'the Time novel', and which later became *The Philosopher's Stone*. This was finished in July, after which I went back to a final rewrite of my book on Bernard Shaw, which took until October.

Now I decided it was time for another potboiler to replenish the bank account. Although our bank manager was allowing the overdraft up to £750, and my agent had agreed to lend me £200 whenever I needed it (and would take it back out of the next royalty cheque), we were permanently short of cash. So I began to work on a history of crime, to be called *A Casebook of Murder*. (This might be regarded as a kind of rehearsal for a later book, *A Criminal History of Mankind*.) This, I see from my diary, was started the day after I finished the Shaw book in mid-October, and finished a week before Christmas. I was turning into a writing machine.

The Outsider was not yet published in paperback in America, and when Lawrence Ferlinghetti offered to bring it out as a City Lights book I agreed immediately. But this turned out to be a rash promise, for my American agent wrote to say he had already sold it to another publisher. By way of an apology to Lawrence, I decided to write him a short book on mysticism, and give it to him as a present. Originally entitled *Poetry and Zen*, this was started a week before Christmas and finished on 3 January 1969.

I immediately began a new version of *The Black Room* but became bogged down after two weeks. It was then I recorded in my diary: 'Hopeless day on *Black Room*, but suddenly got an idea for a third Sorme novel.' I began work on it the next day.

The idea, I seem to recall, came from a leading article in the *Daily Telegraph*, which deplored the amount of pornography that was being published, and cited myself and Brigid Brophy as examples of 'serious' writers who spiced their books with sex to achieve larger sales.

Now in my case it was untrue. My most recent books, *The Mind Parasites* and *The Philosopher's Stone*, contained no sex at all. But the attack made me thoughtful. After all, Terry Southern's *Candy*, written as spoof pornography for Olympia Press, had become a best-seller in America; so had *Portnoy's Complaint*. Then there was *My Secret Life*, the anonymous memoirs of a Victorian gentleman, which had been published by Grove Press. I had bought it at Hollins and had been struck by his single-minded dedication to the pursuit of sex. It was clear that he believed the orgasm could one day bring him to the verge of a kind of mystical insight. I had toyed with the idea of a novel called *The Saint of Sex*, which I saw as an updated version of *The Life of a Great Sinner*, the novel that Dostoevsky had planned but never succeeded in writing.

Another influence on the book was the stories of Jorge Luis Borges, particularly 'Tlön, Uqbar, Orbis Tertius', an attempt to invent an encyclopedia of a world whose language, ideas and modes of thought are completely unlike our own. (I had dedicated *The Philosopher's Stone* to Borges. When I sent him a copy, I received a charming letter of thanks from his mother, who explained that her son was too blind and too ill to reply to me, but sent me his warm regards.)

So out of this mixture sprang *The God of the Labyrinth*, whose title is a homage to Borges.

In America at that time, a new publisher named Bernard Geis had been making a fortune with books that verged on pornography, and it was Geis I had in mind when I began *The God of the Labyrinth*.

The plot was simple. Sorme is approached by an American publisher, who intends to reissue a famous 'banned' book of the eighteenth century, *Of the Deflowering of Virgins*, by an Irish rake named Esmond Donelly. Sorme reads the book and thinks it atrocious and badly written. But since Donelly's family seat is near Moycullen, where Sorme lives in Galway, he agrees to research Donelly's life, and to write an Introduction.

In fact, he soon comes upon some unpublished material by Donelly which convinces him that the 'banned' book is a fake, and that Donelly is a far more interesting and intelligent character than he had realised.

And now, as he continues his quest for Donelly, he begins to experience curious flashes of *déjà vu*, and moments of inexplicable insight into Donelly's life. And it gradually dawns upon him that the spirit of the departed Esmond Donelly is guiding his researches.

These researches reveal that Esmond was a member of a cult called The Sect of the Phoenix, which practised 'sex magic' for purposes of seduction, and which continues to exist in the present time.

It is as Sorme is driving into Dublin that he begins to experience a curious effect of 'double exposure'. He seems to be surrounded by the Dublin of two centuries ago. He 'knows', for example, that in 1765, the year Esmond set out on the Grand Tour, this Conygham Road he is driving along was the Chapelizod Road. At Grattan Bridge he is about to turn right when he recalls that this is no longer the last bridge on the Liffey – that O'Connell Bridge has been built since then.

What I really needed, at this point in the book, was a map of Dublin in the eighteenth century. I recalled that I had bought Joy a book called *Dublin Fragments*, and went in search of it in the attic. I found that it had a map in it, and when I opened it, my hair prickled. It was dated 1765, the precise year I was interested in. It was at that point that I began to wonder whether Esmond was taking me over too.

The weird coincidences continued after *The God of the Labyrinth* was published. I had introduced into the novel a nineteenth-century rake called Edward Sellon, whose pornography is discussed in Spencer Ashbee's *Bibliography of Prohibited Books* (1877). Reviewing a book on sex magic by Francis King in March 1972, I learned that Sellon was, in fact, a student of tantric sex magic. And a correspondent wrote to me to say that there *was* a sexual sect in nineteenth-century England called The Society of the Peacock. So again, my invention had been remarkably close to the truth.

But my hope that *The God of the Labyrinth* would become a bestseller came to nothing. My new agent, Scott Meredith – introduced to me by Norman Mailer – sent it to Bernard Geis, who turned it down in April 1969 explaining 'that it is not so much that it is too intellectual (though it is) but that it is too offbeat and too subtle to respond to our piledriver kind of promotion'. It was published by Hart Davis in England in 1970, and probably sold around my usual 10,000 copies. Several more American publishers found this tale of literary detection too erudite, and after many rejections, the book appeared, heavily cut, as a Signet paperback under the title *The Hedonists*.

The delay in placing *The God of the Labyrinth* imposed a strain on our finances. Urgent action was required. The solution was provided by an American friend named Millen Brand. Millen was an editor at Crown Publishers, who were about to issue my early autobiography, *Voyage to a Beginning*. Millen had written a remarkable psychiatric novel called *Savage Sleep*, based on the work of Dr John Rosen, a Freudian psychiatrist who developed techniques for curing psychotic patients – that is, patients who are apparently so 'mad' that most mental hospitals make no attempt to cure them. I had read this while I was finishing *The God of the Labyrinth*, and decided to try my hand at a psychiatric novel.

What Millen's book made me realise was that a psychiatric novel would permit me to be unprecedentedly frank about the development of a sex criminal. My own predilections suggested that he should be a panty fetishist. So on 2 May 1969, I began writing *Lingard* as a 'non-fiction novel', and continued at an average of three thousand words a day. It was finished four weeks later, the final thirty-six thousand words (144 pages) being written in six days.

My British publisher insisted on certain cuts, including two rapes, and in changing the title to *The Killer*. But the American edition, under its original title *Lingard*, was uncensored.

I read it again recently, to write an Introduction to a new English edition, and was surprised to realise that it is probably among my best novels – it certainly shows no sign of the haste in which it was written.

In the year since returning from Seattle I had written six books: *The Philosopher's Stone*, *Bernard Shaw*, *A Casebook of Murder*, *Poetry and Zen* (later re-titled *Poetry and Mysticism*), *The God of the Labyrinth* and *The Killer*.

It seemed absurd to work as hard as that simply to make a living, and I gave a great deal of thought to other possibilities – for example, persuading the BBC to follow up Kenneth Clarke's *Civilisation* and Bronowski's *Ascent of Man* with a history of crime and civilisation. For a while this looked promising, but finally it fell through. Another possibility was to find myself a permanent academic job in America – there seemed to be plenty of universities who might have been interested. The problem here was simply my reluctance to move to another country. I preferred to stay at home, where I could be among my books and records, and watch my children growing up in the countryside.

But there was at least one interesting future prospect. In the year we returned from America, Scott Meredith had approached me with a proposal for a commissioned book on a subject in which I felt very little interest: the occult. And this would, in fact, change my life.

CHAPTER 18

The Occult

As a child, I had been fascinated by ghost stories. My grandmother was a spiritualist, so I accepted the idea of life after death from the age of six or so.

In the early days of the Second World War, the *Sunday People* had published a series by Air Marshall Dowding, in which he discussed the after-death experiences of an airman, as relayed through a spirit medium. The next world, the dead airman claimed, was not all that different from this one, except that there were no discomforts; grass, trees and sky all looked much as on earth, but when he tried swimming, the water was not wet, so it felt rather like swimming in cotton wool. I read the series avidly every week.

Our local library in Leicester, St Barnabas, had an excellent section on psychical research, and I read all I could find by Harry Price – *The Most Haunted House in England*, *Confessions of a Ghost Hunter*, and *Poltergeist over England*.

But at the age of ten I was seized by a new passion: science. It was – as I said earlier – like a religious conversion, a release from the narrow, stifling world of a working-class childhood into the vast realm of stars and planets and atomic physics. Years later, in the *Autobiography of Bertrand Russell*, I found a passage from a letter to Constance Malleson that expressed it precisely:

> I must, I *must*, before I die, find *some* way to say the essential thing that is in me, that I have never said yet – a thing that is not love or hate or pity or scorn, but the very breath of life, fierce and coming from far off, bringing into human life the vastness and the fearful passionless force of non-human things.

Which explains why the world of the supernatural struck me suddenly as irrelevant and rather silly, and life after death an expression of wishful thinking.

It was when my interest in science started to evaporate at the age of sixteen that I began to dream of becoming a writer. I continued to feel a revulsion towards the world of spiritualism and the supernatural. The problem of why we are alive certainly tormented me, but the notion that the answer might lie in some dubious realm of spirits seemed illogical.

When travelling around America in the 60s, I had often bought paperbacks about ghosts and reincarnation at airport bookstalls, for much the same reason that I bought books on Atlantis or flying saucers: to keep me amused on a long journey.

Therefore when Scott Meredith suggested I should write a book on 'the occult' for Random House, I felt that it would have to be written with my tongue in my cheek. The 'occult boom' of the 60s had started with the publication in 1960 of *The Morning of the Magicians*, by Louis Pauwels and Jacques Bergier, and it had become a worldwide best-seller. I bought a copy, and found it an outrageous hotch-potch of flying saucers, Atlantis, alchemy, Aleister Crowley, H. P. Lovecraft, and speculations about whether Hitler was a member of a secret occult brotherhood. It was all so nonsensical that I was unable to finish it.

However, I needed the money, and it didn't matter that much to me if the book turned out to be a compendium of how many unbelievable things you could believe before breakfast. Random House was offering a $4,000 advance (about £1,500), half on signature. And my British agent soon found me a London publisher, Hutchinson, who was willing to commission it.

Now it so happened that in the summer of 1968, we had been visited by a novelist named Robert DeMaria. He was a friend of Pat Murphy, and we had met him on Long Island, where both taught at the C. W. Post University. Bob told us that the university was setting up an extra-mural department called Dowling College, to teach creative writing, which would be situated on the island of Majorca, and invited me to spend three months there as Writer-in-Residence. The prospect of a long holiday in the Mediterranean sounded marvellous after writing six books in a year, and I lost no time in accepting.

I had another motive. The college would be in a village called Deya, where Robert Graves lived. I had been impressed by Graves's book *The White Goddess*, in which he argued that the ancient 'magical' cult of the moon had been displaced by the solar, intellectual cult that went on to create modern science, and I wanted to ask Graves's advice about the occult book.

So in September 1968 we set out with our children for Majorca. My part-time secretary Bunny decided to come with her own three daughters; she was experiencing marital problems, and hoped that three months away from home would sort them out.

In Deya, we were assigned a house halfway up a hill called the Vina

Vieja, which ran out of the main square. It had a stone-flagged courtyard and a garden at the back, and the drinking water came from a well in the hallway, which collected rainwater from the roof.

The first night we were awakened by a tremendous racket from above our heads, as if a crowd of urchins was playing football with a melon. But a sound of pattering feet indicated that it was rats. The noise kept us awake half the night, until they got tired of whatever they were playing. The next day we learned that they were fruit rats, and regarded as quite harmless. But it was several nights before we grew accustomed to the noise and could sleep through it.

The prevalence of rats was explained by the fact that Deya was divided by a deep stream known as the *torrente*, which dried up completely during the summer. Then the locals simply dumped their household waste into its bed, providing a perpetual feast for the rats. When the winter rains came, they carried the refuse out to sea. But that was still some months away.

At the bottom of our hill, a few hundred yards from our front door, there was an excellent bodega with a restaurant upstairs; carafes of red and white wine cost as little as lemonade in England, and the food was also cheap but superb – I developed a passion for squid. A meal for the seven of us cost as little as a meal for two in Cornwall. I began to see why Robert Graves had moved to Deya.

At this stage I had not met Graves. He was a friend of Bob DeMaria, whose novel *Clodia* is written in the tradition of *I, Claudius*. Bob offered to introduce me, but I decided to leave it until my Shaw book arrived, when I could present Graves with a copy. Meanwhile, I spent my days working in the bedroom – which was lighter than downstairs – revising *The Killer*, and expanding *Poetry and Mysticism* into a book-length study by adding chapters on Yeats, Rupert Brooke and Kazantzakis, as well as on a local Cornish poet and historian A. L. Rowse, whom I had got to know well in recent years.

I met Graves finally at a party at the home of his son William, Can Gelat (which was also the headquarters of Dowling College). We exchanged only a few words, but I told him I would take a copy of my Shaw book to his house, which was outside the village. He was a tall man with an untidy mop of grey hair and a broken nose. The voice was that of an Oxford-educated Englishman, and there was something soldierly about the way he carried himself.

The following day I walked over to Graves's house, Cannelun, and met his wife Beryl, a charming, attractive woman who told me Graves was at the beach. However, I signed a copy of the book and left it with her.

To be honest, I was not now sure how much I really wanted to meet Graves. I had, of course, read the Claudius books, and the novel *King Jesus*.

But I knew Graves regarded himself primarily as a poet, and I had never succeeded in enjoying his poetry; it seemed to me to lack music. And in his Oxford lectures on poetry he had attacked Yeats, who was perhaps my favourite poet of the twentieth century. So I was inclined to wonder whether Graves and I really had anything in common.

The next morning I received a note from Beryl Graves, asking me to go over for a drink later in the day, and perhaps for a swim with her husband. Accordingly, I walked over there at about three that afternoon. Graves was alone, and he showed me around the garden. When I asked him a question about T. E. Lawrence – whom he had known well – he was distinctly unforthcoming, as if implying: do you expect me to talk about an old friend to a total stranger?

Conversations between two writers who are meeting for the first time are always cautious, like two boxers sizing one another up. So as we walked down to the beach – about a mile from the village – I left him to do most of the talking. He was explaining that most old Mediterranean villages are built inland because of fear of pirates, and that Deya had been raided many times.

On the beach we changed into swimming trunks, and Graves asked me if I would like to try the 'traverse'. He was pointing at the cliff face over the sea, and I could see no path. But I indicated I was willing to try anything.

He led me over some sharp rocks, then showed me a handhold and foothold on the face of the cliff. He climbed up himself, then told me to follow. It was important, he said, to put my hands and feet exactly where he put his, otherwise I would find the next step unnegotiable, and might fall on to the rocks below. These were not more than twelve feet away, but since they were jagged would have caused some damage.

As we moved cautiously over the cliff face, it quickly dawned on me that this was a kind of test. But he was also kind about it, explaining very precisely just how to place my feet, and how to reach out for the next handhold. And when finally we stood on top of a rock overlooking the sea, he dived in gracefully, and I followed suit rather less gracefully – I have never been a good diver. But as we clambered up the beach he slapped me on the shoulder. 'You'll do.' I knew I had passed the test.

From then on, his constraint disappeared, and he treated me as someone he knew and liked.

Back at Cannelun he poured me a glass of wine. There was a photograph of him on the shelf, with his hair looking as if it had been in a tornado. It was by a distinguished photographer, and he asked me what I thought of it. I said: 'It makes you look like the Great Grey Poet.' He laughed and pretended to punch me in the stomach with his clenched fist. It was clear that I had been accepted.

In a book of his love poems that he gave me, he wrote: 'Colin Wilson from Robert Graves. Glad to meet you at last and find you wholly misrepresented'.

The following afternoon Joy and I walked down to the beach, and this time I did 'the traverse' on my own. Provided you followed Robert's instructions, it was less dangerous than it looked. I ended by diving – or perhaps just jumping – into the sea. Later, Robert came to the beach – wearing a vast cowboy hat – just as we were leaving. He asked: 'Did you do the traverse?' and when I said yes, he looked pleased.

A couple of days later I came back from a class and found Robert in our kitchen. He was teaching Damon how to split a banana into three lengthwise segments with his thumbnail. He later gave Damon a signed copy of his book *The Poor Boy Who Followed His Star*. And when, years later, Damon became an addict of the *I, Claudius* series on television, he was impressed to learn that it was written by the tall man who had taught him to split a banana.

On another of our walks, Robert made a comment that stuck in my mind: that true poetry is written 'in the fifth dimension'. It was a long time before I figured out that the fifth dimension is freedom.

Graves also made an interesting comment when he was talking about the occult – that many young men use a form of sorcery to seduce women. In fact, I am convinced that practised seducers use something akin to telepathic hypnosis. I understood what he meant; I had noticed that if I felt strongly attracted by a girl, as I was by Joy, and subsequently by girls I met in the Coffee House, I merely had to fix my mind intently on seduction, and it would sooner or later occur as if I had set in motion some chain of 'magical' force.

Robert himself had always been, like all romantics, fascinated by women, and inclined to treat them as muses or embodiments of the eternal feminine. He was a typical Leo, with all the drive and dramatic flair. Bob DeMaria told me that his susceptibility – recorded in his poetry – occasionally caused Beryl some moments of anxiety. There was in the village a beautiful dark-haired teenager, the daughter of a wealthy American (Deya was full of rich Americans) who was Robert's current 'muse'. She also came to some of my classes and lectures, and seemed to me a sweet, good-natured girl who was slightly bewildered by the admiration of this elderly poet, and had no desire to be anyone's muse. (Robert was eighty-four, and told Bob DeMaria that when he fell asleep at night, he was never sure whether he would wake up in the morning. In fact he lived to be ninety.)

When we had dinner with Robert and Beryl, he told us that he was convinced that the Teix (pronounced Teesh), the mountain range that ran around Deya, had some magnetic property that influenced people who came to live there, and unsettled those who were not used to it. (One student from the Institute had a psychotic episode and threw stones through the Graves's windows.) This was many years before I heard of ley lines and earth forces.

It was during that first afternoon walk that I told him I had been commissioned to write a book on 'the occult', and asked his advice. He gave it in one word: 'Don't.'

But in fact, Graves's own views on the occult would play a crucial part in the argument of my book: specifically the distinction he makes, in *The White Goddess*, between 'solar knowledge' and 'lunar knowledge'. Solar knowledge is the kind of rational, daylight knowledge that is the basis of science; lunar knowledge is the kind of intuitive, instinctive knowledge that is the basis of poetry and mysticism.

The cult of the Lunar Mother-goddess, Graves says, was the original religion of mankind, but it was gradually eroded by the 'busy, rational cult of the Solar God Apollo', which has cut off modern man from his deep instinctive roots.

It seemed to me obvious that if man is to evolve, he needs to be able to re-access that 'lunar' part of his being. When that happens, he will create a new kind of science, based on intuition as much as logic. This vision could be expressed in the phrase: 'magic is the science of the future'.

While I was in Deya, I also learned to appreciate Graves's poetry, realising that it is the poetry of a highly disciplined man who did not (like so many poets) wear his heart on his sleeve.

Although it is Graves I remember most when I think of Deya, there were other writers there. One of these, an American professor called George Cockcroft, told me the plot of a novel he was writing as we walked to the post office in the upper town. It was about a man who feels so incapable of making decisions that he throws a dice to make up his mind. A few years later, when a publisher sent me the proof of a novel called *The Dice Man* by Luke Rhinehart, I realised that George had finally succeeded in publishing it. The novel became a bestseller and was filmed.

I liked George, but he seemed to me in every way the typical college professor – liberal, vaguely intellectual and basically unsure of himself. And as I lectured to his classes, or drank wine with him in the bodega in the square, it became clear that he found my ideas – and perhaps my personality – somehow worrying. He saw my preoccupation with human evolution and the development of consciousness as in some way danger-ous and threatening, not at all the kind of thing a decent American liberal should be thinking about.

One evening, George invited Bunny, Joy and myself to his house for a picnic meal. About twenty of us sat on the floor in a large room and drank wine and ate off paper plates. And when we had finished eating, George called for silence, then said: 'I have asked you all here this evening because I want to talk about the ideas of Colin Wilson, and explain just why I think they are dangerous and unhealthy.'

I was outraged. And as he talked on about the 'fascistic' undertone of my ideas, evoking shades of Nazism, and representing my dislike of emotionalism as a denial of ordinary humanity, I was inclined to interrupt him, or get up and walk out. But I felt instinctively that this would be to hand him the advantage. So I suppressed my irritation, and listened quietly. And, as I expected, his own ability to formulate his ideas soon degenerated into vague generalities. And when he stopped, I began to answer reasonably and precisely, pointing out the false assumptions that underlay much of what he had said, and his failure to make a logical case. As I continued to argue, it became clear that I had completely undermined his own case and left him with no more to say.

The episode sticks in my mind as one that taught me the importance of self-discipline in argument, and of not giving way to the impatience to which I am prone.

There were other writers at Dowling College, including the poet Diane Wakovsky, and the novelist Anthony Burgess. I had never met Burgess, or read any of his novels, but our talks over a carafe of wine in the bodega revealed him to be in many ways a man after my own heart – sensitive, widely read and very intelligent – and a good musician and composer. (He had even turned Joyce's *Ulysses* into an opera.)

On the afternoon of his first lecture, I wandered along to hear it, curious to discover his views about literature and language. I knew he was an admirer of Joyce – as I was myself – and looked forward to what he was going to say.

In fact, he soon had me thoroughly confused. He began talking about the basic units of language – not syllables, but phonemes and allophones, the units of sound, and of the importance to fledgling writers of knowing the difference between an autosemanteme and a synsemanteme (whatever they were).

To me this was preposterously untrue. I watched the class sink into boredom, and when Anthony paused to see if we were following him, I asked politely what all this had to do with the making of literature. My own feeling was that his book on Joyce had been too obsessed with the importance of language, as if language was a magic tapestry that was important quite apart from the meanings it conveyed. But surely literature was more than merely playing games with language?

He replied that as far as he was concerned, literature and language were inseparable.

To me that was absurd. Surely words were merely attempts to pin down meanings? For example, the word orange expressed a specific colour and a specific taste – a taste that was quite unlike lemons or limes. If our eyes became capable of seeing a new colour, we would need to invent a new word. But the word would have no importance in itself; it would be, so to speak, the address of a certain meaning. If science discovers a new particle, then we have to invent a new word for it – say muon or quark. But what matters is not the word itself, but its meaning, and that is important only because it leads us on to other meanings . . .

My mention of science was like a red rag to a bull. For Anthony, science was the Antichrist, for which he had nothing but contempt. And by the time we had done arguing, it was time for the class to finish. So we strolled down to the bodega – since it was half past five – and continued the argument over a carafe of wine.

I liked Anthony, but found him in some ways irritating and self-important. He seemed determined to play the part of the multi-talented genius – scholar, composer, linguist – and to impress us with how much he knew. I later came across a hostile review of one of his books that referred to him as 'a pompous know-all', and that struck me, on the whole, as a fair description.

Whenever I came across this kind of attempt to impress – like Braine's 'let me tell you' – I suspected an underlying lack of self-belief. This seemed to be confirmed as I learned that Anthony was one of those people who are always running into problems and complications; somehow, fate seemed determined to make things go wrong for him. The electricity in his house broke down, then his water supply. He and his wife Liana succeeded in falling into the *torrente* when returning home from a bibulous party.

When he told me that he suffered from a kind of 'free-floating guilt', I saw this as the real cause of his problems. Free-floating guilt is another name for low inner pressure, the kind of painful lack of self-assurance found in the heroes of Aldous Huxley's books. And because Burgess was prickly and defensive, the world took pleasure in sticking out its foot and tripping him up.

I think it worried him slightly that I obviously liked him – I like most people – because there was an element in him that disliked me. And I would identify this as the same thing that worried George Cockcroft, and that caused Ronnie Laing and David Gascoyne to gang up on me at the Plymouth lecture: the feeling that anyone who can be cheerful and optimistic must be shallow. There is a kind of Graham Greene-ish gloom in Burgess's view of the universe (like Greene he was a Catholic), and I am inclined to feel that it sprang, like Greene's pessimism, out of weakness.

Joyce himself had this prickly defensiveness, this determination to be taken at his own high valuation. In *Time and Western Man*, Wyndham Lewis puts his finger on it with wicked accuracy. Stephen Dedalus has to be shown to be effortlessly superior to Mulligan, the Rabelaisian Irishman, and Haines, the inhibited Englishman, so he always talks 'quietly' and does things 'wearily'. In the library scene, in which he expounds his theory about Shakespeare and Hamlet, he speaks with an abstruse complexity and parade of learning that would be impossible in a spontaneous conversation (unless he had learned it by heart). *Ulysses* is a book by a man determined to get his own back on a great many people for not showing him enough respect. And Burgess was, in his own way, as thin-skinned as Joyce.

One evening in Deya, he and I were chosen to lead teams in a quiz. I devised most of my team's questions, some of them musical, i.e. who wrote Mozart's 37th symphony? Answer: Haydn (Michael, not Josef). Who wrote Haydn's Toy Symphony? Answer: Mozart (Leopold, not Wolfgang). Anthony let down his team on both questions. His own musical contribution was to sit at the piano and ask us to identify musical themes, but since I often played this game at home with music-loving guests, I knew most of them.

In the end, my team won, largely with the help of a student with an encyclopedic knowledge of films (so he could answer: 'What car did Steve McQueen drive in *Bullitt*?') and another who knew all about pop music. Yet although it was merely an evening's entertainment, I had a feeling that Anthony took his team's defeat very badly. For him, life was a game of one-upmanship, and he had lost this one.

Finally, Anthony and Liana left Deya, tired of disasters. I never saw him again. But a few years later, I was sent the first volume of his autobiography, *Little Wilson and Big God* (his real name was John Wilson), and I was impressed by his account of his working-class childhood, and gave the book a warm review. Anthony, in turn, gave my book *The Misfits* a good review in the *Observer* in 1988, although, as usual, he could not resist pointing out that I had omitted to mention Mario Praz and Ian Gibson's definitve book, etc., etc. I was glad to see that I was wrong in supposing he was unfriendly.

In this I was mistaken, as I discovered when the second volume of his autobiography, *You've Had Your Time*, appeared in 1990. The passage describing our period in Deya is waspish – and inaccurate. I am described as 'a kind of guru', and alleged to have thrown off asides such as 'a major author like myself', which would actually have made me cringe with embarrassment. Like George Cockcroft, Anthony seems to feel that '[Wilson's] presence among the impressionable American young was perhaps dangerous because they were only too ready to throw over the rational'. And he claims that after attending his lecture on Shakespeare 'Colin Wilson . . . had something to say about the pity of history's unkindness to Shakespeare in not allowing him to be born late enough to benefit from reading the works of [Colin Wilson]', which is ponderous satire.

When we returned to England in late November, I decided to read some Burgess novels. I found I was irritated by a kind of pretentiousness, a point that was underlined when a friend who found *Earthly Powers* impressive told me – by way of praising it – that he often had to break off reading and look up a word in a dictionary.

Kingsley Amis seems to have experienced similar reactions in trying to read Burgess. He tells in his autobiography how Anthony gave some of Kingsley's own novels favourable reviews, but was obviously irritated when Amis failed to reciprocate. Amis says that he tried hard, but simply found them oddly unreadable.

Although anxious to get on with *The Occult*, I first of all had to rewrite *The Black Room* yet again. After three months of struggle, I find an entry in my diary: 'Have basically solved *Black Room* problem, with passage on planaria.'

What I meant by this was that the 'double ambiguity planaria', those who were forced to put twice as much energy into the learning process, *never* regressed; as soon as the water was drained out of the tube, they would rush off searching for more water, and never became bored. Boredom was obviously a function of a kind of 'spoiltness'. And since it is a kind of boredom that causes moral collapse in the black room, the answer must lie in a kind of training that demands increasingly urgent effort.

After that insight, the novel proceeded swiftly to the final chapters.

Two days after finishing it, on 17 April 1970, I began writing *The Occult*.

By now my attitude to the paranormal had changed, from amused scepticism to a willingness to take it seriously, and Joy was partly responsible for this. She was reading Osbert Sitwell's autobiography, *Great Morning*, and showed me a passage relating to the period just before the outbreak of the First World War. A group of brother officers had been to see a celebrated palmist, but each described to Sitwell how she had looked bewildered and said: 'I don't understand it. After two or three months the line of life stops, and I can read nothing . . .' All these officers had been killed during the first months of the war.

Sitwell's father, Sir George Sitwell, had been famous for his scepticism – he enjoyed unmasking fake mediums. So Sitwell's story impressed me. And after this I came across case after case that seemed to exude an obvious authenticity – examples of precognition, telepathy, out-of-the-body experience, second sight, premonitions, and what Jung called synchronicities.

An example of the latter occurred while I was writing the book. I needed some reference to alchemy, which I knew to be in a row of books opposite my desk. (They are still there thirty years later.) I was tired and did not want to make the effort of dragging myself out of my chair – I was not even sure which book it was. But I forced myself to stand up, and went and took a book off the shelf. And the book I was looking for fell off the shelf next to it, open at the right page.

The same kind of thing happened as recently as this morning (27 July 2002). I always wake early, and today, opened my eyes soon after 4 o'clock. I began thinking about this chapter of the book, and of the best way of explaining why I had become so convinced of the reality of the paranormal, and decided that I ought to emphasise synchronicity. I have a digital clock beside my bed, and when writing a book on UFOs a few years ago, noticed the strange frequency with which it showed treble figures when I woke up in the night: 1.11, 2.22, 3.33, 4.44 . . . This morning, at this point, feeling uncomfortable on my left side, I stretched and turned over. The clock was showing 4.44.

Of course it could be coincidence. But when I was writing *Alien Dawn*, it happened with such regularity that I began to feel it was more than that. And on the day I was going to finish the book, I awoke some time after 4, wondered about the time, and again felt: I bet you what you like it's 4.44. I turned over and indeed it was 4.44. After that it stopped happening, and now treble figures have become a rarity – in fact, as often as I would expect from a one in sixty chance.

When I had signed the contract for *The Occult*, I had expected to have to write about ghosts with their heads under their arms and families haunted by a banshee that foretells death. And I am as naturally sceptical about such tales as any scientist. But what happened when I began writing *The Occult* was that my emphasis began to change as I found myself stumbling on examples of unusual powers of certain individuals.

At one point I was writing about an example from Sir Alexander Ogston's *Reminiscences of Three Campaigns*. He was in a hospital suffering from typhoid, and in his fever the walls seemed transparent. He had 'seen' a surgeon of the Medical Corps in a remote part of the hospital who became very ill and died, after which his corpse was taken out silently by men in their socks, so his death should not be generally known. When Ogston mentioned this to the nursing sisters, he was told that it had happened just as he had seen.

I was particularly impressed by an incident related to the researcher Arthur W. Osborn (and recounted in *The Future is Now*) by a music master at a public school. He used to drive to London one afternoon a week to give piano lessons, and in the morning was standing by the piano, listening to a pupil playing Bach, when the music paper seemed to vanish, and he saw clearly a certain spot on the road he would have to pass that afternoon. It was at a sharp bend in the road, and a car came round it so fast that it was on the wrong side.

Imagining he had dozed off for a moment, he ignored this incident until he was on his way to London, approaching the same bend, when an instinct made him pull across the road. A car swerved round the bend on the wrong side, and he would have hit him head-on if he had stayed on his own side.

These stories are, of course, anecdotal, and could not be regarded as valid scientific evidence. But I also discovered many cases that have been verified and documented by many witnesses. This was the original aim of the Society for Psychical Research – to build up a body of documentation that demands to be taken seriously. And so, for example, two of its early publications, *Phantasms of the Living* and *Human Personality and Its Survival of Bodily Death* (each in two massive volumes) contain hundreds of cases that have been exhaustively witnessed and documented.

As I read dozens of books, it was suddenly clear to me that 'the occult' is a reality, and that the only reason so many people refuse to accept it is that, unlike me, they have simply not taken the trouble to look into it. But then, I was in that same position before I began *The Occult*, and it was clearly my job now to spread as widely as possible my certainty that the paranormal is a reality, and that the evidence for it is overwhelming.

The odd thing is that even before beginning my research, I accepted certain incidents of the paranormal without question. For example, Yeats tells how he was thinking intently about a fellow-student for whom he had a message. Two days later he received a letter from his friend, saying that he, Yeats, had approached him in a crowded hotel lobby, looking quite solid, and told him that he had a message for him, and would return later. Yeats, the student said, had then returned in the middle of the night and given him the message. Yeats had no knowledge of any of this.

I accepted this story as true before I wrote *The Occult*. So how could I feel vaguely sceptical about the paranormal? Obviously, I had not tried to face up to the logical implications of my attitude. And that, I realised, is true of most people.

Yeats's anecdote raises another question. If he could 'appear' to his fellow student, then why do we not all appear to people we think about? The answer lies in Yeats's comment that he was thinking *intently* about his friend. The implication seems to be that our minds have far more power than we realise, but we simply fail to make the effort that would trigger its activity. And of course, we fail to make the effort because we are not aware of any such power. We simply don't think about it. Therefore, it seemed to me, it is extremely important that we should be persuaded to think about it.

Why? What difference does it make? Well, I suspect that it could make a basic difference to our picture of reality, and therefore to what we do with our lives.

Let me give an example. Graves's story 'The Abominable Mr Gunn' speaks about the maths teacher at his public school. A boy called Smilley, who was in Graves's class, could see the answer to complex mathematical problems *instantaneously*. While the rest of the class was slaving away, Smilley would simply write down the answer. When Mr Gunn asked how he obtained it, Smilley would say: 'It just came to me, sir.' But Mr Gunn was convinced he was cheating, and sent him off to be caned.

The strange thing is that some people have this ability, and it is as baffling, in its way, as precognition. There is no simple method of telling whether a large number is a prime (i.e. cannot be divided exactly by any other number, as 13 or 23 cannot). So if you wanted to know if some giant number was a prime, you would have to do it by patiently trying to divide it by every smaller number. Even a computer would have to do it 'the long way'. Yet some calculating prodigies can instantly tell if the number is a prime or not; the Canadian prodigy Zerah Colburn was able to state in seconds that a giant number was not a prime because it could be divided by 261.

What Graves is implying is that our minds have some strange power of 'knowing' things that cannot be solved by logic. And he gives a personal example. When he was sitting on the roller outside the school cricket pavilion, 'it occurred to me that I knew everything. I remembered letting my mind range rapidly over all its familiar subjects of knowledge, only to find that this was no foolish fancy. I did know everything. To be plain: though conscious of having come less than a third of the way along the path of formal education, and being weak in mathematics, shaky in Greek grammar, and hazy about English history, I nevertheless held the key of truth in my hand, and could use it to open the lock of any door. Mine was no religious or philosophical theory, but a simple method of looking sideways at disorderly facts so as to make perfect sense of them.'

Graves told me that the story was autobiographical when I was asking him whether he had ever had any experiences I might include in *The Occult*. Did he regard his experience as 'mystical', an insight that turned the universe – as opposed to his own experience – into a unified whole? Clearly not. Otherwise he would not have compared it to Smilley's mathematical talent, which was plainly non-mystical.

I believe that Graves's insight was of the same nature as some of my own, as described in this book: that is, they suddenly *made sense* of one's own experience. Graves was a schoolboy and, as he makes clear in other autobiographical writing, a conventional, well-brought-up child. He accepted the world of adult values. So a sudden glimpse of 'Faculty X', the ability to grasp the reality of other times and places, would indeed fit his description of 'a method of looking sideways at disorderly facts so as to make perfect sense of them'.

This is why the paranormal is so important: because it implies that there is something wrong with our ordinary plodding, rational way of looking at the universe. We are somehow leaving a whole dimension out of account – what Graves would have called 'lunar' (intuitive) as opposed to 'solar' (rational) knowledge.

The Occult turned into a very big book, as it had to. I had been commissioned to write 150,000 words and ended by writing a quarter of a million. I often wrote ten pages a day. The result was that the book took from mid-April 1970 until mid-August. And a few days before I received the proofs, on 26 May 1971, our youngest son, Rowan, was born. I took it as a good omen for *The Occult* that he was born on the sixteenth anniversary of the publication of *The Outsider*.

My British publisher, Hutchinson, was apprehensive about its size, and suggested that I cut it by 100,000 words. The very idea outraged me. Fortunately, my agent David Bolt soon found another publisher, Hodder, who were not only untroubled by its size, but offered a larger advance. They even proposed to issue a pamphlet about the book and about me. I must admit that after years of indifferent reviews and unspectacular sales, I thought: poor devils, they'll lose their money.

To my surprise and delight I was wrong. *The Occult*, dedicated to Robert Graves, came out on 4 October 1971, and received excellent reviews: Philip Toynbee in the *Observer*, Cyril Connolly in the *Sunday Times* and Arthur Calder Marshall in the *Sunday Telegraph*. Toynbee and Connolly had, of course, launched *The Outsider* with good reviews, and then had both recanted. Toynbee had called *Religion and the Rebel* a rubbish bin. And here they were, virtually apologising. Toynbee began: 'Colin Wilson has been much battered by reviewers, including, at times, the present one. But what nobody can deny is his staying power, his resilience, his indefatigable curiosity. The book under review seems to me to be marred by the familiar faults, but it displays, more fully than any other Wilson book that I have read since *The Outsider*, the full array of his amiable virtues.' He went on to compare me to 'the headmaster of some appalling school who contrives, in his innocence and benevolence, to find a good word in his report on even the most outrageous of his pupils . . .'

Calder Marshall called it 'the most interesting, informative and thought-provoking book on the subject I have read, and should secure Mr Wilson a success even greater than he won with *The Outsider*'.

In the *Sunday Times* Cyril Connolly declared: 'I am very impressed by this book, not only by its erudition but by the marshalling of it, and above all by the good natured, unaffected charm of the author whose reasoning is never too far-fetched, who is never carried away by preposterous theories. Mr Wilson's mental processes are akin to Aldous Huxley.'

And so, after sixteen years in the wilderness, it seemed I was back again.

Interestingly enough, my father had experienced a conviction that *The Occult* was going to be a success from the moment I told him the title, and now it gave him some satisfaction to say, 'I told you so.' I was also delighted on dad's behalf because by 1971 it was clear that he was ill – he spent a great deal of time going in and out of hospitals, having stomach operations. I suspected that I was to blame, for it had been my idea to get him to come and live in Cornwall in 1957. Freedom had disoriented him so he ceased to enjoy it, and might well have turned him into an alcoholic. But he hated his enforced return to Leicester and the shoe factory, and his decline began from then.

He died shortly before his sixty-fifth birthday, in August 1975. My mother was with him at the end. She told me that his last words to her were: 'I've had a good life.' When she told me, I was incredulous. He had spent most of his adult life at a workbench in a shoe factory. How could he say that he'd had a good life?

But then, I wonder if, a few moments before dying, he experienced that same flash of sheer affirmation as Tolstoy's Ivan Ilyich, the sudden certainty that there is no such thing as death? It would certainly comfort me to think so.

CHAPTER 19

Breakdown

I had been driving myself hard for years, with no sign of ill effect. In fact I enjoyed hard work, and came to recognise myself as a workaholic. I also took plenty of exercise, mowing the lawns, walking the dogs, and in the summer swimming in the sea.

With three children, Joy had to work as hard as I did – especially during the summer, when guests were inclined to arrive unannounced. The invasion usually began at Easter (with my own family from Leicester), and continued until September or October. I often felt frayed, but Joy always seemed calm and good-tempered.

In December 1971, Westward, our local independent television station in Plymouth, asked me to drive up to discuss a new monthly arts programme. We decided it would be called *Format*: although the name meant nothing whatsoever, it was short and easy to remember. It was to be in three parts, one on literature and music, one on theatre and cinema, one on art and architecture. I presented literature and music; the actor Jack Emery presented theatre, and a charming west-country character named Clive Gunnell presented art.

Clive had had a traumatic experience in 1955. He had been walking out of the Magdala public house in Hampstead with a friend named David Blakely when Blakely's lover, a nightclub hostess called Ruth Ellis, shot him down with a revolver. And as Clive knelt over Blakely, she pointed the gun over his shoulder and fired more shots. She then pointed the gun at her own temple and pulled the trigger, but it was empty. A jury found her guilty of murder and she was hanged – the last woman to be hanged in England. And the unfortunate Clive had a nervous breakdown.

Oddly enough, I was writing about the Ruth Ellis case, in a book called *Order of Assassins*, when I was working with Clive on *Format*, and he was able to tell me several things about Ruth Ellis that I did not know – for example, that Blakely was only one of several lovers.

The first time the *Format* team got together in the studio to record the programme, I had an unnerving experience. As I stood in front of the camera, prepared to speak my lines, my heart began to pound, and my voice came out sounding choked and strangulated. The studio manager stopped the recording, and I apologised. We had to start my section all over again, which involved setting the programme clock back to nought. And watching the hand click forward second by second, my heart again began to pound, and again my voice trembled. Twice more we tried it, and finally I managed to say my lines. Everyone was supportive, but I felt deeply ashamed. And when I finally watched the transmission, and my nervousness was obvious, I felt humiliated.

What on earth, I wondered, was happening? My own explanation was that I had spent the past ten years in a state of overwork, grinding out hundreds of thousands of words, and trapped inside my own head. And now I was suddenly standing in front of a camera in the glare of television lights; I felt like a mole that has been dragged into the light of day.

I asked my doctor if he could give me anything to calm my nerves. Andrew Crawshaw, an old friend and fellow-wine enthusiast, gave me some tranquillisers, and told me to take them just before we started recording. But he emphasised that I was only to take one at a time, and must on no account drink alcohol with them or they would knock me out.

On the next recording date, I had to drag myself to Plymouth, feeling like a man in front of a firing squad. I remembered that Shaw had felt a similar nervousness the first time he had gone to a social gathering to play the piano, and had had to walk around the block several times before he worked up courage to knock on the door. He commented that he would have run away 'if I had not been instinctively aware that I must never let myself off in this manner if I meant ever to do anything in the world'. I now thought about Shaw, and gritted my teeth.

We did a camera rehearsal in the morning, and I took a tranquilliser before we began. It made no difference; I was as nervous as ever. So I went to the toilet and took another. It was still as bad. At lunchtime I drank several glasses of wine, and before the recording took another tranquilliser. It all made not the slightest difference, and I had to fight a desire to run out of the studio as I watched the clock ticking towards the start of the opening music. And when it was all over, I was aware that the tranquillisers had had no effect whatever.

When I saw the transmission a few days later, I felt that my performance was terrible, but that at least I did not look so terrified.

Each month thereafter I went through the same struggle. When I was merely making a preparatory interview – with guests such as Ken Russell or Spike Milligan – I was calm and normal, but as soon as I stepped into the studio, a watery sense of panic began to invade my stomach, and I had to resist the desire to flee.

Every recording date brought the same fear, and the more I fought it, the worse it became. I was aware that what I ought to do was to employ what Viktor Frankl called 'the law of reverse effort', deliberately *trying* to be nervous. But when I came to stand in front of the camera, I had to struggle to make myself think of something else, and try not to trigger the flood of adrenaline into my bloodstream. Little by little, like a horse under fire, I began to get better at it.

Since publication of *The Occult* my writing schedule had been as full as ever. First, the book on Maslow (who had died recently) called *New Pathways in Psychology*, written at his own suggestion; then *Order of Assassins*, a sequel to the *Casebook of Murder*; then a police procedural novel called *The Schoolgirl Murder Case*, with a detective named Saltfleet; then a book about wine, which became *A Book of Booze*. After that, I began to research a book about Wilhelm Reich.

At least *The Occult* had improved our cash flow. The American edition had been taken up by a book club and sold well; the British edition went into a bilious green paperback, with a stupid line on the cover declaring it was 'a book for those who would walk with the Gods'. When I went to Leicester to see my parents, and went into Lewis's, the department store where I had met Joy, I found a gigantic rack full of the paperback *Occult* in the window.

Inevitably, the publisher of *The Occult* had asked me to write a sequel, and this was also commissioned by my American publisher, Random House. So far, it was untitled, and I had no idea of what it was going to be about.

It was Joy who solved the problem. I had picked up a second-hand copy of a book by T. C. Lethbridge called *Witches*, written in a casual, personal style by a man who was obviously a scholar as well as an archaeologist and a dowser (in fact, he used his dowsing rod to explore archeological sites). I had sent Lethbridge a copy of *The Occult*, care of his publisher, but received a letter from his wife Mina saying her husband Tom had just died, and offering to return the book. Naturally, I told her to keep it, and we subsequently became friends.

I now bought all the Lethbridge books in print, but it was Joy who read them first. She had made herself a divining rod out of two whale-bones from an old corset, and proved to be an excellent dowser. And now, following Lethbridge's advice, she began to use a pendulum. And it was she who told me that Lethbridge had discovered that if the pendulum was adjusted to different lengths, it would detect different substances. A twelve-inch pendulum would detect charcoal, a twenty-two-inch pendulum silver and lead, a twenty-nine-inch pendulum gold. But it would also respond to emotions and ideas, such as sex (16) love (20) male (24) female (29). Lethbridge and Mina threw stones, and the pendulum would accurately distinguish those thrown by Mina and those thrown by Tom.

This seemed to me tremendously important, and I tried dowsing – with a rod – myself. I went down to the circle of standing stones called the Merry Maidens, and approached them holding the rod (which has two 'arms') with its ends turned inward so as to impart a spring to it. As I drew near the stones, the rod twisted upward in my hands. I tried it again and again to see whether I was causing it by unconsciously changing pressure on the rod; the answer was no – it did it anyway.

Scientific tests have shown that what happens when the rod 'twists' is that our striped muscles contract. But it would seem that these muscles are responding to some force from the standing stone or the ground. The conscious 'I' is unaware of the force, but the unconscious 'me' recognises it.

When writing *The Occult* I had come to recognise that most of the secrets of the paranormal lie in the unconscious mind; synchronicities like the book falling off the shelf had taught me that this unconscious aspect of 'me' is far more powerful than I realise. Now I felt I was learning some important basic secret of the universe. The 'I' who had despaired of the meaning of life in my teens had been the rational, conscious layer of me, and now I was learning that understanding the deeper meanings was a matter of relaxing and penetrating to a deeper layer entirely.

This subconscious 'other self' sometimes proved useful. One morning, I had gone to pick up our cleaning lady in Mevagissey. About to make the difficult 45-degree turn into our drive, I suddenly thought: wait – suppose the post van is coming down the drive? In fact, this had never happened in all my years in Tetherdown. But I slowed down and went into first gear. And the post van braked within an inch of my bumper.

By introducing me to the work of Lethbridge, Joy had increased my awareness of this unconscious component. In doing so, she had handed me the solution of the problem of what the 'occult sequel' should be about.

But I was still a long way from being ready to start it. I was writing the book on wine, whose starting point was my suggestion that the discovery of alcohol, and the imaginative glow it induces, may have been one of the causes for the evolution of intelligence in our Cro-Magnon ancestors. I was also doing a great deal of television. (I had more or less conquered my attacks of panic, but still had difficulty overcoming that initial explosion of nerves.)

I had added one more chore to my overcrowded schedule. In November 1972, I became involved in plans to launch a part-work on crime. A part-work is a magazine that is designed to run to a specific number of issues, and then collected and bound up in volumes to form an encyclopedia. An old friend named Joe Gaute, a publisher who was also an expert on murder (with an amazing crime library), came to stay with us, and we spent two days sketching out the plan that became the twenty-volume encyclopedia *Crimes and Punishment*. We decided that each 22-page issue (a hundred in all) should contain a famous murder case (such as Jack the Ripper), a famous trial (such as Landru) and a general article on crime detection.

At this time I was asked to join the panel of the South West Arts Association. They met once every six weeks in Exeter, from about eleven in the morning until four in the afternoon. Our chairman was the music critic Eric Walter White, and others on the panel included the poets Ted Hughes, Peter Redgrove and Ronald Duncan, and the novelist Alexis Lykiard. Our job was to give away several thousand pounds of the government's money to such events as the Cheltenham Festival of Literature and various theatre companies in the West Country. To my surprise I found I enjoyed working as part of a committee.

Towards the end of February 1973, a new complication was introduced into my life with the arrival of Kathie, the American girl who had got drunk on the boat in Long Beach. She had invited herself to Cornwall for two weeks. I knew this was going to be difficult, since she made no secret of being infatuated with me, and had no inhibitions about showing it. In fact, one of the first things she said to Joy as she came in was: 'I've come now, so you can go.' Joy, being a gentle and non-confrontational girl, only nodded and smiled as if Kathie had said good afternoon.

Kathie's train arrived late, and she was in hysterics, having lost her case on the journey from London. It arrived the following day, as we had assured her it would, but meanwhile it cost us an enormous effort to soothe her.

In the car, driving from the station, I had noticed that Kathie was wearing a peculiarly penetrating perfume that reminded me of a shoe factory. This, she told us, was musk, and was designed to make the wearer irresistible to men.

It was soon clear to me that the episode on the boat – when her skirt proved to have a huge hole in the back – *had* been designed as an attempt at seduction. When Joy left us alone together on her second day in Cornwall, Kathie lost no time in placing her head on my knee, then raised her face to mine and said: 'Kiss me.' I had no wish to appear a prude, and knew it would only provoke hysterics if I refused, so I obliged. After some heavy tongue-probing, she groaned and said: 'I'd like to eat you.' I assumed this was just a manner of speaking – as when a mother says it of her baby. But it seemed she meant it in the American sense, and proceeded to unzip me.

It was an impossible situation, for the average male finds it hard not to respond to a girl caressing his penis. Fortunately, there was the sound of the car engine as Joy returned from school with the children, and Kathie hastily withdrew to her own chair. But I realised this was going to be a problem for the next fortnight. I certainly did not wish to become Kathie's lover – common sense told me it would be disastrous. But neither did I want to spend two weeks repelling amorous advances, like Fielding's Joseph Andrews – it would have felt silly and undignified.

From then on, Kathie would seize her opportunity when we were in the car, unzipping my fly, and observing with satisfaction that my penis automatically stiffened. And I would say something like: 'That lorry driver will be able to see straight into the car when we pull alongside,' and she would restore me to decency. But as soon as we were on the open road again, her fingers would move down to my zip. If the road was really empty she would bury her face in my lap. I found being fellated an oddly nondescript sensation.

When she realised that I had no intention of going further, and regretted having gone so far, she began throwing hysterical fits, and telling us that she intended to commit suicide during the night. Although heartily sick of her, neither of us wanted that to happen, and I was forced to relent and try to show affection. Joy, of course, knew exactly what was going on – I told her that every time she left us alone, Kathie would reach for my trousers. She seemed to find it all mildly funny, and in any case, obviously felt that it was my own fault.

That two weeks seemed an eternity. I would take Kathie out for a drive to some picturesque town like St Mawes, and do my best to talk her into good spirits, and after a while, feeling that she was engaging my full attention, she would become cheerful and normal. But by mid-afternoon she was depressed again, and by evening was having hysterical attacks and threatening suicide.

The day Kathie left, I was due to drive to Exeter for a meeting of the Arts panel. Significantly, she presented Joy with her bottle of musk perfume as she said goodbye. Then I took her to the train and kissed her goodbye, telling her not to cry, waving to her as the train left, and then climbed into the car with a sudden marvellous sense of freedom.

Alas, this soon evaporated. When I tried to get out of the car in Exeter, I was unable to straighten my back. I clambered on to the pavement on all fours – luckily the small back street was empty – then pulled myself to my feet by grasping the wing mirror, and I limped to my meeting. When I got home that evening, Joy offered to give me a 'back walk' – which meant I had to lie on the rug while she sat in her armchair and moved her feet up and down my spine. This only made it worse – when I woke up in the morning it took me five minutes to stand up. I had to roll off the bed and get up on all fours.

I assumed – rightly, I believe – that the unconscious was at work, and that I was paying for two weeks of self-division with Kathie. For the back pains came and went quite unpredictably. When I went to London to lecture at Scotland Yard (about the role of dominance in crime), all my pains vanished as I talked, and did not return that day. But when, on the night train, I mistook Bodmin Road station for St Austell, and rushed frantically to get dressed, it all came back again and I arrived home unable to bend.

The back pains lasted about a month, then vanished as abruptly as they came.

As to Kathie, we saw her only once more, when I was lecturing in Milwaukee in 1987. She was living with a boyfriend, but when we took them out to dinner she treated me as her own property. She committed suicide with an overdose of sleeping tablets about two years later.

The meetings in London for the crime part-work continued, interspersed with days at Westward Television and committee meetings of South West Arts. I also finished my 'Maigret', *The Schoolgirl Murder Case*. I had been hoping, like Simenon, to be able to learn the technique of writing a detective novel in a few weeks, and then being able to return to more serious work for the rest of the year. But I found that writing detective fiction bored me, and after one more attempt, gave it up.

Crimes and Punishment had been holding fire because the backers – Longines – were taking time to make up their minds. But in June 1973, they finally gave the go-ahead, and I was asked to write my first article – on sex killers – for the first issue. They were paying £75 for a 3,000-word article, not bad pay for that time, when I hoped to make £7,500 a year. A hundred articles for *Crimes and Punishment* would bring that much without even writing a book.

I was the only member of the editorial team who had the general knowledge – and the research skills – to cover subjects from piracy to war crimes, espionage to gangsters. This is why I was the obvious choice to write the leading article in each issue. And provided I had the material at hand, I could write a 3,000-word article in two days.

Looking at my diary for this period, I see that many days are left empty. This was because the part-work publishers were increasing the pace, and I had no time to fill it in. From one or two articles a week, I was soon having to write three or four. That meant I could no longer take a leisurely two days for each article; it had to be written in a day, starting at eight in the morning. One sign of this increasing strain was frequent sexual failure.

On 11 July 1973, my diary records that I attended the magistrates' court in Truro to get a divorce from Betty. She had always refused to divorce me, but now that we had been separated for almost twenty years, I was able to divorce her. And since I had found half the money for her to buy a house, and our son Roderick was now twenty-two, I had no further financial obligation to her. (She, in any case, worked as a school nurse.) I often felt guilty about her, for I still felt protective, but there was little I could do. I could certainly not have said to Joy; 'Off you go now – I'm going back to my wife.'

It was Joy's mother who had insisted on the divorce, and paid for it. (Joy's father had unfortunately died earlier in the year.) Joy, oddly enough, was less than enthusiastic about legalising her status. Since we had been perfectly happy for twenty years in an unmarried state, she was afraid that becoming a wife might bring bad luck. Fortunately, she proved to be wrong. We married a few weeks later, our daughter playing truant from school so she could come to the registry office.

In late July, a Dutchman called Slot came to Tetherdown to study the biographical tapes Maslow had recorded for me; our friend Kay put him up. He went off a week later taking the tapes with him, as well as all Kay's signed copies of my books. We never heard from him again.

By this time, the publisher of *Crimes and Punishment* was demanding seven articles a week. This was appallingly hard work, since it also involved research. (The London Library here proved invaluable.) But at least I was earning more than £500 a week – which was as much as my publisher used to advance me on a single book.

Then the publisher rang me to say they needed ten articles a week – 30,000 words, which amounts to about a third of the average book. But on the £750 a week this paid me I felt rich. I would begin an article at 8 o'clock in the morning, finish it by two in the afternoon, and begin another article immediately, writing a half before the end of the day.

Although I was overworked, I was taking it all in my stride. The only problem that worried me was the influence on my sex life. With increasing frequency, I began to experience what Stendhal calls 'le fiasco'. But even that was worth it for £750 a week.

The breaking point came when two young men from the National Broadcasting Corporation of Canada came to interview me. They were both very talkative, with the result that when I went to bed at 11.30, I had drunk far too much wine, listened to far too much boring conversation, and knew I had a busy day in front of me. This began early, with more interviewing for NBC, after which I had to have a passport photograph taken. On my return I did some lawn-mowing, and wrote the last five pages of a book called *Strange Powers*. Then the *Spectator* rang me to ask if I could do a book review in a hurry, and the editor of *Audio* magazine rang to ask me for an article about Verdi for the following week.

In the evening I took Joy and Kay out to dinner, then to see the film *Cabaret*, and was in bed before midnight. I woke up at four in the morning, and began thinking about the review I had to do, the *Audio* piece, and seven articles I had to write for *Crimes and Punishment*. I felt tired and overtense, and unable to relax. It was as if I was lying there holding my breath. It even came into my head that perhaps I should go down to my workroom and begin one of the articles, but realised that this would be the first step towards a nervous breakdown and dismissed the idea.

As I lay fighting this increasing tension, my heart began to beat faster. Suddenly, the blood rushed to my head, and my cheeks and ears began to burn. And at that point I made a serious mistake: I tried to overcome the problem by willpower. My heart began to pound so fast that I was afraid I was having a heart attack.

I went to the kitchen and got a drink of orange juice, then sat on the lavatory and looked at a classical atlas until I began to feel calmer. Then I went back to bed. Instantly, I felt strangely light-headed, as if my head was swelling like a balloon. With a buzzing noise in my ears, I went into the sitting room, and tried to read. But there was an underlying feeling that something terrible had happened, as if I had had a heart attack or a stroke. I was now trying to soothe myself like a frightened horse. But undermining these attempts was a fear in case all this signalled a nervous breakdown, and that I would have to tell my publisher that I could write no more articles. And the fear reinforced itself, so I became afraid of fear itself.

In *Savage Sleep*, Millen Brand had talked about psychotics going into 'exhaust status', and I could now see how easily this could happen. My energies were rushing away, as if someone had opened the floodgates of a dam.

From somewhere outside I could hear the bleating of sheep, and the thought of lambs being reared, then slaughtered to provide human beings with their dinner, seemed horrible. It was as if the whole world reeked of innocent blood.

Finally, just before dawn, I decided to go back to bed. It was clear to me that I had to stop this energy-leak. So I lay beside Joy, staring at the grey square of the window, and refusing to allow my thoughts to move, as if holding my breath. And finally I dropped off to sleep.

I woke up feeling exhausted and uneasy. I did not tell Joy about the 'panic attack'; there seemed no point in worrying her, and she would only beg me to stop working so hard. Instead, after a light breakfast (we usually had tea and toast in bed), I went downstairs, and wrote an account of what had happened in my journal. This calmed me and restored a sense of normality, and I went on and did my usual day's work. By afternoon I felt quite normal and cheerful.

The problem came back in the evening, when I was tired. I began to worry in case the panic should start again when I went to bed. It was like the panic I had experienced in the previous year facing the television camera – an irrational nervousness in which fear seemed to feed on itself. And indeed, after half an hour in bed, I was more wide awake than ever. I began to think with nostalgia of the days when I could climb into bed and fall asleep immediately. It seemed horribly ironic that I had based my life on the belief that consciousness *could* be controlled, and that I now seemed further from it than ever before.

The day after the attack, I worked as hard as ever on an article on traitors, and the day after that wrote the piece on Verdi, and another crime article. The next day I wrote the *Spectator* review (on primitive religious movements), and over the next few days wrote five more articles.

My journal records that I continued to have milder versions of the first panic attack, particularly if I was overtired. In that case, it rose in me as if I was going to be sick, and I had to struggle to repress it, like someone struggling to close a door that is blowing open in a gale. And even when I should have been relaxed, sitting in my armchair drinking a glass of wine, it was horribly easy to slip into 'negative feedback' in which fatigue and anxiety entered into a conspiracy to drag me down into a state of gloom. When that happened, it was important to apply the lesson I had learned that first day, when I wrote it all down. As soon as I could feel detached, my identity was transferred to a higher level of control, and suddenly everything was fine.

The problem was that as soon as I yawned and became forgetful, I was suddenly back in the 'basement' again. It was exactly like being two people.

I learned that if it happened in the middle of the night, the best way of dealing with it was to wake myself up fully. I recognised that basically all this fear was an absurdity, that what was happening was something I was causing myself. I called this trick 'the schoolmistress effect' because it was like a schoolmistress walking into a room full of quarrelling children, and clapping her hands – and suddenly there is instant silence.

So I continued to push myself hard, and in the first week of October wrote ten crime articles. Then I took the family on a holiday to France, and we drove around Normandy. We went on to Tours and Chinon, then to see Urbain Grandier's church in Loudun. Looking at the spot where Grandier had been burned alive, it struck me that I really had nothing to complain about, and I felt suddenly relieved and cheerful. This was the technique that I called 'the St Neot Margin trick' – pushing the mind to a higher level by recognising that things could be ten times as bad.

The attacks continued for months – in fact, my pocket diary has no further entries for the remainder of 1973 because my energies were so low. But a visit from Bob DeMaria cheered me up. He told me he had also been through a period of panic attacks, and had gone to see a psychiatrist about them. This man was honest enough to say: 'Look, I could charge you a lot of money to try to find what is causing the trouble. But it would be wasted, because panic attacks never last more than six months anyway.' And, said Bob, he proved to be right.

In fact, by fighting hard to maintain control, I could minimise the attacks. But it was an exhausting business. For much of the time I was in the state that Graham Greene described before his Russian roulette experiment – a feeling of greyness and suffocation. Yet it could disappear quite suddenly. One day, when I had been struggling with this feeling of tiredness and fatigue, I began to chop wood for the fire and, as I split the logs, cautioned myself to be careful, since it would be disastrous to chop off the end of a typing finger. The oppression burst and, by the time I made the fire, I was feeling perfectly normal again.

On another occasion, I was staying with John Michell, before returning to Cornwall. John, the author of *The View Over Atlantis*, lived in Notting Hill, and was an old friend of Bill Hopkins. In the middle of the night, I was suddenly overwhelmed with a feeling of alienness, of 'what am I doing here?' and the sinking feeling that was the beginning of a panic attack. I wrestled with it until dawn, then sneaked out of the house, leaving a note apologising for not staying for breakfast, and took the next train back to Cornwall.

One day in the midst of all this I began to urinate blood, and was afraid that it might be cancer of the bladder. But a hospital check revealed that it was simply a few gallstones, which were removed.

One of the worst attacks came when I was on my way back from London on the night sleeper, having chaired a Savage Club dinner. After a brief doze, I woke up, and again the sense of alienness plunged me into a panic attack. It was a feeling like milk boiling over, and a fear that if it went too far, I would collapse into 'exhaust status' and be permanently damaged. The simplest solution seemed to be to get off the train at the next stop, and walk until I felt calm again. This decision helped release some of the tension. But half an hour later it was clear that the next station was going to be a long way ahead. By this time, I had fought off the rising panic, and succeeded in relaxing a little. Further struggles gradually brought me back to a sense of normality. And at that point, I had the thought: if I have been able to relax myself this far, why not simply *go on* relaxing? I did this, focusing all my attention on shallow breathing, until I felt so calm that my heart seemed to have stopped beating. And it was at that point that it dawned on me that I had, in fact, solved the problem of the panic attacks: the answer lay in teaching myself how to induce this deep feeling of relaxation, then using it as a springboard for optimism.

A few days later I learned another method. One afternoon, at about five o'clock, in a state of fatigue and depression, I was driving down to the postbox – driving because the post left in five minutes. Halfway down the drive, I saw a car shoot past the end, and reflected suddenly what it would be like if I had failed to brake in time, gone a foot too far, and been hit by the car. The thought of the massive inconvenience of swopping insurance companies and addresses suddenly jerked me to a higher level of alertness, and the tiredness and depression vanished. And once I had got the hang of this 'trick', the panic attacks virtually ceased.

But they had left behind a great deal of fatigue, and I noted this when we spent three months in Philadelphia in the late spring of 1973. Again, I had been offered the post of 'visiting professor', and we swapped houses with a professor who was on a sabbatical. We lived in a pleasant northern suburb of Philadelphia in a clapboard house, and on most days of the week I drove downtown to take classes at Rutgers University, in the area where Walt Whitman had once lived. I was also writing a few articles for *Crimes and Punishment*, although this had almost run its course. At the end of a day's work, I often felt so drained that I could do nothing but collapse into a chair and listen to music or watch television. Once, when I had been invited out to a local club for dinner, the whole evening passed in a state of disconnection and unreality, as I struggled with sheer exhaustion.

It was at Rutgers that I shared a platform with Allen Ginsberg and was struck again by a thought that had occurred to me repeatedly at Hollins and in Seattle – that living in America would be a far more relaxed form of existence than churning out book after book. Allen was able to lead a pleasant, casual life wandering around campuses. The only thing that bothered me about that notion was the prospect of leaving my parents behind, and all the books and records I had accumulated in the past eighteen years.

After Philadelphia, we accepted an invitation from my Arab publisher to go to Beirut. I was aware that my books had been pirated in the Arab countries for years. But my Beirut publisher, Dr Idries, now offered to pay me royalties in exchange for a written agreement naming him as my only official publisher, and he gave me £500 for my signature.

Flying over the Mediterranean there was another of those minor synchronicities that interested me. I had remarked casually to Joy that we ought to be flying over the island of Santorini, which the archaeologist Marinatos thought might be the site of Atlantis. (The measurements were oddly similar to those Plato had given, except reduced tenfold, and the suggestion was that some copyist had added a nought too many to Plato's text.) Just as I said this, Joy pointed below. 'There it is!' (The same thing had happened when we were flying over Arizona and I remarked that perhaps we would see the meteorite crater – it proved to be right below.)

When we landed in Beirut, the stewardess came and told us that we were to be the first off the plane, and shepherded us to the door. We were puzzled until we climbed down the steps, and found that we were being met by a deputation that was headed by the mayor of Beirut, and that we had to walk beside him down a red carpet. It was then that I discovered for the first time that I was one of the most widely read foreign authors in the Middle East. This was confirmed a few days later when our Palestinian hosts drove us to Damascus, and took us to the house of the Syrian War Minister, General Tlas. The general told me how, when he and his brother officers had been imprisoned by the previous regime, they had read the Arabic edition of my *Ritual in the Dark* by tearing out the pages and passing them from hand to hand, so they could all read it at once.

After our return home, I received an invitation to Iran for a lecture tour. (This, of course, was in the days of the Shah.) But it struck me as pointless to lecture in a country where everything I said would have to be translated, so I declined.

Soon after our visit to Beirut – whose relaxed and civilised atmosphere impressed us – the city was overtaken by the Arab–Israeli conflict, and my publisher went out of business.

The panic attacks had started a train of thought that was to prove highly fruitful for my next book, the 'Occult sequel'. For it was very obvious to me that these attacks had pushed me up to a higher level of self-control. If a glass fell on the floor and broke, I did not even flinch. It then struck me that most people never mature beyond a certain stage. A point comes where they feel they have learned all they have to learn, and from then on they live mechanically and repetitively, doing their daily work and then relaxing in the evenings and weekends.

These panic attacks had achieved for me what the 'double ambiguity' experiment had achieved for Rubinstein and Best's planaria, forcing them to make greater efforts as a matter of habit. They had forced me to overcome my own 'mechanicalness'.

At that time, I had been approached by the BBC to introduce a series of television programmes called *A Leap in the Dark*, each of which told a tale of the paranormal, usually filmed on location: stories of ghosts, poltergeists, precognition, second sight, and so on. One of these programmes was a strange tale of multiple personality involving a patient whom Dr Morton Prince, who recorded the case, disguised under the name of Christine Beauchamp (actually it was Clara Fowler). After a bad shock that plunged her into depression, Christine began to experience periods of amnesia, during which she could be taken over by a personality who called herself Sally – a bright, mischievous child who loved playing tricks. Sally would 'take over' Christine's body and go for a long walk in the country, and Christine would 'wake up' and find herself far from home.

The problem of Christine Beauchamp, and the dozens of other cases of multiple personality that have been recorded, fascinated me, for they all originated in depression – just like my panic attacks. I had pulled myself out of this depression by deliberate concentration, and seemed to have created a stronger personality. This left me wondering: do we all contain many 'selves', many personalities? After all, we grow up from childhood through a whole series of 'selves', and the person who emerges – for example, in adolescence – is almost like a butterfly emerging from a chrysalis. Do we have many stages, like a butterfly? And could that explain what happened to Christine Beauchamp, who developed two other distinct personalities beside Sally?

It seemed to me that our biological urges transport us up the lower rungs of the 'ladder of selves', and it costs us no real effort to develop through childhood to adolescence and adulthood. But at that point, the life force ceases to subsidise our development; if we want to go on developing, we have to do it by painful effort, what Gurdjieff calls 'intentional suffering'.

It is as if the 'ladder of selves' is not like a normal ladder, with parallel sides, but more like an elongated triangle. The higher you go, the shorter the rungs become, and the more effort you have to compress yourself into the next rung. Of course, most people see no reason whatever why they should make any effort. If they can establish a stable lifestyle, with a home and family, they are perfectly contented to remain for the rest of their lives on the same rung. But some people dislike remaining static. They experience an obscure inner urge to go on climbing. These are the people I had labelled 'Outsiders'.

In that sense, the 'Occult sequel' could be regarded as an extension of my early work.

When I was three quarters of the way through the book, I came upon a piece of information that had a tremendous impact on my theory of the paranormal. A friend named Ira Einhorn, whom I had met in Philadelphia, arrived at my house with a book called *The Origin of Consciousness in the Breakdown of the Bicameral Mind*, by Julian Jaynes. And what that book had to say about the left and right side of the brain came to me as a revelation.

A science called split-brain physiology leaves no doubt that we all have two people living inside our heads, in the right and left hemispheres of the brain. The one who lives in the left deals with language and logic – you might say he is a scientist. The one who lives in the right deals with shapes and patterns – you might say he is an artist. But the person you call 'you' is the scientist.

When doctors trying to prevent epileptic fits decided to split the brain – by severing the knot of nerves that join the two halves – they quickly discovered that 'you' lives in the left hemisphere. If a split-brain patient bumped into a table with the left side of the body – which happens to be connected to the right brain – he did not notice it.

A patient whose left brain had been destroyed would not be able to speak, but could still recognise faces and appreciate art and music. A patient whose right brain had been destroyed would be able to speak normally, but his sense of beauty and meaning would be non-existent.

I had already concluded that we have an 'other self' inside us, and that this other self is responsible for paranormal faculties like dowsing, telepathy, precognition and 'second sight'. Now it seemed to me that this 'other self' might be the right brain. And obviously, the right brain is very closely linked with the unconscious mind.

When, in due course, I began writing the 'Occult sequel', I began with an account of my panic attacks, then went on to develop the theory of the 'ladder of selves', or 'hierarchy of personalities', with accounts of many cases of multiple personality. In *The Occult* I had pointed out that many poets – perhaps the majority – seem to possess paranormal abilities. Now I was raising the question: could such abilities be explained by this concept of a hierarchy of selves?

I then went on to tell the story of Tom Lethbridge, and his belief, based on his experiments with the pendulum, that there are also many levels of reality co-existing with this one.

The 'Occult sequel' appeared in August 1978 under the title *Mysteries*. It went on to sell well in England and America. I was no longer publishing with Random House because an editor there had asked me to cut the book from a quarter of a million words to 150,000, and since I had done so much work on it, and was convinced of its importance, I was unwilling to scrap a hundred thousand words. So I transferred to Putnams, and under their imprint *Mysteries* finally went on to sell very nearly as many copies as *The Occult*.

These two works of the 1970s, *The Occult* and *Mysteries*, had established my reputation as a writer on the paranormal, and the BBC *Leap in the Dark* series was only one of many projects in which I became involved. Another was a series of books called *A New Library of the Supernatural*, published by Aldus Books, which was run by a charming Viennese called Wolfgang Foges.

I would take the night sleeper to Paddington, arriving at 5.30 in the morning, then take a taxi or walk to Queen's Gardens, where Bill Hopkins had a ground floor flat. He would leave the key for me under a dustbin in the basement area, and I would let myself in, and get another two hours sleep on a bed-settee that his wife Carla had made up for me.

It was when dozing off one morning that I had a kind of semi-dream in which I saw a vast spaceship. It was fifty miles long and two miles high, and full of holes made by space debris.

I woke up immediately, thinking: my God! A kind of Dracula's castle in the sky! and in a quarter of an hour had planned my next novel, *The Space Vampires*.

I told Bill and Carla the plot over breakfast. A spacecraft exploring the asteroid belt becomes aware of this giant space derelict, which probably set out centuries ago from another galaxy, and was struck by a meteor.

A scouting party enters a hole torn in its side, and finds itself in a kind of vast metal cathedral, with columns as tall as skyscrapers, and immense catwalks that stretch over gulfs.

A greenish glow leads them to the centre of the ship, where they find a square, transparent building. Inside this are human beings in glass coffins – probably in suspended animation.

Three of these are taken back to earth for examination – two males and a female, all naked. But they seem to be dead. An enterprising reporter succeeds in getting into the isolation unit, and is obviously excited by the beauty of the woman's body. He caresses her breast, then bends over her, obviously contemplating necrophilia. But as his lips touch hers, there is a flash, and he writhes in agony, and sinks to the floor. And the woman sits up slowly in her coffin. The face of the reporter has changed into that of an old man – the woman has sucked the life force out of his body. And when guards arrive a few minutes later, all three humanoids have vanished.

The girl is found in Hyde Park, strangled and raped, apparently the victim of a sex crime. It is only later that investigators realise that the female vampire has simply changed bodies with a man, then raped and strangled herself.

The problem: how to catch vampires who can change bodies at will . . .?

A few hours later, after my board meeting at Aldus, I called on my publisher, Mark Barty-King, whose office was only two blocks away, and told him the story. He commissioned the book. And in due course, it became the first of my novels to be filmed.

It was Wolfgang Foges, the managing director of Aldus Books, who asked me to fly to Barcelona to spend a few days with the psychic Uri Geller – Foges wanted me to write a book about him. It was through Geller that I became convinced beyond all doubt that certain individuals possess psychic powers.

In fact, I had already met Geller when the impresario Robert Stigwood asked me to write a film script about him. Uri and I went out to lunch, and he quickly demonstrated his ability to bend spoons by rubbing them gently. But that, I realised, could have been sleight of hand – I had already seen Geller's chief detractor, 'the Amazing Randi', do the same thing without claiming paranormal powers. But Uri then went on to do something that left me completely convinced.

He asked me to make a drawing on the back of the menu card. He turned away while I did this, and I watched him carefully to make sure he could not see what I was drawing. This was a little cartoon character I had invented to amuse my children, which I called a 'woozie'. When I had finished it, Uri asked me to cover it with my hand, then asked me to stare into his eyes and try to transmit the drawing. I followed his instructions, re-drawing it in my head. And after some hesitation, Uri seized a pencil and reproduced my 'woozie'. I could have no doubt whatever that he had read my mind.

So when I flew to Barcelona to meet Uri, I already knew what to expect. Over two days, I witnessed several strange events, like a light bulb falling from the empty air, and a broken spoon pinging past us as we walked downstairs.

Since that visit I have met Uri so many times, and witnessed so many strange phenomena that I do not have the slightest doubt of his genuineness.

I duly wrote my book about Uri. And when it came to the matter of explaining his peculiar powers, I reached what then seemed to me a logical conclusion, based on my own theories of the paranormal. I was firmly convinced that poltergeists – 'banging ghosts' – are due to the unconscious powers of disturbed teenagers. I had even made a television programme about a poltergeist that caused havoc in a lawyer's office in the German town of Rosenheim: it had made electric lights bulbs fall out of their sockets, shattered neon tubes, moved filing cabinets and turned pictures on the walls. The paranormal investigator Hans Bender, whom I interviewed for the programme, had no doubt that all this was caused by 'spontaneous psychokinesis' (mind over matter), centred on a teenage filing clerk called Anne-Marie Schaberl, who had a psychologically disturbed background. And when Anne-Marie moved elsewhere, the 'poltergeist' followed her.

As a result of that case, I had come to accept that poltergeists are caused by the unconscious minds of disturbed adolescents. And since many of the phenomena that happened when Uri was around looked very like poltergeist effects, I concluded that Uri's own unconscious mind must be causing spoons to bend and light bulbs to fall out of the air.

Shortly after the programme on Rosenheim, I had received a letter from a Bristol psychic who called herself Madame Rose, and who assured me that the Rosenheim poltergeist was the spirit of a murdered girl, with whom she herself had been in contact. In my reply, I explained that I was inclined to reject the notion that poltergeists are ghosts, and that I favoured the 'spontaneous psychokinesis' explanation: I had no doubt that she was talking superstitious nonsense.

And so in *Mysteries* I had continued to argue that most paranormal events are a form of unconscious psychokinesis. It is true that psychokinesis usually takes place on an extremely small scale – the Russian Nina Kulagina could move fragments of coloured paper by staring at them, while the American Felicia Parise could move corks. Uri could move a compass needle by staring at it. Moving filing cabinets, as the Rosenheim poltergeist did, is quite outside the powers of these psychics.

But then, I had seen a dowser using a huge fallen branch of a tree as a divining rod, from which I reasoned that earth energies can have tremendous force when canalised through a dowser, so perhaps the energies of the poltergeist came from the earth?

Of course, most modern psychical investigators held the view that poltergeists were manifestations of the minds of disturbed teenagers, so I was in respectable company.

I was about to be forced to change my mind.

In the summer of 1980, I received a phone call from a local historian who lived in Pontefract. He asked me if I would be interested in collaborating with him on a book about a local poltergeist case. It had taken place in the 1960s in the house of a couple called Joe and Jean Pritchard, and the poltergeist had smashed just about every breakable item in the house.

It sounded fascinating, and I decided to go and see for myself.

Joy and I set out in late August, 1980. Since I had been invited to lecture on the paranormal at the Hayes Conference Centre at Swanwick, in Derbyshire, we spent the night there on the way. I noted that one of my fellow speakers would be Guy Lyon Playfair, with whom I had exchanged a few friendly letters, and I looked forward to meeting him. But it turned out that he was not going to arrive until about 3 o'clock on Sunday afternoon, and we had hoped to be on the road by that time. However, I decided that meeting Guy was more important than getting to Yorkshire, so we stayed around until mid-afternoon. In retrospect I can see it as one of the most important decisions of my life.

Guy finally arrived – a slim, fair-haired man of about my own age, with something vaguely military about him. I was not surprised to learn that his father was an army officer.

I told him that we were on our way to investigate a poltergeist case in Yorkshire, and then asked casually: 'What do you think poltergeists are?'

'Footballs,' said Guy, without the suspicion of a smile.

'Footballs?' I could hardly believe my ears.

Guy went on to explain that when people get upset and frustrated, they often exude a kind of vital energy, which forms itself into droplets, like rain. But, being so much lighter than water, this energy forms droplets the size of footballs.

Still baffled, I asked: 'But how does that smash things?'

'Well, a couple of spirits with nothing else to do come wandering past the window and see the football. And, like bored schoolboys, they go and kick it around, smashing windows and knocking ornaments off the mantelpiece.'

'So poltergeists are spirits?'

'Oh yes, I think so.'

And then, said Guy, the football turns into a pool of water . . .

He went on to explain that poltergeist cases always follow a certain pattern. They may begin with scratching noises, like rats under the floorboards. Then come pools of water. Then bangs and raps. Then the movement of objects – things appear and disappear. Sometimes poltergeists graduate to whisking off the bedclothes and throwing people out of bed.

Not all cases, he explained, include each of these stages; some of the stages may be missed. But they always follow in the same order.

And at that point, I suggested, an exorcist may have to be called in.

Guy shook his head. 'Poltergeists usually ignore exorcism.'

As Joy and I drove away towards Pontefract, I shook my head. 'Poor chap – he's as mad as a hatter.'

The following day, we called at the home of the Pritchards, who had arranged for me to interview various people who had been involved in the case which had ended some ten years earlier. We listened with amazement to tape recordings of the incredible racket the thing made – like a mad drummer.

It was when I asked Jean Pritchard: 'How did it all begin?' and she said: 'Well, there were these odd pools of water on the kitchen floor . . .' that I remembered what Guy had said – and suddenly knew that he knew far more about poltergeists than I did.

And when the Pritchards' daughter Diane described how the poltergeist had dragged her upstairs by her throat, leaving dark bruises, I knew beyond all doubt that this was not her own unconscious mind – it was some kind of 'spirit'. In other words, a poltergeist was a ghost that could express itself by using the energy exuded by upset and disturbed people, often teenagers on the verge of adolescence, and seething with explosive sexual energies.

As I drove back to Cornwall, I realised that my whole theory of the paranormal had been stood on its head.

To begin with, if 'spirits' really existed, then presumably they had to be spirits of dead people. In which case, there could be no avoiding the conclusion that there must be life after death.

I was reluctant to take this leap, which went against my natural scientific scepticism. But unless I could think of some other plausible explanation of the Pontefract case, there was no honest alternative. And the more I studied other poltergeist cases, the more I had to conclude that they pointed to life after death.

Moreover, Guy Playfair's experiences as a member of the Brazilian equivalent of the Society for Psychical Research left him in no doubt that 'black magic' also works, and that this again involves 'spirits'. According to Guy, local witch doctors – 'umbanda' specialists – can put spells on people by conjuring up spirits, and the only way to get rid of the spell is to call in another umbanda magician to take it off again.

Spirits, black magic, witch doctors – whether I liked it or not, I seemed to be plunging deeper and deeper into a world of wild absurdity, which any civilised westerner would reject with contempt. Yet as I reflected on the experiences that had led me to this conclusion, none of them left the slightest room for doubt.

There was worse to come. Guy told me that one of the most important books on such matters was *The Secret Science Behind Miracles* by Max Freedom Long. I had actually seen it on the shelves of Watkins's bookshop off the Charing Cross Road, but had found the title so offputting that I had not even glanced at it. Now I bought it and found that it was, as Guy had said, a pivotal work for anybody wanting to understand the paranormal.

Long was an American schoolmaster who arrived in Hawaii in 1917, and became interested in its ancient Huna religion, which had been virtually displaced by Christianity. Its priests, called Kahunas, were said to be able to kill enemies by a 'death prayer'. Long discovered the diary of a Christian minister who had challenged a Kahuna magician to a contest of prayers, and the diary described how member after member of his congregation died mysteriously. Finally, the minister persuaded someone to teach him the death prayer, and the magician died within three days.

Long discovered that, according to the Kahunas, man possesses three souls or minds: the lower, the middle and the higher self. The lower self corresponds roughly to Freud's Unconscious, the middle self is our ordinary everyday consciousness, and the higher self is the super-conscious mind, which can foresee the future.

Long mentions that the three souls are literally distinct personalities, and that the low self – which he calls 'George' – has the natural penetration of a child, and can recognise instinctively when people are untrustworthy or dishonest. When Long needed advice about some new acquaintance, he asked George's opinion, and invariably found the answers correct.

After death, the three selves may become separated, and the lower self often becomes a poltergeist. The middle self may become a ghost.

Long also discusses multiple personality, and cites a typical case of a California girl with two personalities, which took over the body for years at a time. When a psychiatrist tried to integrate the two by hypnotic treatment, a third personality appeared and told him that if he persisted, the two personalities would be withdrawn and the girl would die. Long believes that this third personality was the girl's 'higher self', and that this was a case of 'possession'. The girl, said this other personality, should be left as she was, with two spirits sharing the body.

Long had me convinced that many so-called 'paranormal powers' – like precognitions, premonitions and 'second sight' – are not 'powers' in the strictest sense, but often due to spirits. Even 'spirit possession' could be literally what it claimed to be, and not, as Aldous Huxley suggested, mere sexual hysteria. If Long was correct – as Guy believed he was – then perhaps the 'Devils of Loudun' was really a case of demoniacal possession. Even William James, a psychologist I admired enormously, finally came to believe something of the sort.

And so, as I wrote *Poltergeist, A Study in Destructive Haunting*, I found myself being dragged deeper and deeper into a world that I was unwilling to accept, yet which I found impossible to reject.

CHAPTER 20

Criminal History

Although I had learned to abort the panic attacks, to 'stop the milk from boiling over', so to speak – I still experienced ominous twinges of 'the sinking feeling' if I pushed myself too hard. This happened again in 1981, while I was writing *Poltergeist*.

While I was researching the book in February, my agent rang me to say that Reader's Digest had offered $18,000 (about £7,000) for a short novel about Rasputin. And the same day, a small press had offered £3,000 for a text about witchcraft, to accompany a book of illustrations by the artist Una Woodruff. Since we had a £2,000 overdraft, this prospect of £10,000 was very attractive.

The only problem was that I had agreed to deliver *Poltergeist* by the end of June, and they wanted 110,000 words. That meant writing a total of 220,000 words in less than five months. If my publisher could be persuaded to give me an extra month to deliver *Poltergeist*, it would greatly ease the pressure. So I asked my agent to see if New English Library would agree to let me deliver at the end of July.

The answer was no; their tight schedule meant they had planned to have it in proof by mid-August.

The morning this reply came, I went to see my doctor to have my blood pressure checked, and he told me it was far too high – about 155 over 115 – and that unless I got it down, I would be in danger of a stroke or heart attack. He advised me to lose at least twenty pounds.

I came back home feeling thoroughly gloomy, and went to my basement to settle down to the witchcraft book. I was writing an appalling account of the torture of medieval witches – pouring gallons of water down their throats with a funnel and burning them with hot irons – which depressed me further. And at a certain point I had to consult a book that I thought was somewhere in my basement workroom. It was not, and I was inclined to give up the search; but I forced myself to go and look in a bookshed outside. And there my depression became so overpowering that I began to fear that I was on the edge of total inner collapse. Was there a point, I wondered, when all my nervous energies would drain away and I would plunge into a kind of insanity? I felt as if I was sinking into a swamp of black mud.

I had still not found the book, and sheer refusal to give in made me go and look in a book case in the hall. There I finally found it, and I went back to my desk, sunk in depression but still determined not to give way.

As I sat down, a pencil rolled on to the floor, and I forced myself to bend down to pick it up. And as I did so, the depression suddenly popped like a bubble and vanished. It was as if some negative entity had been trying to drive me into surrender, and when I refused, suddenly decided to release its stranglehold.

The relief was enormous; I felt like a general who has won a battle.

And so I ground on day after day, finishing the witchcraft book in a month, then going on to the Rasputin novel, and starting *Poltergeist* in mid-May. By this time, the publishers had told me that if I could deliver all but the last chapter by the end of June – so an editor could begin work on it – I could have another two weeks to write the final chapter. I finished the book with a day to spare.

While I was finishing *Poltergeist* I had a piece of good news. Two years earlier, *The Space Vampires* had been optioned by a film company called Cannon; now we learned that they had decided to go ahead and make it. They paid us $13,000, the largest sum we had received to date. We used £3,500 of this to pay off the mortgage on our house, and experienced a marvellous sense of relief. Now finally we had some security to offer the bank manager against the overdraft.

Looking back on that depression-attack in the bookshed had made me aware of something of which I had been only half-conscious: a recurring pattern in my life that I needed to face. It looked as if 'the angel that presided at my birth' had decided that the way to get the best out of me was to keep me constantly struggling. The problem with human beings is that success causes them to become mechanical; it seemed that my fate involved being driven to further effort by a demonic overseer.

My teens had been an endless struggle against discouragement, reaching a low point when I decided to commit suicide. During the worst period, I had maintained a basic optimism by telling myself that things were bound to improve – and so they did. But the success of *The Outsider* demanded a completely different kind of self-discipline: to maintain a sense of focused purpose in spite of pleasant distractions. My reaction was to escape the distractions and move to Cornwall. The violent criticism of my second book brought a new problem: how to keep on making a living as a writer with a reputation that seemed damaged beyond repair. And this problem refused to go away for the next twenty years. I had been forced to write book after book, and live off the advances. I sometimes felt like someone bailing out a leaking boat with a teacup.

The success of *The Occult* brought temporary relief – and then a new kind of problem when overwork induced the panic attacks of 1973. There could be no question of giving in to them and having a nervous breakdown: I had a family to support. So I had to deal with the problem through learning psychological self-control.

I came to see that, in a sense, the attacks were my own fault. When I am working, I tend to hurl myself at the task with a kind of impatience – this explains how I could write a book like *The Occult* in less than six months. But if I am interrupted during that frantic flow of activity, I become frustrated and impatient, and feel that the task 'isn't worth the effort'. The result is a loss of inner pressure, like letting down a tyre.

This is the feeling that Auden meant when he wrote:

> Put the car away; when life fails,
> What's the good of going to Wales?

It is an extremely dangerous state, for if it persists for any length of time, it makes all life seem pointless and futile. And once our inner pressure has been reduced too much, it is extremely difficult to raise it back to normal.

Faced with demands that seem excessive, we sink into a state that is akin to deep boredom. Suddenly, everything in life becomes too much for us. And it is then we experience panic, as if about to be drowned in a stormy sea.

My panic attacks taught me to cut off that 'sinking feeling' before it drained away all my energies. But that was only part of the solution. The next part was to recover a sense of enthusiasm and purpose. The simplest way of doing this is to contemplate some imaginary disaster – Graham Greene chose an even more straightforward method by playing Russian roulette.

In theory, it should be possible for human beings to reach any level of happiness or intensity they choose, by using 'the mind itelf' and recognising how many awful things *haven't* happened. The first person to learn to do this easily and naturally will have achieved the basic aim of our human evolution.

Now I could see that what was being demanded of me was that I should learn to keep on coping with these complexities. I just had to get good at it, and not allow myself to experience that sinking of the heart.

I quickly discovered that when I did this, things tended to go right. When I didn't, they tended to go wrong.

One of the signs that they were going right was synchronicities. When that book fell off the shelf during the writing of *The Occult*, open at the right page, I had just forced myself to overcome my laziness and get out of my chair. It was as if some invisible force was trying to teach me something.

One of the most unaccountable examples of this occurred when Joy and I were driving back from the pub one evening. (We often go to a local pub on Saturday for a glass of wine and a sandwich, but leave early, before it becomes crowded.) I remarked to Joy that one of the basic human problems is that we take things too much for granted. For example, we took it completely for granted that this car would get us home . . .

As I spoke, the car began to slow down, then stopped. I was baffled. The fuel gauge showed it was almost full. I pulled out the choke and turned the key. It started for a moment, then cut out again.

There was little traffic on the road, but when a car approached, I waved it down, and asked the driver if he could give my wife a lift to Gorran Haven. And within a quarter of an hour, Joy was back, driving the Land-Rover. I attached a tow rope, and within ten minutes we were home.

At the local garage, the proprietor told us that the engine had developed a rare fault he had never seen before.

When I remembered the way the car had slowed down, then stopped, just as I was commenting that we took it for granted that it would get us home, I had a feeling that it was as if something was trying to tell me something. Like the book falling off the shelf, it was saying: yes, you're right – life isn't a matter of pure chance. And the lesson was not driven home too painfully; what had happened was only a slight inconvenience, and we were not more than half an hour late getting home. I took heed of the message.

Two weeks after finishing *Poltergeist*, we set out for Finland, where I was to give a series of seminars. It was there that I made some interesting new discoveries about the powers of the right brain.

We drove up to Heathrow to take a plane to Helsinki. From there we were headed for a remote settlement in the forest called Viitakivi. The thought of escaping to Finland after writing three books in four months was agreeable; for me the very name conjured up lakes and pine forests and the music of Sibelius.

The bearded man who met us off the plane had a slight American accent, and introduced himself as Brad Absetz. And as we sat in an old-fashioned tea shop that looked as though it was unchanged since the days of Ibsen and Strindberg, Brad told us about Viitakivi. It sounded rather like Esalen, in California, and was subsidised by the Finnish government. The subjects taught there ranged from world religions to organic farming.

On the train to Hameenlinna, I asked Brad if he did any writing – the kind of polite question one asks a travelling companion just to make conversation. His answer: 'A little poetry', was also what one expects of a travelling companion – except that he added: 'If you could say I wrote them.'

Oddly enough, I understood immediately what he meant, and made a mental note to ask him more later; at present, with the children asking what was the Finnish for crisps and lemonade, this was no time to open a conversation about split-brain physiology.

The next day Brad dropped in a sheaf of his poems to our cabin, which overlooked an immense lake. I found them remarkable – curiously non-literary, and devoid of any attempt to impress. Two hours later, as we sat together on the top step of a steaming sauna, I told him how much I liked them, and Brad began to tell me a story that was so fascinating that I knew immediately that I would have to write a book about it.

In 1961, Brad and his wife had decided to adopt a new-born baby. But the child had received very little love or attention since birth, and was now not only unresponsive, but screamed all the time.

When the child was four and a half, he was found to have an abdominal cancer. Although they had four other children, Brad and his wife decided to give him their full attention, to try to make up for lost years. They took turns sitting up with him all night. And when the child died, eighteen months later, they were shattered.

Brad's wife took it badly, and sank into depression. She would lie on the bed for hours, plunged in a state of misery and guilt. Brad would lie beside her, ready to help during one of her rare excursions back to reality.

He never slept, for he wanted to be there if she stirred. But gradually, he learned to sink into deep relaxation. And one day, he felt an impulse in his right arm, as if it wanted to move. As he, in effect, gave it permission, the arm rose gently into the air. A few minutes later, the other arm did the same, while Brad looked on like a bystander.

On subsequent occasions his legs did the same thing; his breathing patterns also changed. And one day as he stood in a queue in the dining room, his hand reached out and took food he did not normally choose. When he allowed it to do this regularly he began to feel healthier than he had ever felt in his life. His weight dropped by twenty pounds.

Brad concluded that some 'other self', some part of his unconscious mind, was trying to teach him something.

One day when he came in from the first skiing of the year, his legs aching painfully, the 'other self' made him lie on the bed, then caused his legs to make a series of movements which quickly caused the discomfort to disappear.

When his little daughter was making crayon drawings, she asked Brad to draw something. Again, 'the other self' took over and created a series of beautiful flower drawings, each one quite different – he did dozens. Finally came two remarkable drawings which he labelled 'The Fire Ball' and 'The Ice Crystal', which seemed to have a quality of finality. After that, the drawings stopped.

The poetry was written in the same way, his hand writing without effort. But when, one day, his handwriting changed, and some 'entity' indicated that it wished to communicate, Brad said: 'No, go away. This is for me' – and it never happened again. Once more, at a certain point, the poetic impulse died away.

The 'other self' even led Brad to become a bee keeper, and he did this with extraordinary success, producing excellent honey and never once being stung. It was as if the 'other self' entered into some perfect harmony with the bees.

All this fascinated me. It was obvious that Brad had succeeded in establishing direct communication with his right brain. And this is extremely rare. Of course, all men of genius possess the power to communicate with the right brain – Mozart said that tunes just walked into his head, and all he had to do was write them down. A painter like Jackson Pollock obviously did much the same thing. But most artists have to exercise far more left-brain control.

In my own case, teaching myself to write had been a long and very discouraging process. In those early days, I would often spend an evening writing quickly and fluently, but when I read what I had written the next day, it made me groan with embarrassment. But I persisted, merely because I felt that becoming a writer was my only way of escape from dreary jobs. And one day I read what I had written the evening before, and saw that this *was* what I had been trying to say. It was obvious that the two persons inside my head were working together in perfect harmony, like two good tennis players, or two lumberjacks at either end of a double-handled saw. Now I realised that these were my right and left brain, with the right brain flinging up the insights, and the left turning them into words and writing them down.

I began to see that the most important part of the secret was *knowing* that the 'other self' is there, ready to help. Most people spend their lives in states of unhappiness and tension because they believe, quite wrongly, that they are alone – just as I had during my panic attacks. And since I was still, to a minor extent, experiencing that uneasy sense of nervous tension while I was in Finland, I saw that Brad had something important to teach me.

Which is why, on my return to England, I wrote a book called *Access to Inner Worlds*, and gave half the proceeds to Brad Absetz.

I made another interesting discovery at Viitakivi. One of my students, a middle-aged woman, told me she often felt depressed, and I addressed this subject in class one morning.

After speaking about Husserl, and explaining that all moods are 'intentional', I told them to induce a mood of depression by thinking of the most depressing things they could remember. Within about a minute, they were looking thoroughly gloomy. At this point I said: 'OK – now un-depress yourselves.'

They looked puzzled. I said: 'Look, you've just depressed yourselves deliberately, so it must be possible to un-depress yourselves in the same way.'

It took longer this time, but eventually they all looked cheerful again.

In these exercises of mind control we also made use of the 'pen trick' – concentrating on it to induce a peak experience.

One day, about half an hour before lunch, I decided to complicate the exercise by introducing another factor: Reichian breathing. This had been taught to me by a pupil of Reich's, Constance Rooth-Tracey. She told me to lie on my back, and breathe in as deeply as possible, envisaging that I was breathing in vital energy – Reich's orgone energy. Then, as I breathed out slowly, she told me to repeat: 'Out – down – through', as if forcing this energy down through my body. The 'out' is from the lungs, the 'down' the solar plexus, and the 'through' the genitals and down to the feet. I discovered that Reichian breathing induces a curious glow of vitality.

Now I told my students to combine the 'pen trick' with Reichian breathing: to focus hard as they breathed in, then release the tension as they said: 'Out, down, through.'

I half-expected the pen trick and the Reichian breathing to cancel one another out. But on the contrary, they reinforced one another, and induced a deep sense of happiness and relaxation, which was almost like floating off the floor. As we were lying there in this blissful state, I looked at my watch and realised that lunch had started half an hour ago. As I recalled them to the present, we all stood up slowly, feeling that lunch was not nearly as interesting as what we had been doing.

Am I, then, suggesting that it is the right brain that communicates with spirits?

That seems to me the logical conclusion: that when a medium goes into trance and speaks with 'spirit voices', the 'entities' gain entrance through the right brain. The same, I think, must be true of tribal shamans. That other person inside us – what Maurice Maeterlinck called 'the unknown guest' – can hold conversations with beings who belong to another world.

Oddly enough, at the time I wrote *Access to Inner Worlds*, I was far from convinced of life after death.

During this period – the early 80s – a murder trial suggested that the problem of the split brain might have some interesting implications for criminology. This was the case of the Hillside Stranglers, who between October 1977 and February 1978 had murdered and raped a dozen women in the Los Angeles area. One year later, two students in Bellingham, Washington State, became the victims of a sex murderer after they had been asked to do a 'house sitting' job by a security guard named Kenneth Bianchi, who insisted that he had no knowledge whatever of the crimes. But since the evidence pointed clearly to Bianchi, he was arrested and charged with the murders. It soon became clear that he might also be involved in the Los Angeles murders, together with his cousin Angelo Buono.

Since Bianchi insisted that he had no memory of the murders, a psychiatrist began to wonder if he might be a case of multiple personality, and asked him to allow himself to be hypnotised. Within minutes, Bianchi was speaking in a strange, low voice, and had introduced himself as 'Steve'. Steve claimed to be a part of Bianchi who hated 'Ken', with whom he had to share the body; he was a highly unpleasant character who spoke in a sneering voice and used a great deal of obscenity.

Bianchi convinced several psychiatrists that he was a 'multiple'. If he could also convince a judge, then Bianchi would be sentenced to a few years in a mental hospital. And he would not be allowed to testify against his cousin Angelo.

But Bianchi made a mistake, which proved he was only pretending to be a multiple personality. When, under hypnosis, he was told that his defence lawyer was sitting in an empty chair, he immediately jumped to his feet to shake hands. The hypnotist had never seen this before – hypnotised subjects try not to touch their hallucinations.

But Bianchi made an even greater mistake. Asked his surname, 'Steve' said it was Walker. And the policeman in charge of the case had discovered that Bianchi had stolen the identity papers of a psychology graduate named Steve Walker, and had used them to get a false diploma. So Bianchi was revealed as a clever con man, and in due course, he and Buono were both sentenced to life for the Hillside murders.

But although Bianchi proved to be a fake, at least one other criminal of the period, the rapist Billy Milligan, was generally accepted by the psychiatrists who examined him as having twenty-three sub-personalities, some of whom were more talented than Billy was himself. And one of these, a central European, actually spoke languages that Billy could not speak. As I studied Daniel Keyes's book *The Minds of Billy Milligan*, I found myself more and more inclined to accept that these were not 'sub-personalities', but other people – spirits.

And so the subject of split-brain physiology, which I had written about in *Access to Inner Worlds* and *Frankenstein's Castle*, turned my mind once more in the direction of crime and criminals. Which is why, thinking in terms of some large volume that could stand beside *The Occult* and *Mysteries*, I began to think about writing a comprehensive history of crime and civilisation.

Britain was in the midst of another of its economic crises, and it was reflected in the publishing world. I had heard from fellow-writers that it was becoming harder and harder to get books commissioned. But I had been lucky. My publisher was Granada, and my editor, Mark Barty-King, had become an old friend. It was to Mark that I put the idea of writing a world history of crime, and was delighted when he commissioned it for an advance of £15,000.

The book would have a basic unifying theme: the psychological motivation of criminality. And this was a subject on which I had received a vital clue from my friend A. E. Van Vogt, after meeting him at the Hollywood Science Fiction Convention in 1966.

Van had made a truly amazing discovery about a type of person he labelled the Right Man – so called because his desire to save face is so great that he will never, under any circumstances, admit he is in the wrong. If you prove to him that he is wrong, he will hit you in the face rather than admit it. This is why Van also labelled him the Violent Man.

In 1956, in the course of planning a non-SF novel about a Chinese prison camp, Van noted the behaviour of the Right Man. His basic desire is to be a despot with absolute power. But if the worst comes to the worst, he will make do by behaving like a petty dictator with his wife and family. They have to behave with slavish obedience, for the least questioning of his decisions leads to an explosion of rage and physical violence.

He may be flagrantly unfaithful to his wife, for sexual conquest is immensely important to his self-esteem. But if his wife so much as smiles at another man, she may end with a black eye.

He reserves this side of his character for his family; to other people, he often seems a normal, likeable man.

The Right Man seems to have one strange characteristic. If his wife actually leaves *him*, he may have a nervous breakdown, or even commit suicide. She has kicked away the foundations of his sandcastle of illusion. Hitler, a typical Right Man, came close to suicide when his niece – and mistress – Geli Raubal killed herself to escape him. For when a Right Man has found a woman who is submissive and admiring, it fills him with a new self-confidence and a sense of his own worth. He can then create his fantasy of power and greatness. If she walks out on him, the whole structure threatens to collapse, together with his sanity. Van Vogt points out that it is necessary to feel a certain sympathy for the Right Man because he is 'struggling with an unbelievable inner horror'. Trapped in the carapace of an insatiable craving to be recognised and admired, he is like a man who is suffocating to death in a sealed room. Acts of violence can bring temporary relief, but it only lasts for a few hours before the suffocation starts again. This is precisely the same 'horror' that Conrad's Mr Kurtz suffers from in *Heart of Darkness*.

Right Men are incredibly common. When I talked about it in my classes in America, many of the girls said: 'My God, my father was like that,' or, 'That's just like my ex-husband.'

What causes Right Man-ishness? Well, every member of the dominant 5 per cent feels the craving to express his dominance. But not all dominant males have 'what it takes' to be successful. So, like a Romantic poet who needs to escape reality, they take refuge in imagination.

But if you can find someone else to join you in your imaginative game, it becomes ten times as satisfactory. That is why the submissive woman is so important to the Right Man. She is a guarantee that he is not a mere fantasist.

Oddly enough, success makes no real difference to the Right Man. Once the obsession has taken a hold – early in life – it is almost impossible to dislodge. Hitler and Stalin and Mao were all Right Men. So, as I discovered, was the actor Peter Sellers. The book by his son Michael, *PS I Love You*, reveals that deep lack of inner self-assurance, and the selfish and violent behaviour, that mark the Right Man.

The truth is that there can be few males who cannot, if they are honest, recognise traces of the Right Man in themselves. Provided he is aware of it and keeps it under control, this hardly matters. It is the man who is unaware of it who is a danger to himself and other people. And I quickly recognised that this is the key to criminal psychology. The Right Man is like a spoilt child who is determined to get his own way. He is trapped in a world inside his own head. And if he also lacks social conscience – or the caution that keeps most people inside the law – then he can behave appallingly and do society a great deal of damage.

I had also noticed many cases in which the Right Man becomes truly dangerous only after he has found a submissive woman to control. The obvious example was Ian Brady, the Moors Murderer, and his partner Myra Hindley. Brady, who had been in Borstal for burglary, was not interested when the teenage Myra came to work in the same office, for she was obviously not a member of the same high-dominance group as Brady and, as Maslow discovered, high-dominance people prefer a partner in their own dominance group. But when he realised she was infatuated with him, he changed his mind. And once they were lovers, he found the sheer intoxication of being adored so addictive that it affected him like a drug. The Right Man suddenly had a partner to share his fantasy. And since Brady's fantasies involved paedophilia, the 'game' played by the two of them became the abduction and murder of children.

Myra herself, although not of the 'dominant 5 per cent', had some unpleasant characteristics due to the psychological insecurity of her upbringing. The arrival of a sister, when Myra was four, meant that she spent much of her childhood with her 'gran', who lived just around the corner. Myra grew up a bully, who loved tormenting younger children. This is why she became the ideal partner for Brady. Like some starry-eyed convert to Nazism, she developed the mentality of a concentration camp guard, and took to murder and torture with enthusiasm. She aided and abetted Brady in the kidnap, rape and murder of three children and two teenagers.

As was almost inevitable, they were caught. Brady had tried to extend his sphere of influence to a young male admirer, the husband of Myra's sister. But the sight of Brady murdering a teenage homosexual with a hatchet was too much for David Smith, and he went to the police.

Brady still regards Smith with unremitting hatred, as I learned when I became engaged in correspondence with him in 1991. A girl had asked me to help her with an autobiography in which her correspondence and friendship with Brady played a central part. Brady wrote to ask me about the rumour that I was helping her write a book about him, and we began to exchange letters. I was impressed by his intelligence and his wide reading, and jumped to the conclusion that a man as intelligent as this could be objective about his own crimes. It was soon obvious that I was mistaken. For Brady was a Right Man, and nothing could persuade him that he had been wrong to kill children. Like his favourite writer, de Sade, he believed that 'everything is lawful'. It was society that was wrong, because society was corrupt and rotten. It made no difference for me to point out that two wrongs do not make a right; he had persuaded himself that he was the victim of a vicious and immoral society.

In due course he wrote a book called *The Gates of Janus*. I added an Introduction and found him a publisher. It is a remarkable document, for it is the only work in world literature in which a criminal Right Man argues his case that society is really to blame for his crimes.

The publication of the book – in 2001 – also marked the end of my correspondence with Brady. His prison, Ashworth Hospital, demanded that some of his accusations about the way he was treated should be removed. They were finally contented with a brief erratum slip, without which the distributor refused to handle the book. But even this was too much for Brady, who exploded with rage because he felt the hospital had 'won'. I was not too concerned when he ceased to correspond, for we had, in fact, exhausted all we had to say to one another. But *The Gates of Janus* remains as a unique Right Man document, paranoid, obsessive and wrong-headed.

Writing the book that became *A Criminal History of Mankind* was an important experience for me, for it was my first attempt to grapple with history. The historian A. L. Rowse had remarked to me in the 1970s that I ought to learn more about history, but I had felt that the subject offers little opportunity for my kind of psychological analysis. Writing the *Criminal History* proved me wrong. It soon became apparent to me that every time human beings have tried to create a society based on peace and cooperation, criminals have immediately used their dominance to gain control.

Rome itself is an example of a civilisation that was taken over by plunderers and gangsters. For my chapter on Rome, I borrowed the title 'No Mean City' from a novel about Glasgow gangsters – the original quotation is St Paul's 'I am a citizen of no mean city', referring to Rome.

It struck me as interesting that the original Christianity of Jesus should have been an attempt to create a genuinely non-criminal society, based on love and mutual aid, and that as soon as the emperor Constantine made Christianity the official state religion in AD 313, the Christian Church should have immediately become another massively corrupt and criminal institution, based upon power and wealth.

One day, when I had actually finished writing the book, and was re-reading the typescript, I was struck by the way that civilisation has steadily increased its pace, from its slow and gentle beginnings to its present headlong rush. It started like a broad, slow river with the earliest humanoid apes. With our ancestor *Homo erectus* it seemed to enter a valley, and became a fast-flowing stream. With Neanderthal and Cro-Magnon man, it is as if the river has entered a canyon and become a torrent. With the building of cities, the raft that carries mankind entered a narrow gorge full of dangerous rapids. And now man flies along between towering walls, surrounded by drifting wreckage and bodies struggling in the water, he is having to concentrate as never before.

As I added a passage to the book in which I said this, I noticed the parallel to my own position, and the steadily increasing pace at which I had been forced to work. The panic attacks had almost flung me among bodies struggling in the water, but so far I had managed to cling on and continue to steer. If I meant to survive, I also had to concentrate as never before.

The writing of the *Criminal History* brought two more important insights that were to play a central part in my subsequent work. The first was that all human sexuality is based on 'the sexual delusion'. To recap, the effect of sexual attractiveness on human beings is very much like the effect of the Pied Piper on the rat population of Hamelin, or of the song of the Sirens on Ulysses: it creates an overwhelming feeling of desire that overpowers the senses like an intoxicant. This recognition – that sexual desire is literally a delusion – threw an entirely new light on the problem of sex crime.

It also made me realise the extent of the part played by the sexual delusion in my own development. Considering those powerful feelings that had made me pull on my mother's knickers long before I knew anything about sex made me aware that I had been dominated by the sexual illusion since I was born. In my teens it divided me into two: the romantic who dreamed of some incarnation of the eternal feminine, and the realist who read of the crimes of a rapist with muted envy. Like the hero of Hermann Hesse's *Steppenwolf*, I was both a man and a wolf. The human part was the part that loved Joy and the children, but the wolf continued to growl and slaver in the background whenever a girl in a mini-skirt bent over and showed her nylon-clad behind.

At least, as I grew older, the self-division had ceased to be quite so painful. I recognised the desire as a kind of drug addiction. I could count half a dozen friends who had given way to it, and wrecked their marriages and their lives. But I am not sure whether I was becoming more moral, or just more cautious.

The other realisation came when I was writing about the birth of the modern novel in the eighteenth century. It was invented by a printer named Samuel Richardson, who had decided to tell a story in the form of letters. They are from a servant girl named Pamela, whose master, Squire B, is determined to seduce her. When she is undressing, he leaps out of a cupboard and throws her on the bed. Only the entrance of the housekeeper saves her. Then he sends her to a brothel, and tries to rape her as the procuress holds her hands, but she goes into convulsions and he gives up again. Finally, overcome by her sweetness and goodness, he marries her.

Nothing like this had ever appeared – a moral tale that read rather like pornography – and *Pamela* became a best-seller. Clergymen praised it from the pulpit. And soon novels were being read in every middle-class household. Lending libraries sprang up all over Europe.

What Richardson had done was to invent a kind of magic carpet that would transport readers to a land of dreams. So far, human beings had shared the fate of animals, and been tied down to mere physical existence. For most people, the only escape from the dullness of everyday life was when they went to church on Sunday and listened to the vicar telling them stories from the Bible. That was why the best-sellers of the time were volumes of sermons.

By 1780 a bored housewife could curl up in a window seat and simply forget who she was. Instead, she spent the next hour or so in the world of the author's imagination, and shared the problems and dangers of the heroine. It was as startling as if human beings had learned to leave their bodies and float around in space. There is a sense in which the novel was the most important invention since the wheel.

I felt that this was one of the greatest insights I had ever had. Julian Huxley had said to me that I ought to give some thought to the vital role art has played in human evolution. Now I understood what he meant. The novel taught human beings to dream. And of course, it also made them develop a taste for another world – the world of mystery and beauty and romance. The romantics wanted to turn their backs on the ugliness of everyday life, and find a richer and more exciting reality. In the nineteenth century, this craving caused many tragedies, from the deaths of Keats and Shelley to the suicide of Van Gogh. In fact, this 'eternal longing' ushered in the age of 'Outsiderism', and of what Karl Marx called alienation.

It is significant that in Richardson's even more popular second novel, *Clarissa*, the heroine is raped as well as abducted, and dies of shame. From then on, writers quickly discovered that sexual fantasy has a ready audience, and the genre we call pornography was launched in 1745 with John Cleland's *Fanny Hill*. By 1820, pornography was a flourishing industry – the production of what one writer called 'books that one reads with one hand'.

Yet oddly enough, there was very little of what we would now call 'sex crime'. One reason is certainly that among the poor, so many women were forced to sell their bodies that cheap sex was generally available, and it would have been pointless to risk jail for it. It was only in the second half of the century, when Victorian prudery had endowed sex with the allure of the forbidden, that sex crime in our modern sense appeared. It struck the Victorians as so bizarre that they did not even recognise the murders of Jack the Ripper as sex crimes – the favourite theory being that he was a 'religious maniac' with a hatred of fallen women.

In other words, sex crime came into its own in the nineteenth century, with the sudden increase in the 'sexual delusion'. The pornographers who followed in the steps of de Sade had invented what might be called 'super-heated sex', and this would bring about a slow but complete transformation of human nature, until we find ourselves living in the age of the serial killer.

The writing of *Criminal History* was also important for me because it placed the ideas of my 'Outsider cycle' in a historical context. Suddenly it was possible for me to see the direction of the stream of my work since *The Outsider*. I had recognised from the beginning that we are living in an 'age of defeat', and that this defeat is based on the disappointment of the hopes of the romantics. Goethe and Schiller thought that man has a god-like potential. H. G. Wells wrote a novel called *Men Like Gods*. In *Back to Methuselah*, Shaw forecast a time when humankind will be virtually immortal. Yeats said that the aim of art is the 'profane perfection of mankind'. Yet all this had collapsed into the pessimism that is the foundation of literature from Graham Greene to Beckett, and philosophy from Heidegger to Derrida and the post-moderns.

Yet Maslow had seen the basic solution: that the 'peak experience' is the driving force of all creative individuals, and that this remains untouched by negative thinking.

The *Criminal History* was finished early in 1983, after an almost complete rewrite. The sheer length of time it had taken meant that our finances were in the usual crisis – we were £10,000 overdrawn.

My bank manager asked me to go in and see him. He was a nice man – I had occasionally given after dinner speeches at his rotary club – but obviously worried about the situation. 'The problem is that this loan is unsecured.' 'Unsecured?' I was astonished. 'But surely you have the deeds to our house?' He shook his head.

Joy, it seemed, had simply forgotten to hand them over when we paid off the mortgage. (A certain sweet vagueness was the price she paid for her serene, easygoing nature.)

He asked me: 'What kind of house do you have?'

'A fairly large bungalow standing in two acres of building land.'

'Oh, in that case, you can have what you like!'

We agreed that a £15,000 overdraft would serve for the time being, and I drove home in a state of euphoria.

I needed the sense of financial security, for I had decided to bring my mother down to live with us. Ever since the death of my father in 1975, she had been living alone in Leicester. Just before dad's death she had suffered a stroke and collapsed in the street – obviously due to the stress of nursing him. By the time he died, she had recovered, and I was looking forward to bringing her to Cornwall for long holidays, perhaps even taking her for trips abroad. But she soon had another stroke that made her vague and absent-minded. Living in Leicester made her nervous – she read in the paper about the increase in burglary, and used to lie awake at night. I decided that bringing her to Cornwall was the only solution.

Joy was not entirely happy – what if my mother had another stroke and needed full-time nursing? But we decided to take the risk, and in the spring of 1983 I drove to Leicester to fetch her.

Our anxieties proved unnecessary. She was the perfect guest, quiet and unobtrusive. I was delighted to have her living with us, for I think most males are deeply protective about their mothers, and it gave me real satisfaction to see her sitting on the settee opposite me and reading or dozing.

Even her death was quiet and unobtrusive. One Saturday evening in October 1991, we took her to the pub as usual for an early drink. When we got home, we had supper, and watched a television programme about life after death, in which two women spoke of their absolute certainty of human survival. The next morning, mum failed to make her usual appearance at about 10.30, but we assumed she had overslept. Finally, Joy went into the bedroom, and found her lying on the floor; she had died of a stroke as she dressed.

Joy called me – I was writing an Introduction to an American edition of my poltergeist book – and I went into the bedroom, where she was lying on the carpet. I suddenly felt deeply sorry that I had never shown her how much I loved her. Our family is emotionally reserved, and although I show endless affection to my wife and children, some working-class inhibition had always made it hard to show it to my mother. I recalled that, only a week before, as I brought her a cup of tea, she had said: 'Oh, I do love you, m'duck', and now I regretted not pushing aside the inhibition and replying: 'And I love you.' Instead, I had smiled awkwardly and gone out.

Now I tried to make up for it by kneeling beside her, kissing her soft cold cheek, and saying: 'I love you mum.' I hoped she was somewhere nearby, to hear me say it. Then I lifted her on to the bed – she was very light – and as I did so she sighed, and I thought she might not be dead after all. But it was only the air coming out of her lungs.

I wish I had told her I loved her while she was alive.

Back in the practical world, the next problem now was to think up a subject for my next book.

At that point, I remembered something I had overlooked in *The Occult* and *Mysteries*: psychometry. This is the curious ability that some people possess to hold an object in their hands and 'read' its history.

They may not even realise they possess this power. In 1921, a group of people met in Paris to test a clairvoyant. Among them was a novelist named Pascal Forthuny, who was a total sceptic. And as someone was passing a letter to the clairvoyant, Forthuny grabbed it and said: 'It can't be difficult to invent something that applies to anybody.' He held it against his forehead. 'Ah yes, I see a crime . . . a murder.' And when he had finished his improvisation, the owner of the letter said: 'That was written by Landru, at present on trial for killing a dozen women.'

Forthuny then held other objects, and was able to describe their history with amazing accuracy. He had not dreamed he possessed the power of psychometry.

The word was invented around 1840 by a young American professor of medicine named Joseph Rodes Buchanan. He happened to be talking to a bishop named Leonidas Polk, who mentioned that he could detect brass, even in the dark, because it produced an offensive metallic taste in his mouth when he held it in his hand.

Buchanan decided to test it out on his students, and discovered that a number of them could not only detect brass, but various other metals like iron and copper, and some could even distinguish sugar, salt, pepper and vinegar.

Buchanan concluded that our fingers must have the same ability as our tongues to distinguish tastes. He felt he had made an interesting scientific discovery.

His next step was just as exciting. He handed one of his 'sensitives' various sealed envelopes containing letters written by people of strong character. The 'sensitive' was able to describe the character of the letter writers with remarkable accuracy.

Buchanan still felt that all this could be explained scientifically. Photography had only recently been discovered. And a photograph is, after all, only a kind of painting made by light on the sensitive chemicals of a photographic plate. So if a person happens to be 'sensitive', why should he not be able to register the effect of a strong personality, like a photographic plate?

The next step was slightly more controversial. Buchanan put photographs in sealed envelopes and handed them to his sensitives. Once more, the results were impressively accurate. But how could that be, since photography is a purely mechanical process? Then the answer occurred to him. Most people would have handled their own photographs, leaving the imprint of their personality, which would then be picked up by the 'nerve aura' of the sensitive.

This theory was disproved when he tried using newspaper photographs, and his sensitives were just as successful in identifying them. How could a newspaper photograph carry the imprint of the sitter's personality?

The only possible answer was that human beings possess powers of perception that are far greater than they suppose. And in 1848, Buchanan chose a name for this 'new faculty'; he called it 'psychometry', meaning 'mind measurement'.

Buchanan's discovery should have made him famous among his medical colleagues, for it had been established by a careful series of scientific experiments. Unfortunately, he was about to be overtaken by a wholly unforeseen disaster.

In that year, the home of the Fox family, in New York state, was shaken by a series of baffling disturbances – bangs and crashes that made the house tremble. We would now call these poltergeist phenomena. Neighbours who established communication with this entity – by means of a code of raps – were told that it was a peddlar who had been murdered and buried in the cellar by a previous owner. The publicity spread nationwide, and soon dozens of 'mediums' (as they had become known) were holding seances in darkened rooms and apparently talking to ghosts. In 1849, the first 'spiritualist' association was set up in Rochester, N.Y. As the craze swept around the world, scientists became furious at what seemed to them a return to the superstition of the Dark Ages. Understandably, Buchanan found himself tarred with the same brush. This is why 'psychometry' failed to achieve the acclaim it deserved.

But Buchanan had at least one disciple. Nine years Buchanan's junior, his name was William Denton, and he was the Professor of Geology at the University of Boston. He came upon one of Buchanan's original papers on psychometry, and was fascinated by a paragraph that suggested that a psychometrist ought to be able to hold a piece of a dinosaur fossil, and see the dinosaur 'rise before his eyes'.

His sister Anne seemed to be a highly sensitive person, so he began by handing her sealed letters written by people with strong personalities. Impressed by her accuracy, he tried her with a piece of limestone full of tiny fossil shells, and wrapped in paper. Her reaction was 'Oh, what shells, small shells: so many . . .' And she described the place on the Missouri River it came from.

He tried handing her a fragment of volcanic lava from Kilauea, in Hawaii, concealed in paper. She saw 'an ocean of fire pouring over a precipice' and making the sea boil. She also saw ships on the sea; and the lava had been ejected in the eruption of 1840, when the US Navy was in the bay.

He tried a fragment of bone on his wife; she saw a creature with a thick skin, and a horned head rather like that of a sheep. What she seems to have described was a plesiosaur, the species to which the Loch Ness monster is supposed to belong.

A fossil from Cuba brought a description of a tropical island. A piece of Indian pottery brought an image of Red Indians. A piece of meteorite brought visions of empty space. A pebble from a glacier produced an impression of being frozen at a great depth. A piece of rock from Niagara brought the sound of a torrent, and looking into a deep hole with something boiling up in it – the psychometrist guessed a hot spring.

And so they went on – visions that seemed to indicate that psychometry was a kind of telescope into the past.

To make sure she was not reading his mind, Denton mixed up specimens in parcels until he no longer knew what was what. The visions were still accurate. And one experiment seemed to prove conclusively that this was not telepathy. Denton handed his wife a piece of mosaic pavement from the villa of the Roman orator Cicero, hoping for a description of Cicero. She 'saw' helmeted soldiers in a villa, and a fleshy man with blue eyes who was obviously not Cicero (who was tall and thin). Denton only found out later that the the emperor Sulla had also lived in the villa, and fitted the description exactly.

These experiments seemed to show beyond doubt that Buchanan's 'psychometry' was a genuine human faculty that no one had suspected –

one more curious power of the right brain. Yet because it seemed to smack of spiritualism, it failed to attract the attention of scientists.

There was, of course, another problem. If psychometry worked even with newspaper photographs, it could not be a 'natural' faculty like the bloodhound's sense of smell. Which meant that scientists like Buchanan and Denton found themselves being dragged, much against their will, down the slippery slope of 'occultism' – precisely as I had been myself. Once you admitted the possibility of some anomaly like psychometry, dowsing or multiple personality, it was impossible, if you were honest, not to find yourself compelled to admit the possibility of a great deal more. (I have known only one scientist who managed to pull himself back from the brink – Professor John Taylor, a physicist who studied Uri Geller and dowsing, then suddenly reaffirmed his total scepticism and rejoined the fold of the respectable.)

In deciding to write a book about psychometry, I was trying to revive a 'science' that had been forgotten for more than half a century. The problem, of course, was what such a book should be called. *Telescope into the Past* would have been ideal, but would have failed to interest most readers – and the paperback publisher Pan Books, who commissioned it, wanted a 'selling title'. So, not for the first time, I had to compromise, and accept *The Psychic Detectives*.

In June 1985, the film of *The Space Vampires*, now retitled *Lifeforce*, finally reached the screen.

It had been directed by Tobe Hooper, an associate of Stephen Spielberg, and some vast sum – running to millions of dollars – had been spent on 'special effects'. When Joy and I heard that it was being filmed on the same set as *Star Wars*, we allowed ourselves to daydream of a whole series of my novels being optioned by Hollywood, and the end of living off an over-draft.

A few days after its New York premiere, we heard that it had been a flop. When I finally saw it – at a special screening for myself and my family in Plymouth – I understood why.

Whatever the merits of *The Space Vampires* as serious literature, it is a good story, and moves on logically, step by step, from the initial discovery of the vampires in the wrecked spacecraft, to the problem of how the pursuers could track down and corner aliens who can transfer themselves from body to body. In that sense it has the structure of a detective story.

The trouble with the film was that it tried to move too fast. If I had been given a chance to work on the script, I would have drawn a lesson from the original *King Kong*, with its long, slow build-up of suspense, which is suddenly released as the giant ape rampages out of the jungle. In *Lifeforce*, from the moment the vampires kill the guards and walk out into modern London, the pace accelerates until it is like a gramophone record being played at twice its proper speed. And the audience, bombarded and stunned by absurd special effects, soon lapses into a state of exhausted indifference.

John Fowles had once told me that the film of *The Magus* was the worst movie ever made. After seeing *Lifeforce* I sent him a postcard telling him that I had gone one better.

CHAPTER 21

Dreaming to Some Purpose

In July 1986, Joy came down to my work room to say that a Japanese friend was on the phone, asking if we would like to fly to Tokyo, and go on a tour of Buddhist monasteries. Joy was included in the invitation, and they were offering to pay all travel expenses – first class – and a fee of several thousand dollars. Naturally, I accepted.

Ever since *The Outsider* was published in Tokyo in 1957, the Japanese had been enthusiastic about my work, and translated virtually everything – even magazine articles. One delightful day in 1976, when I had just staggered home exhausted from making a television programme in Bristol, Joy had said: 'You're not going to believe this,' and held out a cheque for £10,000. My Japanese publisher was bringing out a new edition of *The Occult*, and this was payment in advance. The money came just in time for a holiday we had booked in France, and for the next two weeks we stayed in the best hotels, ate the best food and drank the best wine. Understandably, I felt considerable affection for the Japanese.

In mid-1986 I was in need of a long holiday. Since finishing *The Psychic Detectives*, I had written a novel called *The Personality Surgeon*, a short biography of Rudolf Steiner, and a study of the evidence for life after death called *Afterlife*. And at the time of the phone call from Tokyo, I had recently finished a fantasy novel called *Spider World*.

This had come about through my meeting with a neighbour called Donald Seaman, a retired foreign correspondent from the *Daily Express*. When the spies Guy Burgess and Donald Maclean had defected to Moscow in 1951, Don had been asked to cover the case, and had ended by writing a book about it. And since the spy novels of John Le Carré and Len Deighton had become so popular, Don had decided to apply his knowledge of espionage to writing a thriller. The result was *The Bomb That Could Lip Read*, which sold a respectable number of copies and established his name as a spy novelist. So when he was offered early retirement and a 'golden handshake', Don decided to move to Cornwall and supplement his income by writing a thriller every year.

He and his wife Irene found themselves a beautiful little cottage in a hamlet called Penare; a wishing well in the garden made it look like a set from a Walt Disney film. Unfortunately, the cottage was owned by the National Trust, and Don spent most of his golden handshake renting it on a long lease. His next four spy novels were reasonably successful, but by the time I met him in 1983, he was already beginning to experience the difficulties of most authors who try to live by writing alone.

Don and I used to walk our dogs on the cliffs between Gorran Haven and Penare every afternoon, and discuss our work and current problems. His were mainly financial, and one day, when he was in urgent need of money to pay the rates, I suggested that we might collaborate on a sequel to the *Encyclopedia of Murder* I had written with Pat Pitman in 1960. The same publisher – Weidenfeld – accepted it, and the advance enabled Don to clear his debts.

Don had travelled all over the world as a foreign correspondent, and had some amazing stories. I often suggested that he should, like Negley Farson, write his autobiography. But the truth was that Don lacked Negley's drive and charisma. His idea of heaven was simply to walk on the Dodman – the peninsula between Gorran Haven and Penare – twice a day, and relax with a glass of whisky in the evening.

After *An Encyclopedia of Modern Murder*, Don suggested that we might write an encyclopedia of scandal. The idea struck me as too journalistic, but the more I thought about it, the more interesting it seemed – after all, there were some marvellous historical scandals, like the South Sea Bubble and the Dreyfus affair and Queen Caroline's adulteries; so we got the book commissioned, and once again Don was able to pay his rates and tax bill. The only problem was that he was a far slower writer than I was, so I ended by writing two thirds of both books.

Bored with writing spy thrillers, Don decided to transfer his scene to the late nineteenth century, and write about a plot by the IRA to assassinate Queen Victoria. His agent was enthusiastic, and assured him that the book – called *Chase Royal* – would transform his lifestyle. It did – but in the wrong direction, and poor sales made his financial problems worse than ever. I sometimes had to lend him the money to avert severe crises – to Joy's disgust, since our overdraft was far larger than Don's. But we had collateral, since we owned our house, and Don hadn't.

He toyed with the idea of writing a science fiction novel, about a nuclear-powered spacecraft that crashes into a Canadian lake and causes nightmarish mutations, but his heart was not in it. One evening, after watching a television programme about insect defence, I had a flash of inspiration. And the next day I said: 'I think I've got it. A novel called *Spider World*, about a future date in which the earth is taken over by giant telepathic spiders, who breed human beings for food.' But Don wrinkled his nose. 'It doesn't sound my cup of tea.' But by now I had become enthusiastic about the idea. 'Then why don't we write it together? I'll get my publisher to commission it, and give you the first part of the advance.'

My publisher accepted the idea, and paid us £5,000, half the advance, which I gave to Don. We agreed that we would write alternate chapters, and that I would write the first. I began *Spider World* at the end of March 1985.

I set the first scene in an underground burrow in the desert, where a small family of human beings, including the seventeen-year-old hero, Niall, hide from the spider balloons that patrol overhead. The spiders are telepathic, and can pick up the thought-vibrations of humans. And for some unknown reason, they regard humans with a virulent hatred, and are determined that none shall remain free. As their thought-beams scan the desert like radar, the humans have to learn to restrain their panic, which would give them away immediately . . .

As I wrote, I found myself becoming increasingly absorbed. I had done a great deal of research on deserts and their inhabitants, such as tiger beetles and trapdoor spiders – which hide underground and leap out on their prey – so there was no shortage of interesting, and often rather gruesome, material. And as I wrote I experienced a sensation like an aeroplane taking off. I had never felt so completely gripped by anything I had written.

Every other day Don would ask me: 'Would you like me to start writing my bit yet?' and I would answer: 'No, let me do a few more pages . . .' Then one day, Don said: 'Look, you're obviously enjoying this so much that I don't want to interrupt you. Why don't you go ahead and do the whole book?' I agreed that he could keep the advance we had received, and I told my publisher that *Spider World* had ceased to be a collaboration, and would appear under my name only.

The main problem was that the book was going to be far longer than I had intended. It was supposed to be a hundred thousand words – about 250 pages. But by the time I had reached a hundred thousand words, it was obvious that I was not even halfway through. Niall's family have been captured by the spiders, and taken to the spider city, where they are enslaved. Niall escapes, and makes his way to a strange white tower in the centre of the city, which proves to be a kind of time capsule, left by an earlier race of human beings before they abandoned earth to escape the impact of a giant comet. And as Niall learns about his forebears, he begins to grasp the possibility of restoring the human race to freedom . . . And at that point there was still a long way to go. The book was not finished until the end of February 1986, exactly eleven months after it had been started.

My publisher was impressed with it, but said that it was obviously too long – a quarter of a million words. The solution was to publish it in two volumes. And, to my delight, Grafton also agreed to double the advance. We used this to pay a tax bill of £5,400.

By the time we received the invitation from Tokyo, I had already started my next book, an *Encyclopedia of Unsolved Mysteries*. This had been commissioned by Harrap (who had already published an anthology of my work called *The Essential Colin Wilson*) and they paid an advance of £10,000, half on signature. This I decided to write in collaboration with my son Damon, who was now twenty-one, and had still not quite decided what he intended to do with his life. I felt that collaborating with me would be the easiest way of teaching him to write.

'Teaching him to write' sounds more laborious than it was; in fact, my main piece of advice was simply to go through every sentence and strike out each unnecessary word.

It cost me a struggle with my conscience not to ask Don to collaborate, for I knew he needed the money. But his financial problems were unending, and I had my own family to think about.

When Don's bank manager wrote to him forbidding him to write any more cheques, I had to rescue him again, to Joy's indignation; but I felt I owed him a debt for allowing me to take over *Spider World*.

Joy and I set out for Japan in late October 1986; by that time, Damon and I had completed the *Encyclopedia of Unsolved Mysteries*, and he was already writing like a professional.

The friend who had arranged our trip was an interpreter named Kazue Kobata. I had met her when she came to interview me for Japanese *Playboy*. Our hosts there were to be the monks of Koyasan, one of Japan's greatest Buddhist monasteries, which was celebrating its thousandth anniversary. It had been founded by a monk named Kobo daishi or Kukai, whose sect was known as Shingon (or Esoteric) Buddhism.

Although I had been deeply influenced by Buddhism in my teens, my attitude towards it had become slowly less wholehearted. It seemed to me that compared to Hinduism, whose aim is union with God (or Brahman), Buddhism seems basically negative. The legend tells how the parents of Prince Gautama decided that he should be protected from all knowledge of evil, and so kept him in their palace. But one day the boy was out with his tutor when they saw a sick man. The prince asked, 'What is wrong with him?' and the tutor replied, 'He is sick – it is something that happens to everyone.' The next day they saw a very old man, and again the prince asked, 'What is wrong with him?' and the tutor replied, 'He is old – it happens to everyone.' Finally they saw a dead man's funeral procession. Again, the prince asked, 'What is wrong with him?' and was told: 'He is dead – it happens to everyone.' And Gautama was so shocked that he began to wonder how human beings could escape misery and death.

His answer was the eightfold path, which involves a high level of religious self-discipline. This enables men to achieve complete detachment from their desires, and to attain the state of nirvana, union with the absolute.

Yet it had always seemed to me that the aim of self-discipline is not detachment: it is an attempt to understand the unknown potentialities of human consciousness – those amazing potentialities of which I had become aware through the study of subjects like psychometry, precognition and out-of-the-body experience. Yeats, I felt, was right: the aim is 'profane perfection of mankind'.

Now shortly before we set out, I had read a book about Kobo daishi, the founder of Esoteric Buddhism, which had been sent to me by my future hosts, and had been delighted to see that one of his main teachings is 'enlightenment in this very life'. This, surely, described my own aim. Which is why, when we caught our flight from Heathrow, I felt much happier about what lay ahead of me.

Our plane took off at 2.45 in the afternoon, and we halted in Anchorage, Alaska, at 3 pm local time. It seemed strange to be in blazing sunlight when my body knew it was midnight. It was even stranger to have dinner on the plane at 2 o'clock in the morning, and stranger still to arrive in Tokyo at 8.30 in the morning London time and discover that it was 4.30 in the afternoon. I felt completely disoriented. We then caught a flight to Osaka – the nearest city to the monastery of Koyasan – arriving at 7 o'clock in the evening, although my body knew it was only 11 in the morning.

Two hours later, we sat down to dinner with the Reverend Matsunaga, the rector of Koyasan University, another monk, a representative of Mainichi newspaper, which was sponsoring our trip, and our friend and interpreter Kazue. The Japanese dinner consisted of courses of raw fish, sea weed, turtle soup and rice, washed down with saké. That night I slept very badly, largely because my body could not understand why I had gone to bed at three in the afternoon. (I should have asked my doctor for sleeping tablets – it would have saved me a great deal of maladjustment.)

After a press conference at which I was dopey with fatigue, we were given lunch and taken to look at Osaka, after which we caught a train to Koyasan. The monastery lies ten miles up a mountain, and on the cable car, which climbed at 45 degrees through lovely autumn woods, I disregarded Kazue's advice and fell asleep, a mistake that would cost me another night's sleep.

It was cold at Koyasan, so that after our vegetarian dinner we retired to the Reverend Matsunaga's room, where we sat around a table covered with a thick cloth that reached the floor, and a hot stove under the table close to our knees. The monks had a taste for scotch whisky, which they drank in surprising quantities. I, being a wine drinker, avoided it and stuck to saké. After that, I took a bath in a huge stone tub, with water about four feet deep. A young Japanese professor named Hirose Yoshiji (who asked me to call him Hiro) joined me in the steaming water, and startled me by remarking: 'Ah, Mr Wilson, in England you must be as famous as Charles Dickens!' He was too young for me to suspect him of sarcasm, and when I replied: 'In England, few people have heard of me,' he looked astonished.

That night I slept on a mat in a small room in a temple, and after two hours sleep lay awake for the rest of the night. The result was that when I dressed in the morning I felt not only exhausted but also hung over.

An 'English breakfast' consisting of two cold fried eggs on toast did nothing to improve it. After that we were taken on a tour of the temple complex, which was vast. In a kind of cemetery, consisting of elaborate tombs, I felt like nothing so much as lying down on one of them and falling asleep. (Joy, who had been sensible enough to keep herself awake on the train, was wide awake and full of curiosity.) A point came where I realised that I had to make a real mental effort to throw off this fatigue. So I concentrated very hard, and did the 'St Neot Margin trick' – awakening myself to a sense of crisis. To my relief, it worked, and I suddenly began to feel less like a zombie. The Master Kobo daishi was obviously right – the answer lay in the mind itself.

Nevertheless, it was a relief to catch a cable car back to Osaka around midday, then take the 'bullet train' – which travels at 120 miles an hour – to Tokyo. Mount Fuji looked unbelievably beautiful as we passed. We were in Tokyo by six, and took a taxi past the Emperor's palace (Hirohito was still alive), and arrived at the magnificent Akasaka Prince Hotel, where we had a suite that overlooked the whole of Tokyo. There Kazue presented us with our air tickets to Australia, the next leg of our journey (for which our generous hosts had also paid), and a further million yen (more than £4,000) as my fee for coming to Japan, as well as 'pocket money' of about £50 a day (each) for lunch and dinner. (In 1986, Japan was at the height of its economic boom and the sense of wealth was awe-inspiring.)

I was worried in case I was still suffering from jet-lag when I had to deliver my first lecture at midday the next day. But all went well: I got a good night's sleep, and woke at nine the next morning, feeling greatly refreshed, and ate an English breakfast of bacon, egg and tomato. My guardian angel was back on the job again.

Lecturing to a vast audience who were all listening through earphones was an unsettling experience, for I had to speak slowly so Kazue could translate. The result was that there was no 'response' from the audience. But I was used to talking into a tape recorder – I had been keeping my diary on cassette for the past three years – so it came easily. But it was good to hear later that my lecture had been received with enthusiasm.

That afternoon, after a late lunch of sushi (eaten out of a square wooden box with a sliding lid), we were taken on a shopping expedition to the

Ginza, then back to the hotel to attend a symposium on mandalas. I was by now so tired that I wanted nothing except to go to my room and rest. I knew I was due to attend a reception in the evening, but since most receptions consist of standing around holding a glass and accepting canapés from trays I felt I would hardly be missed.

I was just drinking a glass of French wine that I had been able to buy at a reasonable price in the Ginza when the phone rang. It was Kazue asking where we were. So we hurried down – and discovered that everyone was waiting for us to arrive. When we appeared, they clapped, then we had to walk between two lines of applauding guests to our place at the table. I had not been so surprised since 1973, when I arrived in Beirut to find the mayor and corporation waiting for us.

It took me some time to realise that in Japan I was as well known as I had been in the Middle East, and that Hiro had been perfectly serious in assuming I was as famous as Charles Dickens. When I appeared at a large bookstore, the queue for my lecture stretched around the block, and many had to be turned away.

Another charming Japanese custom was to hand me an envelope after press interviews or broadcasts, which contained anything from £50 to £250. In Hiroshima, where I lectured and made two television appearances in the Peace Park, they paid me more than £800. Joy, who felt we ought not to be making money out of the miseries of Hiroshima, wanted to donate the money to the Hibakshi – survivors of the atom bomb – but our hosts flatly refused to take it.

During the rest of that tour I had to make constant use of the 'St Neot Margin trick': arousing my mind to a state of intense concentration by envisaging some crisis. (That episode of losing Sally in Cheltenham was a useful starting point.) It was not the temples that caused my vitality to slump – they were often fascinating, with their rock gardens and pools and demon guardians. The problem lay in the lunches, even if they were only noodles and beer. After this there might be hundreds of steps to climb, often covered with cherry blossoms, to reach a temple that looked down on a precipitous valley with a waterfall. There was no point in climbing mechanically; the mind had to be concentrated until all this was more than a kind of dream.

This point had struck me forcefully after reading a passage in the writings of Kobo daishi. It was a discourse by the Taoist monk Kyobu, after listening to the remarks of a Confucian monk. He explains that, in olden times, people drank the blood of a sacrificial animal and made a vow before listening to the doctrines of the Emperor Huang, and were therefore in the right state of attentiveness to absorb them. Wisdom cannot be attained by merely listening to words of wisdom without preparation.

So when I entered a temple, I did my best to still my mind completely, to achieve simultaneously a state of relaxation combined with wide-awakeness, as if listening for some very faint sound, or perhaps to the silence itself. And if I did this for a few minutes, my relaxation would deepen – my panic attacks had taught me how to do this – and the silence would seem to yield new depths, as if I had penetrated to the other side of silence. I believe it was the temples themselves that caused this to happen. Centuries of prayer and meditation had imprinted themselves on the place itself, so that I responded to it like a dowser to water. It made no difference if I was tired after climbing hundreds of steps; a state of deep inner calm would descend fairly quickly. And in this state, I occasionally experienced brief flashes of an underlying reality that was not normally accessible to the senses, the timeless reality I had occasionally glimpsed in my teens when meditating on the *Bhagavad Gita*.

I was also struck by Kyobu's remark: 'When you see a beautiful girl with a slender waist, think of her as a devil or ghost.' Kobo daishi recognised what had become increasingly clear to me since writing the *Criminal History*: that sex is an illusion that is designed to persuade us to propagate the species, and that it does so by filling us with a kind of fever. At that time, the American murderer Ted Bundy was much in my mind, since I had written about him in the *Criminal History*. Bundy had been passing a lighted window on the campus of the University of Washington, in Seattle, when he had glimpsed a girl getting undressed. It had produced such a violent fever of desire that from then on he had spent all his evenings peering through windows. He had, in his own words, 'turned it into a project'. Inevitably, he finally began breaking into the bedrooms and attacking the women. Then he graduated to abducting the girls, driving them to some distant place, and spending hours violating them. And now, at the time I was in Japan, he was on Death Row in Florida, awaiting execution – an appalling example of a man who had been dragged down to the depths by the sexual illusion.

On that first trip to Japan, I met a man who had been caught in the same whirlpool. His name was Issei Sagawa, and ten years before he introduced himself to me at a book signing, he had killed a girl and eaten parts of her body.

He had been a student at the Sorbonne at the time, taking a degree in literature, and had become fascinated by a Dutch classmate named Renée Hartevelt. Ever since he had been a teenager, Issei had dreamed about beautiful blondes – not making love to them, but killing them and eating them. One day he invited her to his flat, ostensibly to teach him German, and, as she sat reading poetry aloud, shot her in the back of the neck. Then he undressed her, raped her, sliced off one of her buttocks and ate part of it raw. He told me that as he did so, he was in an intense state of sexual excitement.

He dismembered the body in the bath, then bought two suitcases with wheels, and asked a taxi driver to take him to the Bois de Bologne. When a couple approached, he fled, leaving the suitcases, and the mystified pair looked inside . . .

He was easily caught – the taxi driver took the police to the flat. In the refrigerator, they found more of Renée's body, wrapped in greaseproof paper.

At first investigators assumed it to be a *crime passionel*. But when he told the examining magistrate about his lifelong desire to eat a girl, he was certified insane and confined in a mental home. Eventually he was released and returned to Japan, where he became a celebrity. A book he wrote about the murder sold hundreds of thousands of copies.

What fascinated me as I listened to his story was his explanation of how it had all come about. He had been born prematurely, so was always a tiny child. When he was three, his father and uncle had played a game in which his uncle was a wicked giant and his father a good knight. They fought over Issei and his brother, and the good knight was killed, and the two children placed in a cooking pot.

From then on, Issei's daydreams were about being cooked and eaten, which gave him a peculiar sexual thrill. And when, as a teenager, he began to experience sexual desire, it was not to make love to a girl, but to eat her. In Paris, he stared at the bare arms of girls in cafés, and dreamed of how they would taste. Finally, with only a few weeks to go before he returned to Japan, he felt it was time to act. That was when he bought a carbine, and invited Renée Hartevelt back to his flat.

On a later visit to Tokyo, I agreed to do a long interview with Issei for a magazine. It took place in my hotel suite. Joy was horrified at the idea of meeting him, and went out for the afternoon. But when she returned, Issei was still there. As I introduced her she shrank away and did not offer her hand. And when she heard me inviting Issei to the Press Club for dinner, she drew me aside and whispered: 'If they recognise him they'll order you both to leave.'

She was wrong. We had an excellent dinner – I think Issei ate raw lamb – and Joy sat next to him. He was small, with hands like a child, and obviously shy and nervous. And after we had put him in a taxi, she said: 'What a delightful man!' She had recognised – what I knew from the beginning – that Issei was not a monster, but simply a man who, for reasons even he did not understand, had been hypnotised by the sexual illusion.

Such thoughts were in my mind as we visited the temples. I recall attending an official meal when a geisha knelt beside me, refilling my glass or replenishing my plate. It was easy to see how, in this culture where women occupied a subordinate position, such a girl might also be expected to perform sexual services. And since she was slim and pretty, the thought induced a pleasant excitement. Yet another part of me, the part that had learned to sink into deep relaxation in the temples, looked on with total detachment, aware that she was like a sticky sweet that would make me feel sick.

Compared to these insights, the actual ceremony to celebrate the thousandth anniversary of Koyasan seemed almost anticlimactic. The temple was vast, and open on four sides. The three guests – myself, Lyall Watson and Fritjof Capra – sat in the centre of this temple, with an enormous mandala behind us, so that three quarters of the audience could not even see us. In the morning there was a Buddhist service, and we watched the monks parade in. It was cool, but I was wearing a leather overcoat and scarf, and when my feet got cold, I slipped them into my hat. Lyall Watson and Capra were thinly clad and sat there with their teeth chattering. At 2 o'clock they rushed back to their rooms for warm underwear.

In the afternoon I opened the symposium by briefly explaining the 'pyramid of consciousness', a concept I had developed in my book on Wilhelm Reich: that everyday consciousness has a disjointed quality that could be compared to a billiard table covered with scattered balls. When we concentrate, they come together in the middle of the table. But in moments of intense concentration, it is as if the balls started climbing on top of one another to form a second layer. If we could concentrate so hard that they formed a pyramid, it would never collapse, for sheer intensity would create a feedback effect that would make it permanent. This, I said, was probably close to what Kobo daishi called 'enlightenment in this very existence'. And later, in a longer address, I expanded the concept by talking about Faculty X – when we are in a state that induces an awareness of the reality of the past.

Meanwhile, the audience of a thousand or so sat in the cold, most of them unable to see the speakers, while Joy and I thanked our lucky stars that we were among the guests of honour who had been provided with blankets to cover our knees, and small bags of chemicals which glowed like hot water bottles. That afternoon made me realise that the monks who founded Koyasan must have had enough discomforts to turn them all into saints.

Forty-eight hours later, Joy and I landed at Sydney, and there we separated, Joy on her way to see her brother Neil in Townsville, and I for Melbourne.

There I immediately became aware of the contrast between the manners of the Japanese and those of the Australians. I needed a phone card, and went into the office of the airline to ask where I could buy one. The girl behind the counter stared at me as if I was mad, then told me I would have to apply to the telephone company. I walked fifty yards down the concourse and enquired at the newsagent; they immediately sold me one. So on my way back to my gate, I called in the airline office and told the girl that if anyone asked about a phone card in future, she could simply direct them to the newsagent. She glared at me virulently and snapped 'Oh *thenkyou!*'

In Melbourne I was scheduled to give more lectures, the main one being at Latrobe University, where my friend Howard Dossor, who was writing a book about me, was an administrator. He was waiting at the gate to meet me, and beside him was my old girlfriend of my Coffee House days, Carole Ann – still, in her mid-forties, as pretty as ever.

After our affair in 1955, Carole Ann had gone to a singing teacher, and discovered she had an excellent soprano voice. She met an Australian actor named Terry Gill, married him and emigrated to Australia. In Melbourne they opened a restaurant and music hall called The Naughty Nineties, and became a celebrated husband and wife team. They enjoyed performing duets from light operas, and musicals like *The Phantom of the Opera*. I spent a pleasant evening there and was amazed that Carole Ann had become such a fine soprano.

Terry was a big, good-natured man who reminded me of my younger brother Barry, so I liked him instantly.

I had seen Carole Ann in London over the years, for she was the kind of person who likes to keep in touch with old friends. She had kept her figure trim with daily workouts in the gym, whereas I had put on a great deal of weight – a writer's occupational hazard.

As to Howard Dossor, who had arranged this lecture trip to Melbourne, he had written to me two years earlier, and then come to see me. Before becoming a university administrator, he had been a clergyman – a profession that might be guessed from his gentle, earnest manner. Then he had become ill with cancer, and been told that he had only a year to live. He had always been interested in my ideas, and now decided to devote the time he had left to writing a book about me. The cancer had been cured, but by then he had lost his Christian faith – an outcome he attributes partly to me, and partly to his study of the Greek novelist Nikos Kazantzakis, whom I also admired. So he became an academic, and also began a collection of my work which must be the largest in the world.

Latrobe University proved to be a beautiful campus, green and spacious. But what startled me about it was the amount of litter that had been left lying around. This was not due to the lack of janitors or of litter bins, but to the fact that students preferred to throw newspapers, plastic bags, beer cans or paper cups on the ground or in a flower bed when there was a litter bin a few feet away. After the cleanness of Japan's streets and campuses, there was something oddly shocking about this untidiness, and I made a note in my journal for the book on serial killers I was planning, to the effect that this lack of a sense of responsibility is the beginning of criminality.

The point seemed to be underlined by a murder case that was making the headlines on the day I landed. A married couple from Perth, David and Catherine Birnie, had been arrested and charged with the abduction and murder of four women in the past four weeks. Birnie, a slightly built man in his thirties, was apparently sexually insatiable, and needed sex six times a day. He worked in a car-wrecker's yard and sold spare parts. And when a 22-year-old student came to the house to buy tyres, Birnie was unable to resist, and forced her into the bedroom at knife-point, then raped her while his wife looked on. She was then taken to a secluded place, where he raped her again, then strangled her. The same thing happened to three more girls, the only difference being that Birnie kept them captive for days while raping them. One was strangled by the wife, who felt her husband was taking too much interest in her. A fifth victim, a seventeen-year old girl, succeeded in escaping after three days, and gave the alarm.

Birnie was the perfect example of what I meant by the sexual illusion. My friend Ronald Duncan had often questioned me about my interest in crime, evidently suspecting some sinister perversion. He could not understand that when I studied a murder case I suddenly became aware of this problem of illusion and reality. In Koyasan and the other temples I caught a clear glimpse of reality; such glimpses are not easy to find in the modern world. But a murder case made me aware of these values by their absence, like a shadow cast on a whitewashed wall. I experienced the same thing to a far lesser degree looking at the beer cans on the Latrobe campus. It was not, of course, that Australia lacked these values more than England or America, but that the contrast with Japan made it more obvious.

Where evil was concerned I had always been a platonist – that is, I felt that there is no evil as such, but that everyone is striving towards his own ideal of good. But the Birnie case raised some doubts, and I found myself wondering whether this might be more than a case of clinical hypersexuality, and be some kind of 'possession' by an active force of evil.

Another story I heard in Melbourne strengthened that suspicion. Howard Dossor introduced me to a remarkable painter called Bert Tucker, whose work was as highly regarded as that of Sidney Nolan. And Bert told me of an extraordinary experience that made me deeply thoughtful.

Some years earlier, Bert had spent an evening eating dinner at the home of friends, and set out to walk home late at night. He was living in a room in a boarding house. But as he came closer to home, he began to experience a curious sense of reluctance to go back. He told himself this was absurd, and forced himself to walk on, yet the feeling became stronger and then, as he mounted the stairs, overpowering. As he walked into the room he was assailed by a revolting stench – like the smell of hot, wet fur in zoos. As he stood fighting off terror – still convinced that this was all absurd – he saw something on the coverlet of his bed. It was a dead mouse. It was lying with its legs spread out, and a trail of urine behind it that had still not soaked into the bedsheet. And when he reached out and touched it, the body was still warm – it had only just died.

Suddenly he knew that if he spent the night in the room he would not walk out alive. So he hurried back to his friends and spent the night there.

What was it? He told me that the landlady had an idiot son, who was in an asylum most of the time, but occasionally came home for the weekend. He was home that weekend, in the room below Bert's. His presence, Bert felt, had brought something evil into the house.

And some other force – perhaps his 'guardian angel' – had done its best to warn him. And, when he refused to accept that warning, had killed the mouse on his bed.

The conclusion, it seemed, was that there are indeed forces of good as well as evil, and both could intervene actively in our world.

It was a good time to start thinking again about the problems of the paranormal, for my editor at HarperCollins, Jim Cochrane, had asked me if I would like to write another book on 'the occult'. At the time, it was the last thing I wanted to do; I felt I had said everything I had to say in *The Occult* and *Mysteries*. But my experiences in Japan, and Bert's story about the mouse, made me feel there was still a lot I had overlooked. I spent a great deal of time during that week in Melbourne and the journey home thinking about the new book.

A good starting point seemed to be an extraordinary story told to me by my friend Mark Bredin, a concert pianist. One late evening after a concert, he was returning home in a taxi along the Bayswater Road, when he suddenly knew with *absolute certainty* that at the Queensway traffic light, a taxi would try to jump the light and hit them sideways. He wondered if he should tell his driver, then felt the man would think him mad. But at the next traffic light, a taxi tried to jump the light and hit them sideways.

How could he know the future? Presumably because he was totally relaxed and was using some odd ability we all possess. The historian A. L. Rowse had told me how one afternoon, in his college rooms, he suddenly knew that if he crossed two quadrangles and went into the library, he would find two young men embracing. He hurried there and found them, as he expected, in one another's arms.

Another friend told me a story that seemed equally strange. Kay Lunnis, who often spent days in our house helping Joy to look after the children, told us how, when she was seriously ill in hospital, she had felt herself rise above her body so she could look down on it. I would once have dismissed this as a hallucination due to fever, but I had come across too many such cases of 'out-of-the-body experiences' since I began studying the paranormal.

I had used these stories in *The Occult*, yet it had never struck me that it implies some unknown power of the human mind, which becomes available when we are deeply relaxed. How could I call myself an existentialist if I failed to take such powers into account?

T. E. Lawrence was obviously in the same state of relaxation when he experienced that feeling of complete wakefulness as he set out in the dawn that awakened the senses before the intellect. Relaxation seems to be the common denominator of such experiences.

But I was also aware that too much relaxation can be dangerous. I recalled an impressive story told to me by my friend Joyce Collin-Smith, the sister-in-law of one of Ouspenky's most brilliant disciples, Rodney Collin. In August 1960, she became a follower of the Hindu guru, the Maharishi Mahesh Yogi, who was convinced that the world could be transformed by 'transcendental meditation'.

She described how she had gone to the house the Maharishi had rented near Regent's Park, taking a flower as an offering. The Maharishi, a little man with a high voice and a sing-song Indian accent, taught her a brief mantra in Sanskrit, which immediately brought a strange, deep sense of peace. He told her to go and sit near the window, on the carpet. As she did so, the mantra seemed to be repeating itself in her brain without her volition. Time slipped peacefully by – three hours – before she noticed the evening traffic in the street, and realised she had to get home to cook her husband's dinner.

From then on, the mantra would plunge her into the same deep state of blissful serenity. She saw the Maharishi do the same thing repeatedly – once a long queue stretched down the corridor of a hotel in Oxford, and the Maharishi saw each person in turn, accepted the flower, then touched the donor on the forehead and told him to go and sit down – and all obviously experienced the same instantaneous feeling of peace.

Joyce was by then acting as the Maharishi's unpaid secretary, and it was she who took a phone call from the management saying that an old lady who lived on the same floor was complaining about the noise and threatening to leave. Joyce asked the Maharishi: 'What shall we do?' 'Do nothing,' said the Maharishi, smiling benevolently. 'It will be all right.' And so it was. They heard nothing more from the old lady.

This was one of many examples of the Maharishi's powers, which were to some extent telepathic – as was illustrated on another occasion, when he read Joyce's mind as she sat in the audience listening to him, and answered the question she meant to ask.

Every one of the Maharishi's followers seemed to be happy and light-hearted; he was surrounded by an atmosphere of gaiety. But Joyce soon noticed that not all was well. Some of the disciples began spending more and more time sitting in a state of bliss, and it was obvious that they were becoming less capable of coping with everyday life. They didn't want to come back and face reality.

Joyce herself began to experience something more disturbing. She found it increasingly difficult to focus her mind, and seemed to see too deep into the underlying reality of things. She had always understood *intellectually* that everything changes, but now she could actually see it happening. Looking at her hands, she would see them change into the hands of a child, and at the same time into the hands of an old woman, then into a skeleton. Looking at a chair, she could see it as new timber still smelling of sap, and as a worn-out old chair about to be thrown on the bonfire. Everything fluctuated all the time.

Finally she could stand it no longer, and decided to commit suicide. She took a rope and went to a tree in the garden.

But as she looked at the rope, she suddenly noticed that it was *staying still*, remaining unchanged. Instead of dissolving into strands, then into flax, or becoming old and frayed, it was holding steady. The emergency had shaken her subconscious mind awake. Which meant that she had to set out to train her mind to fix her attention on the present. And as soon as she learned to do this, the problem went away.

By this time she was becoming disillusioned with the Maharishi, who was changing from a child-like guru into a super-tycoon, so she left the movement.

Joyce had discovered same trick I had learned to control the panic attacks: *focusing* the mind to prevent it from wavering. The answer lies in one word: attention.

The Japanese master Ikkyu was asked by a workman to write something on his tablet. He wrote: 'Attention.' The workman looked disappointed. 'Can't you write something else?' So Ikkyu wrote: 'Attention, attention.' The workman asked: 'But what does attention mean?' Ikkyu replied: 'Attention means attention.'

In fact, concentrated attention enables us to push the mind up to the level that I have labelled 'higher focus'. And in states of higher focus we experience a rush of energy.

So I began writing the book that would become *Beyond the Occult*, into which I tried to put everything about mysticism and the paranormal I had learned in the past twenty years. I regard it as my best book. It contains two insights that I feel are among the most important I ever had.

The first illustrates how difficult it is to recall such insights later.

It came when I was driving up to Plymouth to meet someone at BBC Television to discuss a series about the paranormal. As it flashed into my head, I saw at once that it was one of those basic unifying insights that I ought to make an intense effort to remember. Luckily, I had a pocket tape recorder with me, and talked into it as I drove along. Then I had lunch with the producer, drove home – and completely forgot about the insight.

Some months later, I was driving again to Plymouth when I recalled that I had had an important insight on this same stretch of road. But it simply refused to come back. Then I remembered the tape recording. It was hard to find – I had made several tapes since then – but I finally located it. And I realised that it was, indeed, a major insight, and that I had come close to losing it permanently.

I called the insight 'upside-downness', meaning the state in which negative emotions can stand us on our heads, producing a mild form of insanity. A person suffering from frantic jealousy is suffering from upside downness; so is someone consumed by hatred or egoism or envy.

When we are 'the right way up' we see the world practically and rationally. Strong emotions or unpleasant physical sensations can completely distort our normal view of things.

You could say that most of us can be divided into three people, and these correspond to the mind, the emotions and the body. In our social lives, the mind is, in effect, the ruler. If we become very ill – if, for example, we are suffering from high fever – the body becomes the ruler. But this is rare, and in any case, we are accustomed to the body's vagaries, so it doesn't bother us all that much.

Emotions are a different matter. Strong emotions can be like a violent storm that sweeps away all rationality. And if *we allow ourselves to be taken in by them*, it is exactly as if our feet have turned into gas-filled balloons and we suddenly find ourselves floating upside-down.

We might turn this into a parable in the manner of Confucius, and say that when the intellect is the emperor, and the emotions the grand vizier, the kingdom is harmonious and happy. But when emotions usurp the throne and force the emperor to become their servant, the kingdom descends into misery and chaos.

Moreover, when we allow upside-downness to provoke us into doing something absurd and self-defeating, we invariably tell ourselves that we were justified because we were placed under intolerable pressure.

Here is an example. An American friend of mine, who had been a close friend of the film star James Dean, told me that he had become so angry at being stuck in a New York traffic jam that he simply a-bandoned his car and went into the nearest cinema. Of course, he was heavily fined – but he told me it was 'worth it'. He genuinely felt that he had made a justified protest, in the true spirit of James Dean, against New York traffic.

Many serial sex killers operate on the same logic, declaring that all women are whores, and deserve what they get. Without exception, they are 'Right Men'.

Of course, such instances convince you and me that *we* are not in the least like that. But we are forgetting that 'being the right way up' requires a kind of effort similar to the effort a baby has to make to walk upright; most people experience dozens of brief episodes of upside-downness every day, while some apparently normal people are like it most of the time.

The appalling truth is that upside-downness is one of the worst perils we face. You could almost imagine it as a kind of homicidal demon whose job is to depress and discourage us, and whose ultimate triumph would be to make us commit suicide. He seldom shows his face, preferring to inject depression and weariness by stealth. But his activities are easy enough to observe when you feel energetic and confident – that is, in a state of 'spring morning consciousness'. Then you notice how easy it is to slip into fatigue and self-doubt. And before you know where you are, the vizier has tossed the emperor off the throne and taken his place.

As a teenager I woke up almost every morning with a watery feeling of anxiety in the pit of my stomach, expecting the day to bring unspecified miseries and humiliations. That was upside-downness. But the sense of revelation that came on spring mornings was a sudden glimpse of man's future destiny – consciousness *without* upside-downness. This is why Maslow's students had had peak experiences as soon as they began to talk and think about peak experiences: they saw that consciousness without upside-downness is a normal potentiality of human beings. And the moment they saw this they turned the right way up.

The second of my insights came when I was in California in 1987.

Two friends had driven me from San Francisco to the Esalen Institute at Big Sur, where I had to lecture. As I climbed into the car for the return drive, I began thinking about levels of consciousness, and seeing how many I could distinguish.

I decided to begin with the basic state of non-consciousness we experience in deep sleep, and to call this Level 0. So Level 1 is the dream state, which shades off into the hypnagogic (semi-waking) state.

Level 2 is 'mere awareness', as when you are gazing blankly out of the window, thinking of nothing. In a sense, 'you' are not really there at all.

In Level 3 we have become self-aware, but consciousness is dull and heavy. Sartre calls it 'nausea'. Every act of will costs a tremendous effort.

Level 4 is our ordinary everyday consciousness. But life still seems a hard battle, and it is easy to sink back towards 'nausea'. This is what Christina Rossetti meant when she wrote:

> Does the road wind uphill all the way?
> Yes, to the very end . . .

But as you struggle on, sheer doggedness seems to generate a feeling of strength, and at about halfway up Level 4, you begin to get a suspicion that perhaps you *can* win after all. Consciousness ceases to be dull and passive, and suddenly becomes active. And a rising feeling of optimism often culminates in the peak experience. This might be regarded as a kind of spark that leaps the gap between Level 4 and Level 5.

So what is Level 5? This is the state I sometimes call 'spring morning consciousness' – a bubbling sense of vitality, a feeling that 'all is well'. Life suddenly becomes self-evidently rich and infinitely exciting. This is the state Graham Greene experienced after playing Russian roulette.

Level 6 could be called 'magical consciousness'. It is what a child often feels on Christmas Day. Or imagine two honeymooners on a balcony overlooking a moonlit lake, with dark shapes of mountains in the distance, and a feeling that life is good and will continue to be good. In Level 6, just being awake seems to be a continuous mild peak experience.

As to Level 7, this is what I have called Faculty X, a state in which we are aware of the reality of other times and places. They seem as real as the present moment.

Level 7 is the highest level that need concern us as human beings – that is, the highest level we can achieve by sheer effort. The level that lies beyond this, Level 8, is 'mystical consciousness, and is so paradoxical and self-contradictory that it lies beyond the reach of the will. The only person I can recall who offered a more or less comprehensible description is Gurdjieff's disciple P. D. Ouspensky. It is to be found in his book *A New Model of the Universe*, in a chapter called 'Experimental Mysticism'.

Ouspensky does not tell us the details of how he achieved his states of mystical consciousness, but his biographer James Webb is probably correct in assuming that he used yogic and magical methods combined with the use of some sort of drug, almost certainly nitrous oxide – 'laughing gas'. Ouspensky states that the change took place more quickly and easily than he had expected. The account that follows is one of the most important and detailed in the whole literature of mysticism.

'The unknown', Ouspensky says, 'is unlike anything that we can suppose about it. The complete unexpectedness of everything that is met with in these experiences, from great to small, makes the description of them difficult.' And he goes on to make an observation of central importance:

First of all, everything is unified, everything is linked together, everything is explained by something else and in turn explains another thing. There is nothing separate, that is, nothing that can be named or described separately. In order to describe the first impressions, the first sensations, it is necessary to describe all at once. The new world with which one comes into contact has no sides, so that it is impossible to describe first one side and then the other. All of it is visible at every point . . .

Here we have one of the most basic assertions that all descriptions of mystical experience have in common. Everything is seen to be connected. And the word 'seen' deserves to be underlined. This world of infinite relationships, in which everything is connected with everything else, is seen all at once – from a bird's-eye view, as it were. And language instantly becomes useless, because it can only pin down one thing at a time. 'A man becomes lost amidst the infinite number of totally new impressions, for the expression of which he has neither words nor forms.'

What seems equally strange is that the normal sense of the distinction between objective and subjective disappeared:

Here I saw that the objective and the subjective could change places. The one could become the other. It is very difficult to express this. The habitual mistrust of the subjective disappeared; every thought, every feeling, every image, was immediately objectified in real substantial forms which differed in no way from the forms of objective phenomena; and at the same time objective phenomena somehow disappeared, lost all reality, appeared entirely subjective, fictitious, invented, having no real existence . . .

He goes on to say that this strange world resembled more than anything else 'a world of very complicated mathematical relations'.

This vision of infinite meaning made it very difficult to carry on a conversation, for between each word of the sentence so many ideas occurred that it was difficult for Ouspensky to remember what he intended to say next. He began a sentence with the words, 'I said yesterday . . .' but could simply get no further. The word 'I' raised hundreds of insights about the meaning of I, the word 'said' raised just as many ideas about speech and self-expression, each of which produced 'an explosion of thoughts, conjectures, comparisons and associations', and the word 'yesterday' led to endless thoughts and ideas about the nature of time, so that he was left with a feeling of breathlessness that made it impossible to continue.

Something strange also happened to his sense of time, so that when his companion spoke, there seemed to be an immense gap between each of his words. 'When he had finished a short sentence, the meaning of which did not reach me at all, I felt I had lived through so much during that time that we should never be able to understand one another again, that I had gone too far from him.'

All this, says Ouspensky, was accompanied by immensely powerful emotional states. 'I took in everything through feeling, and experienced emotions which never exist in life.' His inner world became a kaleidoscope of 'joy, wonder, rapture, horror, continually changing one into the other'. The state seemed to allow access to infinite knowledge, but when he looked for the answer to any particular question, it 'began far away and, gradually widening, included everything, so that finally the answer to the question included the answers to all possible questions'. He encountered the same problem when he looked at physical objects: an ashtray seemed to arouse an infinite succession of meanings and associations, so that he scrawled on a slip of paper: 'A man can go mad from one ashtray.' And the ashtray, like everything else, seemed to be communicating with him, almost as if it had a voice.

The remainder of Ouspensky's description is too long and detailed to quote here even in summary. His experiments usually ended in sleep, and his awakening the next morning was a dreary and disappointing experience. The ordinary world seemed unutterably dull:

. . . this world contained something extraordinarily oppressive: it was incredibly empty, colourless and lifeless. It was as though everything in it was wooden, as if it was an enormous wooden machine with creaking wooden wheels, wooden thoughts, wooden moods, wooden sensations; everything was terribly slow, scarcely moved, or moved with a melancholy wooden creaking. Everything was dead, soulless, feelingless.

They were terrible, these moments of awakening in an unreal world after a real one, in a dead world after a living, in a limited world, cut into small pieces, after an infinite and entire world.

In other words it is as if man found himself stranded on a planet whose gravity was so enormous that he was unable to stand upright – unable even to crawl on his hands and knees without immense effort. (Gurdjieff once said that our world is the cosmic equivalent of Outer Siberia.) In this iron world even thought is trapped by the tremendous gravity, so that it has to drag itself along the ground like a wounded animal. For the most part consciousness is little more than a mere reflection of the environment, and life is basically a mere succession of visual images, of being 'here and now'. This is why our world seems to be 'cut into small pieces', why its basic characteristic is 'separateness'. If you were utterly exhausted as you read this page it would dissolve into separate words, and even if you succeeded in grasping the meaning of an individual sentence the total meaning of the paragraph would still elude you. This is what our world is like. Everything stands separate and disconnected, and we have become so accustomed to this state of affairs that we assume that it is natural and inevitable. Yet it is not natural, any more than it is natural to fail to grasp the meaning of a sentence. And we realise this every time a spring morning fills us with a sense of the sheer interestingness of the world. 'Separateness' is unnatural; the true and natural state of affairs is a basic 'connectedness', just as Ouspensky realised during his mystical experiments.

In short this world, which seems to us so oppressively real, has been robbed of a dimension of reality by the feebleness of human consciousness and its inability to function efficiently in the powerful gravitational field of our universe. This is only a part of the problem. What turns a difficult situation into a dangerous one is that our mental numbness deprives us of all sense of direction, so that most human beings have given up any attempt to see things as a whole. In effect most of us waste our lives battling against the difficulties of the present moment, and when life offers us the occasional breathing space we are inclined to waste it in boredom or the search for amusement. This is why man, who is fundamentally a well-disposed and sociable creature, is capable of so much evil where his fellow-creatures are concerned. The harsh Siberian environment has made him brutal and short-sighted. Yet every flash of poetic or mystical insight makes us instantly aware that such a view is, quite literally, an absurdity.

One thing seems clear: the world glimpsed in these moments of insight is more real than the world of everyday reality. And everyone who has experienced these glimpses has seen the same thing; it always involves a sense of no longer being at the mercy of circumstance, of being a slave of material reality and our own bodies. We possess 'hidden powers', tremendous reserves of unsuspected strength.

Equally fascinating are Ouspensky's insights about time. In his 'Experimental Mysticism' chapter, Ouspensky offers some clues about how these ideas were developed. He speaks of the curious feeling of a 'lengthening of time', a speeding up so that seconds seem to turn into years or decades. He emphasises that the normal feeling of time remained as a background to this 'accelerated time', so that he was – so to speak – living in two 'times' at once. Our ordinary time merely has 'duration', but the second time has 'speed'. And since time has a flow from past to future, it would also seem to possess a third dimension – 'direction'.

It is because we are stuck in time that it seems inevitable that one event follows another like the notes on a piano keyboard. But, says Ouspensky, if time has three dimensions, if it is a 'cube' and not a line, and its forward flow can go up or down or sideways within a three-dimensional space, this obviously means that the next point on the line is not rigidly predetermined. It might go up or down or sideways. Life is full of non-actualised potentialities, says Ouspensky in the 'Eternal Recurrence' chapter of *A New Model of the Universe*, and when it comes to an end it starts all over again, so we go on living the same life for ever. Yet within this repetitive pattern there is room for infinite freedom.

So it does not have to be exactly the same: only dull and lazy people live the same life over and over again. More determined people strive to actualise their potentialities, and although the events are predetermined, like the notes of a symphony, they can be transformed by a great conductor. So their lives are changed infinitesimally each time.

It follows that the future is, to a large extent, predetermined. On one occasion Ouspensky asked himself whether communication with the dead was a possibility and immediately 'saw' someone with whom he urgently wanted to communicate. But what he 'saw' was not the person but his whole life, in a kind of four-dimensional continuum. At that moment Ouspensky realised that it was pointless to feel guilt about his own failure to be more helpful to this particular person because the events of this person's life were as unchangeable as the features of his face. 'Nobody could have changed anything in them, just as nobody could have changed the colour of his hair or eyes, or the shape of his nose . . .' In other words, what happened to the man was his 'destiny'.

It was also during these experiments that Ouspensky had a clear premonition that he would not be going to Moscow that Easter, as he fully intended to. He was able to foresee a sequence of events that would make his visit impossible. And in due course this sequence occurred exactly as he had foreseen it in his mystical state. Ouspensky, therefore, had no doubt that precognition is a reality. (J. B. Priestley borrowed Ouspensky's idea for his third 'time play', *I Have Been Here Before*, in which a thoroughly unsatisfactory character who has committed suicide out of self-pity makes a determined effort the 'second time round', and makes an altogether better job of his life.)

So, excluding the weird and paradoxical Level 8, I had worked out the basic 'normal' levels of consciousness. The above, I believe, gives a fairly complete account of my view of human consciousness and its potentialities. The interesting thing is that up to the halfway point – Level $4\frac{1}{2}$ consciousness is passive. Beyond $4\frac{1}{2}$, it is as if you have reached a mountain top, and the going is now all downhill; consciousness has become *active*.

To grasp this is obviously of immense importance, for once you *know* that a certain effort will take you to Level 5 and beyond, you become unstoppable. There is a law of consciousness which states: the stronger it becomes, the stronger it is capable of becoming. And the method involves focused attention.

Upside-downness and the seven levels of consciousness are central to the argument of *Beyond the Occult*. But most of the book is taken up by examples of 'strange powers', like the ability to foresee the future or have out-of-the-body experiences.

Equally important are the many 'mystical' glimpses that have been experienced under everyday circumstances. In a book called *A Drug Taker's Notes*, R. H. Ward describes his experience under dental gas – nitrous oxide – and says: 'I passed after a few inhalations of the gas directly into a state of consciousness already far more complete than the fullest degree of ordinary waking consciousness.' And the following is an account by a sixteen-year-old girl as she was walking up a lane towards a wood:

'I was not feeling particularly happy or particularly sad, just ordinary.' As she stood in the cornfield looking towards the wood, everything changed.

Everything surrounding me was this white, bright, sparkling light, like the sun on frosty snow, like a million diamonds, and there was no cornfield, no trees, no sky, this *light* was everywhere . . . The feeling was indescribable, but I have never experienced anything in the years that followed that I can compare with that glorious moment; it was blissful, uplifting, I felt open-mouthed wonder. Then the tops of the trees became visible once again, then a piece of sky, then the *light* was no more, and the cornfield was spread before me. I stood there for a long time, trying in vain for *it* to come back, and have tried many times, but I only saw it once; but I know in my heart it is still there – and here – around us.*

This, it seems to me, is the kind of experience we need to recall when we discuss philosophy and the nature of reality. *This*, as Blake knew, is what reality is really like.

In August 1989, Joy and I went on a trip to a little French town called Chaise Dieu, in the Auvergne. We were travelling by bus with a group from the Torquay Gramophone Society, to hear the Bach St John Passion in the medieval Abbey Church. The day before we left, we were taken on a trip to a volcanic mountain called the Puy de Dome, above Clermont.

On the bus Joy was reading a French newspaper, when suddenly she began to shake with laughter. The item described how a group of East Germans who had taken refuge in Hungary (which was then a Communist country) had been given permission to picnic close to the border with West Germany, and lost no time in hot-footing it across the frontier and vanishing into the distance.

*From *Seeing the Invisible: Modern Religious and Other Transcendent Experiences*, ed. Meg Maxwell and Verena Tschudin, Penguin 1990.

Neither of us had the least idea that we were seeing the beginning of the downfall of Communism. Yet I should have had an inkling. In a symposium called *Marx Refuted* (1987), which I edited with Ronald Duncan, I had foretold the downfall of Communism two years before it happened. On the last page of the book, I had written:

The attempted uprisings in Hungary and Czechoslovakia suggested that [the downfall of Communism] might not take as long as that: that human nature itself might revolt long before prosperity made it inevitable. Now in the 1980s, we become aware of a more startling possibility. Events in Chile, in Afghanistan, in Poland, suggest the possibility of a world in which communism has simply vanished, overturned by the masses it is supposed to represent. History is not always gradual. The 'witchcraft craze' collapsed quite suddenly, in Europe and America; at one moment it seemed as strong as ever; in the next it had disappeared . . .

And so, during the next two years, I watched with awe as something I had never dared to hope actually came about. I told my mother: 'You're lucky. You've lived long enough to see the downfall of the Soviet Union.'

But then, she had never been much interested in politics, so was not all that impressed.

CHAPTER 22

The Ancient Ones

It was on that first trip to Japan, when I was in a hotel in Nara, the site of the largest Buddhist temple in Japan, that I had received a phone call from New York asking me if I would go there the following year to lecture at the Open Center. This had been founded in the belief that New Yorkers are as interested in New Age thought as Californians, and this had proved correct. During the next ten years I was to return there many times. I would also return to Japan and Australia. But since travel bores me, and writing about it bores me even more, I shall not describe these.

Back from our travels we were met off the train by Don Seaman. He was in his usual financial straits, and I had to lend him £2,000 in anticipation of the Japanese advance on the scandal book. But he repaid me by giving me an excellent idea for a new book, asking: 'Why don't you write a book called *The Sexual Misfits*?' And since my mind was full of the notion of the sexual illusion, this struck me as an ideal subject, and I lost no time in persuading my publisher to commission it.

I felt it was high time to write a sequel to *Origins of the Sexual Impulse*. And I had an ideal starting point: an extraordinary Hungarian lady called Charlotte Bach, who in 1971 had sent me a vast and incomprehensible typescript on sex. When I finally succeeded in working out what she was talking about, I discovered that it was highly original: that all men are possessed by a basic urge to *become* women, and all women by an urge to become men. She saw the inner tension created by this urge as the force behind evolution, as well as all human creativity. Those who give way to the compulsion and become transvestites release the tension, and destroy their potential creativity. Those who struggle with it may become great artists, or even saints and mystics. One man Charlotte had interviewed claimed to have had an orgasm that lasted for eight hours, and this, she thought, was because these inner forces were perfectly balanced at a very high level.

In due course I met Charlotte – a big lady with huge bosoms and a deep voice – and even interviewed her for a magazine called *Time Out*, for her ideas were beginning to attract attention. I also wrote a section about her theories in *Mysteries*.

Then, in 1981, Charlotte was found dead in her room, and when she was undressed, proved to be a man. She had died of cancer – afraid to consult a doctor because it would betray her secret.

I spent the first two chapters of *The Misfits* discussing her life and ideas, then used them as a springboard to speak of various sexual 'Outsiders' from Sade to Wittgenstein and T. E. Lawrence. I wrote it after writing a short book about Aleister Crowley, another man whose life was dominated by the sexual illusion.

All this still left me feeling that I had not got to the bottom of the problem. But I felt that I had taken an important step in the right direction in *Space Vampires*, when I had suggested that sex is somehow an exchange of vital energies. Which is why, for a long time, I had planned a sequel that would deal more comprehensively than anything I had ever written about the sexual impulse.

This sequel was to be about the grandson of Olaf Carlsen, the hero of the previous novel, who realises one day that he has inherited 'vampirism' from his grandfather. (The latter had been in contact with a female vampire – the premise being that, as with blood-drinking vampires, a person who has been 'bitten' by an energy-vampire turns into one.)

The problem was whether I could afford to write it. My publishers, HarperCollins, had commissioned a second part of *Spider World*, and I had written the first volume, called *The Magician*. But I felt that my imagination was beginning to flag. *The Tower* and *The Delta* had practically written themselves, but this second part was far harder. I felt that I needed a rest – a year, perhaps two years, perhaps longer.

That is why I decided to embark on the *Space Vampires* sequel. But HarperCollins were not willing to commission it, for they wanted me to finish *The Magician* first. So there was nothing for it but to write the sequel by increasing my overdraft, and hoping I could sell it for a reasonable advance. It was a risky venture, but I had spent most of my life taking risks. So I began the book in July 1992, intending it to be roughly the same length as its predecessor.

Its hero is understandably shocked by his recognition that he is a vampire – until he discovers that there is a whole colony of them in New York, descendants of the original space vampires, and that they are in no way dangerous. They absorb vital energy from other living creatures, although never enough to cause them harm.

Carlsen soon begins to understand that when a man and woman are involved in lovemaking, they exchange energies by a process not unlike a mutual blood transfusion. He becomes convinced that if all human beings could learn the trick, most of our problems would disappear – wars, murders, suicides, mental illness. For nearly all negative human activities are due to the frustration of this energy-flow. It seems clear to him that if everybody could be converted to 'vampirism', humanity would have made an advance towards sanity and optimism.

And it is at this point that he is horrified to realise that there are still many of the old destructive vampires left – those who experience a craving to absorb someone's energy to the point of destroying them.

What followed was my fullest exploration so far of the sexual illusion. And as Carlsen is taken on an astral journey to the three planets of the Rigel star system, I found myself creating alien worlds and their inhabitants in an explosion of sheer inventiveness. Soon the book was longer than *The Space Vampires*, and as it continued to grow, I began to experience doubts. But I clung on, like someone going downhill on a toboggan.

I finished it in July 1994, two years to the day after starting it. By then it had grown to a quarter of a million words, the same as the original *Spider World*. But my publisher had solved that earlier problem by dividing it into two volumes. There was no convenient way of dividing *Metamorphosis of the Vampire* into two volumes, or even three.

The result was that it failed to find a publisher. The remainder of 1994 was thoroughly depressing as the vast parcel went off again and again, and was rejected. Both my British and American agents advised me to shorten it, but after spending two years on it, I was damned if I was willing to cut a single word.

By the autumn of that year, I was lying awake at night, worrying about the overdraft, and wondering if things were really as bad as they looked. Why did no one seem to share my opinion that it was an important book? Had my judgment completely deserted me?

I began to consider selling the house and finding somewhere smaller. Or perhaps moving to America and trying to find a university post. At least my children were now grown up, and my mother had been dead for three years. But I would hate to have to abandon all my books and records.

Then one night, when I had awakened at two in the morning, and was unable to get back to sleep, I found myself asking whether I really believed that we were on the brink of disaster. Then, as I thought of those black days in my mid-teens, when I had contemplated suicide, and recalled that curious feeling of optimism that surged up in me as I re-stoppered the cyanide bottle, I suddenly knew that this gloom was unnecessary. Provided I kept going and remained optimistic, the problems would be resolved. And with a curious feeling of confidence and relief I fell into a peaceful sleep.

It was shortly after that, when *Metamorphosis of the Vampire* was still being turned down repeatedly, that some earlier plans began to come to fruition. This was a commission for a book about my long-time interest in the age of the Sphinx.

It had started as long ago as 1979, when I had reviewed a book called *Serpent in the Sky* by an American named John Anthony West. It was a study of the ideas of a rebel Egyptologist, René Schwaller de Lubicz, who had spent years studying the temple at Luxor. But Schwaller had also come to the controversial conclusion that the Great Sphinx of Giza was eroded by water, not by wind-blown sand, as historians have always believed. And, since heavy rain is so rare in Egypt, the Sphinx could be thousands of years older than anyone had supposed.

Moreover, since Egypt is among the most ancient civilisations known to history, this seemed to indicate that there must have been a 'founder civilisation' long before 2500 BC, the date usually ascribed to the Great Pyramid and the Sphinx.

What Schwaller had suggested was that this 'forerunner' was Atlantis.

This is not as wild as it sounds, for Schwaller pointed out that by 2500 BC, Egypt had already achieved a remarkably high level of culture in science, in medicine, in mathematics, in architecture and in religion. Surely all this was not created in the mere five or six centuries since Egyptian civilisation is supposed to have started?

I had already come across the same suggestion in Gurdjieff's *Beelzebub's Tales* – that ancient Egypt was founded by survivors from the destruction of Atlantis, which, according to Plato, had happened about 9600 BC.

Now three years earlier, in 1991, the film producer Dino de Laurentiis had asked me to write an outline about Atlantis. My first thought had been to try to make it more historically realistic than most Atlantis stories, and to base it on Schwaller's ideas.

In November 1991 I was in Tokyo, lecturing at a symposium, and I happened to mention my Atlantis project to my host in the Press Club, Murray Sayle. And Murray remarked that he had recently seen a paragraph in a Japanese newspaper that claimed that new evidence had been found to support Schwaller's view of the age of the Sphinx. Unfortunately, he was unable to lay his hands on it. But a week later Joy and I were in Melbourne, and I happened to mention the problem to the editor of the *Age*, Creighton Burns. The next day he handed me a photostat of the item, taken from the *Los Angeles Times* of a few weeks earlier. This said that the Sphinx had been studied by a geologist called Robert Schoch, and that Schoch had concluded that it could date back to about 7000 BC.

This notion had been presented at a meeting of the American Geological Society in San Diego, California, and although orthodox archaeologists had been hostile, the geologists in general had been surprisingly sympathetic.

Back in Cornwall I wrote my film outline and sent it to Dino de

Laurentiis; and, typically, heard no more of it. Then I plunged into *Metamorphosis of the Vampire*, and put the Sphinx out of mind.

But in 1993 I was reminded of it when, out of the blue, I received a copy of a magazine from John Anthony West containing an article about the Sphinx. It seemed that West had been behind Robert Schoch's investigation of the Sphinx two years earlier. And he had decided to pursue the matter further. Most Egyptologists accept that the face of the Sphinx is that of the pharaoh Chefren, who built the second pyramid at Giza. This identification was based upon a bust of Chefren that was found under the floor of the Sphinx Temple, which stands in front of the Sphinx. But of course, the face of the Sphinx is badly damaged, so the resemblance is far from obvious.

Now West had decided to call upon the services of an American forensic artist named Frank Domingo. It was Domingo's job to make sketches of criminals from witness's descriptions. West wanted him to go to Egypt, study the face of the Sphinx and the bust of Chefren, and state whether they could be the same person. Domingo warned that he might conclude that they were, but West said he was willing to risk that.

So Domingo went to Cairo, and quickly concluded that they were not the same person. The chin of the Sphinx was bigger than Chefren's, and the line from its ear to the corner of its mouth sloped at a different angle.

I was interested because a publisher had asked me if I had any ideas for a volume in a series about 'the occult', and I told him the Sphinx story. He liked it, and I sketched out an outline of the book, arguing that civilisation probably dates back thousands of years earlier than we have always believed.

It had been complete coincidence that John West had decided to send me his article about Domingo. We had never met, or even corresponded. The coincidence struck me as propitious. I wrote back mentioning that I would be in New York in a few weeks' time, and we agreed to meet.

This came about on 28 September 1993, when I was in New York with my family. John proved to be a thin, bespectacled man who radiated that terrific vitality of the enthusiast. Like all genuine enthusiasts he was generous with his ideas and his time; there was none of the paranoia that I have encountered in writers who think that everybody is out to steal their ideas. He had with him a first 'rough' videotape of a television programme about the Sphinx, and we watched this at the home of the playwright Richard Foreman and his wife Kate. It seemed to us that it established beyond all possible doubt that the Sphinx was weathered by rain, and that since there had been little rain in Egypt for thousands of years, that meant that the Sphinx must date from some earlier rainy period.

When, over dinner, we discussed my projected book – which had the provisional title *Before the Sphinx* – John mentioned that I ought to contact another writer, Graham Hancock, who was just now completing a book on ancient civilisations. He also mentioned another name, Rand Flem-Ath, who had written an unpublished book arguing that Atlantis had been situated in Antarctica.

This made sense, for the American professor Charles Hapgood had written a book called *Earth's Shifting Crust*, in which he produced convincing geological arguments that the whole crust of the earth had slipped about two thousand miles southward around 10000 BC. This could explain why Atlantis – which Plato described as being in the mid-Atlantic – was now so far south.

Moreover, Hapgood had written a later book called *Maps of the Ancient Sea Kings*, a study of ancient seafaring maps called portolans (meaning 'from port to port'), one of which – the famous Piri Re'is map – showed the coast of Antarctica in the days before it had any ice. So did many other portolans. That meant that the original ancient maps on which the portolans were based must have been made around 5000 BC – the last time the coast of Antarctica was free of ice. But a map is no use without some kind of writing, and historians place the invention of writing (by the Sumerians) around 3500 BC, fifteen centuries later.

Besides, other maps studied by Hapgood show most of the *interior* of Antarctica before it was covered with ice. But who would bother to map the interior of a continent except people who lived there?

So, on my return to Cornwall, I lost no time in writing to Graham Hancock and Rand Flem-Ath. Both of them let me see their typescripts. And when I read Hancock's – called *Fingerprints of the Gods* – I was dismayed to realise that he had virtually pre-empted my own book, producing some highly convincing proofs that civilisation may date back long before 10000 BC. (For example, he cites evidence that Tiahuanaco, in the Andes, was built around 15000 BC.) But on reflection I decided that there was still plenty for me to say – for example, about the date man first appeared on earth, and about the megaliths.

As to Rand Flem-Ath, his notion that Plato's Atlantis was situated in Antarctica struck me as highly plausible. He told me that the book was now being considered by a Canadian publisher, and I told him that if it would help in getting it published, I would be happy to write an introduction. He accepted my offer, and the book was duly published in Canada, then in England.

By this time, my own book on the Sphinx had been commissioned by Virgin. They had been delighted that a book called *The Serial Killers*, which I had written with Don Seaman, had done well – and so, of course, was Don. But I was still only halfway through *Metamorphosis of the Vampire*, so for the time being, Virgin would have to wait.

In early September of the following year, 1995, Graham Hancock came to visit me in Cornwall, together with his wife Santha, and John West.

Graham struck me as having the same kind of drive as John, although less sheer enthusiasm. He and his family were having a thin time of it. They had spent much of the advance on the book on visiting the sites described in it, and were now waiting anxiously for its publication the following spring. I took them all out for tea in my Land-Rover, to a little village on the coast called Portloe. When we had ordered tea, I found myself wondering if I had enough money, and asked Graham to lend me five pounds until we got home. He looked uncomfortable and explained that he did not have five pounds. Neither did John West. Fortunately, the money I had on me was enough to cover the bill and the tip.

A few months earlier I had reviewed a book called *The Orion Mystery* by Robert Bauval, who had made a striking contribution to the debate. Bauval had noticed that the rather unsymmetrical arrangement of the three Giza pyramids on the ground reflects precisely the arrangement of the three stars of Orion's Belt in the sky. Pointing out that the Egyptians regarded their land as a reflection of the heavens, Bauval suggested that the three pyramids were constructed by the Nile as an image on earth of the Milky Way and the stars of Orion's Belt. However, the stars of Orion are no longer a true reflection of the pyramids, for precession of the equinoxes, due to the wobble on the earth's axis, causes them to twist slightly over the ages. The last time the pyramids *exactly* reflected Orion was in 10500 BC, and Bauval went on to make the breathtaking suggestion that the pyramids were planned – and partly built – at that date.

So if Bauval was correct, there was a sophisticated civilisation in 10500 BC. I lost no time in getting in touch with Bauval, a Belgian engineer who was also cast in the same mould as John West. But Graham had already been in touch with him, and the Orion theory played an important part in *Fingerprints of the Gods*.

The latter appeared in April 1995, and became an instant bestseller, solving Graham's financial problems at a stroke and making him a millionaire within a year.

As to me, I had begun writing my Sphinx book in December 1994, still struggling with a £25,000 overdraft due to the non-acceptance of the vampire sequel. Admittedly, the Russians had published it – but then, the Russians never paid.

I had followed this with a book about charlatan messiahs I had been planning for several years, and whose latest starting point had been the fiery death of David Koresh and his Branch Davidian Sect at Waco in April 1993. This was finished just before I began the Sphinx book, and then ran into the same problems as the Vampire novel, and was rejected by several publishers. I was keeping afloat by working on the Japanese version of *Murder Casebook*, but only just. And out of sheer cussedness I began to write the messiahs book for the third time.

It was one of those years when everything seems to go wrong. For some time I had been experiencing bladder problems, with a need to relieve myself with increasing frequency. On a business trip to London these had become acute, and I once more noticed blood in my urine. I rang Joy and asked her to book me in for an examination at our local hospital, and travelled back the next day. I was, of course, worried that it was cancer – the thought of dying was doubly disagreeable when I thought of leaving my family with a large overdraft. But the hospital visit brought relief. When I woke up from the anaesthetic, the doctor told me that he had discovered two large gallstones, and removed them both. And after an uncomfortable day or two with a catheter inside me, I was allowed to go home. I went back to rewriting the book on messiahs.

A Japanese television company wrote to ask me if I would be willing to go to the Middle East to make a programme 'In the Footsteps of Lawrence of Arabia'. Joy and I were in New York at the time – I was lecturing at the Open Center – and our son Rowan phoned us to tell us about the letter. They were apparently offering seven million yen. We quickly looked up the exchange rate in the *New York Times* and discovered that this was about £50,000. We told Rowan to email the television company and accept immediately. But when I arrived home, and contacted them to ask if they were *sure* they were offering seven million yen, I got an abjectly apologetic reply explaining that they had included one nought too many. They were offering 700,000 yen, about £5,000 – a reasonable sum, but not, as I had been hoping, enough to clear the overdraft. After some discussion they increased the offer – but not to anything like £50,000. And in June, Joy and I travelled to Jordan and Syria, and I made the programme, and I got the opportunity to see all those places I had read about so often in *Seven Pillars of Wisdom*.

Back in England, an old friend named Nick Robinson, who ran Robinson Publishing, asked me if I would be interested in writing a series of small paperbacks, on such topics as UFOs, spies, ghosts and famous love stories. In fact, I and my children – Damon and Rowan – had already written a number of these potboilers for Nick. Even our daughter, Sally – now in her thirties – decided she would like to try her hand at writing the book on great love affairs. I did a volume on UFOs, which I dictated on to tape and got my part-time secretary to type up. But the children, being less experienced writers, were much slower, with the consequence that in October I found that I had their three typescripts to read and edit – one on spies, one on royal scandals, and one on great love affairs.

Now editing someone else's work is, in a sense, more stressful than writing your own book, for if there is something clumsy about a sentence, the editor has to brood on it until he can see the best way of smoothing out the lumps. I worked on grimly through three books, determined to get the damn things finished and get back to the Sphinx book, which was behind schedule. The editing bored me, but it had to be done. And on the day I finished the final book – Sally's volume on great love affairs – I stood up, and found I could not straighten my back. Like the previous occasion – after Kathie's visit – this was obviously due to hypertension. I limped upstairs, bent double, and Joy advised me to go and lie down. But I had to take the dogs for a walk, and was sure the problem would go away once I was out on the cliff.

It did not go away. It was as if I had broken some hinge in the middle of my spine, and both legs became so stiff that I had to begin walking with a stick. And to make it worse, I had contracted one of the worst colds of my life, which dragged on for month after month, and made my chest wheeze so loudly that I could not sleep at night.

In the middle of 1995, I had been approached by a publisher called Dorling Kindersley, who produced large, glossy volumes, to ask me if I would be interested in writing a volume on the sacred sites of the world. I explained that I first had to complete a book on the Sphinx, but then would be glad to go ahead with the sacred sites book. I made a trip to London to meet the team, and they proved to be young, enthusiastic and friendly. And when December came, and I had still not finished the Sphinx book, I began working on the sacred sites for two days a week, and the Sphinx for the rest of the week. It was fortunate that the panic attacks had taught me to control anxiety when overworking.

I was a month late with the Sphinx book, for I thought I had until the end of December 1995, but my contract specified delivery by 5 December – publication day was 12 May. I sent them all but the last chapter, then went on working on the two books at once. I finished the Sphinx book on 31 December, and sent off the final chapter the following day. Virgin had told me they wanted to call it *From Atlantis to the Sphinx*. I was not over-joyed at the title, but had to agree that it was probably more explanatory than *Before the Sphinx*.

In early May I had been invited to Glasgow to lecture to the Scottish Society for Psychical Research, at the invitation of an old friend, Archie Roy, who had been Scotland's Astronomer Royal. The train journey from Cornwall was immensely long – from 8.15 in the morning until 5 in the afternoon. The following day, which was free, we decided to go to Edinburgh, to meet Graham Hancock's uncle, Jim Macaulay. He took us to lunch at his golf club, then drove us to a place called Rosslyn Chapel, of which neither of us had heard. Rosslyn had apparently been built by a Templar named William St Clair, in the mid-fifteenth century. What was odd about the place, Jim told us, was that its walls were covered with sculptures of vegetation – implying paganism – and that these included corncobs and aloes cactus, both exclusively American vegetables. The strange thing was that it was decorated nearly half a century before Columbus discovered America. And this could only mean one thing: that someone else had sailed to America before Columbus.

The Knights Templar were one of the most powerful and wealthy orders of medieval chivalry. But their wealth was coveted by Philip the Fair of France, who ordered their arrest in 1307. A few days before this mass arrest, someone must have tipped off the Templar fleet in Le Havre: it sailed away and simply vanished. Some ships are believed to have found their way to Scotland, but the evidence of the corncobs and the aloes seems to indicate that others reached America.

It was a fascinating afternoon, and the trip to Rosslyn was serendipitous, for the visit would provide information for future work. While at Rosslyn, we saw a copy of a newly published book called *The Hiram Key*, by Robert Lomas and Christopher Knight, and I bought a copy for Joy. This would also provide important material for my next book.

We arrived back in Glasgow in time for a glass of wine with Archie Roy before my lecture. And there I received some cheering information. Archie had tried to order more copies of *From Atlantis to the Sphinx*, but was told that it was now reprinting. It had already sold out its first impression.

It went on to sell a great many copies – not as many as Graham's *Fingerprints of the Gods*, but enough to clear our overdraft.

After one of the most disastrous years of my life, it looked as if things had started to look up at last.

In September 1996 I was invited to lecture at a symposium on 'Ancient Knowledge' at the University of Delaware. It was sponsored by the Society for Scientific Exploration, and speakers would include Graham Hancock, Robert Bauval, Robert Schoch, Rand Flem-Ath and Paul Devereux. It proved to be a pleasant trip, since *Atlantis to the Sphinx* was still selling well, and we felt we could relax and enjoy ourselves.

I was delighted to see Rand Flem-Ath there, for it was the first time we had met – and also the first time he had delivered a lecture in public. Rand was a balding, squarely-built, bearded man, and I took an immense liking to him from the first. I thought his lecture, in which he set out to prove that Atlantis was the continent of Antarctica, was admirable. From the beginning I felt great affection for him, as if he were a younger brother.

At the same conference I met a charming Dutch television producer named Roel Oostra, who told me he would like to make a programme based on *Atlantis to the Sphinx*, and asked me if I would be willing to travel to Egypt, Mexico and South America to film it. I said I would be delighted – provided I could take Joy with me.

Making the programme would also involve a trip to Los Angeles and Washington – Los Angeles to film the famous 'tar trap of La Brea', and

Washington to go to the Library of Congress and film the room where Charles Hapgood had first examined the 'maps of the ancient sea kings'. Since this part of the trip would only occupy a long weekend, there was no point in Joy coming. So on 22 November I flew from Heathrow to Los Angeles, a twelve-hour flight.

I had the following morning free – we were due to do a camera rehearsal at the George C. Page Museum in the afternoon. And since Roel intended to go and see someone in Santa Monica, I took the opportunity to beg a lift: I wanted to go and see my old friend John Wright, for whom I had lectured on my last trip to Los Angeles.

In fact, John's bookshop was no longer situated at the same address. But as I strolled along Santa Monica Boulevard, I stopped outside a bookshop that was still closed, and saw John behind the counter. He welcomed me in and gave me a coffee. I felt that finding him like this, by pure chance, was a good sign.

And indeed it was, for John's shop contained a large selection of books on flying saucers, and Virgin had just asked me if I would write a book called *Alien Dawn* that would survey the history of UFOs.

It was not, to be honest, a subject in which I was deeply interested, even though I had written a short paperback about it in the previous year. I was simply not much interested in flying saucers. However, with John's guidance, I took the opportunity to select a couple of dozen books about them, and asked him to parcel them back to Cornwall.

In the Library of Congress I had the unexpected pleasure of seeing Rand again, and we filmed the section of the programme about Hapgood. There was something very decent and reassuring about this squarely built, bullet-headed man, and as I said goodbye, I felt an odd sadness at the thought that I would probably never see him again.

In December 1996 it was time to make the second leg of the Atlantis programme, in Mexico. The aim would be to try to show that, at some time in the legendary past, white men had come from the east, led by a blond, blue-eyed Caucasian known as Viracocha or Quetzalcoatl, who had brought civilisation to Mexico and South America. The implication, of course, was that these white men were the survivors of the Atlantis catastrophe, and that others fled to Egypt.

This time Joy came with me; we flew from Gatwick to Mexico City. There Roel met us, and we spent two days filming at Teotihuacan, the sacred site that had once been as big as ancient Rome. There I had a hair-raising journey down a long, low tunnel underneath the Pyramid of the Sun, not a place for anyone who suffers from claustrophobia, and filmed in a tiny chamber whose purpose is unknown.

The next day we went on the Tollan, and filmed among its great stone figures known as Atlantides, probably named after Atlantis. Then to Oaxaca, associated with D. H. Lawrence and Malcolm Lowry, and its sacred hill called Monte Alban, where there are stelae that show the castrated corpses of white men – quite clearly not Indians. After that, to Puebla, site of the greatest of all pyramids, Cholula, now merely a heap of rubble. Finally to Villahermosa, to film those huge stone heads that look unmistakeably negroid.

Ten days after leaving home, we were back in Cornwall, where the parcel of books from John Wright was awaiting me.

The next stage of our journey, the following January, was to Egypt, which I had never seen. Standing in front of the Great Pyramid, I was struck forcibly by the problem of how it was constructed. It consists of two and a half million blocks, mostly weighing about six tons each. It would not be difficult to build the first half dozen courses, using levers and muscle power. But how would they have gone on raising these blocks as the pyramid got higher? Some kind of ramp? But a ramp to reach 203 courses would have to contain more blocks than the pyramid itself . . .

Like everyone else, I was also fascinated by the King's Chamber, and the riddle of its great stone sarcophagus. This must have been placed in the chamber as the pyramid was being built, for it is too big to have been taken through the passageways. But why has it no lid? And why was the 'burial chamber' empty when the first explorer, the Caliph Al-Mamum, entered it in AD 803?

The interior of the pyramid was far too hot. Even so, I had a brief flash of a sense of being connected to some knowledge that has been long forgotten.

Looking at the walls of the Sphinx enclosure, which surround it on three sides, I could see why Robert Schoch claimed that they were weathered by rain, not wind-blown sand. They consist of parallel strata, like a layer cake, some hard, some soft, and the soft layers cut deep into the rock, because both rain and wind-blown sand would cut more deeply into the soft layers than the hard. But wind-blown sand would not create those channels running vertically from the top; that had to be rain. So I could see in front of me proof of Schwaller's belief that the Sphinx was far older than dynastic Egypt.

Since it seemed pointless to go to Egypt without visiting its ancient capital, Thebes (Luxor), Joy and I flew there, and I had a chance to see the temple in which Schwaller de Lubicz spent so many years of his life. We hired a guide to take us around its vast sister temple at Karnak, since it would otherwise have taken us a whole day. I felt guilty at rushing around these places like a tourist; nevertheless, I felt it was important to form an impression of them for future work.

Two months later, in early March, we embarked on the last – and most impressive – stage of our journey: to Bolivia and Peru. We flew to Buenos Aires, then on to La Paz, in the Andes. This is 12,000 feet above sea level, and we noted immediately that the thin air made us tired and slightly dizzy – in spite of a tea brewed from coca leaves (the basis of cocaine) provided by the hotel. Roel, unaffected by the altitude, continued to rush around and organise permits; Joy and I decided it would be more sensible to retire to the bar and drink margaritas.

That night, after I had fallen asleep, Joy woke me up to say she was suffering from heart palpitations. I knew there was an oxygen cylinder available in the lobby, and had to go down and explain my needs in sign language, since I spoke no Spanish. I had morbid visions of having to return to England with Joy in a coffin, but the oxygen mask proved effective, and she got a normal night's sleep. In spite of which, she decided not to come with us to Tiahuanaco the next day – since it was another 500 feet above sea level – but to stay in the hotel.

This was a pity, for the ruins of Tiahuanaco are extraordinary. The main part of the temple is an immense courtyard called the Kalasasiya, which contains the famous 'great idol'. Professor Arthur Posnansky, who spent his life studying Tiahuanaco (and wrote the classic book on it), concluded from the astronomical alignments of the temple that it must have been built in 15000 BC – five thousand years before the end of Plato's Atlantis. Scholars were horrified at that remote date, and a German team checked Posnansky's measurements with Teutonic thoroughness – and found them accurate. Nevertheless, in the small museum opposite the temple, its date is given as 500 BC.

In front of the Kalasasiya there is a sunken temple that I nicknamed 'the swimming pool' since that is what it looks like. And in its centre there is a statue of a bearded white man (Indians cannot grow beards), who is supposed to be the white god Viracocha, who according to legend landed on the east coast of Mexico after tidal waves had signalled some great catastrophe in the mid-Atlantic.

Equally remarkable is the statue known as 'the Friar' (El Fraile) which stands in a remote corner of the great courtyard. It is obviously a fish god, with huge eyes, and scales on the lower part of its body. I was fascinated because I knew that the Dogon, a tribe in Mali, East Africa, had declared that civilisation was originally brought to earth by 'fish gods' from the star Sirius. And the Dogon knew something that was then unknown to astronomers – that Sirius is a double star, which has an invisible companion made of matter far heavier than any on earth. In fact, Sirius's invisible companion, Sirius B, is a 'white dwarf', made of immensely heavy elements that have collapsed in on themselves.

As I looked at 'the Friar', I realised that there was a simple link between my arguments in *Atlantis to the Sphinx* and the projected *Alien Dawn*. This statue seemed to be evidence that aliens had come to earth in the remote past.

But most impressive of all is the port area, known as the 'puma punka', or Puma Gate. One construction block weighs 440 tons, and we have no idea of how it could have been moved. The great blocks on the site are joined together by metal clamps that must have been made in a portable forge and poured in while still molten. The builders of Tiahuanaco obviously possessed a sophisticated technology.

Fortunately, Joy had a chance to see Tiahuanaco after all, for Roel decided to return the next day to finish shooting. I persuaded her that if she took half of one of my blood pressure tablets, it should compensate for the low atmospheric pressure. It worked, and she was able to spend a perfectly comfortable day high up in the mountains.

We went on to Cuzco for more filming, including the giant stone walls of Sacsahuaman, as baffling in their way as the Great Pyramid, many of the blocks too large to be lifted by even the largest modern crane. And finally Joy and I spent half a day in a rickety train that chugged along mountain valleys and through the jungle, to drop us off at the station below Machu Picchu, the hidden mountain stronghold where the last Inca hid from the Spaniards. As with Tiahuanaco, its date is unknown. Scholars assume it is fifteenth century AD, but Graham Hancock quotes the German astronomer Rolf Müller as saying that its alignments suggest that it could be 6,000 years old.

As to why it matters if civilisation is far older than we assume, the answer is that it doesn't if the mentality of these remote ancestors was more-or-less the same as our own. But the more I saw of ancient sites, the more I became convinced – as I argued in *Atlantis to the Sphinx* – that it was fundamentally different from our own way of grasping reality. It amounts to Robert Graves's distinction between lunar and solar knowledge: lunar knowledge is more intuitive and visceral than solar knowledge, and it can, as Graves said, 'leap straight from problem to answer'. And this, I felt fairly certain, was the kind of knowledge posessed by ancient man. It explains, for example, why, from Neanderthal onwards, they seemed to have some strange and comprehensive knowledge of the heavens.

Such knowledge explains what I meant in *The Occult* by the phrase 'Magic is the science of the future'.

Three days later, we were back in Cornwall, and I was becoming increasingly excited about the UFO book. What I had seen in South America convinced me that the Dogon could be right, and that the earth has probably been visited in the remote past by beings from other worlds. Of course, Däniken had said the same thing in his *Chariots of the Gods*, but his books were so full of absurdities – and in one case, downright untruths – that I had dismissed him and his 'ancient astronauts' out of hand. Now I saw it was a mistake to throw out the baby with the bathwater.

When I settled down to study the pile of books from Los Angeles, I began to grasp the nature of the problem. 'Flying saucers' were first reported in 1947, when I was a sixteen-year-old schoolboy. Since my mind was full of gloom about the meaning of human existence, I dismissed them as irrelevant – they were not going to answer the question of why I was here on earth.

Now I began to see that it is not as simple as that. The problem with UFOs is that although many reports are deeply convincing because attested by many witnesses, others have a preposterous element that can only be called 'deliberate unbelievableness', as if they are *designed* to create scepticism, like a con man who is trying a double-bluff.

One example will suffice: the 'siege of Hopkinsville'.

In the early morning of 21 August 1955, two carloads of frightened people arrived at the police station in Hopkinsville, Kentucky, and alleged that they had been besieged in their remote farm by little shining men, who somersaulted backwards when struck by bullets, but were otherwise unharmed. Police drove seven miles to Sutton Farm, but could find nothing, and left. Then the little men came back and peered in the windows, and the 'siege' continued for the rest of the night.

Neighbours heard the shooting. One of them saw some craft landing nearby. And two carloads of people do not drive seven miles as a joke. Something undoubtedly happened at Sutton Farm that night – but what?

It was my friend Jacques Vallee, the world's leading UFO expert, who first pointed out that there is a fundamental similarity between some reported UFO cases and tales of medieval fairies and goblins. And the more I read of UFO cases, the more I was inclined to agree that there seems to be some curious 'paranormal' element.

And what of the hundreds of cases that began to command attention in the mid-1980s, of people who realised that several hours were missing out of their lives, and then gradually remembered that they had been abducted by strange-looking grey creatures with large eyes? Again, the simplest explanation is they were suffering from delusions. But this simplistic theory will not work. A friend of mine, Professor John Mack, a Harvard psychologist, had been approached by an investigator named Budd Hopkins, and asked if he would look into reports of 'missing time' by people in the Boston area. His first reaction was to dismiss it all as absurd, but fair-mindedness led him to look into a few cases, all involving apparently sane and normal people – students, housewives, secretaries, businessmen, even psychologists – that ended by convincing him that they were telling the truth. The result was a book called *Abduction* that almost cost him his job, since the University of Boston does not like its professors being held up to public ridicule.

His ultimate conclusion was certainly alarming to academic colleagues. He speaks of our everyday experience as 'consensus reality', and argues that there is no way of making sense of UFO reports 'within the framework of our existing views of what is real or possible'.

Since *The Outsider* was about people who feel that there is something deeply wrong with 'consensus reality', and that we need to broaden our views about what is real or possible, I experienced an instant rapport with his conclusions. I ended by coming to believe that although UFO phenomena seem to contradict consensus reality, they do not contradict the reality described by quantum physicists. Or, for that matter, mystics. All the evidence seems to show that we should not regard UFOs as 'space craft', but as unknown energy forms.

I ended by agreeing with Jacques Vallee and John Mack: the purpose of UFO phenomena seems to be heuristic – that is, they are designed to *teach* us something, to change our attitude towards reality. H. G. Wells had written a novel called *Star Begotten* in which he argues that evolution is creating a new type of human being. He calls these new men 'Martians'. And at the end of my three-hundred-page study of the UFO phenomenon, this was in fact my own conclusion. Something is trying to alter and widen our concept of reality.

My conclusion was reinforced by an odd series of events that came about while I was writing the book, and which I have touched on earlier. I have a digital clock beside my bed with illuminated figures. While I was writing *Alien Dawn*, I often glanced at it in the night and found that it was in treble figures – 1.11. 2.22. 3.33. 4.44. The chances of this kind of coincidence are obviously one in sixty; but during the writing of *Alien Dawn* it occurred again and again. And on the day I was due to finish the book, I woke around 4 o'clock, then dozed off again. Then, as I woke, I thought: I bet you what you like it's 4.44. I turned over, and indeed it was 4.44.

Once the book was finished, the phenomenon became as rare as it had been before. I concluded that Jung was correct: synchronicity tells us something important about the nature of reality. In the case of *Alien Dawn*, it was trying to tell me that I was on the right track.

When Roel Oostra's programme on Atlantis was broadcast, I emailed Rand to ask if he had seen it, and learned that he had not. So I sent him a video-tape. Soon after that, I received an email from him asking me if I might consider collaborating with him on a book about his own latest theories on ancient civilisation. Naturally, I was immensely interested. And when Rand sent me an outline of his ideas, I knew immediately that this was a book I would want to write.

The reason he needed a collaborator, Rand explained, was that his wife Rose, who had co-authored *When the Sky Fell*, now wanted to be able to devote her full time to the novel she was writing.

I had known that Rand had corresponded with Charles Hapgood, and that Hapgood had died after a car accident. But Rand had not told me the full story, and when I heard it, I instantly felt that this was best-seller material.

As already described, Rand had become interested in Atlantis by chance, and had started to research it in 1976. He soon began to speculate whether Atlantis might have been Antarctica. Then he read Hapgood's *Maps of the Ancient Sea Kings* and *Earth's Shifting Crust*, and his Antarctic theory was reinforced. If, as Hapgood said, the ancient maps proved that there had been a civilisation around or even before 7000 BC, this could be Atlantis – although Hapgood, as a respectable academic, did not dare to say as much. Rand sent Hapgood a paper discussing his ideas, and Hapgood said that 'it was the first truly scientific explanation of my work that has been done'. Rand and Rose decided to move to London, where he could do his research in the British Museum.

From London Rand wrote to Hapgood, and received an amazing letter. Hapgood told him: '. . . in recent exciting discoveries I believe I have convincing evidence of a whole cycle of civilisation in America and in Antarctica, suggesting advanced levels of science that may go back 100,000 years . . .'

Rand was staggered. *A hundred thousand years?* That is about fifteen times the present estimate of the age of civilisation. He wrote back immediately asking for further details. His letter was returned labelled 'Deceased'. Hapgood had walked in front of a car, and died in hospital.

What on earth could Hapgood have meant about a hundred-thousand-year-old science?

This was the question Rand wanted me to try and help him answer. He had studied Hapgood's papers at Yale, and found no hint of an answer; neither could Hapgood's friends or relatives offer any help.

Hapgood's assertion excited me so much because it reinforced my own conviction that intelligence did not make its first appearance on earth with the coming of the Cro-Magnons, around fifty thousand years ago, but was already present in the form of some deeper power of intuition that, as Graves said, 'can cut out all routine processes of thought and leap straight from the problem to the answer'.

Rand had already stumbled on an important clue. Running approximately north out of Teotihuacan, in Mexico, there is a two-mile avenue that has become known as the Way of the Dead. But it is 15.5 degrees off true north. And when Rand discovered that there were forty-nine other Central American sacred sites that had the same misalignment, he had a flash of inspiration. Could it be that these sites were aligned on the *old* North Pole, before the earth's crust slipped two thousand miles south?

But Hapgood believed this 'slippage' occurred between 15000 and 10000

BC. If so, then these temples must have been built long before civilisation came into existence in the Middle East.

It is true that archaeologists have dated many of these as far more recent than that. But that proves nothing, for such sites are often built one on top of another. I had learned while writing my own *Atlas of Sacred Sites* that this is true of many temples, and we know that no less than nine Troys have been discovered in successive layers.

So it looked as if Rand had discovered the most convincing proof yet that civilisation may be thousands of years older than anyone thought.

Rand and I began planning the book immediately. Our first problem was finding a publisher. This was solved for us by Graham Hancock's agent, Bill Hamilton, who asked Rand to come to London so we could go and 'present' the idea to various publishers. I lent Rand the fares across the Atlantic, and we spent a week doing our 'presentations'. The result was an excellent offer of £110,000 from Little Brown. We then did our presentations in New York, and this time received an offer of $75,000 (about £50,000). I lent Rand my part of the initial advance, so he and Rose could buy a house.

However, early in the project, Rand discovered that his theory was not as watertight as he thought. When the curve in the earth's surface was taken into account, his sacred sites were not precisely aligned on the old North Pole in Hudson Bay. But he had made an equally important discovery: that sacred sites are placed symmetrically on the earth's surface, as if in a grid pattern. I was deeply impressed when his theory led him to locate a place that ought to be a sacred site in British Honduras, and where indeed there proved to be a Maya temple – at a place called Lubantuun, where the famous 'crystal skull' is alleged to have been discovered.

Next I needed to do some 'field work'. The ideal opportunity arose in November 1998, when I was invited on a trip down the Nile, together with other writers who were interested in ancient civilisations: John West, Robert Bauval, Robert Temple, Michael Baigent, and others. We had all agreed to give lectures on the boat.

The cabin next door to ours was occupied by a couple named Walton – Gurth and Maria. And after I had given my lecture, they asked me if I knew a book called *Our Cosmic Ancestors* by Maurice Chatelain, and lent me their copy. Chatelain was an aeronautics engineer who had worked on the Apollo moon project.

Chatelain explains that when European nineteenth-century archaeologists had excavated the ruins of Nineveh, in what was then Mesopotamia, they discovered tablets inscribed with huge numbers, one of them containing fifteen digits: 195,955,200,000,000. No one could imagine what the ancient Assyrians wanted with such vast numbers. Then Chatelain had an idea. The ancestors of the Assyrians were the Sumerians, and the Sumerians had invented seconds, minutes and hours. Could this enormous number be in seconds? He worked it out to 2,268 million days, or just over six million years.

He now recalled the precession of the equinoxes, that slight wobble on the earth's axis that takes just under 26,000 years to complete its cycle. And when Chatelain tried dividing the fifteen-digit 'Nineveh number' by the length of the precessional cycle, he knew he was on the right track, for it divided exactly 240 times.

He wondered if the Nineveh number could be what ancient astronomers had called 'the great constant of the solar system', a number that would be a multiple of the revolution of each and every body in the solar system, including moons. He tried it and again it worked.

So these ancient astronomers must have had an awe-inspiring understanding of the solar system – far, far greater than anyone suspected. They knew as much about the heavens as Isaac Newton did, and probably more.

The Nineveh number provided such accurate estimates of the revolution of the heavenly bodies that Chatelain was puzzled when he found a very slight discrepancy when he compared the earth's revolution according to the Nineveh number to its length as measured by a modern caesium clock. It was only a twelve-millionth of a second per year, but the Nineveh number had been otherwise so accurate that he felt there must be some explanation.

Then he remembered something. The earth is slowing down very slowly – a mere sixteen millionths of a second per year. This could explain the tiny inaccuracy. But if he took it into account, the implications were staggering. The Nineveh number *would have been totally accurate 65,000 years ago*. What this implied is that there were men on earth that long ago who computed the Nineveh number. It looks as if Hapgood could be right when he suggested 'advanced levels of science that could go back 100,000 years'.

But if so, what could it mean? What intelligent beings were there on earth 65,000 years ago? Chatelain was convinced they were visitors from space, and I was certainly not willing to rule out that possibility, in view of that statue of 'the Friar' in Tiahuanaco.

Now in a book called *Hamlet's Mill*, Georgio de Santillana and Hertha von Dechend had demonstrated very convincingly that most ancient cultures knew all about the precession of the equinoxes.

This did not surprise me, for I had always been fascinated by the ability of mathematical prodigies. In the nineteenth-century a five-year-old boy named Benjamin Blyth was out walking with his father, and asked him what time it was. His father told him. A few minutes later, Benjamin said:

'In that case I have been alive . . .' – and he named the number of seconds, about 158 million. Later, back at home, his father did the calculation on paper and said: 'You were wrong by 178,000 seconds.' 'No I wasn't,' said the child, 'You've forgotten the two leap years.'

So it *is* perfectly conceivable that our ancestors might have been able to handle immense figures in the same way. It is probably a natural 'right brain' ability.

This also seems to rule out Daniken's belief that 'ancient astronauts' created our civilisation. For surely the space men would have explained to human beings that the precession of the equinoxes, to which they attached such immense mystical significance – assuming it to be a glimpse into the mind of the gods – was merely due to a wobble on the earth's axis. But then, this is no ultimate argument against 'ancient astronauts' – only against the belief that they created civilisation.

It should be noted that Hapgood did not say that advanced levels of *civilisation* existed 100,000 years ago, but advanced levels of *science*. And that would certainly apply to the Nineveh number.

Now a psychologist friend of mine named Stan Gooch, had written a book called *Cities of Dreams*, arguing that Neanderthal man was not a shambling ape, but was an astronomer who possessed a genuine culture. Was it possible, I wondered, that Hapgood may have had Neanderthal man in mind?

This was confirmed one day when I was still writing the early chapters of the book. I had been contacting Hapgood's friends, to try to find out if he had told any of them about the 'hundred-thousand-year-old science' – so far, with no result. Then someone advised me to try a retired academic who lived in Massachusetts – I shall call him Carl (although that is not his name) for reasons that will become apparent. And when I rang him, he took my breath away by telling me that it was he who had convinced Hapgood that civilisation is tens of thousands of years older than we have assumed.

When I asked him why he thought so, he mentioned two reasons. First: that the measurements of the earth prove that ancient man knew its exact size long before the Greeks. Second: that there is evidence that Neanderthal man was far more intelligent than we give him credit for.

The first had been pointed out by a geographer named A. E. Berriman, in his 1953 book *Historical Metrology*. Berriman noted that although the Greeks did not know the size of the earth until about 200 BC, when the astronomer Eratosthenes worked it out, the polar circumference of the earth is exactly 216,000 Greek stade (the latter being about the length of a football pitch).

Now a stade consists of 600 Greek feet, and if we want to know how many stade there are in one degree of the earth's circumference, we divide

216,000 by 360 degrees, and the result is 600, the same as the number of feet in a stade. That cannot be chance. It can only mean that, centuries before Eratosthenes, some unknown civilisation must have known the exact size of the earth. The Greeks merely inherited that knowledge through the size of their stade.

As to Neanderthal man, I was delighted that Carl seemed to confirm the ideas Stan Gooch had put forward in *Cities of Dreams*.

I expected Rand to be delighted that I had stumbled on the solution to this mystery, which answered the main question of our book. To my surprise, he was at first dubious, then dismissive. Shortly thereafter, he told me that, after conducting some investigations into Carl's background, he had concluded that he was a fraud.

This astounded me. After many long conversations with Carl – he was an inveterate phone talker – I was also dubious about some of his ideas on ancient man. But he knew too much to be a fraud. He was one of the most erudite men I had ever encountered.

As to the notion that Neanderthal man was far more intelligent than we believe, Rand was totally dismissive. He told me he had mentioned the idea to a female colleague and she had burst into screams of laughter.

I remained convinced that Hapgood had been speaking about Neanderthal man, and became even more so when I found a report from Tarragona University that fifteen Neanderthal furnaces had been unearthed near Barcelona, one of them a blast furnace. Since then, another report has established that Neanderthal man invented a kind of superglue, a pitch made from birch heated to 300–400°C, to secure flint axe blades to wooden handles. So in spite of Rand's fierce objections, all this went into the final two chapters of *The Atlantis Blueprint*.

I had also been making some interesting discoveries about Hapgood. While still a professor, he had seen a psychologist hypnotising students and 'regressing' some of them to 'previous lives'; Hapgood then learned hypnosis, and was amazed when he found he could not only regress students into the past, but get them to prophesy future events with remarkable accuracy. He soon came to the conclusion that the human mind possesses a far wider range of powers than we recognise. He was intrigued by Cleve Backster's experiments with plants connected to a lie detector, which seem to show that plants can read our minds. His final conclusion was that primitive man possessed paranormal abilities.

This, it seemed to me, was probably an important part of the explanation of Hapgood's conviction that advanced levels of science existed 100,000 years ago. This is the case I proceeded to argue in the final chapters of *Atlantis Blueprint*. Rand expressed no objections about these chapters – on the contrary, he sent me a warmly congratulatory email about the chapter on Hapgood's later researches.

Finishing a 150,000-word book in a year was not easy, but I finally did it at the end of December 2000, and sent it to Little Brown. In February, the edited typescript came back for a final reading. Five months later, in July, the proof arrived.

Since I was proof-reading another book, I left the parcel unopened. But when I finally looked at the proof, I saw instantly that this was not the book I had written. To begin with, it was much shorter. It did not take long to discover that enormous, sweeping cuts had been made, including the whole of its last two chapters.

I sent Rand an angry email, asking the reason for what seemed to me an incomprehensible act of treachery. Rand was obviously furious and sent back an email beginning in capitals, stating that I had libelled him in an outrageous manner, and telling me that he had submitted all his suggestions to me, down to the smallest comma. He said that it was my own fault for not bothering to read his suggestions.

So I spent two days, with Joy's help, reading every email Rand and I had exchanged in recent months, without success. Finally, I had to write to him asking for the date of the email in question. His reply was 'June 1st'.

I turned to this and found an email entitled 'last of it', in which he heaves a sigh of relief that the book is finished at last, and tells me that his dogs had run away because of fireworks, with many more items of pleasant gossip. He ends 'with affection, Rand', then goes on to page after page – nine in all – of details of latitudes and longitudes and appendices and notes. And in the midst of all this he comments that he feels the book would be greatly improved with 'a slight restructuring . . .' Then, after outlining these changes in a single long paragraph, he goes back to listing the latitudes and longitudes and notes for the appendices. Was it surprising that I missed his suggestions?

He had also removed all my references to Neanderthal man, and in one place changed it to 'people like us', implying I meant Cro-Magnon man.

What made me so indignant was not simply that he had, to my mind, ruined the end of the book by leaving the mystery of the 'hundred-thousand-year-old science' unanswered, but that he had also suppressed my conviction that a high level of human intelligence had existed long before Cro-Magnon man came on the scene. And this was absolutely central to my thesis.

In due course, *The Atlantis Blueprint* was published in its hacked form, with my most important conclusions excised. I felt it was like an Agatha Christie thriller with the last chapter missing.

As to Rand, it was a sad end to a friendship I had regarded as important. The only thing that cheered me was the reflection that, since Rand had removed such a vast amount of the book, he had at least left me plenty of material on which to base a sequel.

Just before I went to London for the publication of *Alien Dawn*, I had been proof-reading a book that was about to be published in America: *The Books in My Life*, whose title I had borrowed from Henry Miller. It was dedicated to Frank DeMarco, a publisher I had met in New York, and who was to become a close friend. It was he who offered me the opportunity of writing the long-delayed fourth volume of *Spider World*.

I had met Frank when I had been in New York to lecture at the Open Center. One afternoon Joy and I had been invited to a party at the home of the paranormal researcher Alexander Imich, to meet a group of people interested in the same field. There I was introduced to a dark-haired, youngish man, who said he had travelled from Virginia to meet me. He ran a small New Age publishing house called Hampton Roads, and told me that he was deeply interested in the work of a researcher named Robert Monroe.

I had written about Monroe in *Mysteries*. He was a radio engineer who had been dozing on the settee one Sunday afternoon, his hand resting on the floor, when he felt his fingers go through the floorboards. And after that, to his confusion and bewilderment, he found that he could float outside his body and wander around the neighbourhood. His book *Journeys Out of the Body* had become a classic, and a number of respectable parapsychologists have studied Monroe's case and accepted he was genuine.

Monroe had concluded that his out-of-the-body experiences might have been induced by some experiments he had been doing on sleep learning. These involved playing synchronised sounds through two headphones at the same time, the aim being to establish a perfect balance between the right and left hemispheres of the brain so they could absorb knowledge during sleep. He called it his 'hemi-sync' process. And he later set up an institute to teach people how to use the hemi-sync process to achieve unusual states of consciousness, including out-of-the-body experiences.

When he took his first course at the Monroe Institute three years earlier, Frank's aim had not been primarily to achieve out-of-the-body experiences, but to explore the hemi-sync process. And he had found that sinking into states of deep calm, using a 'black room' and various mind-control techniques, he had quickly acquired the art of 'mental projection'.

For example, some time earlier, Frank had visited Emerson's house in Concord, and had instantly felt that he had been there before. Now, using the Monroe technique, he 'projected' himself to Emerson's house, and instantly felt as if he was watching a film with realistic playback. He saw himself – as a certain Dr Atwood – arriving at the back door, to be introduced to Mrs Emerson. Their conversation was interrupted by Thoreau, who was then living in the Emerson household. Later he talked to Emerson, and was convinced that this was actually a memory of a real conversation rather than some kind of dream or free fantasy.

I, of course, have no way of knowing whether Frank's experiences are fantasy. But having read Monroe's three books, I am reasonably convinced that he found a method of projecting himself out of our physical reality and exploring realms beyond the body. Of course, shamans of all nationalities have made the same claims, and their techniques have been extensively explored and documented by many researchers, such as Mircea Eliade and Jeremy Narby. A large part of my recent *Atlantis and the Old Ones* is devoted to shamanism. But I believe Monroe can claim the credit for being the first westerner who has developed techniques for exploring other levels of reality. And if Monroe's experiences are true, and not some kind of subjective fantasy, then he must be regarded as one of the greatest paranormal investigators of the twentieth century, a man who taught us as much about the non-physical realm as Columbus and Vasco da Gama taught us about our physical globe.

What neither Frank nor I knew that day we met was that Robert Monroe had just died. It was 5 March 1995.

When Frank asked me if I had any work he might publish, I mentioned *The Books in My Life*, a series of essays that I had written for a Tokyo magazine called *Litteraire*. I had just finished proof-reading it when I went to London for the publication of *Alien Dawn*.

In October 1998 Joy and I flew down to Charlottesville for publication of *The Books in My Life*.

Frank was living in a house about thirty miles outside Charlottesville, but within only a couple of miles of the Monroe Institute. And on my third day in Virginia, I went to see the Institute.

Frank was anxious that I should take one of the 'Gateway' courses and learn how to achieve out-of-the-body experiences. My own reaction was a curious reluctance, feeling perhaps that 'this was not for me' – much as I had felt when I took mescalin.

But I spent some time in the 'black room', and tried the 'hemi-sync' process, in which different sounds are played into either ear to synchronise the left and right halves of the brain. This produced a deep sense of peace and relaxation that brought back memories of the Japanese temples.

Back in Cornwall, I reread *Journeys Out of the Body*, and was again impressed by a feeling of the author's total honesty. Then I went on to *Far Journeys*, then the third – and strangest – of the series, *Ultimate Journey*, which I found so fascinating that I read it slowly to make it last.

A year after my visit to the Monroe Institute, Frank began to send me chapters of an autobiography he was writing. This impressed me so much that, in spite of a heavy work schedule, I printed up every section as he emailed it, and read it immediately.

My interest had been seized by a passage describing the effect of taking mescalin as a student. The drug produced the effect described by Aldous Huxley in *The Doors of Perception*: a deepened sense of reality. He writes: 'If I were looking at a candle, say, I would really look at it, really see it, for the first time in my life.' Looking at a painting of a boat, it was as if the front half of the boat was sticking out into the room.

What really excited me was: 'The walls, I realised, were alive! Literally. What I had been taking for dead matter was something much more exciting: it was somehow alive in a way I couldn't fathom, but couldn't doubt.'

I recalled a passage from a book called *The States of Consciousness* by an American scientist, C. Daly King, a follower of Gurdjieff, who described how he had been standing on a New Jersey railway platform, practising 'self awareness', when 'Suddenly the entire aspect of the surroundings changed. The whole atmosphere seemed strangely vitalised . . . The most extraordinary alteration was that of the dun-colored bricks . . . all at once they appeared to be tremendously alive; without manifesting any exterior motion they seemed to be surging almost joyously inside and gave the impression that in their own degree they were living and actively liking it.'

It is obvious that what had happened to Frank and to Daly King was that they had ceased to be 'robotic'; suddenly the 'real me' was looking out of their eyes. But then, most of us experience that – when we set out on holiday, or go walking on a spring morning. Frank and Daly King had somehow achieved an even deeper degree of freedom from the robot, and were suddenly aware that everything is seething with its own life.

Frank also describes how the mescalin made him aware that there is no such thing as chance in human relations: 'Several times in the course of that long Saturday afternoon I watched the interaction of five people come to perfectly orchestrated peaks and lulls. I refer not to anything externally dramatic, but to the temporary clarity of vision that showed me (beyond later doubting) that more went on between individuals than their ordinary consciousness realised. Thinking about the orchestration I saw then, I for a while referred to God the Great Playwright.'

This is that odd conviction of meaning we experience when some outrageous synchronicity occurs, the feeling that our apparently dis-organised world is less chaotic than it looks.

In the first chapter of this book I described my experience when driving back through the Lake District, and felt as if the hills had become somehow transparent, and I could see what lay on the other side. This is an example of what I later came to call Faculty X, that sudden sense of the *reality* of other times and places. In this case it was due to the upsurge of optimism I felt as I realised I had less far to drive than I thought. It is typical of what Maslow meant by the peak experience, when energy bubbles over like an effervescent drink poured hurriedly into a glass. According to Maslow, such 'overflows' are a matter of chance, and cannot be deliberately induced.

But my experience driving back from Sheepwash in the snow proves otherwise. Here sheer concentration caused my mind to go into a kind of lower gear, inducing a strong sense of control. The result was that most of the drive back was a sustained peak experience, demonstrating that Maslow was mistaken, and that they *can* be induced by effort.

What misled Maslow, I suspect, was his failure to add another of his discoveries to the equation: that students who talked about their peak experiences began to have peak experiences all the time. Why? Because they induced a mood of *optimism* that acted as a springboard. In the case of my drive back from Sheepwash, it was the pleasure of finding myself back on the main road that transformed concentration into the peak experience.

It was my subsequent recognition of the seven levels of consciousness that provided the final clue: that Level 4 – 'ordinary consciousness' – can be easily transformed into Level 5 – 'spring morning consciousness' – by optimism. And since I am an optimistic kind of person, I have in recent years found it increasingly easy to access Level 5. Moreover, since it is a *perception* of meaning – like the view from a hilltop – it is not difficult to maintain.

I have also noted that when I am feeling cheerful and optimistic, I often have a clear sense of some presence or presences who are pulling the strings.

I see my task as a writer to explore, and at times to create, what Rhea White calls 'exceptional human experience'. In studies like *The Outsider* and its sequels I focused on individuals who experienced a deep dissatisfaction with what Heidegger calls 'the triviality of everydayness'. And in works like *The Mind Parasites*, *The Philosopher's Stone* and *Spider World*, I concentrated on trying to create my own version of exceptional human experience, and to enable readers to absorb that experience through the medium of imagination.

Until three years ago, one of my major efforts in this direction, *Spider World*, was unfinished and seemed likely to remain so. Then Frank DeMarco wrote to me and told me that he intended to launch a series of fantasy novels, and asked me if I would like to write one. I replied, asking him if he had read *Spider World*, and, when he said he had never heard of it (the American edition having been issued in a cheap paperback), sent him the first three volumes. I was delighted when, a few weeks later, he told me that the books had been read by most of his staff, and had aroused enthusiasm. So I began writing Volume 4, *Shadowland*, planned ten years earlier, while Hampton Roads began reissuing hard-cover editions of the first three volumes.

I had broken off because the effort of writing the third volume, *The Magician*, had left my imagination exhausted. Now, to my relief, I discovered that ten years of lying fallow had allowed it to recover, and I was writing with the same excitement as when I began it. It took eighteen months, six months longer than I had intended.

As I write these words on 3 December 2003, I have just received a parcel containing my author's copies.

And that, I feel, is probably as good a place as any to end this autobiography, since it is four o'clock on a winter afternoon, and time to take my dogs for a walk.

Epilogue

Wittgenstein once said: 'Whatever is the purpose of human existence, it is not to be happy.' When I was an adolescent that thought would have depressed me. Now it seems self-evidently true – not merely in Shaw's sense: 'I don't want to be happy, I want to be alive and active' – but in the sense that being alive is grimly hard work, and that this applies to all of us, including kings and millionaires.

When I was thirteen I daydreamed of a marvellous future in which I was rich and famous and universally admired. When *The Outsider* came out, it looked as if I had made a good start. Since then, it has become clear that the aim was never realistic. Moreover, I can see that it was always the wrong goal, and that even if I had achieved it, I would have remained unhappy, like someone who has eaten a large meal and still feels empty. Most of our human aims are so naïve that they do not deserve to be fulfilled.

Yet I have not fallen into the negative position of believing that all life is an illusion. It seems to me quite clear that certain things can be achieved. I have described in this book the experiences that led me to this belief – for example, that intensification of awareness I reached when driving back from Sheepwash through the snow. In these cases I somehow pumped consciousness up to a higher level of pressure, and could immediately see that this is the real aim.

There is another related problem: we spend most of our lives in 'mono-consciousness', a narrow state in which we are aware mainly of the present moment. It could be compared to being in a picture gallery but being forced to stand with your nose within an inch of the canvas. When we set out on holiday we go into duo-consciousness, and our minds are *in two places at once*: back at home, and in their new surroundings.

But then, I also experienced it when *The Outsider* was accepted, and when we lost and then found Sally in Cheltenham.

When I think back on those experiences, I can see that what I had done is to 'close my leaks', and prevent my mind from drifting like a balloon. But plainly, long and continuous effort is not necessary, as Maslow realised. If we think of his housewife watching her family eating breakfast, and then having a peak experience as the sun came out, we can see that the sunlight simply made her 'focus', and this closed the leak instantaneously, and catapulted her into the peak experience.

I have a hydraulic car jack which is quite small, but which can lift an enormously heavy weight. I merely have to tighten a screw to trap the air inside, and pump the handle up and down. All that Maslow's housewife did was to give the screw a half turn, and she went into the peak experience. The glimpse of sunlight made her momentarily 'unrobotic', and it was this that induced the peak experience.

It is extremely important to grasp how far we are slaves of the robot. There is a television game in which rapid questions are fired at contestants, who are not allowed to reply yes or no, or to nod or shake their heads. Yet few can control this automatic reaction for more than half a minute. It is a remarkable demonstration of Gurdjieff's assertion that we are machines.

In this book I have not said half as much as I intended to about Gurdjieff. Let me say here that I regard him as by far the greatest teacher of the twentieth century. And, as bizarre as this sounds, I suspect that Gurdjieff himself may be aware of this. Sometime in the late 1950s, when I was living in Old Walls, I received a letter from a medium who explained she was passing on to me a message from someone called Gurdjieff – she had no idea who this might be. And the message, in Gurdjieff's fractured English, certainly sounded exactly like the Master. After more than fifty years I can no longer recall exactly what it said, but it was more or less an exhortation to keep on going in the same direction. I am ashamed to say that the message – in the medium's handwriting – was lost long ago (as later was my correspondence with writers like Aldous Huxley. Karl Popper, Henry Miller and Robert Ardrey), since in those days I had no filing system.

Goethe once said: 'Beware of what you wish for in youth, because you will get it in middle age.' He had noticed this interesting fact that people tend to get things they want *deeply*. The great trick is to want the right things.

When I look back on my own life, I am aware that I wanted much the same kind of thing as the nineteenth-century Romantics: enough peace and solitude to be able to devote myself to what interests me more than all else: the 'moments of vision'. Publication of *The Outsider* made me aware that this 'success' was not at all what I wanted. Instead, I found most of my time taken up with other people. It was not until I moved to a cottage in Cornwall that I could finally concentrate on my work. Then I had to pay a high price: to have my ideas ignored or attacked. But it was basically a fair price, for I had once again achieved the conditions in which I wrote *The Outsider*, and another dose of 'success' would have wrecked me. Besides, to have a home and a family was a tremendous bonus.

As I move into my seventies, I realise I have developed an unexpected conviction: that there is something in our minds that can alter our lives – the 'something' that causes synchronicities, for example. Wells makes Mr Polly say: 'If you don't like your life you can change it.' But Wells was speaking of practical change, the way we live. I am convinced that there is another way of changing our lives: using this curious power of the mind that we hardly understand.

When I first read *Back to Methuselah*, I saw that Shaw is right: the only way to make human life less stupid and futile is for us to live longer. But how? Shaw said it would 'simply happen' – but I suspect this is not the solution. What becomes clear to me as I get older – and at three score and eleven I have already passed the biblical limit – is that the only way to live longer is to be driven by a strong sense of purpose. Human beings die for the same reason they fall asleep – because they no longer want to make the effort to stay awake.

It seems to me that the most important statement in this book is Gurdjieff's comment that human beings live in the equivalent of outer Siberia. We find ourselves in an appallingly harsh environment and, to add to our problems, are dragged down by a gravitational force that makes every step an effort. And why are we here? Oddly enough, because – I believe – we chose to be. We are like explorers on some remote planet, whose only contact with home base is a poor and crackly radio. Our most dangerous problem is forgetting why we are here and becoming confused and directionless. Then anything can happen; we become bored or lazy, or even angry at what we feel our undeserved misfortune. Such people waste their lives. And when they get back to home base, and the amnesia vanishes, they will suddenly feel like kicking themselves for their stupidity.

And why *are* we here? In our moments of optimism and enthusiasm, this is something we know instinctively. The purpose is to colonise this difficult and inhospitable realm of matter and to imbue it with the force of life. T. E. Hulme, the philosopher who was killed in the First World War, said that consciousness is trying to force an entry into matter, as the sea might try to force a small hole in a dyke. 'In the amoeba, then, you might say that the impulse has manufactured a very small leak through which free activity could be inserted into the world, and the progress of evolution has been the gradual enlargement of this leak.' A dog or cat is a bigger leak still. But man is the biggest leak so far.

He has discovered new techniques for enlarging the leak: art, intellect, imagination. And eventually he will be so certain of his purpose that he will never lose sight of it even for a moment. The grey dawn in which we now live will be transformed into the clear light of midday, and consciousness will have made an impregnable bridgehead into the world of matter.

Ouspensky and R. H. Ward had the same insight: that this world of matter is not our home. That lies behind us, in another world. But for those with enough strength and imagination, it will *become* our home. And when that happens the purpose of human existence will have been achieved.

My own life has been a whole series of clues to the purpose of human existence.

The first was on that journey to Peterborough when I coined the phrase 'the St Neot margin', meaning that recognition that our minds can be jarred out of indifference by a sense of crisis. Since then, the 'St Neot margin trick' has become the most useful in my armoury of devices to 'shake the mind awake'.

But the Sheepwash experience and the train journey to Northampton offered me the second important clue. The mind can be focused and concentrated into a state of non-leakage. But unlike 'moments of vision' and flashes of illumination, this does not simply fade away when we relax the mind. Once the state has been achieved, another simple act of focus immediately restores it. On the drive back from Sheepwash I was able to do it again and again. The 'trick' had lodged in some kind of physical memory, and could be recalled at will.

In fact, even writing about these experiences in this chapter brought them back again. It brought back a state of 'duo-consciousness' which lasted for the remainder of the day, during which I went down to Vault beach for a swim. As I was swimming in the sea I saw clearly that duo-consciousness is a 'trick' we can master.

An example of what I mean is the Miss Verity case of 1882, when her fiancé Beard decided to 'appear' to her by an act of will, and succeeded in doing so on two occasions. Beard said:

> Besides exercising my powers of volition very strongly, I put forth an effort which I cannot find words to describe. I was conscious of a mysterious force of some sort permeating my body, and had a distinct impression that I was exercising some force with which I had hitherto been unacquainted, *but which I can now at certain times set in motion at will*. [My italics.]

John Cowper Powys obviously mastered the same trick, for he was able to tell Theodore Dreiser that he would 'appear' to him later that evening, and did so. Is it coincidence that Powys lived to be ninety-three?

When driving from Sheepwash in the snow I had a reason for

concentrating hard – the danger of landing in the ditch. And as I experienced this 'force permeating my body', I realised that it is a 'trick' that can be learned.

And the basis of that trick is a feeling of optimism, the knowledge that, ultimately, it is the mind that controls what happens to us.

Index